Windows 2000 Enterprise Storage Solutions

Windows® 2000 Enterprise Storage Solutions

J. Peter Bruzzese
Chris Wolf

San Francisco London

Associate Publisher: Neil Edde

Acquisitions and Developmental Editor: Chris Denny

Editors: Kim Wimpsett, Sharon Wilkey

Production Editor: Kylie Johnston

Technical Editor: Dan Renaud

Book Designer: Bill Gibson

Graphic Illustrator: Tony Jonick

Electronic Publishing Specialist: Jeff Wilson, Happenstance Type-O-Rama

Proofreaders: Dave Nash, Laurie O'Connell, Nancy Riddiough

Indexer: Ted Laux

Cover Designer: Ingalls & Associates

Cover Illustrator: Ingalls & Associates

Copyright © 2002 SYBEX Inc., 1151 Marina Village Parkway, Alameda, CA 94501. World rights reserved. No part of this publication may be stored in a retrieval system, transmitted, or reproduced in any way, including but not limited to photocopy, photograph, magnetic, or other record, without the prior agreement and written permission of the publisher.

Library of Congress Card Number: 2001094596

ISBN: 0-7821-2883-1

SYBEX and the SYBEX logo are either registered trademarks or trademarks of SYBEX Inc. in the United States and/or other countries.

The Mark Minasi Windows 2000 Series is a trademark of SYBEX Inc.

TRADEMARKS: SYBEX has attempted throughout this book to distinguish proprietary trademarks from descriptive terms by following the capitalization style used by the manufacturer.

The author and publisher have made their best efforts to prepare this book, and the content is based upon final release software whenever possible. Portions of the manuscript may be based upon pre-release versions supplied by software manufacturer(s). The author and the publisher make no representation or warranties of any kind with regard to the completeness or accuracy of the contents herein and accept no liability of any kind including but not limited to performance, merchantability, fitness for any particular purpose, or any losses or damages of any kind caused or alleged to be caused directly or indirectly from this book.

Manufactured in the United States of America

10 9 8 7 6 5 4 3 2 1

Dedicated to my wife Jennette. The book you bought for me in Germany says it best: "...Right up to the moon...and back again."
—*McBratney.*

—*PB*

This book is dedicated to Mike Dahlmeier, my friend, mentor, and absolute storage guru. "It is the supreme art of the teacher to awaken joy in creative expression and knowledge."
—*Einstein.*

—*CW*

Acknowledgments

First of all, I'd like to thank Mark Minasi for putting us in his series. It's a privilege to have his name attached to this book. Second of all, I'd like to thank all of the Sybex staff members who have contributed to the completion of this tremendous project. Specifically, I'd like to thank Chris Denny, Neil Edde, Dan Renaud, Kim Wimpsett, Kylie Johnston, Maureen Forys, Jeff Wilson, Ted Laux, and especially Tony Jonick, who created the artwork, which is incredible compared to the stick figures I put together. Again, thank you.

When teaching storage classes, I often tell students that I'd prefer not to be labeled as an *instructor*. In reality, I am merely a window into the knowledge of others. I hold that to be true within this book. Quite a number of people have allowed their knowledge to be displayed. So, I'd like to thank all of the engineers at CommVault Systems who have contributed greatly to this book: Lisa Hess for her knowledge of SCSI and SANSs; Michael Dahlmeier for his knowledge of, well…everything; Jim Powers for his real-world NAS scenario; Joe Masi for his Verizon experiences; Norman Lunde for his instruction on Network Appliance filers; Gaylord Friend for his knowledge of redundant Exchange Server configurations; and Kevin Low for his configuration assistance, especially with the XP/.NET and Exchange lab configurations.

Along with thanking my colleagues, I'd also like to thank Michael Alvarado from Network Appliance; Ava Schutzman from EMC, Paralan Corporation; Gary Fields (the king of SCSI); Cyndie Behrens from Brocade; Jeff Lietner from IBM; Fred Richardson from SanSite.com; and George McNamara from WestWorld Productions, Inc. All of these people (in addition to the ones Chris mentions below) have contributed to this book in one form or another; they deserve credit for allowing us to present as clear a picture of storage as possible in one collective work for working administrators. Thank you.

Finally, I'd like to thank Ronald Barrett for collaborating with me on a couple of the earlier chapters. His gift for teaching clearly shows through in the way he writes, and I look forward to future projects together. I'd also like to thank Timothy Duggan and Patrick Geisz for their research assistance.

—PB

Several people contributed to my portion of this reference, and they certainly deserve recognition. First, I would like to thank Kevin Low for his assistance in acquiring the hardware and software necessary to document the vast world of storage. Next, I would like to thank these fine members of CommVault Systems who contributed directly or indirectly to this book: John Teti, Audrey DeNovio, Victor Abyad, Mike Kelly, Lisa Hess, Fran Shields, Steve Brooks, Terry Krull, Suresh Reddy, Tom Massano, Juan Paulino, Jim Power, John Tosh, Stan Lau, Laura Norton, Tom Kresic, Doug Gengler, Stacy Nekervis, Jonathan Cragle, and Jeff Rembish.

—CW

Contents at a Glance

Introduction xvii
Chapter 1:   Windows 2000 Storage Overview 1
Chapter 2:   Storage Terminology 15
Chapter 3:   Windows 2000 Storage Enhancements 41
Chapter 4:   Working with Removable Storage Manager 73
Chapter 5:   SCSI Solutions 119
Chapter 6:   Storage Area Networks (SANs) 145
Chapter 7:   Network Attached Storage (NAS) 171
Chapter 8:   RAID Technology 201
Chapter 9:   Cluster Technology 221
Chapter 10:   File System Backup and Recovery 267
Chapter 11:   Operating System Rebuilds: The Gotchas 297
Chapter 12:   Exchange 5.5/2000 Backup and Recovery 331
Chapter 13:   SQL 7/2000 Backup/Recovery 379
Chapter 14:   The Future of Storage 419
Glossary 427

Index 443

Contents

Introduction xvii

| Chapter | 1 | **Windows 2000 Storage Overview** .... 1 |

Storage Growth 2
    Microsoft Takes the Challenge 3
    From Then 'Til Now... 3
    NTBackup 4
Storage Grows Beyond Itself 7
    Direct Attached Storage (DAS) 8
    Network Attached Storage (NAS) 9
    Storage Area Networks (SAN) 10
Windows 2000 Storage—It Begins 11

| Chapter | 2 | **Storage Terminology** .... 15 |

Defining Storage Terms 16
    Understanding General Terms 16
    Understanding Media Terms 17
    Understanding Drive Terms 18
    Understanding Library Terms 18
    Understanding Enterprise Storage Terms 19
Defining Your Backup Strategy 20
    Your Backup Options 21
    Defining Rotation Methods 23
    Your Company Is Your Data 28
Understanding Media Types 28
    Magnetic Tapes 29
    Optical Discs 33
    Magnetic Disks 35
Managing Media 35
    Examples of Media Management 36
    Library Capacity 38
But What About...? 40

Chapter 3   **Windows 2000 Storage Enhancements** **41**
    Removable Storage Manager (RSM) 42
    Remote Storage Service (RSS) 43
    Reparse Points 45
        Using Linkd 45
        Using Delrp 47
    Volume Mount Points 48
    Windows File Protection 51
        Improving WFP Performance 52
        Using the System File Checker Tool (sfc.exe) 53
    The Change Journal 54
    Indexing Service 55
        Starting the Indexing Service 56
        Defining Folders to be Indexed 56
        Searching Indexed Files 57
    Sparse Files 57
    Single Instance Storage (SIS) 58
    File Replication Service (FRS) 59
        Authoritative versus Nonauthoritative Restores 59
        Using the Robust File Copy Utility Robocopy 61
    Distributed File System (Dfs) 62
        Enabling Dfs 63
        Adding Dfs Links 64
        Creating Replicas for Fault Tolerance and Load Balancing 65
    Encrypting File System (EFS) 66
        Using the Cipher Utility 68
    Disk Quotas 68
        Monitoring Disk Usage with Diskuse 69
    System State 70

Chapter 4   **Working with Removable Storage Manager** **73**
    Configuring RSM 73
        Media Pools 74
        Physical Locations 79
        Work Queue 88
        Operator Requests 89

Removable Storage Administration 90
  Inventorying Libraries 91
  Importing and Exporting Media 91
  Adding a Cleaning Cartridge to a Library 91
  Cleaning a Library or Single Drive 92
  Configuring a Zip/Jaz Drive 92
  Configuring a CD-ROM Jukebox 93
  Using the RSM Database Integrity Checker (rsm_dbic.exe) ...93
  Using the RSM Database Utility (rsm_dbutil.exe) 94
  Performing RSM Database Backup and Recovery 96
  Using the rsm.exe Command-Line Utility 99
Configuring RSS 100
  Installing RSS 100
  Configuring Remote Storage Service for the First Time 101
  Configuring RSS Volumes 101
  Adding New Volumes 104
  Configuring RSS Properties 104
  Configuring RSS Media 105
Administering RSS 107
  Copying RSS Data 108
  Using Task Scheduler to Automate RSS Media Copy Operations ..108
  Browsing Remotely Stored Data 109
  Supporting Down-Level Client 111
  Using the Remote Storage File Analysis Utility (rsdir.exe) 112
  Using the Remote Storage Diagnostic Utility (rsdiag.exe) 112
Backup and Recovery of the RSS Database 114
RSS and Dfs 114
  How It Works 115
  Configuring a Stand-Alone Dfs Server 116

Chapter 5 SCSI Solutions 119
What Is SCSI? 120
  A History of Evolution: From SASI to SCSI-3 120
  SCSI Terminology 122
What Exactly Is the SCSI Bus? 122
  Narrow and Wide Buses 123
  SCSI IDs and LUNs 124

	The Parallel SCSI Interface 125
	SE, HVD, LVD 125
	Termination 129
	Cables 132
	Stubs 133
	Internal and External Cables 133
	SCSI Speeds 134
	Terminology Summary 136
	Troubleshooting SCSI 137
	Final Thoughts 142
Chapter 6	**Storage Area Networks (SANs)** **145**
	The Benefits of a SAN Solution 146
	Understanding Fibre Channel 148
	Benefits of Fibre Channel 148
	The Two Flavors of Fibre Channel 149
	Fibre Channel Specifications 151
	Understanding Fibre Channel Topologies 154
	Point-to-Point 154
	Arbitrated Loop 154
	Fabrics 156
	Exploring SAN Components 157
	The Brocade Perspective: Protecting Your Data 158
	SAN Benefits 159
	The Brocade Family 164
	Vendor Options 166
	Additional Details for SANs 167
	Dynamic Drive Sharing 167
	SAN Appliances 168
	So Much to Learn… 169
Chapter 7	**Network Attached Storage (NAS)** **171**
	What Is NAS? 171
	NAS vs. SAN 174
	NFS and CIFS 176
	Understanding Network File System (NFS) 176
	Understanding Common Internet File System (CIFS) 177

What Is NDMP? ...178
   NDMP Arrives ...178
   How Does NDMP Work? ...178
   Compliance Benefits ...180
Backup Strategies for NAS ...182
   Backing Up over the LAN (without NDMP) ...183
   Backing Up the Filer to a Locally Attached Library ...184
   Backing Up from One Filer to Another (Three-Way) ...184
   Backing Up from the Filer to the Server ...185
   Backing Up from the Server to the Filer ...185
   Who Supports What? ...185
NAS: The Microsoft Way ...186
   Windows-Powered NAS? ...186
   What's Wrong with This Picture? ...188
NAS by Network Appliance ...189
   Snapshots 101 ...190
   Implementing Your Network Appliance Filer ...193
EMC NAS ...199
NAS and the Future ...199

Chapter 8 RAID Technology ...201
Just a Bunch of Disks (JBOD) ...202
   When to Use JBOD ...202
   When JBOD Is Not the Answer ...203
Redundant Array of Inexpensive Disks (RAID) ...203
   RAID 0 ...203
   RAID 1 ...204
   RAID 5 ...206
   RAID 10 ...207
   RAID 50 ...208
Hardware RAID ...209
Windows 2000 Software RAID Solutions ...210
   Basic versus Dynamic Disks ...211
   Creating a RAID 0 Striped Volume ...213
   Creating a RAID 1 Mirrored Volume ...214
   Creating a RAID 5 Volume ...215
   Creating a Spanned Volume ...216

		Moving Disks 216
		When Good Volumes Go Bad 217
		Recovering a Failed RAID 1 Mirror 218
		Recovering a Failed RAID 5 Array 220
Chapter	**9**	**Cluster Technology** **221**
		Clustering Essentials 222
		Configuring Clusters 222
		Server Clusters 223
		Network Load Balanced Clusters 225
		Component Load Balanced Clusters 226
		Configuring Resources and Groups 227
		Addressing Single Points of Failure 228
		Planning Cluster Deployment 229
		Checking Compatibility and System Requirements ..229
		Choosing the Right Model 230
		Planning for Resource and Group Configuration ..236
		Planning for Failover 238
		Planning for Active Directory Issues 239
		Installing the Cluster Service 239
		Making Final Hardware Preparations 240
		Configuring the Final Network Settings 241
		Creating a Domain Account for the Cluster Service ..242
		Assigning Drive Letters to Shared Storage 244
		Installing the Cluster Service 245
		Verifying Failover 247
		Administering the Cluster Service 248
		Using the Cluster Administrator 248
		Using the Cluster Command 259
		Using the Cluster Command 260
		Using the Cluster Group Command 262
		Using the Cluster Network Command 263
		Using the Cluster Node Command 263
		Using the Cluster Resource Command 265
Chapter	**10**	**File System Backup and Recovery** **267**
		Creating an Emergency Repair Disk 267
		Creating an ERD 268
		Using Windows 2000 Repair 269

    Performing Backups 274
      Full Backups: The Foundation 275
      Effect of Open Files on Backups 277
      Setting Up a Backup Schedule 278
    Restoring Windows 2000 Systems 284
      Restoring Files, Folders, and Volumes 285
      Restoring the System State 287
      Recovering Domain Controllers 288
      Restoring Active Directory Objects 294

Chapter 11 Operating System Rebuilds: The Gotchas **297**

    Overlooking the Obvious 298
      Using Diskmap 299
    Restoring to Different Hardware 300
      The Longer but Safer Road to Recovery 301
    Encrypting File System 303
      Encrypting Data 303
      The Gotchas of EFS Management 304
    DHCP Database Recovery 320
      Using DHCP Server Conflict Detection 320
      When Trouble Arises 322
    SIS Volume Recovery 324
      Rebuilding a SIS Volume 325
    Dfs Recovery Considerations 326
      Dfs Structure Table 326
      Recovering Dfs Replicas 327
    Losing WINS 327
      Configuring Automatic Backup 328
      Restoring the WINS Database from a Backup File 329

Chapter 12 Exchange 5.5/2000 Backup and Recovery **331**

    Understanding Exchange 5.5 Architecture 332
      Exchange 5.5 Log Files 332
      Exchange Database Structure and File Locations 334
      Putting It Together 335
    Backing Up Exchange 5.5 336
      Understanding Offline Backups 337
      Using Windows Backup for Online Backups 340

Backup/Restore Strategy for Exchange 5.5 347
   Performing a Full Server Restore with 5.5 347
   Restoring a Mailbox 351
   The Full Recovery Server Issue 356
   Best Practices for Exchange 5.5 Recovery 359
Understanding Exchange 2000 Architecture 360
   Active Directory and Exchange 2000 360
   System State 360
   Understanding the New Storage Structure 361
   Exchange 2000 Reminders 362
Backing Up Your Exchange 2000 Server 363
   Restoring Your Exchange 2000 Server Databases 365
Backup/Restore Strategy for Exchange 2000 369
   Full Server Restores of Exchange 2000 369
   Restoring a Mailbox 371
Best Practices for Exchange 2000 Recovery 376
Going Forward 377

Chapter 13 SQL 7/2000 Backup/Recovery 379

Understanding SQL Basics 380
   Defining SQL Databases 381
   Defining Transaction Logs 382
   Defining Data Files 383
   Defining Filegroups 384
   Enterprise Manager 385
   Transact-SQL (T-SQL) 385
What's New with SQL 2000? 386
   Multiple Instances 387
   Log Shipping 387
   Fast Differential Backups 388
   Copy Database Wizard 388
   Recovery Models 389
Backup and Recovery Planning 390
   Backup Types 391
   Backup Strategy 393
Backing Up SQL Databases 398
   Configuring Logical Backup Devices 398
   Running Backups with Enterprise Manager 399

	Running Backups with T-SQL 402
	Configuring Log Shipping on SQL 2000 Servers 405
	Copying SQL 2000 Databases with the Copy Database Wizard ... 409
	Restoring SQL Databases 411
	System Database Restore Issues 412
	Rebuilding the Master Database 413
	Restoring Databases with Enterprise Manager 414
	Restoring Databases with T-SQL 416
Chapter 14	**The Future of Storage** **419**
	Exploring Windows XP/.NET 420
	Volume Snapshots 420
	ERD Replaced with ASR 421
	System Restore 421
	Looking at Future Technologies 422
	Tunneling and iSCSI (IP Storage) 422
	Millipede Technology 423
	Optical Improvements 423
	Holographic Storage 424
	Virtualization 424
	Additional Technology 425
	Where Do You Want to Go Today? 426
Glossary	.... **427**
Index	.... *443*

Introduction

Think for a moment about a world without storage management. On September 11, 2001, after a horrific attack on the World Trade Center, many organizations had to implement their disaster recovery solutions. Following the collapse of the two towers, many websites went down, with organizations losing up to a million dollars a minute. Although this is such a small story—and certainly insignificant compared to the lives lost on that day—it still speaks volumes about the importance of storage management in the enterprise.

So, to continue with the story, after losing nearly all their hardware, many organizations were able to rekindle their web operations within a day. This is a true testament to what you can accomplish with proper planning and management of storage. By contrast, although some companies were able to quickly recover within hours, others were down for weeks.

With storage management in the enterprise, those who are aware of and use the current storage technologies certainly had an advantage over those who didn't. But it isn't just having the latest and greatest technologies that equates to a speedy recovery. How you use modern technology is just as important as merely having it. For example, we have worked with organizations that back up their terabyte NAS filers over the LAN. This is an approach that usually does not lend itself to speedy backups and recovery.

That is where this book comes into play. In this book, we will not only explain the current storage technologies, but we will also provide you with plenty of examples on how to use those technologies in an enterprise-level environment. If you are managing a small office, or several small offices, you should also find our examples on the use of Windows Backup useful, as well.

With the Windows 2000 architecture, countless new storage technologies do much more than just complicate your backup and recovery strategy. Many of these technologies will actually make storage management on your network much simpler. Although you may at this point have all of these technologies properly implemented, can you guarantee you will be able to recover everything in a failure? Your enterprise storage software undoubtedly promises to bring everything back, but does it deliver? Can it successfully bring back files such as the RSM database, Active Directory, encrypted files, or the IIS metabase? For answers to these questions, take a look inside this book.

What's in This Book

From this point, you might want to pick and choose your starting point. This is a reference book—one absolutely essential to making administrative decisions for storage and to carefully implementing the new storage-related features in Windows 2000. If we included all the storage knowledge available right now, this book would be thousands of pages.

These are the most important topics:

Chapter 1, "Windows 2000 Storage Overview" This chapter is a great way to catch up on modern improvements to storage. It includes an overview of the progress Microsoft has made in its operating system from times past into the present with Windows 2000. It's also a review of the differences between DAS, SANs, and NAS.

Chapter 2, "Storage Terminology" This is a great chapter for those who have little to no background in storage terms. Tape, DLT, magnetic, RAID, NAS, SAN—are these foreign terms to you? Then move onto Chapter 3.

Chapter 3, "Windows 2000 Storage Enhancements" Windows 2000 has several tools and services that will make your life easier. This chapter explains each of these tools and operating system improvements.

Chapter 4, "Working with Removable Storage Manager" See how Windows 2000 RSM enables you to maximize your storage resources. You will also see real-world examples of Windows 2000's HSM product, Remote Storage Service.

Chapter 5, "SCSI Solutions" SCSI is the current key to connectivity of tape libraries and drives. Get the ins and outs of SCSI specifications in this chapter, whether you've worked with SCSI for years or are just getting started.

Chapter 6, "Storage Area Networks (SANs)" Imagine a network set aside for storage, running over Fibre Channel. What is Fibre Channel, and what is a redundant storage solution? The experts answer these questions, and Brocade pitches its hat into the ring.

Chapter 7, "Network Attached Storage (NAS)" NAS appliances are quick and easy to set up. Learn how they work and how Microsoft is using Windows 2000 to create appliance solutions.

Chapter 8, "RAID Software" One of the fastest-growing backup mediums is a RAID array. This chapter explains how to configure disk arrays by using either hardware or the Windows 2000 operating system.

Chapter 9, "Cluster Technology" Get everything you need here to fully recover and rebuild a cluster server. You will see what to look out for from both a backup and a restore perspective.

Chapter 10, "File System Backup and Recovery" This chapter takes you through what is thought to be simple file system backup and recovery. You will also see how to safely recover domain controllers and how to restore individual Active Directory objects.

Chapter 11, "Operating System Rebuilds: The Gotchas" Restoring the operating system is the easy part. Restoring the operating system and having everything work as it did before is not as easy. When rebuilding a server, such as a WINS or DHCP server, you must be aware of the effect that the rebuilt server will have on existing clients. This chapter tells you everything you hadn't thought about when backing up and recovering Windows 2000 Servers.

Chapter 12, "Exchange 5.5/2000 Backup and Recovery" One chapter to handle two distinct platforms. How do we do it? Just the facts, ma'am.

Chapter 13, "SQL 7/2000 Backup/Recovery" As with Exchange, we give you the bare-bone essentials for recovering SQL servers. These pages provide everything you need to plan, to protect, and to actually recover a SQL database or server.

Chapter 14, "The Future of Storage" Storage is still changing. In this chapter we explore IBM's work on iSCSI as well as other developing technologies.

Don't Go Out Naked

For those of you who are aware of the Hans Christian Anderson story, *The Emperor's New Clothes*, you know it is the story of an emperor who hires some tailors to design him an outfit. Months go by with the tailors living it up; finally the Emperor demands to see his threads. The tailors build it up verbally and speak so highly that when they open the closet doors and nothing is inside, the Emperor is too proud to admit he can't see the clothes. He goes out in the parade in the outfit. Finally, a young child has the guts to tell him he's naked, and the Emperor has the tailors killed.

Great story, but how does it relate to storage? Modern solutions are complex and often require a full storage dictionary to understand. Marketing and technical discussions tend to be very high-end, and most people who talk about storage solutions aren't the ones actually working with them. Most are too proud to ask questions when the yarn is spinning wildly around them, filled with crazy words like *heterogeneous*, *SAN*, *NAS*, and *Fibre Channel*. We need to admit sometimes that we are barely clothed with the knowledge of storage that we need. Don't let the marketing hype overwhelm you. Don't go out naked. Read this book and make sure you're getting a full set of clothes from vendors. And if any of the terminology catches you off guard within the book, learn to overcome the habit to simply let it pass; instead, turn to the Glossary to understand the proper context and usage of storage terminology.

Windows 2000 Storage Overview

OK, there is a good chance you're reading the first line of this book in the store right in front of about 10 other books about enterprise storage solution. Look at them for a moment. Can we sum up the lot of them in a single word? Boring. Say it with us: *Boring*.

Well, you might think storage is not exactly the most exciting topic—but is that true, or is it just that most books present the wrong angle? For example, if you wanted to learn to ski, would you read a book about the incredible uniqueness of snow and then study the many crystal-like shapes it forms? Most likely not. So then why read a book about the formation of Fibre Channel standards that reads like toothpaste ingredients when you need to know about real-life implementation?

Allow us to show you how wild a ride storage solutions can turn out to be. All right, skip that—let us at least teach you the real ins and outs of storage management and give you that edge in the workplace as you master what most industry experts are saying will be the biggest field in the first decade of the 2000s: storage.

> **NOTE** It's important to state at the outset that storage comprises three major factors, as opposed to the standard "backup of data" concept that most people have. Storage consists of the management of data, the continuous availability of that data, and the restoration of data in the case of a loss. Expanding the definition to include these avenues may begin the process of broadening the understanding of storage solutions.

Storage Growth

The need for storage solutions has always been a part of an enterprise network infrastructure. The recent growth in this segment of the market, however, is primarily a result of the dot-com boom, coupled with average brick-and-mortar companies realizing the importance of storage technology and implementing it within their network designs. Fortune 500 companies have also realized the benefits of transcending regular marketplaces and have taken to the Internet to increase business. A final contributing factor to corporate awareness of data management solutions is fear. A company is based upon data and if that data is lost, the company is lost with it.

> **NOTE** *Brick and mortar* is a term used in e-commerce to define a traditional business, such as Macy's, Kmart, Barnes & Noble, and so on. It mainly pertains to businesses with physical locations that customers visit to purchase merchandise. However, that doesn't limit a company to that form of business only; for example, Barnes & Noble also has a strong web clientele.

You might try to imagine the moment when the first corporate webmaster went running to his boss and screamed, "Where in the world are we going to keep all this information we're putting on the Web?" In fact, it reminds us of a *Star Trek* episode: "Captain, the main drives are at maximum—they're gonna blow!" "Add more hard disk space, whatever it takes!" But we digress: The point is that there was a beginning to this increase in data management needs.

There was a time when computers were just for employees who performed a specific task or ran a special application (that is, accounting, word processing, and so on). This is no longer the case. The introduction of the Internet, intranets, e-mail, and the increasing number of end users have also contributed to the massive amounts of data that need to be stored.

And let us not forget the role that broadband has played in the evolution of streaming and downloadable media. All in all, this makes for a lot of data, and this data needs to be managed and maintained. (That's not to say you need to support and condone your users' fetish for MP3 downloads.)

So, data is growing and the need to manage that data is growing with it. We're not talking about 100MB Zip drives here; we're talking terabytes of information populating every nook and cranny of the Internet. Enterprise storage is not crawling forward; it's flying. Some companies are estimating a 50-percent growth rate a year; others are crying 100 percent. Where to put it all?

Microsoft Takes the Challenge

Microsoft's enterprise network solutions are beginning to be taken seriously with Windows 2000. On February 17, 2000, with the release of Windows 2000, Microsoft solidified their claim to enterprise networking. It only makes sense that, in addition, they've made strategic moves to become storage ready.

A recent white paper by Microsoft (*Enterprise Class Storage in the Next Generation of Windows NT*) estimates that the quantity of data being stored on NT-based servers has reached 39 petabytes worldwide and that by 2002, Windows 2000 Server data is projected to exceed 260 petabytes. This is a staggering number when you consider that Microsoft is but one competitor in the network operating systems market. In this book, we discuss how Microsoft has answered the call for better storage solutions and has risen to the challenge that companies are facing as their data is more than doubling each year. Windows 2000 is ready to handle enterprise storage solutions now and in the future.

From Then 'Til Now...

Before we begin discussing Microsoft's storage solutions for Windows 2000, we should give you some background. Let's start with a brief history (or lack of history) on Microsoft's storage solutions prior to the release of Windows 2000.

When Microsoft went out on its own (after its partnership with IBM over DOS), they began their venture with a desktop operating system called Windows. We all know the effect that Windows 3 and its predecessors had on the personal-computer market. It's an effect still being felt today. Most desktops are running some form of Windows, from Windows 95/98 to Windows Millennium Edition (for the Home) or Windows NT/2000 Professional (for Business).

However, although Windows overtook the desktop operating system market from the beginning, Novell NetWare and the various flavors of Unix remained the backbone network operating systems (NOSs). That began to change with the release of Windows for Workgroups 3.11.

Windows for Workgroups was not the ultimate network operating system, but it showed that Microsoft had definitely turned its attention toward the benefits of networking resources. They also turned their attention toward a huge segment of the personal-computer market. Microsoft said, "Show me the money!" and they got it.

Windows for Workgroups offered some of the features of a real network operating system, but was, in reality, still a workstation-based operating system that relied upon a separate backbone. Although this offered easier interoperability with Netware and Unix servers, it still relied upon integration with a third-party NOS.

Enter Windows NT. Microsoft at last had forayed into the network operating system marketplace. NT was to be Microsoft's answer to Novell, Sun Microsystems, and various other Unix vendors. This was a full embodiment of what an NOS was supposed to be, and of course it offered the graphical user interface (GUI) Windows environment that has been the cornerstone of Microsoft's success.

With the introduction of NT, Microsoft finally addressed the server side of a network infrastructure. NT could offer the benefits of shared resources, user administration, redundancy, and storage. Prior to NT, there were no storage solutions because, as we've said, Windows had been a desktop or workstation operating system.

This history lays a good foundation for what this book is all about. It is now easy to understand and even perhaps forgive Bill & Co. for their previous lack of depth in the area of storage solutions. Microsoft is, after all, a babe at the game of developing storage strategies.

Windows 2000 has made vast improvements. You'll be amazed at some of the changes. Even if you've been working with Windows 2000, watch and see how much it can do that you were completely unaware of. However, we need to return to our little history lesson for now.

NTBackup

At the heart of Microsoft's storage solutions are New Technology File System (NTFS) and the NTBackup utility. NTFS was developed as a means of supplying security, disk recovery, support for long Unicode naming schemes, and large volume support. The importance of NTFS in storage solutions has more to do with architecture than implementation. And NTFS 5 for Windows 2000 plays a major role in storage solutions by providing new storage enhancements that we will cover in detail in Chapter 4, "Working with Removable Storage Manager," and Chapter 5, "SCSI Solutions." But for now, we are focusing on the history of storage solutions, and so let's take a deeper look at the NTBackup utility of old.

NTBackup was introduced with the release of NT 3.5 (Microsoft's first true NOS release). NTBackup offered a rudimentary storage and disaster recovery utility for the system administrator in the form of tape backup. Although this was cost-effective and offered an easy interface for quick and simple backups, NTBackup was better known as a "disaster" rather than a "disaster recovery solution" and storage utility. NT 4 followed suit with the inclusion of NTBackup.

Of course, in the interest of getting a product to the market, Microsoft did what anyone would have. They sacrificed the less important functions and utilities for those that were more in demand. After all, a network operating system did not have to necessarily be a network storage solution as well. However, some basic components were essential, and NTBackup did address these to a degree.

NTBackup also supported FAT and NTFS. These were the default file systems for NT, so it only made sense that NTBackup was able to handle them. (HPFS was also supported in NT 3.5 but was dropped with 4.) Another advantage was that NTBackup was included with the operating system, which made it theoretically more stable. (Note the word *theoretically*. Go to Microsoft's Knowledge Base and research NTBackup and see how many problem articles surface. Then reconsider the word *stable*.) Although NTBackup took care of some of the administrator's basic needs for creating an effective backup, it had many more drawbacks.

Let's review these drawbacks quickly.

Drawback Number 1

The first drawback of NTBackup was that it supported only tape (specifically SCSI tape drive) backup. This means you couldn't use a hard disk (magnetic), a CD-R/CD-RW drive, a DVD-RAM drive, or a network drive to create a backup. (Although these technologies didn't exist initially, as they became more widely available in the market, it was obvious they were missing support from NTBackup.) Although this might not seem that bad at first, the ability to create a backup onto media other than tape affords system administrators with alternatives if a tape drive breaks down and a substitute is not immediately available.

Drawback Number 2

NTBackup lacked the capability to easily schedule backups. Now when you think of scheduling within a backup utility, some might think of just a time schedule for backups. This is essential but strangely absent from NTBackup. You *could* write a batch file along with various switches, but that would only start the backup process. You would then need to use the AT command and yet even more switches to enable you to schedule a time to start the backup. Although this worked, it must be said that it was a long and cumbersome process.

An additional pitfall related to the lack of scheduling was NTBackup's inability to handle tape rotation methods and media management computations. These features are addressed further in Chapter 2, "Storage Terminology."

The ability to have an authorized user alerted if the backup job should fail was also missing from NTBackup. This is an invaluable tool as it offers the option of returning to the site either that day/night or early the next morning to get a backup. Without this feature, an administrator has no recourse except to wait for the next scheduled backup.

Drawback Number 3

NTBackup does not have the ability to back up open files. This was and is imperative in an environment that uses SQL or Exchange. In addition to SQL or Exchange, a network may have NT as its backbone but may be using Lotus Notes, Oracle, SAP, or any other application that remains active during a backup and can be affected by this lack of ability.

Third-party companies offer agents, for a price, that can back up open databases and open files, such as a SQL database. In many companies, this is the principal data that needs to be protected by backup. NTBackup provided no function for backing up this critical data. Agents provide the ability to copy this data in real time and add it to the backup.

Drawback Number 4

Another of NTBackup's shortcomings was that you couldn't back up a remote system's hard drives or registries. There was a workaround to this also, of course. You could map the remote drive to the server. In a small environment, this might not be that bad. But in an enterprise environment with multiple servers, you would need to either physically attach a tape drive to the system or map the drive with the resources to the backup server.

Drawback Number 5

Last, and by far perhaps the worst problem with NTBackup, was that it required you to catalog a tape to view its contents. The problem was that every time you closed NTBackup, it deleted the temp file, which contained the catalog. The only workaround was to move the file from the temp folder and close NTBackup, and then return the file to the temp folder when you needed to browse the catalog. If you forgot to do this, NTBackup would go through the process of scanning the tape and creating the catalog all over again. This could waste valuable time. So you had to know that the file was being copied to the temp folder in the first place and that its name ended with U01, or enjoy the wait.

Final Word on History: It's, Well...History.

NTBackup, while offering a simple, cost-effective solution for storage management, left too many "what-ifs" to make it worthwhile. Therefore, it has stood as an unused and hopefully unneeded utility that just happened to be packaged with Windows NT. Most system administrators cringe at the mere mention of NTBackup.

With few or none of the features that were sought by system administrators, NTBackup was not really a storage solution at all. It was merely a utility. Limited in functionality, NTBackup was to be used only in cases of severe emergency.

Want the shorter version of the last couple of pages? These are the advantages of NTBackup with NT 4:

- It's free! Hey, let's face it, free is sometimes what we need. We can't all be working on GHz systems with flat-screen monitors.
- NTBackup is relatively easy to use.
- It can use full, incremental, and differential backup strategies.
- It can handle NTFS or FAT.
- You can schedule backups with a little work.

These are the disadvantages of NTBackup with NT 4:

- It has no online catalogs or databases to perform restores.
- Open or locked files or folders will not back up.
- Each NT system has to be configured separately for backups.
- Tape libraries are not supported.
- Tape devices are the only supported medium.

Storage Grows Beyond Itself

To pretend that the storage world begins and ends with NTBackup is foolish. This is but one poorly designed backup application embedded into the NT operating system. Where storage issues really begin is with the need for more storage. Another growing dilemma is the need for storage to have less of an effect on a production network. Herein lie the issues.

According to a study completed by the School of Information Management and Systems at the University of California, Berkeley, an estimated 635,480 to 2,120,539TB of unique data is being generated each year worldwide. Of this information, about

300,000 to 600,000TB are generated by departmental and enterprise servers. For more information, see the *How Much Information?* study at www.sims.Berkeley.edu/research/projects/how-much-info/summary.html.

The solutions are not moving as fast as the data. Every day, technology biggies such as IBM, Cisco Systems, Microsoft, EMC, CommVault Systems, Veritas Software, Legato Systems, and a host of other companies are racing against time to handle the newer issues of storage. To begin to understand the process, let's look into some of the current solutions.

Direct Attached Storage (DAS)

Direct Attached (or Server Attached) Storage is what it sounds like: storage attached directly to a server, either externally or internally. It generally refers to a RAID array (Redundant Array of Independent, or Inexpensive, Disks) or JBOD (Just a Bunch of Disks) solution. Figure 1.1 illustrates Direct Attached Storage.

Figure 1.1: Direct Attached Storage

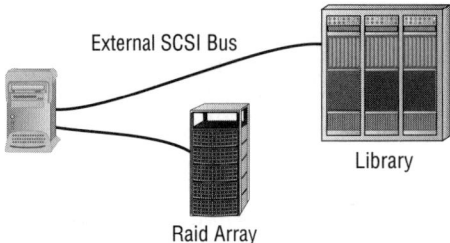

Although this is the most common type of storage in our market, it has some obvious limitations. For one thing DAS relies on the server being available. If, for any reason, the storage is offline, then your data is not accessible by your users. This allows for two points of failure, the server and the DAS device itself.

> **NOTE** Some might say that another drawback is cost, but in reality, when you start comparing prices for storage solutions, it's going to cost you either way. Watch the sales jargon that DAS costs more than other, newer technologies, such as SAN, in the long run. A great deal depends upon your needs. Enterprise solutions are for enterprise corporations. Don't allow the marketing hype to force you into a SAN solution (which you'll learn about later in this section) for your two-server environment, with two servers that sit three feet apart from each other. In that case, a DAS solution is cheaper, easier to implement, and much more reliable.

Another drawback to DAS is that you handle your data on a server-by-server basis. You need to worry about the various volumes of data, provide for fault tolerance for that data (with some form of backup solution), and consider security issues for the server and its contents. These are normal concerns, but the point is that server-by-server management means increased time (and time is money) and less control. In fact, some say more money is spent managing storage than buying it. So, in large environments it's important to consider the extent to which your administrators will manage data. This is one of the reasons that companies have changed their marketing from "Backup Software" to "Data Management Solutions" because the key focus is not so much on simply backing it up but on the centralized control of data, additional security, and fault tolerance on both the daily level ("Oops! I deleted an e-mail I need") and the disaster level ("Oops! I burned down the entire building, and I need to restore the data").

You have less control of individual server usage as well. In a multiple-server arrangement, you might have one server with plenty of space left on it, while another server is completely maxed out. What do you do? Let's say your Exchange server is busting at the seams with data. What is the solution? Logically, even if you have another server with room, you are most likely forced into trying to eliminate unnecessary data on the Exchange server or going out and purchasing more hardware—additional spending for no other reason except that the available space on one server is not transferable to the other in a DAS environment. Interesting, huh?

When we combine the growing importance of data and the increasing volume, there is a need for diverse solutions. Those solutions consist of online solutions (enabling data to be accessible and available $24 \times 7 \times 365$) and offline storage solutions (enabling storage to be restorable $24 \times 7 \times 365$). Perhaps, then, NAS or SAN is your answer.

Network Attached Storage (NAS)

Chapter 7, "Network Attached Storage (NAS)," is wholly devoted to the subject, but let's whet your appetite a bit right here. NAS is a storage pool. In the case of NAS devices or appliances, you attach the storage pool, or appliance, directly to the existing network and therefore remove the server from the equation in terms of management and point of failure for your online storage. Figure 1.2 shows an example of NAS storage.

This solution is not to imply that NAS appliances are ghost driven (that is, without an operating system, of the paranormal) but rather, they hold a very lightweight, task-specific operating system (usually Unix based, and more recently Windows 2000–based), which can quickly and easily be managed.

Figure 1.2: A NAS solution

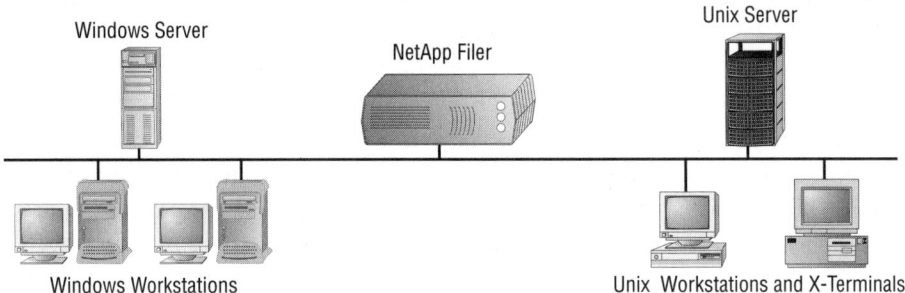

NAS appliances allow for sharing of all types of services between different types of servers, including using NFS and CIFS (formerly SMB), which are file server protocols that Unix- and Windows-based systems use for file access from clients' systems.

The cool features of NAS may not be enough to draw you into this type of solution, but the savings might. By having a system that can contain multiple file types and is easy to install, easy to administer, and easy to back up (NAS appliances can be backed up by using SCSI ports on the back directly connected to offline storage, or through mapped/mounted shares off to another solution)—the bottom line is you save money and time in administration.

In addition, the problem mentioned earlier with DAS concerning diverse storage causing problems with misplaced storage needs is resolved; NAS contains a cost-effective solution of storage located in a single place for all to use. When more storage is needed, simply add it into your existing NAS solution.

Are there downsides to NAS? With NAS you attach a storage pool to your existing (most likely overburdened) production network. That can't be a good thing. With the advent of Gigabit Ethernet and other solutions, this may not be as big an issue, but when your current network structure is already highly utilized, it's good to remember that NAS solutions should be developed in harmony with high-speed network infrastructure changes.

Interested in learning more? Chapter 7 is your next stop then.

Storage Area Networks (SAN)

A Storage Area Network (SAN) solution takes your storage off your production network and places it on a high-speed, dedicated storage network. By creating a separate network, you remove the strain that is put on the production network in terms of input/output (I/O) requests and backup solutions.

The first design/implementation of SAN took existing Ethernet technology to create a secondary network with SCSI devices. This is still an affordable and reasonable solution for many companies. But with the belief that storage could and should be separate came the advent of better, faster methods of data transport. Fibre Channel (not *Fiber*) is the product of those beliefs, allowing for both copper and fiber-optic medium to transport your data on your SAN.

> **NOTE** Although Fibre Channel is gaining acceptance, its still the workings of Fibre Channel in conjunction with SCSI devices and cabling that make a SAN whole. SCSI is a huge part of the storage world that any storage administrator should understand. We help you to increase that knowledge in Chapter 5, "SCSI Solutions.") Others claim that Fibre Channel, due to expense and limitations, will be pushed out by a future technology called iSCSI. True or not? Chapter 14, "The Future of Storage," gives the IBM perspective on the future.

By using a SAN for your storage needs, you can pull the storage out of the production network, leaving the production network to handle client requests and application-intensive needs. Figure 1.3 illustrates the concept of a SAN.

With a SAN, there are many technologies, configurations, and troubleshooting points to consider—certainly a great deal to learn about. This is one of the hottest technologies developing these days, and Chapter 6, "Storage Area Networks (SANs)," goes into greater detail, including SAN deployment, Fibre Channel facts and topologies, and a special report from one of the leading SAN switch manufacturers, Brocade Systems.

Windows 2000 Storage—It Begins

In addition to the changes being made in the underlying hardware and infrastructure technology, software is advancing to handle the needs of the global community. Microsoft has entered the battle of storage with Windows 2000, by including directly within the operating system several key features, including a new backup utility called Windows Backup, a lighter version of Veritas's Backup Exec product. Some may say this isn't new; the tool is still called ntbackup.exe, just like its predecessor. NTBackup was also from Veritas; however, this tool is visibly different, as you'll see.

Windows Backup is an enhanced product as compared to NTBackup that provides support for Active Directory, Removable Storage Management (RSM), automatic system recovery, disk-to-disk backup operations, and new file system objects that come with NTFS 5. It also has a new GUI and wizards that will totally blow you away if you remember the older tool.

Figure 1.3: A SAN configuration

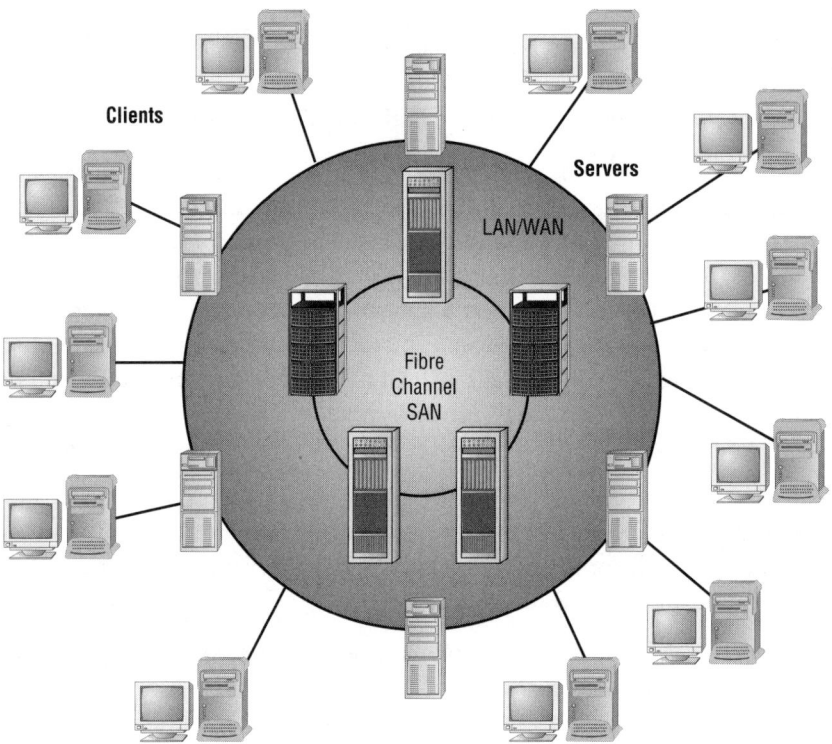

Microsoft steps into the ring of enterprise storage with more than a backup program. There are tons of enhancements to the storage components included with Windows 2000.

Some of the great enhancements include the following:

- Removable Storage Manager (RSM)
- Remote Storage Service (RSS)
- Reparse points
- Volume mount points
- Windows File Protection (WFP)
- NTFS Change Journal
- Indexing Service

- Sparse files
- Single Instance Storage (SIS)
- File Replication Service (FRS)
- Distributed File System (Dfs)
- Encrypting File System (EFS)
- Disk quotas
- System State

If these new features seem a bit new to you, that's great, because Chapter 3, "Windows 2000 Storage Enhancements," teaches you what they are. Then Chapter 4, "Working with Removable Storage Manager," makes you a professional with Windows 2000 RSM and RSS, including the in-depth tips and tricks you need to implement these new features within your enterprise storage solution.

In addition to these features, you might be interested in learning about Microsoft's new cluster abilities, which are covered in Chapter 9, "Cluster Technology." If you are an administrator of a SQL or Exchange environment, then Chapter 12, "Exchange 5.5/2000 Backup/Recovery" and Chapter 13, "SQL 7/2000 Backup/Recovery," will round out your backup/recovery knowledge of these systems.

Storage Terminology

Before we thrill you with the amazing things Microsoft has done with storage for Windows 2000, we need to give you some background on storage and discuss the terminology in this book. If you've been working with storage for a while now, skip to Chapter 3, "Windows 2000 Storage Enhancements"; for newcomers, you should read this chapter before even thinking about working with storage.

Because storage is composed of many different media types, devices, and methodologies, many of the terms used in this book may not be familiar. Unlike Internet, networking, and general computer terminology, storage terms just aren't as commonplace. Moreover, standards are pretty wide open for the storage industry. But that's not to say that no standards exist; there are just many choices. And, as such, storage terminology can be pretty overwhelming for a seasoned information technology (IT) person—let alone a newcomer. So, this chapter covers some basic information that will help you understand the rest of the book. If some of the terms seem to include other terms that you aren't familiar with, check to see if these are also explained in this chapter. Or check the Glossary at the back of the book for more assistance. By the way, we hope you like acronyms B.T.C.H.P.*

*Because this chapter has plenty.

Defining Storage Terms

Let's start by defining what we mean when we use the term *storage*. Storage is a semi-permanent or permanent place for holding data. This refers to tape, disks, or optical media. This does not include volatile media such as Random Access Memory (RAM). The emphasis is on the potential long-term permanency of the data to be held.

OK, you might stop here and say, "What exactly is media, and what are tapes, disks, and optical media?" Good question. These terms are often thrown out in storage conversations, and people usually nod their understanding, but without a real background in terminology, these are usually just high-end conversations. Let's bring them back down to earth. These terms are all covered in the next sections.

Understanding General Terms

These terms relate to storage in general. They will be used throughout the book, so become familiar with their definitions now.

Data Management Software   The high-end way of saying *backup software*. However, most companies want the emphasis to be that the software backs up, restores, remembers where the data is kept, keeps track of the your storage devices, knows when it's time to change drives and tapes, and knows when you should clean those drives.

Fault Tolerance   The ability of a system to continue nonstop even with a hardware failure, without disrupting the flow of data. This term describes many different types of solutions.

Compatibility   Refers to the storage system having the ability to work with many different systems or operating platforms.

Connectivity   The ability of the storage system to interface with multiple hosts seamlessly.

Expandability   Simply put, the ability to expand your storage system without having to purchase an entirely new solution.

Scalability   Refers to the ability to expand your storage system incrementally as needed. This may sound similar to expandability because, well, it is pretty much the same.

Globally Unique Identifier (GUID)   A 32-byte string assigned to both logical and physical media. Running the `Guidgen.exe` (which Microsoft internally uses even though there are other GUID generators in existence) command-line program creates this number. `Guidgen.exe` never produces the same number twice, no matter how many times it is run or how many different machines it runs on.

Every entity that needs to be uniquely identified (such as an interface) has a GUID. These GUIDs are handy for unique IDs for databases or anything else.

Latency   The time when a request is initiated until the time the request is actually implemented by the system.

Port   Point of connection for moving data in and out of a computer. Ports can provide controlled access to a media in a library.

Redundancy   A duplicate of peripherals or components that ensure the continuation of operation should one of the devices fail.

Data Transfer Rate   Measured in megabytes per second, this is the amount of data transferred both in a burst or sustained level in that given period of time.

Availability   The time a system can be accessed by users. The term *availability* within storage usually implies 24/7/365 availability. Companies want all data to be available at all times, no matter what happens.

Understanding Media Terms

Media refers to the place where data will reside. The following terms will help you in understanding the in-depth discussions of media that come up later on in the book.

Physical Media   Refers to a real item that stores data. This is what is mounted and dismounted or inserted and removed from drives and libraries.

Media Type   Defines the fixed or removable object used to store data. Examples are disk drives, CD-RWs, DLT tape, AIT tape, and so on; these are all defined later in this chapter.

Media Pools   A logical grouping of removable media that share management policies. These management policies are created through the use of data-management software.

Sides   Refers to media sides where data is actually stored, such as the sides of a cassette tape.

Available Media   Side of media available to be allocated. Any application that has access to the media or media pool can claim the available media.

Allocated   Reserved for use by an application. Once media is reserved or allocated, it cannot be used by any other application. Only writeable media may be allocated.

Deallocated   A media side no longer reserved for use with an application. This side could then be held for reserve or allocation by another application.

Understanding Drive Terms

Media is used in connection with *drives* that read and write data onto that media. You may work with one drive for your storage needs or you might use a library that contains many drives. The following terms will ensure your understanding of drives.

Drive A device that is able to read and write data onto media. A DLT tape drive is a good example of a device that can read and write to DLT tapes. There are different types of drives, including stand-alone drives or drives inside libraries.

Stand-Alone Libraries A device that holds one piece of media at a time and is operated manually.

Mount The insertion of removable media into a physical drive.

Dismount The removal of tape or disk from a physical drive.

Understanding Library Terms

When drives are combined and a robotic arm is included, you've moved into the more expensive methods of storage: using a library. The following terms will increase your understanding of the various library components.

Library A data storage system, which consists of both the storage media (tape, disk, cartridge) and the hardware device that can read and write to the media. There are two major types of libraries: stand-alone (defined in the previous "Drive Terms" section) and robotic.

Robotic Libraries (Online Library) Can consist of multiple device drives and media. They are automated through a robotic arm, which, to say the least, is cool to watch and, in the case of the TimberWolf Library, is very *Terminator-esque*. There is a door, a bar code reader, and a transport, which is the arm itself.

Slots Storage locations used in a tape library. These are sometimes arranged into collections called *magazines*.

Bar Code A physical label attached to the media, which is machine-readable. This is similar to bar codes on most goods packaged for resale today. It's a way for your data-management software to keep track of which tape holds which data. It's a hateful day when your labels fall off your tapes, because if you mix them up you have a real problem on your hands.

Door Used to gain free access to the contents of a storage library.

Transport A robotic device that gets a medium from its slot to a drive and then back to its slot.

Offline Media   A collection of media that Removable Storage Manager (RSM) has catalogued but is not currently in any library, such as media that have been backed up, dismounted, and stored away from the physical device.

Understanding Enterprise Storage Terms

As your organization grows, you begin to move past the equipment itself as your solution to storage and you begin to look for additional methods to assist in controlling that storage. You may look to a Storage Area Network (SAN), or you may look to built-in Microsoft tools such as Removable Storage Manager (RSM). The following terms will give you your initial introduction into the world of enterprise storage solutions.

Removable Storage Manager (RSM)   Microsoft's built-in service for Windows 2000 that simplifies communication between applications, robotic changers, and media libraries. For more information, see Chapter 4, "Working with Removable Storage Manager (RSM)."

Operator Requests   Used with RSM when human interaction is needed in a robotic library.

Storage Area Networks (SAN)   These involve creating an organized network separate from your production network and only handles storage needs. SANs commonly employ Fibre Channel (copper or optical) to connect your libraries with your servers, enabling multiple access points for your data. For more information, see Chapter 6, "Storage Area Networks (SANs)."

Network Attached Storage (NAS)   NAS devices allow for quick storage solutions that primarily allow you to "plug and play" your storage into your existing Ethernet networks. For more information, see Chapter 7, "Network Attached Storage (NAS)."

Random/Redundant Array of Independent/Inexpensive Disks (RAID)
A disk subsystem that uses two or more physical disks and a controller card (called a RAID card) to provide increased performance and/or fault tolerance. There are also "software" RAID solutions that require no special controller card. Windows 2000 supports several software RAID solutions. For more information, see Chapter 8, "RAID Technology."

Striping   Distribution of data across two or more disks in an array. This reduces the latency that may occur in accessing data.

Clustering   A group of independent servers configured so that they appear on a network as a single machine. This group is managed as a single system, shares a common namespace, and is designed specifically to tolerate component failures and to support the addition or subtraction of components in a way that's transparent to users. For more information, see Chapter 9, "Cluster Technology."

Defining Your Backup Strategy

Performing a backup should become routine, much like bringing your license with you when you drive. Can you get by without it? Sure, it doesn't affect your everyday driving, but don't get pulled over. Backups are similar. You can get by at times without remembering to do them, but what if you forget for a couple of days and the server goes down ? You better start looking for new work.

So, you need to consider a plan of structured protection. To begin with, you need to know the different types of backups available and how each works. The inner workings of many backups begin with the use of a feature called the *archive attribute*.

Simply put, archive attributes are used to determine under certain circumstances if files were backed up. Backup software uses these archive bits to determine which files need to be backed up and which have already been backed up. That is not to say that this is the only method; additional methods are called upon in modern data-management software.

These bits are simply tag attributes (such as hidden and read-only), which reside on files and folders and allow backup software to determine through the bits if a backup has occurred. If it has, then the bit is off, and if it hasn't, then the bit is on. These bits are not the last word in truth, however. In considering the various types of backup options, there may be a time when you've performed a backup, and the bit is still left on.

Moving into Windows 2000 begins a new phase of backup tracking through a Change Journal (although many backup programs still use the archive bit alone).

The Change Journal is a more accurate way to track changes that occur to files and folders and is part of the strong set of features that come with NTFS 5. The Change Journal keeps track of all changes made, including changing the name of the file/folder or changing permissions on a file/folder, which is not a feature of archive bits. A good example of the Change Journal in use is that a data-management application could use the Change Journal to build the list of files needed for an incremental backup because the Journal would know if changes have been made. The benefit of the Change Journal may not be immediately apparent, but it is faster.

Consider the following scenario: One day you perform a full backup, which turns the archive bits off of everything. You decide the following day to change the name of a file on which you've been working. In addition, you change some of the permissions on another file. You go to perform an incremental backup and those files are not included. Why? Because the archive bit isn't flipped when you change a name or permissions of objects. But if the backup application uses the Change Journal, it would back up those files because the Change Journal keeps track of every change, ensuring a clean backup.

Your Backup Options

There are five types of backups:

- Normal
- Incremental
- Differential
- Copy
- Daily

Normal, or full, backups will back up all files you personally select, whether that is a single file or folder or an entire drive. All files backed up have their archive attributes turned off to indicate their safe state. In the case of a full crash with a need for a full restore of all data, the full backup will be the fastest solution. The disadvantage, however, is that full backups take the longest to perform. As the amount of data your servers handle continues to grow, your window for backups shrink and your restore times grow. In other words, if you have a 12-hour backup but only an eight-hour window during the workweek to perform the backup, then you have a problem. You may decide to perform a full backup over the weekend and choose a faster method during the week.

Incremental backups will only back up those files that have changed since the last full or incremental backup. So, if a file was backed up yesterday and it hasn't changed today, then an incremental backup would not back the file up today. If a file was changed, then the incremental backup would note the change and back up the file. Then it would turn off the backup marker attribute.

> **NOTE**   You'll notice that the term *archive attribute* has been used for the most part to describe the archive bit setting. However, this term, along with terms such as *file marker* or *backup marker*, could be used interchangeably when describing the various backup methods.

The end result of this kind of backup is that you require shorter backup windows because you only back up changed data. The negative side is that a restore process, in the case of a failure, would be longer than full backup restores. You would have to restore the last full backup you performed and then restore each additional incremental backup. This could be time consuming.

Differential backups will back up all those files that have changed since the last full or incremental backup. Notice the difference is that a differential backup will back up all changed files but will not change the backup marker. So, if you performed a full backup on one day and files changed the next, the differential backup would back up those files, as would the incremental. The differential wouldn't turn off the backup attribute marker. As files continue to change, the differential backup times increase because it backs up all changed files since the last full or incremental. The positive side is that in the case of a restore issue, you only have to restore the last full backup (any incrementals, if you have used this method) and then your last differential. The negative side is that the backup process begins to grow every day.

Time is money, right? The question is, "Which time, the backup time or the restore time?" That is for you to decide in your environment. Figure 2.1 shows the difference between these backup methods.

Figure 2.1: Choosing your backup type

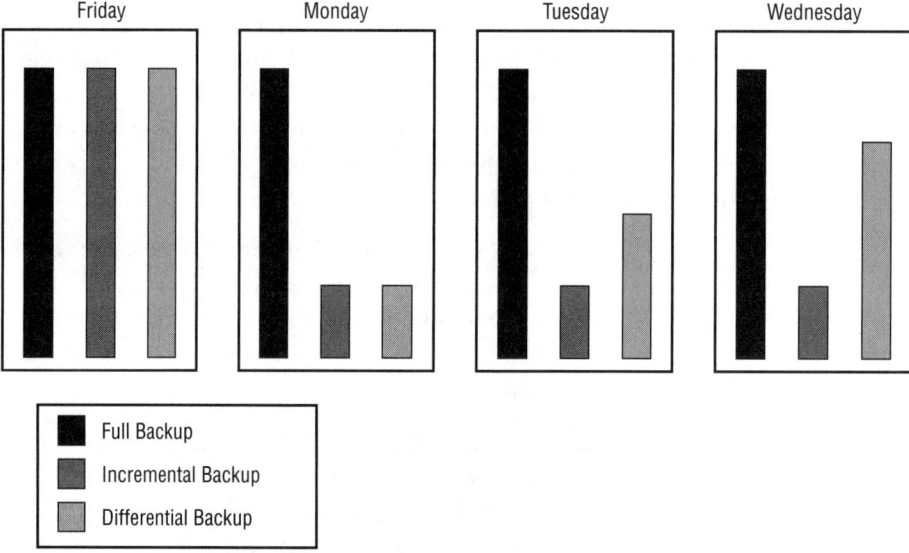

The figure shows an exaggerated view of what really happens, but you can see that the backups vary in size as the week progresses. Fulls remain constant, and the restore will be the quickest. Incremental backups involve less time per day but will require the longest restore. Differential backups involve more time as the week progresses, but to recover will only require the last full backup and the last differential.

The last two types of backups are not as complicated a choice as their predecessors.

Copy will copy (logical, huh?) all files selected without changing the archive attribute to indicate a backup. These are reasonable solutions when you simply want to copy a document but still want to ensure that it gets backed up with your pre-existing routine for backup.

Daily will back up all files that have been worked on within the day, without changing the archive attribute to indicate a backup. This will allow for a quick way to back up a day's work without searching for each document you worked on that day. You might use this type to grab for all documents you worked on to bring home.

Now that you have an understanding of different backup types, we'll look at the two typical types of tape rotation.

Defining Rotation Methods

If you have an unlimited amount of money and you can purchase new media for your backup solution, then you really don't need a rotation method; just back up your data and keep the media flowing. However, much like we usually don't wear a new pair of socks every day (you wash and reuse the ones you have), your media is expensive and cannot always be new. Most companies put a tourniquet on your spending in this regard and yet the job still needs to be accomplished within some degree of reasonability.

With standard media rotation, eventually all of your previous backups are going to be overwritten as new backups are performed and media is overwritten. So, to put this into reasonable terms, if you delete a file today, then it will eventually be completely removed from your backup tapes. Maybe not today, maybe not tomorrow, but soon and for the rest of your life. The method you use for media rotation will determine when that medium is reused.

Here are some methods to help you reuse your media. You can manipulate them to fit your needs.

Grandfather-Father-Son

The Grandfather-Father-Son rotation method is where you would label tapes by the days of the week on Monday through Friday (Saturday and Sunday would only be added if data needed to be backed up over the weekend). Monday through Thursday tapes would be used to perform an incremental backup of files changed since the last daily backup performed. You would use a different tape for each Friday, which should be an incremental backup of all the files that have changed since the last weekly backup. You would also use a different tape for each new month in the year, which should be a full backup. The monthly backup should be performed on new media, which should be used as an archive (that is, saved offsite). The following is an example of the rotation chart for this method:

In this example the numbers indicate the media set for each portion of Grandfather (G), Father (F), and Son (S). So when it says *Tuesday (2S)*, it means that for that day you use (or reuse) the media set (which can be a single tape or many tapes depending on the size of your data being backed up) that is part of the Son portion of your backup. Your Son tapes get reused each week on their specific days, the Father tapes get reused each month on their specific days, and the Grandfather tapes might get reused each quarter or never, depending on how you want to retain your data.

Month 1

1 Monday (1S)	2 Tuesday (2S)	3 Wednesday (3S)	4 Thursday (4S)	5 Friday (1 F)
8 Monday (1S)	9 Tuesday (2S)	10 Wednesday (3S)	11 Thursday (4S)	12 Friday (2 F)
15 Monday (1S)	16 Tuesday (2S)	17 Wednesday (3S)	18 Thursday (4S)	19 Friday (3 F)
22 Monday (1S)	23 Tuesday (2S)	24 Wednesday (3S)	25 Thursday (4S)	26 Friday (4 F)
29 Monday (1S)	30 Tuesday (2S)	31 Wednesday (1 GF)		

Month 2

			1 Thursday (4S)	2 Friday (1 F)
5 Monday (1S)	6 Tuesday (2S)	7 Wednesday (3S)	8 Thursday (4S)	9 Friday (2 F)
12 Monday (1S)	13 Tuesday (2S)	14 Wednesday (3S)	15 Thursday (4S)	16 Friday (3 F)
19 Monday (1S)	20 Tuesday (2S)	21 Wednesday (3S)	22 Thursday (4S)	23 Friday (4 F)
26 Monday (1S)	27 Tuesday (2S)	28 Wednesday (3S)	29 Thursday (GF2)	

Month 3

				1 Friday (1 F)
4 Monday (1S)	5 Tuesday (2S)	6 Wednesday (3S)	7 Thursday (4S)	8 Friday (2 F)
11 Monday (1S)	12 Tuesday (2S)	13 Wednesday (3S)	14 Thursday (4S)	15 Friday (3 F)
18 Monday (1S)	19 Tuesday (2S)	20 Wednesday (3S)	21 Thursday (4S)	22 Friday (4 F)
25 Monday (1S)	26 Tuesday (2S)	27 Wednesday (3S)	28 Thursday (4S)	29 Friday (5 F)
31 Monday (GF3)				

So, if you add up the number of media sets used, you would come up with a total of 12 in this example. A media set could be one tape or several; it really all depends on the size of your backups. For example, one media set, if a full backup, could encompass several tapes, but another media set for the same backup set, if an incremental, might only need one tape to complete the backup.

So, let's try to be reasonable. What are your needs? Do you want an offsite copy? No problem, take your Friday full backups and keep those offsite. Or, if you want to purchase more media, you can buy more media for the daily backup and then you can retain a longer history of data.

On the average, though, to reuse your media, you rotate your daily tapes every new week, you rotate your weekly tapes every month and your monthly tapes every new quarter. If your company requires a longer history than this, simply extend the plan out for as long as you need.

Other variations might involve a need for the weekly full to be held or the monthly full to be held for longer periods of time, and you could purchase more media for this process. You might vary the need for a Saturday tape, or some other facet to the rotation scheme, but the point is that you have a media rotation plan in place that works within your needs.

And now for another media rotation type.

Tower of Hanoi

Named after a popular Chinese game, Tower of Hanoi is a variation of Exponential Backup and uses the mathematical function of powers of two. This creates the need for a minimum amount of media for backup.

For example, three tapes provide eight days of backup, four tapes provide 16, five tapes provide 32, and so on. In the game you have different-sized rings on a pole that need to be moved to another pole. Only smaller rings can go on bigger rings. Therefore, you must manipulate them in a certain way to complete the task. In the backup scheme, you would rotate tapes in this same manner.

Does this sound complicated? You're right, it is. Don't try to remember all of this. It's practically impossible for a human to keep track of the schedules involved. Certain backup applications are programmed to retain schedules you can rely on (but be aware that not all data-management software has included this rotation method in their solution). In fact, it's entirely possible to purchase software that doesn't include any predefined rotation methods, in which case you're on your own. But back to Tower of Hanoi.

Tower of Hanoi typically uses four media sets. These are labeled alphabetically as A, B, C, and D. We mentioned that media sets can be one single tape, or many tapes, depending on the data being backed up. You can see from the following chart that the first day uses media set A. You continue to use A every other day in the rotation. The key is not to use set A two days in a row. The second day of the game (ahem…we mean rotation scheme) uses media set B. The fourth would use media set C. The sixth would use media set B again. The eighth would use media set D for the first time. Then you repeat the process. You could leave it like this, but if you wanted to increase the backup history all you would have to do is change up the D set on day 16 to use an E media set, which will actually double the backup history you retain. This is how the five media sets would be scheduled:

1	2	3	4	5	6	7	8	9	10	11	12	13	14	15	16
A		A		A		A		A		A		A		A	
	B				B				B				B		
			C								C				
							D								
															E

You might wonder about the type of backups you're looking to perform. With A you want to start with a full backup and then perform subsequent incrementals during the retention period of 16 days. The same would be true for B and C, where you perform a full the first time you use those media sets and then perform subsequent incrementals, although the chart clearly shows that you don't use these tapes as often as the A media set. With D and E media sets (or higher if you determine a need for it) you perform full backups. Using these five media sets, you would repeat the cycle on the 17th day and start again.

We could go through the reasons of why this is a good rotation method, but let's cut to the chase: You can use fewer media with this method (however, manually keeping track of your media would be impossible in the Tower of Hanoi). Another positive is that you will always have an older version of a file on one tape. Depending on the number of media sets you use, you can retain copies from the beginning. In addition, if you happen to get a virus within your media sets, you have a variety of sets to choose from to restore at a point where the virus wasn't present.

But let's take this a little further. What if you wanted to retain a longer history? What if, let's say, you wanted 128 days of media rotation? How many media sets would you need? In that case, you would need eight tapes (or media sets of tape), labeled from A to H, which would provide 128 days of history in your rotation. You could have a copy of a file from 128 days ago because of the way you manipulate your tape rotations.

There are also several variations to this rotation. If you did backups twice per day, you would be able to capture work in progress during the day, but you would also only have versions from as long as 64 days ago in the previous example.

It would also be possible to back up to a single tape for a week by doing a full backup and then only backing up updated files during the week. You could increase the number of copies this way but may run out of space on the tape. You could also risk losing up to a week's worth of data if that tape has a problem or is damaged.

Does all of this sound complicated? Remember, if you want to use Tower of Hanoi, then look for this as a feature when choosing your data-management software.

One More Thought

We only promised two, but there is another media rotation method to consider. This is a simple method of backup to implement. You would simply decide how long you would want to keep your backup and how many media sets you want to use. You would then label your media sets by number and rotate them incrementally. Adding and taking away one media set from each week. An example of a typical five-day rotation follows:

Week 1: 1-2-3-4-5

Week 2: 2-3-4-5-6

Week 3: 3-4-5-6-7

Week 4: 4-5-6-7-1

At the end of Week 4, you would insert Tape 1 again.

Now, there are a couple of different ways to handle this. You could do full backups each day, but that might be slow, depending on the amount of data your backing up. You could do a full at the beginning of the week and then incrementals or differentials throughout.

One advantage is that tapes can be added or removed to the rotation, according to your needs, so if you decided to hold a tape for archive you could simply take a new tape and number it with the number of the tape you took out of rotation. You can also expand this rotation to include a seven-day schedule or add more tapes to keep backup information longer.

Your Company Is Your Data

Where are you going to put those backup tapes? Maybe you could put them right on top of the server so that when the fire ravages your building and your systems, the backup tapes go right along with it. OK, that would be foolish, but it's amazing how many companies went out of business from the 1993 World Trade Center bombing because of the lack of preparation for offsite storage—or storage in any form. It's also amazing how many companies learned from that incident so that in 2001, when the Towers (two buildings that I've worked in and loved) were destroyed in a terrorist attack, companies were prepared to continue working. Today, your company is your data, end of story.

For maximum data security, your backup media should be stored in an environmentally controlled (so, your garage that floods or your attic that reaches 150-degree temperatures are not good), offsite location (and offsite *isn't* the trunk of your car). You might even consider storing your backup media in a fireproof vault. Offsite storage provides the maximum protection against fire, flood, and other disasters (such as crazy thieves who steal the server and storage, or purposeful saboteurs who do the same). The added security of vault storage protects your backup media from internal or external theft.

Understanding Media Types

As mentioned earlier, there are three types of media: magnetic tape, optical discs, and magnetic disks. Each is unique in abilities and specifications. This section describes each in detail, including how they compare to each other.

For those of you who consider this a bit strange to read through all the specifications, just look at the graphics. Remember, you're going to see this stuff in the field, so you need to know what you're working with.

Magnetic Tapes

Before going through the different types of magnetic tapes, it would be good to note that two new terms are used in the descriptions: helical and linear.

Helical recording technology is magnetic tape technology that records and reads digital data in diagonal stripes on a magnetic tape while the tape streams past the spinning head, from one end of the tape to the other without interruption. The tape drive wraps the magnetic tape partially around an angled, rotating drum. The read and write heads are aligned in the drum. The heads spin fast while the tape moves slowly. After any read or write operation, the head stops spinning to avoid excessive wear on the tape.

The diagonal recording pattern enables a high data density. The read heads are just behind the write heads for "read-while-write verification," which ensures the data integrity of each data stripe.

The combination of spinning head and moving tape provides equal wear across the media. The time required to stop and start the head spinning and then resynchronize on the data can be many seconds. As a result, helical tape devices are most efficient when they are constantly in use.

VCRs, 8 mm tape drives, and DAT use helical recording.

Linear recording technology is a magnetic tape technology that records and reads digital data in tracks that go the entire length of the one-half inch wide tape. The tape moves past the fixed heads in a straight line. When the end of the tape is reached, the heads are repositioned and the tape moves in the opposite direction to record a new set of tracks on the length of the tape. When the tape stops, neither the tape nor the head is moving. This reduces media wear and also provides a start time well under two seconds.

It has been the primary recording technology for digital data for the last 30 years.

DLT tape, LTO, and QIC technologies use linear recording.

3480, 3490, 3490e, Magstar (3590), Magstar MP

IBM's version of a half-inch, single-hub cartridge similar to the DLT, the Magstar (3590) is the latest in this series of tapes. Developed by IBM in 1984, the original 3480 series was designed for IBM mainframe and midrange systems. This media's backup capacity ranges from 200MB (3480) to 10GB (Magstar 3590). Other than using a linear recording method, the Magstar MP is completely different from the Magstar line. Magstar MP employs an 8mm tape (like AIT, defined next). The starting point for this media is in the middle of the tape rather than the beginning, and this tape is generally used in robotic libraries. The MP cartridge holds up to 5GB of data.

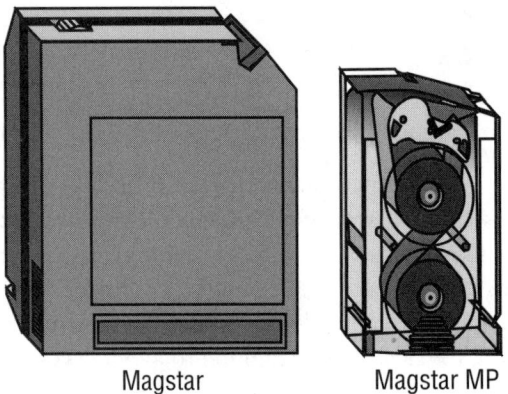

Magstar   Magstar MP

Advanced Intelligent Tape (AIT)

Developed by Sony, AIT uses an 8mm cassette tape that has the capacity to store from 25GB (AIT) to 50GB (AIT-2) of data. This media contains an EEPROM chip, which stores indexing information and tape status information. This EEPROM chip also allows for fast forwarding to a particular partition. AIT tapes also contain a built-in head cleaner. AIT tapes are similar in look to 8mm video camera tapes. They use the helical scan method of recording.

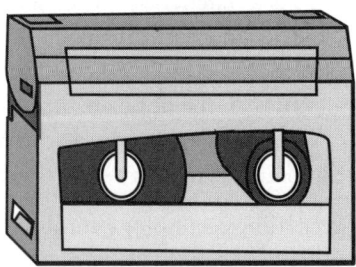

Digital Audio Tape (DAT)

Originally developed for Audio, the DAT was hailed as the new cassette standard for consumers but found a much wider audience with recording studios and technology professionals as a compact but powerful media. The DAT uses a 4mm tape and conforms to the Digital Data Storage (DDS) standard. It's capable of storing 2–20GB of data. DAT uses a similar recording method to videotapes (in other words, helical scan recording). DAT tapes look like a thick but slightly more compact audiocassette tape.

Digital Linear Tape (DLT)

DLT was originally developed by Digital and sold to Quantum. DLT uses a half-inch, single-hub cartridge. DLT tapes store 10–35GB of data; the introduction of SuperDLT increases the maximum storage capacity from 35GB–50GB. As the name implies, DLT writes data in a linear format, writing 128–208 tracks simultaneously. This fast writing capacity (5MB per second for DLT, 10MB per second for SuperDLT) has made DLT the popular choice for mid- to large-sized enterprise Local Area Networks (LANs).

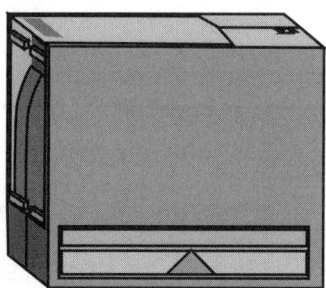

Digital Storage Technology (DST)

Designed by Ampex for use with uncompressed digital video and large databases, DST also uses the helical scan recording method. DST has capacities ranging from 50–330GB. It's based on magnetic storage methods normally used in the broadcast industry. Many of today's large enterprise networks as well as Internet Service Providers (ISPs) or Application Service Providers (ASPs) could benefit from the huge capacity of these tapes.

Digital Tape Format (DTF)

Developed by Sony, DTF is based on its successful half-inch helical scan beta-cam tape. DTF-1 holds 42GB of data with a transfer rate of 12MB per second. And the more powerful DTF-2 introduced in 1999 holds up to 200GB of data and boasts a transfer rate of 24MB per second. Again, due to the large capacity of this media, it is best suited for backup of video and large databases.

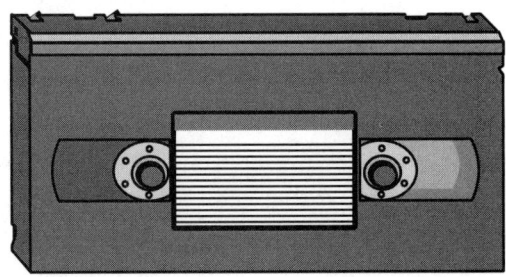

Exabyte 8mm tape

Created by Exabyte Corporation, this 8mm tape has a capacity of 2.5GB–60GB of data. Exabyte is the largest independent manufacturer of tape drives. Although slightly larger than AIT tapes, the size is still only a fraction of DLT tapes.

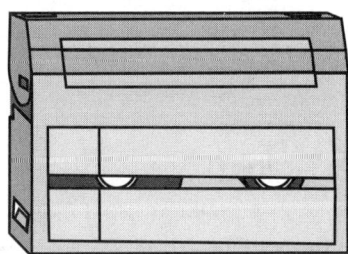

Quarter-Inch Cartridge (QIC)

Getting its name from the size of the tape, QIC comes in two formats: 3.5-inch and 5.25-inch cartridges. With capacities ranging from 40MB (3.5-inch cartridge) to 50GB (5.25-inch cartridge). QIC is a good solution for small- to mid-sized businesses. QIC-Wide, QIC-EX, and Travan are several variations of QIC Travan; for more information, go to www.qic.org.

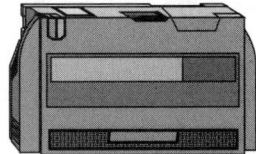

Redwood Tape

This is another half-inch tape, designed by StorageTek. But this tape uses a helical scan recording method rather than a linear recording method. The Redwood stores 10–50GB of data.

Optical Discs

Optical discs use light (laser light) to create pits on the surface of a plastic disc. These pits can be read by a "read laser," and the data is interpreted in this way. The following sections describe the different kinds of optical discs. For more information on how this technology works, visit www.extremetech.com and search for an A–Z on optical disc technology by Alfred Poor.

Compact Disc Recordable (CD-R)

Based on the popular digital compact disc design, the CD-R allows for the storage of 700MB. CD-R drives are fairly inexpensive. CD-R drives write the entire disc at once.

As a result, the media is not rewriteable. Therefore, this media is generally reserved for archiving. The one advantage over other media is that CD-Rs can be read in any CD-ROM drive.

Compact Disc Rewriteable (CD-RW)

Similar to the CD-R, the CD-RW is rewriteable. CD-RWs use a recording method similar to the way a hard disk writes data to a drive. This therefore offers the ability to add or delete data one file at a time if necessary. This also makes CD-RWs more flexible than CD-Rs. The data, however, is still limited to a maximum of 700MB. And because of the rewriteable nature, the media must be formatted, which makes this slower than CD-R recorders.

Digital Versatile Disc Recordable (DVD-R)

Much like the CD-R, this is a one-time recordable media. DVD uses the same familiar disc design as CD-R/CD-RWs, but because of the design of a DVD, a DVD-R has a capacity of up to 7.9GB. This is 12 times more storage room than a CD-R/CD-RW.

Digital Versatile Disc Read/Write (DVD-RW/DVD+RW)

Similar to DVD-R, both these medias are rewriteable. DVD-RW can store up to 4.7GB per side (9.4GB total) and can be rewritten to more than 100 times. DVD+RW can store up to 3GB per side (6.0GB total) but can be rewritten to more than 100,000 times. DVD-Rs have a pink cast.

Digital Versatile Disc Random Access Memory (DVD-RAM)

Again, this is much like DVDs except that DVD-RAMs can be double-sided. Therefore, the disc is placed in a cartridge to protect the media. DVD-RAM stores between 4.7GB of data for single sided and 9.4GB of data for double-sided.

Magneto-Optic Disk (MO Disk)

This disk employs both magnetic and optical methods of recording data. MO disks come in 3.5 inches and 5.25 inches. The 3.5-inch disks can store up to 640MB of data. Although the 5.25-inch disks can store up to 5.2GB of data, they are double-sided and must be flipped and reinserted to get full use of the large capacity. MO disks boast a 30-year shelf life as well as the ability to withstand millions of rewrites.

Write Once Read Many (WORM)

WORM is an optical disk media that can only be recorded to once. There are two types of WORM media. *Ablative* makes permanent change in the optical material, but Ablative is a declining technology. Continuous Composite Write (CCW) is used in 5.25-inch MO drives to emulate WORM. *Firmware* is used to ensure that recorded sections are not re-recorded in CCW mode.

Magnetic Disks

You should know a few more terms related to magnetic disks. However, these may be a bit more familiar to you.

Floppy Disk

A floppy disk consists of a small round magnetic bendable material within a rigid casing. This is the most commonly used removable storage medium since the personal computer's inception. But it is seriously lacking in capacity (only 1.44MB) for today's storage needs.

Zip Disk

A Zip disk is a 3.5-inch disk designed by Iomega and used with Iomega's Zip drive. Zip disks can store 100–250MB (since 1998).

Laser Servo 120 (LS-120)

A new alternative to the floppy disk, the LS-120 records magnetically but uses optical tracks inside the disk to align the heads. This allows the LS-120 to store up to 120MB of data.

High Capacity Floppy Disk (HiFD)

Yet another improvement on the floppy disk, the HiFD is capable of storing 200MB of data.

Fixed Hard Disks

The primary and most widely known storage device, fixed disks use two standards: Integrated Drive Electronics (IDE) and Small Computer System Interface (SCSI).

Jaz Disks

Yet another offering from Iomega, the Jaz disk uses a high-capacity cartridge and stores 1–2GB of data.

Managing Media

There are two philosophies concerning how to manage media in a backup environment, according to Michael Dahlmeier, a Systems Engineer in charge of Special Projects for CommVault Systems. He says the following:

"The first philosophy is *data storage* where all efforts are focused on getting the maximum usage of available media capacity. With this philosophy the cost of the media is paramount, and media management is driven solely by the need to fill each tape to its maximum capacity. Media management boundaries become blurry as retention cycle boundaries are arbitrarily located. This philosophy usually works best for long-term offline data storage.

"The second philosophy is *data protection* where efforts are focused on minimizing data loss from media failure. Media costs are secondary to the value of the data stored and the need to maximize recoverability. Here, media management is governed by tape rotation and retention cycle boundaries consistent with business practices. This philosophy works best for short-term business continuity efforts."

The impact of either philosophy is best demonstrated through the application of the tape usage formula.

A common basic tape usage formula is:

```
Number of tapes = V ( F + DI + A ) /T
```

where the following applies:

    V is a client full backup in GB

    F is the number of full backups retained

    D is the incremental percentage (assumed to be 5 percent)

    I is the number of incremental backups retained

    A is Axiom's Constant (unused capacity, assumed to be 10 percent)

    T is the tape capacity in GB (compressed)

> **NOTE** The estimated hardware compression ratio is hard-coded at 2:1 for all tape media except Exabyte, which is hard-coded at 7:5. The actual compression can fluctuate wildly depending on the type of data being compressed (for example, binary files don't compress as well as text files).

Much of the previous formula should be familiar to you from other parts of the chapter with the exception of Axiom's Constant. This term is used to describe normal waste of capacity resulting from miscalculation of compression, unused space remaining at the end of a tape, and planned or unplanned write to new media before the previous tape is full. Essentially it's a fudge factor to make sure you don't underestimate your need for tapes.

Examples of Media Management

To use the formula in a data storage environment, let's say you keep eight weeks' worth of backups with weekly fulls and daily incrementals. For a 40GB server and DLT7000 tapes with 70GB of compressed data storage (assuming 2:1 average compression), you'd get the following:

```
Number of tapes = 40(8 + (.05 * 48) +.1)/70 = 6 (if it was lower you could
    round up to 6) = 6 tapes
```

This formula assumes one full backup per week, with six incrementals. You could change these numbers to reflect one full with four incrementals or one full with five incrementals; it really doesn't make much difference because that's what variables are for.

If data protection were your focus, you would want to schedule each of the previous full backups to a new tape. That way the loss of a tape affects only one cycle and any media management efforts can be applied specifically to a single cycle. Each tape now will contain one full backup and six incrementals.

```
Number of tapes = (40(1+ (.05 * 6) +.1)/70) = .8 (round up to 1) * 8 weeks
    = 8 tapes
```

So, the data protection method involves more tapes in this scenario (not that it must) because your primary concern is the quick restoration of your data, not storage management.

Even if the formula doesn't make perfect sense right away, you should be able to see how the data storage method, in using six tapes, takes complete advantage of the tapes, making this perfect for using fewer tapes and putting them offsite in a storage vault. That would also mean that the data protection method, using eight tapes, gives more attention to restoration of data and less fear of media failure.

These are two interesting ways of handling the same data. Keep in mind that the data storage method calculates for the data retention time period in total, whereas the data protection method calculates by the week, for the entire data retention time period. Even if the two numbers were the same, the method in which the data is collected will be different.

So, which method is better? With the data storage method, you will start recycling tapes at various times starting at the end of the 10th week. Because retention cycles span tapes, you may use up to 10 tapes before you actually recycle tapes. If you're walking the edge on spare media (as most customers do), having an erratic tape recycle schedule such as this may cause sporadic "Out of Spare Media" problems. Should these problems occur, your options in manipulating tapes are severely limited. You can't just free up any single tape to use because the retention cycle spans multiple tapes. Most data management software will not allow you to disrupt the cycle in the middle of an established retention setting.

With the data protection method, you recycle each tape weekly starting at the end of the ninth week. You end up using nine tapes and you have a consistent recycling schedule. There's more unused capacity, but your media management is more consistent and predictable. If you need to free up a tape to use, you can do so easily because each tape is autonomous in terms or retention cycles boundaries. So, it's an opinion but the data protection method gets our vote.

Library Capacity

Let's take a real-life look at media management from the tape library's point of view. Let's say you're backing up 30 of the same 40GB client described previously. Of the eight weeks of data you want retained, you need to keep the most recent two weeks online and available for automatic restores. The rest can be exported and kept on a shelf.

This is what we are looking at working with in this scenario:

- 30 40GB clients
- Weekly full backups, daily incrementals
- Retaining eight cycles/eight weeks (56 days)
- Keeping most recent two weeks online

You've got a single module ADIC Scalar 1000 with 12 DLT 7000 drives and 118 slots. The following examples consider one day for full backup and six for incremental. You can see that after two weeks, either of the previous methods will generate 60 tapes of backup data.

This is the formula for the data storage method (for the two-week period in total):

```
Number of tapes = 40(2 + (.05 * 12) +.1)/70 = 1.54 (round up to 2) * 30
clients = 60 tapes
```

This is the formula for the data protection method (per week times two for the two-week period):

```
Number of tapes = (40(1+ (.05 * 6) +.1)/70) = .8 (round out to 1 tape) * 2
weeks * 30 clients = 60 tapes
```

> **WARNING** How is it possible that they take up the same amount of tape? They don't. If you see where we round up, that is the killer. The data storage method will eke out every last part of the tape, so rounding out is nice for the numbers, but per client you will use the tapes differently.

Those are your two weeks online, but now you need to continue, up to eight weeks. Consider a three-week portion of tapes.

This is for the data storage method:

```
Number of tapes = 40(3 + (.05 * 18) +.1)/70 = 2.28 (round up to 3) * 30
clients = 90 tapes
```

and this is for the data protection method:

```
Number of tapes = (40(1+ (.05 * 6) +.1)/70) = .8 * 3 weeks * 30 clients = 
90 tapes
```

After three weeks, both methods will give you 90 tapes. Where is the difference between the two?

With the data protection method you can now remove the first week's set of tapes to make room for the fourth week's backup. A weekly media management pattern is now set to have 60–90 tapes containing backup data in the library.

With the data storage method you can't export any tapes yet because the second week's full backup started on the first tape. This occurs because you are more concerned with filling tapes and so you squeeze the data all together. Think of it in terms of recording music back in the good old days (the 1980s, before we had CD burners). You had a 60-minute tape with 30-minutes on each side and you had five Michael Jackson songs and three Culture Club songs. You could put seven songs per side. What do you do? You could put seven on one side and one on the other to save room and add more music, or you could put the five on one side and three on the other to organize your music data. It depends on your ability to get more tapes and your vision of music control. The same is true of these two methods for storage, and in this case you can't pull a week just yet, so you're forced to keep going. So you do another week's backup using the data storage method. This is the formula for the data storage method:

```
Number of tapes = 40(4 + (.05 * 24) +.1)/70 = 3.03(round up to 4) * 30 
clients = 120 tapes
```

Wait a minute. We said earlier that the ADIC Scalar only has 118 slots. You need to make room. How can you make more room? The answer is "not easily." You could possibly start exporting data tapes and importing spares while the fourth week's full backups are running. Otherwise, you need to make a decision on which client will not have the two weeks online requirement met. Either way, it requires you to take action. And what about growth?

This is but one example of the issues that need to be addressed using media management techniques. There will always be trade-offs concerning resource usage and media management. Understanding those trade-offs is important. The solution may not always be the same for each situation.

The real concern with media management is that many administrators think they need to fill up the tapes. Keep in mind that tape is cheap, but your data is not. Data is the most important aspect in storage solutions, so don't worry about filling tapes. Just be concerned with organizing our data in such a way so as to make it easily retrievable.

But What About...?

Granted, every library, specification, and standard is not in the storage terminology chapter. Who wants to read all of that? If you do, the Internet is your best resource for all the different vendors and their corresponding information. And prices, which change every day, have purposely been excluded in this chapter. Again, your best bet is the Internet and eventually the vendor or a reseller.

This chapter was designed to provide the basics about storage terminology. You have data, it resides on one form of media (most likely magnetic disk), and you need to preserve it through the use of either magnetic tape, magnetic disk, or optical media. That preservation includes, in wise cases, movement of your data offsite through the use of backup strategies that will fit within your backup window and recovery window. From this point you can determine your needs for alternate forms of storage solutions such as SANs, or NAS, and so on. Now, if this paragraph makes sense to you, then the chapter did its job.

Where do you go from here? Maybe you think you need to hit a store and start looking for data-management software to handle all of your new needs. Well, that depends. How well do you know what you already have on your Windows 2000 Server? Do you know all the improvements that Microsoft has added to assist you in keeping your network running comfortably and in a recoverable mode?

Keep reading.

3

Windows 2000 Storage Enhancements

In recognizing the growth of data over the last decade, Microsoft saw the need for increased storage management on its new platforms. Microsoft's idea about these enhancements was simple: Provide a more versatile storage-based architecture. Tools such as Removable Storage Manager (RSM) have done just that. By using RSM, the Windows operating system can act as a virtual traffic cop for mass storage devices, allowing expensive equipment such as libraries to be shared by multiple applications simultaneously. In addition to RSM, the storage-related improvements to Windows 2000 are as follows:

- Remote Storage Service (RSS)
- Reparse points
- Volume mount points
- Windows File Protection (WFP)
- NTFS Change (USN) Journal
- Indexing Service
- Sparse files
- Single Instance Storage (SIS)
- File Replication Service (FRS)
- Distributed File System (Dfs)

- Encrypting File System (EFS)
- Disk quotas
- System State

This chapter explains each of these new or improved concepts as they relate to the backup and recovery of Windows 2000 Servers. Many of these features (and accompanying acronyms!) will continue to be mentioned throughout the remainder of this book.

Beginning in this chapter, and following in several others, you will be introduced to extra utilities included with the Windows 2000 Server Support Tools or with the Windows 2000 Server Resource Kit. The Windows 2000 Server Support Tools come with the server installation CD-ROM. The Resource Kit must be purchased separately but is well worth the money. A limited number of Resource Kit tools are available for free at www.microsoft.com/windows2000/library/resources/reskit/tools/default.asp. Both the Support Tools and Resource Kit are easily installed by running setup.exe from their installation disks and then following the prompts for their setup wizards. To install the Windows 2000 Server Support Tools, run setup.exe from the Support\Tools folder on the server installation CD-ROM.

Removable Storage Manager (RSM)

Removable Storage Manager (RSM) is one of the best Windows 2000 storage enhancements. Most storage and file management applications that want to utilize a mass storage device such as a tape library must take ownership of it. Before RSM, the solution to allowing multiple applications to share a library was to purchase a third-party library control package. RSM has made sharing libraries much easier because it enables application developers to integrate their software into one library control package. Now you do not have to worry about compatibility issues, because all new Windows-based storage applications are written to work with RSM. The storage applications will talk to RSM, and RSM will mount and dismount the storage media in the libraries.

Besides providing a common interface for storage applications such as Microsoft Windows Backup, CommVault Galaxy, and Veritas Software's NetBackup, or BackupExec, RSM can also increase the range of hardware accessible by your storage application. Your current storage software probably supports hundreds of library and drive combinations. Unfortunately, you probably have some incompatible storage hardware that you refuse to throw out because of the amount of money you paid for it. With RSM, if your hardware is on the Microsoft Hardware Compatibility List (HCL) and supported by RSM (which most everything is), it probably has new life. As long as your storage application supports RSM, the Windows RSM driver is what communicates with the hardware. All your application needs to do is talk to RSM. Figure 3.1 illustrates this concept.

Figure 3.1: Use of RSM service

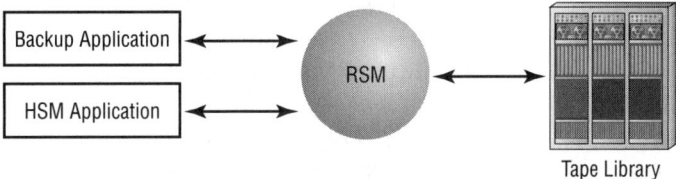

In Figure 3.1, both an HSM application (covered in the next section) and a backup application are able to simultaneously use the same library by interacting with RSM. All the backup applications mentioned earlier integrate with RSM. If you are using a different backup application, you should check with the software manufacturer to see whether your solution supports RSM integration.

> **NOTE** You can find information about using, configuring, and administrating RSM in Chapter 4, "Working with Removable Storage Manager."

Remote Storage Service (RSS)

Remote Storage Service (RSS) is the Microsoft version of a *Hierarchical Storage Manager (HSM)*. HSMs are great for large file servers that are running out of room.

HSMs were designed to free up faster, more expensive storage, such as magnetic RAID arrays, by shifting infrequently accessed files to lower-cost, high-capacity media, such as tapes. Imagine that you have an available library with 10 70GB DLT tapes. With HSM, that would give you an additional 700GB of "virtual" disk space. HSM is smart enough to store on the removable media only files that have not been accessed in quite some time. For these old files, the HSM application presents the appearance that the files reside on a hard disk, when in fact they are stored on some form of removable media.

As the administrator, you are able to use an HSM to archive rarely accessed files off a server, which in turn will increase the server's amount of available storage space and performance. Best of all, the HSM will operate completely transparent to end users.

An HSM gives you the best of both worlds. With an HSM, such as Windows 2000 RSS, you set a maximum capacity (as a percentage) for each hard disk. After the high watermark (maximum capacity setting) percentage is reached, files that meet an age qualification (days since last accessed) are migrated to a form of remote storage media, such as a tape library.

For example, say you set your disk high watermark to 90 percent and set the file qualification limit to 180 days. After the server's hard disk reaches 90 percent of its total capacity, any files that haven't been accessed in six months (180 days) will be moved to the library. Now you're probably thinking, "How do I access the file from the library?" This is why people buy HSM software. When files are migrated to remote storage media, the HSM engine will leave the filename, along with a pointer (reparse point) on the server's hard drive. Sometimes these files are referred to as *stub files*. Figure 3.2 illustrates this concept.

Figure 3.2: HSM at work

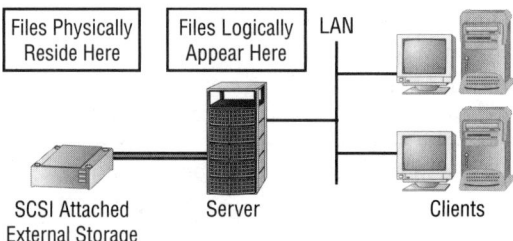

Odds are that you have several servers holding files that have not been accessed in months or even years. Users are reluctant to remove files that they might eventually need. In these cases, RSS can be configured to migrate these files to remote storage media—and as far as users are concerned, the files appear to be on the local hard drive of the server. Although practically transparent to users, files that have been migrated are marked by a clock symbol in Windows Explorer, as shown in Figure 3.3.

Figure 3.3: File migration indication in Windows Explorer

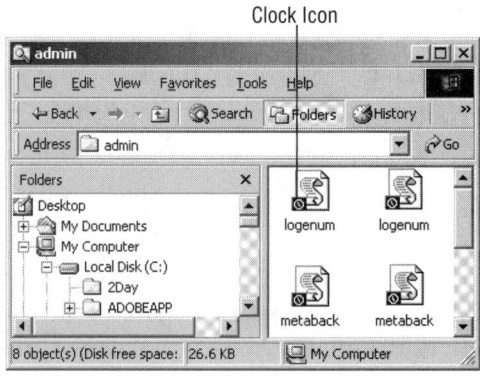

When a user attempts to open a file that has been migrated off the server, the user sees a message that the file is being retrieved from remote storage. The entire process to deliver the "actual" file to the server so that clients can access it may take several minutes, depending on how quickly the medium that holds the file is mounted and the file is retrieved. The key point here is that the user takes the same actions whether accessing a local or remotely stored file—other than a brief wait for the remote one.

> **NOTE** Chapter 4, "Working with Removable Storage Manager," fully explains RSS administration and configuration, as well as alternatives to the RSS solution.

Reparse Points

The preceding section mentioned reparse points. Reparse points are new to Windows 2000, and thus are supported only on NTFS 5 volumes. Although users and applications can also take advantage of their functionality, the Windows 2000 operating system uses them for Remote Storage Service, volume mount points, and Native Structured Storage.

The Microsoft documentation spends pages on reparse points, but we will try to keep them simple. A *reparse point* is a file attribute. They operate mainly at the I/O subsystem level, which basically means that they work with the operating system transparent to the end user.

The functionality of reparse points can be summed up in one sentence: When you click a file or folder that contains a reparse point, you are unknowingly redirected somewhere else to retrieve the file's or folder's data.

Redirection can happen to users or to applications. Another example of the use of pointers would be Windows shortcuts. Shortcuts are just pointers to applications or files that automatically direct users to the application from the Desktop. They are not copies of actual files.

Using Linkd

The Linkd utility creates reparse points to link one folder to another. This utility is included with the Windows 2000 Server Resource Kit. This tool can be useful for redirecting files on one share to another.

Suppose a disk on one of your file servers is filling up. You want to store a portion of a department's data on a new disk, but you do not want to have to reconfigure permissions for that disk. In fact, you do not even need to share the new disk. To solve this problem, you can use Linkd to have a folder on the shared disk point to a folder on the new disk. This redirection will be completely transparent to users.

The syntax of the utility is as follows:

```
linkd <source> [/d] <destination>
```

- Using Linkd with only a source folder specified will list any existing links for that source folder.
- With a source and destination folder specified, Linkd will create a link from the source to the destination.
- With a source specified with the /d switch, the source folder and associated links will be deleted, regardless of whether any links exist for the source.

With a hard disk filling up, you want to redirect users who access the `C:\Marketing\Documents` folder to a new folder on the newly installed G drive. To do this, you do the following:

1. Create a new folder on the G drive called `G:\Marketing\Documents`.
2. Move the contents of the `C:\Marketing\Documents` folder to `G:\Marketing\Documents` folder.
3. Delete the contents of the `C:\Marketing\Documents` folder.
4. From the command prompt, run Linkd with the following syntax:

   ```
   linkd c:\marketing\documents g:\marketing\documents
   ```

Now when users access the `C:\Marketing\Documents` folder, they are transparently redirected to `G:\Marketing\Documents`. If you were to use the `dir` command in the `C:\Marketing` folder, the Documents subfolder would be listed as a *junction point* instead of a folder. A junction point can be accessed from the command line like a folder by using the `cd` command. The easiest definition for a *junction point* is a folder that uses a reparse point. Junction points are accessed like all other folders.

Figure 3.4 shows the commands used in this example.

You could have kept the original files in the `C:\Marketing\Documents` folder if you had wished. Instead of moving all files, you can also use Linkd to create a subfolder that points to a new location. With this approach, you would have to alert users of the new subfolder and its purpose.

Figure 3.4: Using Linkd

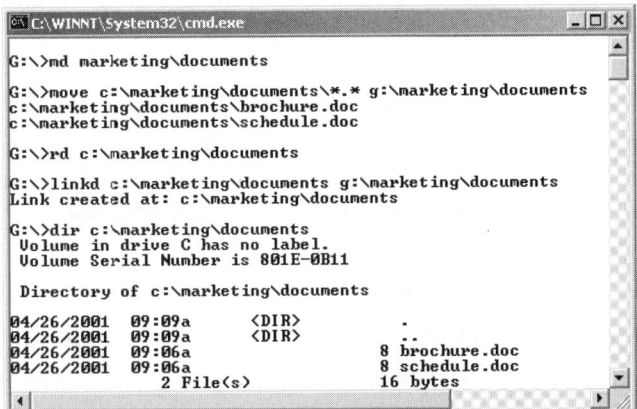

Using Delrp

The Delrp utility is also on the Windows 2000 Server Resource Kit. You just saw how to use Linkd to create junction points. Instead of using `linkd <source> /d` to delete a junction point, you can also use `delrp.exe`. The `delrp.exe` utility can be used to delete a file or folder, along with any reparse points that it contains. You should not assume that simply deleting a file by using Windows Explorer or the `del` command will get rid of its underlying reparse points as well. The reparse point could be followed, and all the files in the folder that the pointer points to could also be deleted! The safest bet is to use either Delrp or Linkd to delete a file and its reparse points.

Here is the `delrp` command's syntax:

```
Delrp <file or folder name>
```

In this example, the command would delete the Documents junction point (folder) and its associated reparse point:

```
Delrp c:\marketing\documents
```

Support for Mapped Drives

You cannot create reparse points that point to mapped network drives. If you use a command such as `linkd.exe` to attempt this, you will get a message that the link was successfully created. However, the reparse point will not work, and you will receive an error when attempting to access the link.

> **WARNING** You cannot create reparse points that link to remote computers.

Support for Virtual Disks

For the most part, reparse points do not work well with the cluster service and virtual disks. As far as what does and does not work, this is what you need to know:

- Remote Storage Service is not cluster aware, and thus cannot manage a shared disk.
- Directory junctions do work with shared disks, as long as their source and target disk resources are in the same group. Also, the physical disk resource that contains the host folder must be dependent on the physical disk resource that contains the linked folder.
- Volume mount points (covered in the next section) do not work on a shared disk.
- Remote Installation Service (RIS) is not cluster-aware, meaning volumes managed by RIS cannot be stored on a shared disk.

Volume Mount Points

Volume mount points are similar to junction points, with the exception that they are used to link a folder to a volume (disk drive) instead of linking a folder to another folder. In spite of this distinction, both junction points and volume mount points are displayed as junctions when viewing them using Dir from the command prompt.

If you are wondering when and where you could use mount points, consider the following:

- Mount CDFS or FAT file systems onto an NTFS 5 volume.
- A FAT volume mounted as a subfolder on a NTFS volume could inherit the NFTS permissions of its parent folder (only when accessed through the folder and not directly accessed).
- For CD-ROMs, mount points refer to the drive and not the media in the drive, so you do not have to mount and unmount a CD-ROM to change its media.
- Mount points actually reference the GUID of a disk drive and not its drive letter. This enables mount paths to remain valid even if a drive letter changes.
- Once created, volume mount points are retained by the operating system. You do not have to re-create them each time the operating system restarts.

You can create mount points by using the Windows 2000 Disk Management administrative tool (found under Computer Management) or you can also create them from the command line.

WARNING To mount a volume into a folder, the folder must be empty.

Using Disk Management to Create Mount Points

For those who love GUI tools, Windows 2000 Disk Management makes it easy to mount volumes inside folders. To do this, follow these steps:

1. Right-click the My Computer icon on the Desktop and select Manage. This will bring you to the Computer Management administrative console.
2. From Computer Management, click the Disk Management folder located under the Storage folder.
3. Right-click the drive that you want to add the mount path for and select Change Drive Letter and Path.
4. In the Change Drive Letter and Paths for Data dialog box, click the *Add* button.
5. In the Add New Drive Letter or Path dialog box, shown in Figure 3.5, type in or browse to the path of the folder in which you want to mount the volume. Then click OK.

Figure 3.5: Adding a mount path for a volume

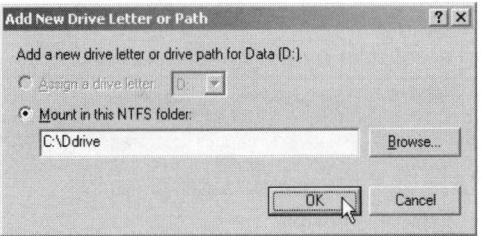

After the mount path is added, if you right-click the volume again and select Change Drive Letter and Path, you will see the volume mount point displayed.

Using Mountvol to Create Mount Points

If you want save precious time and create mount points as quickly as possible, you will find using the command line to be much faster. The Mountvol command-line utility enables you to create, delete, and display mounted volumes for a specified folder. One nice aspect of this utility, compared to Linkd and Delrp, is that it's free! The difference, however, is that it is used to manage volume mount points exclusively, and not reparse points.

The syntax is as follows:

    mountvol displays command-line help and also shows valid volume names for your system.

mountvol [drive]*path* VolumeName creates the mount path.

mountvol [drive]*path* /d deletes the mount path.

mountvol [drive]*path* /l lists the mounted volume name for the specified folder.

Say you wanted to mount your CD-ROM drive (the F drive) to the `C:\CDROM` folder. This will allow users to access the CD-ROM from within the `C:\CDROM` folder. One reason for doing this might be to decrease administrative overhead by mounting drives into folders that are already a part of an existing network share. To create the CDROM folder and then mount the drive, you would perform the following steps:

1. Type **md cdrom** at the command prompt to create a CDROM folder on the C drive.

2. Type **mountvol** at the command prompt to display the GUID for the F drive. In this example, the GUID syntax for the Volume*Name* portion of the command is \\?\Volume{aedd8941-f132-11d4-a69e-806d6172696f}\.

3. Now type **mountvol c:\cdrom \\?\Volume{aedd8941-f132-11d4-a69e-806d6172696f}** to create the volume mount point.

The execution of the command is shown in Figure 3.6.

Figure 3.6: Mounting a volume by using `mountvol.exe`

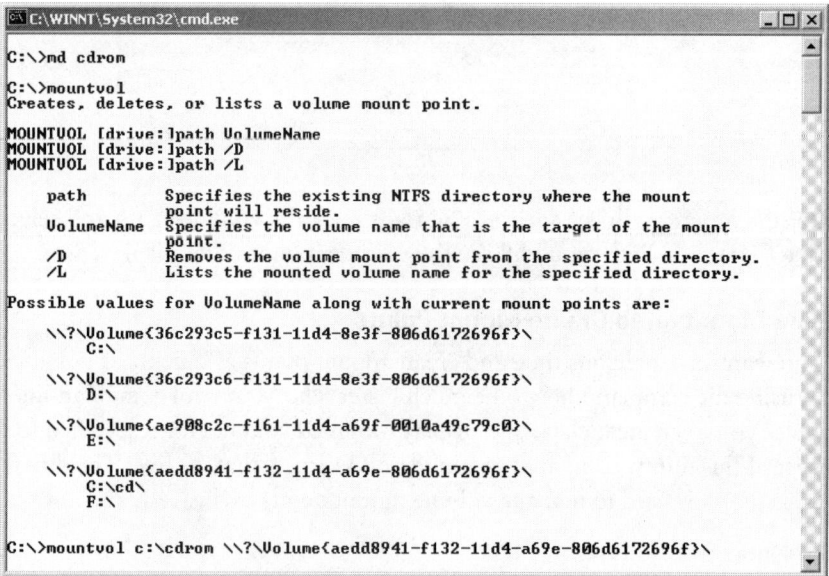

> **NOTE** Check with your backup software vendor to see how your backup software works with volume mount points and junction points. If the software is not aware of the reparse points, it might follow the pointers and back up the contents of the folder that they point to. If you are backing up an entire hard drive, this means you might wind up backing up the same data more than once.

Windows File Protection

If you have worked with Windows NT long enough, you have probably experienced pain after installing an application at one time or another. This pain was often the result of the new application modifying some system DLLs. In doing so during installation, another program that had been using the DLLs might have been affected, or even worse, the application's modifications caused the operating system to crash.

Microsoft realized this problem and devised Windows File Protection (WFP) as the solution with Windows 2000. The operating system runs WFP in the background to monitor a range of "essential" system files that are designated as protected. These files mainly consist of system DLLs, but believe it or not, `pinball.exe` and `solitare.exe` are also protected. All `.sys`, `.exe`, `.dll`, and `.ocx` files that come on the Windows 2000 installation CD-ROM are protected. If the operating system detects an attempt to replace a protected file by a user or application, Windows will check the file signature to see whether it is the correct Microsoft version. If Windows determines that the file does not bear the proper signature (because it was replaced by an application), it will automatically replace the file with the original version. Windows determines the authenticity of a file by checking its file signature against its associated record in a catalog file.

The protected file replacement search order is as follows:

1. Windows searches the DllCache folder (by default, this will be in `%System Root%\System 32 folder`).
2. Windows then checks the `%System Root%\Driver Cache\Platform\driver.cab` file.
3. If the system was installed over the network, Windows will search the network installation path.
4. Windows searches the installation CD-ROM.

If you want to see which files are protected, the easiest place to check is the DllCache folder, which contains most of the protected files. What is unique about this folder is that it is updated as patches, hot fixes, and service packs are applied. The fact that the DllCache folder is somewhat dynamic makes it the most reliable source for listing the most recently protected operating system files.

> **NOTE** As of the time this book was published, not all backup solutions fully supported WFP. Our research has led us to the notion that the restoration of protected files is a dilemma that must be resolved by Microsoft and storage management vendors. Although the operating system normally would not want any protected files replaced, they would need to be replaced as part of a restore operation. As you upgrade by using service packs, some protected files are replaced. If you attempt to rebuild your system by reinstalling the operating system and then performing a full system restore, you may find that not all protected files were restored. You should consult with your backup vendor to see whether they have any known issues and workarounds for restoring certain protected files.

Improving WFP Performance

Although the DllCache folder maintains most of the WFP replacement files, some files do remain on the installation CD-ROM. This means that if the operating system detects that a protected file was replaced, and if the original of that file is not in the DllCache folder, you will be prompted to insert the installation CD-ROM (if Windows was installed from a CD-ROM). WFP performance can be improved by causing all protected files to be placed in the DllCache folder. This way, a replacement for any protected file will be available if needed by the operating system.

To cause all protected files to be cached in DllCache:

1. Run `regedit` and navigate to the `HKEY_LOCAL_MACHINE\SOFTWARE\Microsoft\Windows NT\CurrentVersion\Winlogon|SFCQuota` value.

2. Verify that the `SFCQuota` value is set to `0xFFFFFFFF`. This will cause all protected files to be cached. If it is not at this value, edit the value so that it is.

3. Exit the Registry Editor.

4. At the command prompt, type **sfc /scannow**. This will enable the System File Checker to verify all protected file versions.

5. If prompted, insert the Windows 2000 installation CD-ROM. Once finished, SFC will then add any missing protected files to the DllCache folder.

Using the System File Checker Tool (sfc.exe)

In the preceding example, you saw the sfc command used to enable Windows to check and verify all protected files. Although you have seen one use for the SFCutility, there is quite a bit more that you can do with it as well. In addition to scanning protected files and updating the DllCache folder, sfc.exe can also be used to repair the DllCache folder in the event that it becomes corrupted or unstable.

Here is the syntax:

sfc causes all protected system files to be scanned. Incorrect versions are replaced with the correct Microsoft versions.

sfc /scanonce is used if the DllCache folder becomes corrupted. Scans all protected system files once.

sfc /scanboot creates the SFCScan Registry Key and sets its value to 1. This causes protected files to be scanned each time the system boots.

sfc /purgecache purges the DllCache folder and then scans all protected files immediately afterward.

sfc /cancel cancels all pending scans of protected files.

sfc /quiet causes incorrect protected file versions to be automatically replaced without prompting the user.

> **TIP** Although some sfc commands, such as the /scanboot switch, cause the Registry to be modified, you can also manually edit the Registry to change the system's WFP settings. All System File Checker–related registry values are located in the HKEY_LOCAL_MACHINE\SOFTWARE\Microsoft\Windows NT\CurrentVersion\Winlogon key. Table 3.1 lists the SFC-specific Registry values and their possible settings.

Table 3.1: System File Checker Registry Settings

SFC Registry Value	Type	Possible Settings
SFCDisable	REG_DWORD	0—enabled. 1—disabled, prompt user at boot to re-enable. 2—disabled only for the next boot; user is not prompted to re-enable. 4—enabled; pop-up prompts disabled.

Table 3.1 continued: System File Checker Registry Settings

SFC Registry Value	Type	Possible Settings
SFCQuota	REG_DWORD	Max size in MB of DllCache folder Default = FFFFFFFF = no limit.
SFCScan	REG_DWORD	0—do not scan protected files at boot. 1—scan protected files on every boot. 2—scan protected files once.
SFCShowProgress	REG_DWORD	0—no progress meter is display when SFC runs. 1—progress meter displayed.
SFCDllCacheDir	REG_Expand_SZ	Enables you to specify local path for DllCache folder.

The Change Journal

With previous versions of Windows, incremental backups were slowed by one of two factors: (1) having to check the archive bit of each file, or (2) having to check the date-time stamp of each file. However, the time needed for a backup utility to scan a file system and collect the list of files that have changed since the last backup (in the case of an incremental backup) is relatively minimal. For most servers, this process of checking the archive bit or date-time stamp will last only a few minutes. Compared with the time needed to back up a large file server, those couple of minutes seem insignificant. If we were to tell you that the Change Journal (also referred to as the Update Sequence Number (USN) Journal) enables backup applications to perform incremental backups faster by eliminating the need to scan file systems, you would probably say "Big deal, what's a couple of minutes?" If this was all that the Change Journal did for you, you would be right, but the Change Journal is much more powerful.

For backup purposes, think of the Change Journal as a virtual notepad. Now imagine that someone wrote in the notepad the name of each file as it changed. This means that on incremental backups, the backup applications can get their list of files right from the journal, without having to scan the file system to get their own list. What this also means, however, is that all changed files get backed up. Did you know that before the days of the Change Journal, files that were renamed or had their security attributes changed were not backed up during incremental backups? These two changes do not affect the date-time stamp of the file, nor do they flip the file's archive bit. Therefore, files with these changes would not be backed up during an incremental backup that used the traditional file-scan method. If your backup software integrates with the Change Journal, they will be backed up.

In addition, backup software that is truly Change Journal aware will maintain the journal, pruning its records after each backup, so that it can look at a fresh journal during the next backup.

Indexing Service

Want to provide users with a low-overhead search engine for your file servers? Indexing Service is the answer. With the indexing service, you can define the specific folders that you want to have an index created for, and the service basically takes care of the rest.

> **NOTE** The index itself, located by default in the C:\System Volume Information (or Inetpub for web access) hidden Catalog.wci folder, will size up to 15 to 30 percent of the size of all the files being indexed. Make sure you have enough free disk space before enabling the service, or limit the number of files that are indexed.

The Indexing Service supports the following file types:

- Text
- HTML
- Internet mail and news (newsgroup article, e-mail message)
- All Microsoft Office files (Office 95 or higher)

The service can do the following tasks:

- Search files by content (words contained in the file)
- Provide secure searches via Access Control Lists (ACLs) (users can see only files they have permission to view)
- Search files by properties (creator, date, etc)
- Integrate with IIS to allow users to search the index via a web browser
- Maintain separate indexes for Internet and local searches
- Index network shares, including Unix and NetWare servers
- Support free text search (any combination of words will work)
- Support Boolean searches (AND, OR, NOT)

Starting the Indexing Service

To start the Indexing Service, follow these steps:

1. Open the Computer Management MMC. Expand the tree to Services and Applications/Indexing Service.

2. Right-click the Indexing Service icon and select Start.

3. Click the Yes button for the Indexing Service to start each time the computer is started.

Once started for the first time, the indexing service will scan all folders that have been defined for it to manage. After the first full scan, the indexing service will incrementally update its catalogs as files are added or changed. For you, little overhead is associated with the service.

Defining Folders to be Indexed

Here is how to define folders to be indexed:

1. Open the Computer Management MMC.

2. Expand the tree to Services and Applications/Indexing Service.

3. Click the System/Directories folder (or Web/Directories), as shown in Figure 3.7.

4. To delete a managed folder, right-click the folder and select Delete.

5. To add a managed folder, right-click the Directories folder and select New and then Directory. You can then either browse to or type in the path to the desired folder.

Figure 3.7: Indexing Service Managed Directories

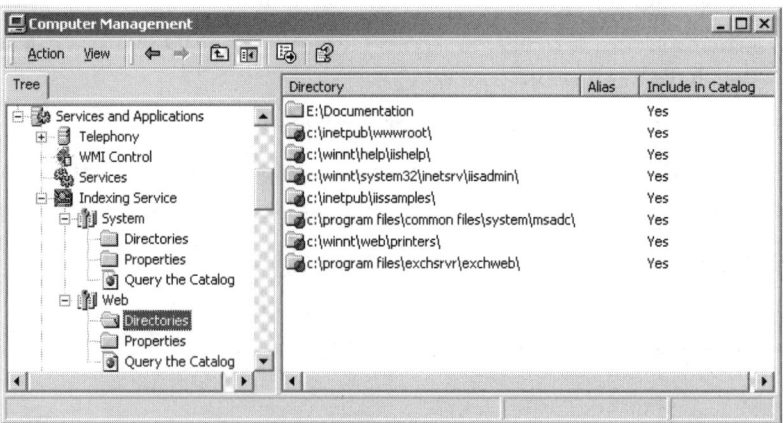

Searching Indexed Files

Users can search indexed local files as well as network shares by using Windows Explorer, or by clicking Start ➢ Search ➢ For Files or Folders. To utilize the features of the indexing service, you could then enter search criteria in the Containing Text field. Figure 3.8 shows an example of a file search using the Indexing Service.

Figure 3.8: Searching indexed files

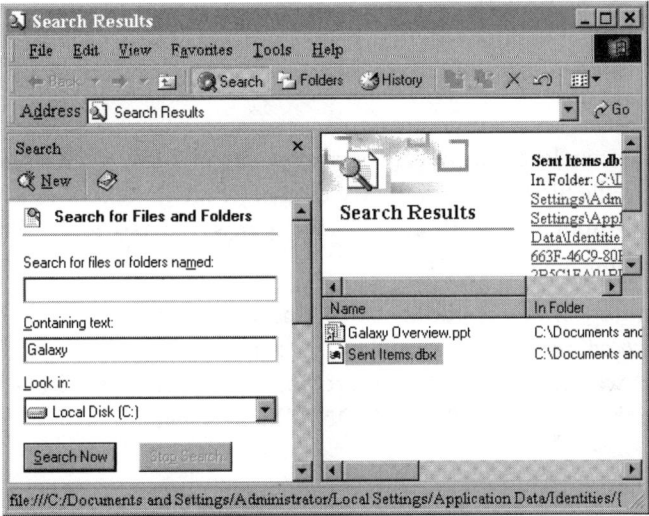

Sparse Files

Files that take advantage of the NTFS 5 *sparse file attribute* can effectively save you a tremendous amount of disk space. Say you have a 500GB data file. If you break it down to the bit level, you are talking about 4,294,967,296,000 bits. That's a lot of 1s and 0s. When this file is requested, every 1 and every 0 must be sent as a stream. With the sparse attribute, data is written and read in a different way. Consider the logic shown in Figure 3.9.

Sparse data is defined as streams of consecutive 0s. If you have data files with large volumes of sparse data, why store every 0? It would save a lot of room if the file system could understand the concept of thousands of consecutive 0s and simply make a note of the sparse strings when the data is saved. It's like buying a dozen eggs. You are told that there are 12 eggs in the container, and you accept that so you don't have to count every egg.

Figure 3.9: Huey and Ed discuss the concept of sparse files.

At the file system level, the operating system can allocate and deallocate 0-filled space anywhere in the file for files that have the sparse attribute set. In using the sparse attribute, the 500GB data file could possibly be saved as 1 to 2MB on the disk, thus saving you quite a bit of space.

If you want to learn more about sparse files, documentation can be found at the MSDN site http://msdn.microsoft.com/library/default.asp; use *sparse files* as the search criterion. You will not find much by searching other parts of the Microsoft site, such as Technet or the Knowledge Base. MSDN is the best bet.

Single Instance Storage (SIS)

Single Instance Storage is a feature that reduces the amount of disk space necessary when multiple Remote Installation Service (RIS) images are stored. If you are using RIS to deploy Windows 2000 Professional, SIS will run in the background on your RIS volume. When RIS is first installed, a SIS Common Store folder is created at the root of the volume managed by RIS. This folder is used by SIS to store files that are common to multiple RIS images. The RIS installation will also create the Single Instance Storage Groveler service, which defaults to an automatic service.

This is how SIS works: SIS monitors RIS images for duplicate files. When a duplicate file is located, SIS stores a copy of the file in the SIS Common Store folder. SIS then makes all other RIS duplicates of the file reparse points. The filenames will exist in each image, but their reparse point will point to the location where the actual data for the file is stored.

The RISetup Wizard will do all the work you need to worry about when RIS is first set up. SIS does not require any manual administration. If you have multiple RIPrep images on the same volume, SIS will certainly be valuable in saving you disk space.

> **NOTE** SIS operates at the physical volume level. If you have other junction or mount points on the volume that contains your RIS images, SIS will not follow the pointers to any other physical volume.

You can find more information regarding backup and restore issues involving SIS in Chapter 11, "Operating System Rebuild: The Gotchas."

File Replication Service (FRS)

File Replication Service is the Windows 2000 replacement for the Windows NT LMRepl Service. In Windows 2000, FRS is used by domain controllers to replicate Active Directory and SYSVOL data. FRS is also used by the Distributed File System service to replicate data between Dfs replica sets. No other Windows 2000 service integrates with FRS. FRS is a multithreaded application, which enables it to replicate different files between different computers simultaneously. Initially, FRS is set as a manual service for member servers. When a server is promoted to a domain controller, the FRS service is changed to be automatic. For servers participating in Dfs replica sets, you should configure the FRS service to be automatic as well.

Quite a bit of information is currently available about FRS administration, including scheduling replication and general administrative settings. FRS does not have its own administrative console, so it is administered through the Active Directory Sites and Services MMC for Active Directory replication, and through the Distributed File System MMC for Dfs replication.

Because you bought this book to learn specifically about enterprise storage issues of Windows 2000, that is what we will concentrate on. Backing up replicated files is not the issue. Any backup application can back up these files and restore them as well. The issue that you must consider, however, is whether you want your restored data to replicate out to all the replication partners of a particular share. In most instances, this is something that you do not want. To understand the underlying restoration issues involved with replicated folders, you must first grasp the concept of *authoritative* and *nonauthoritative* restores.

Authoritative versus Nonauthoritative Restores

FRS is a great service, as it makes sure that a given folder has identical replicas of its files and subfolders in other places around the network. But consider: FRS must *somehow* keep all of those replicas in sync with each other. So let's examine a simple case, of an FRS-ed folder with just two replicas. Let's further simplify things by putting just one file into that folder, a text file called `mystuff.txt`. Let's call the first replica directory A and the second one B.

FRS keeps track of how often a file has changed, giving the file a "version" number. This version number is known as the Update Sequence Number (USN). Thus, when I first created `mystuff.txt`, FRS assigned it a USN of 1. Later, suppose I happen to attach to Replica B and grab the copy of `mystuff.txt` there and modify it. That copy of `mystuff.txt` in Replica B is now USN 2 of `mystuff.txt`. Eventually Replica A and Replica B compare notes and discover a conflict—Replica A has a copy of `mystuff.txt` that's USN 1, and Replica B has a `mystuff.txt` that's USN 2. They're not the same, so which should FRS replicate? As you'd guess, FRS takes the higher USN number.

But now suppose this scarier scenario occurs. I decide to edit `mystuff.txt` and I'm attached to Replica A. Simultaneously, you decide to work on `mystuff.txt`, and you're attached to Replica B. We are both, then, editing different copies of the same text. When we started editing `mystuff.txt`, we had a file that thought that it was USN 2. Therefore, when I write my changes, my copy will think that it's USN 3. Unfortunately, when you write *your* changes, it'll also be USN 3.

When it's replication time, FRS notes two `mystuff.txt` files, probably with different dates, times, and file sizes. So it consults the USN numbers. But they're *both* version 3! When the USNs are the same, FRS must go to the next best thing—the time and date. FRS, then, replicates first by USN, and then by date and time. This is called the "last writer wins" algorithm.

Now consider what that means if you discover that `mystuff.txt` is damaged in some way, and so you need to *restore* a file on an FRS volume. Perhaps you're restoring a backup copy from three days ago, and you restore it into Replica A. When FRS goes to replicate then again it's got a choice—the newer (damaged) file, or the older (correct) file? Well, by default, FRS is going to overwrite the newly restored file with the newer, damaged file.

Clearly we've got to do something about that. That's what *authoritative restores* handle.

Authoritative Restores

When you perform an authoritative restore of replicated data, your restored data will go out and overwrite any like data on all replication partners. This happens because all restored objects will have their USN incremented by 100,000 during the restore. Incrementing an object's USN that much ensures that it will be looked at as the most recent file version, because it is highly unlikely that any object could be modified 100,000 times before you would try to restore the object. Because they overwrite the data on all replication partners, authoritative restores are infrequently used.

You would use an authoritative restore under these circumstances:

- You want to effectively "roll back" data on replicated shares or domain controllers to a time before data was corrupted.
- You made mistakes configuring an AD object such as an Organization Unit (OU) and believe that it will be quicker to authoritatively restore the OU from a previous backup rather than undo your erroneous changes.

Nonauthoritative Restores

Nonauthoritative restores are the most common way of restoring replicated data. When you perform a nonauthoritative restore, files and objects are restored exactly as they were backed up. The restore application does not change the file's attributes or version number. Any files on replication partners that are newer then the restored files will overwrite the restored data during the next scheduled replication.

You would use an authoritative restore in this instance:

- You want to restore a server while minimizing replication traffic over the network. You use your backup software to restore the replicated data. If the backup media is locally attached to the server, the replicated files can be brought back without affecting the network.

The alternative would be to rebuild the server and rejoin the replication set (in the case of Dfs). For domain controllers, you would rebuild the server and then run dcpromo. This approach would cause the rebuilt server to receive all its updates via replication over the LAN. If you are having to restore the data over the LAN anyway, and are not using compression with your backup solution, you are probably better off just rebuilding the system from scratch and not using your backup software at all. Taking this approach will ensure that the rebuilt system is clean. Of course, if you don't have time for this, then that is what you bought your backup software for in the first place.

> **NOTE** If you are wondering how you perform authoritative and nonauthoritative restores, that will be covered in Chapter 10, "File System Backup/Recovery," and Chapter 11, "Operating System Rebuilds—the Gotchas."

Using the Robust File Copy Utility Robocopy

FRS is limited in what it can and will replicate. To maintain data availability, you may just want to setup replication between two network shares. On many occasions, you might want to replicate an application's data in order to retain higher availability of that data. Based on your needs, using Dfs (covered in the next section) might be overkill. FRS by itself does not allow you to define replication between two shares. Within the Windows 2000 Server Resource Kit, however, is a utility that can do this.

Robocopy is a powerful utility that performs replication by acting as a "smart" file copier. When using Robocopy, you define a destination folder to copy a source's file to. Robocopy is "intelligent" enough that if a file in the destination folder is newer than the file it is trying to copy, it will not overwrite the newer file, nor will it prompt you to overwrite the file. If you set up Robocopy to run on two shares, copying data to each other at scheduled intervals, you have in essence set up replication. This might not be the solution for everything, but for small shares that do not need much management, this might prove to be the ideal tool for you.

In addition to copying files, Robocopy can be used to purge files from a share. If you want to maintain two mirrored replicas, you will need to have files that are deleted on one share removed from the other share as well. Robocopy has built-in switches for just this scenario.

Robocopy is a command-line tool. Therefore, you can script Robocopy with other tools or use the Windows Task Scheduler to schedule it to run at regular intervals. Although not complex, the amount of syntax that can be used with the Robocopy utility is quite extensive. If you are interested in this utility, read the robocopy.doc file located on the Windows 2000 Server Resource Kit CD-ROM, or type **robocopy /?** at the command prompt for a brief explanation of its syntax.

Distributed File System (Dfs)

Dfs has been around since the introduction of Windows NT, but is still unused by many organizations. With Windows NT, Dfs was not stable enough to be included with the software and had to be downloaded from Microsoft. Dfs was available only for North American releases of NT.

Once set up, Dfs can make administering network file shares much simpler. An easy way to think of Dfs is as a "share of other shares." Users can access all network shares through a single server. The server, or Dfs root, hosts pointers to remote network shares. Users see folders and subfolders, while in reality each folder can reside on a different physical server. With Dfs, if you want to perform maintenance on one file server, you can change a Dfs link to point users to a different server that has the same data. This enables you to perform file server maintenance without having to alert users to access a different share.

As you read in the preceding section, Dfs also uses FRS. With Dfs, you can create up to 32 replicas of a network share. This helps to maintain data availability, as well as provide load balancing. When you configure the Dfs root (the server that users access as a central point for seeing all network shares), you can set up either a stand-alone or domain-based root.

Table 3.2 shows the features of domain-based and stand-alone roots.

Table 3.2: Domain-based versus Stand-alone Roots

Domain-based	Stand-alone
Uses Active Directory to store Dfs hierarchy.	Provides no Active Directory integration.
Can have multiple levels of Dfs links.	Cannot have multiple levels of Dfs links.
Can have root-level shared folders.	Cannot have root-level shared folders.
Supports automatic file replication (uses FRS).	Does not support automatic file replication.
There can be only one domain-based Dfs root (you can have up to 32 replicas of the root).	You can create as many stand-alone roots as you want.

As you can see, stand-alone Dfs roots are not as flexible as domain-based roots. But their lack of AD integration enables them to remain independent. You may want to have several roots, and thus forego the AD integration of domain-based roots. An example of using several stand-alone Dfs roots is shown in the next chapter.

Enabling Dfs

Dfs is installed by default on Windows 2000 Servers. To enable Dfs, you must first provide some initial configuration information. This is done at the Dfs administrative console, accessed by clicking Start ➢ Programs ➢ Administrative Tools ➢ Distributed File System.

Follow these steps:

1. From the console, click Action and then New Dfs Root.
2. At the Dfs Root Wizard welcome window, click Next.
3. Select either to create a domain or to create a stand-alone Dfs root.
4. For domain Dfs roots, select the domain name.
5. Type the host server name.

6. Select to use an existing share for the Dfs Root, or create a new share and click Next, as shown in Figure 3.10.

Figure 3.10: Specifying the Dfs Root Share

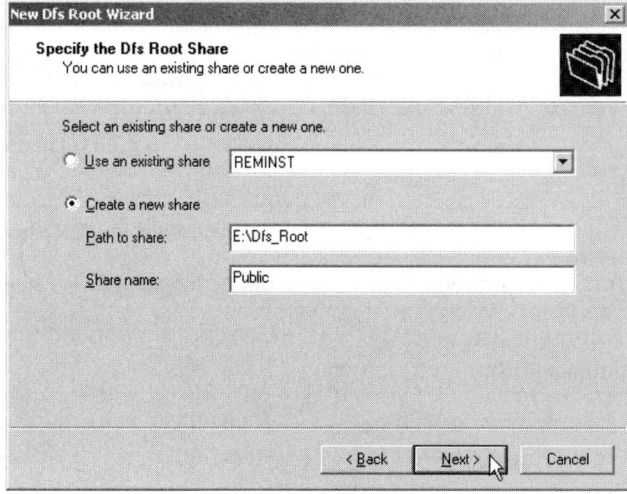

7. If you created a new folder, click Yes to create the folder.
8. Type in or leave the default share name as the Dfs Root name and click Next.
9. Click the Finish button to complete the creation of the Dfs root.

Adding Dfs Links

After you have configured the root, you have created a starting point for users to access all network shares. To enable access to remote network shares, you must create Dfs links. *Links* are pointers that transparently redirect users and applications to other file servers on your network.

To create a Dfs link:

1. Right-click the Dfs root and select New Dfs Link.
2. In the dialog box shown in Figure 3.11, type a name for the link. The name you provide will be the name of the folder that users see when they access your Dfs root over the network.
3. Then enter the path that the link will direct users to. You can browse the network to a share or you can type a UNC path.
4. With all information entered, click OK to create the link.

Figure 3.11: Creating a DFS link

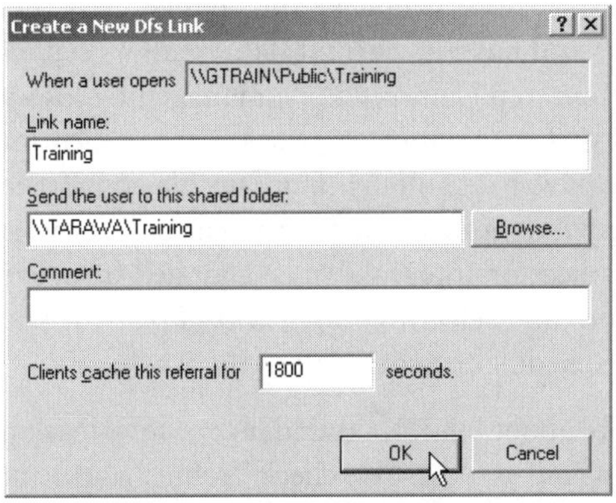

Creating Replicas for Fault Tolerance and Load Balancing

After you have created a link to a share, you can ensure that the Dfs share is always available by replicating its data to another domain share. When you create replica sets for a Dfs link, users will be automatically redirected to one share if the other replica share is not available. The use of replicas for a Dfs link also allows file access directed through the Dfs link to be load-balanced between the replicas.

To create a replica share for an existing Dfs link:

1. Right-click the Dfs link and select New Replica.
2. In the Add a New Replica dialog box, type in or browse to the path for the network share that will replicate the existing Dfs link replica. This dialog box is shown in Figure 3.12.
3. Select either Manual or Automatic replication and click OK to create the replica.

Figure 3.12: Adding a new replica for a Dfs link

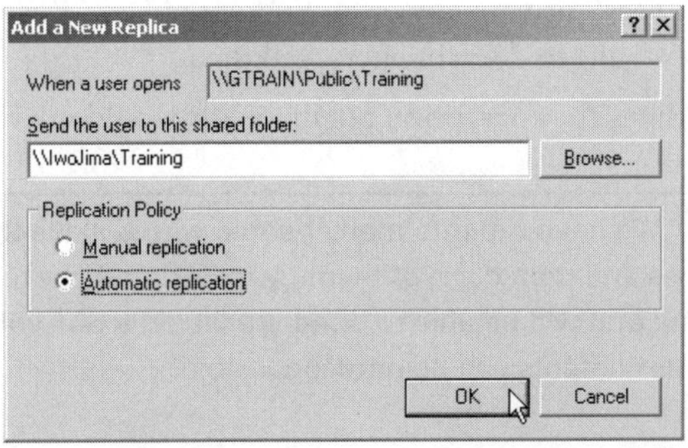

After you create the replica share, the Replication Policy window will open. From here, you can designate one share as master and enable the other share to participate in replication. The master will push its current data to all its replication partners. If you select *automatic* replication, replication will be managed by FRS and will occur every 15 minutes by default. If you use *manual* replication, no replication will occur between replica partners. You will have to manually maintain file consistency between the shares, or schedule Robocopy to handle manual "replication" for you. If you are using automatic replication, the replication interval can be changed from every 15 minutes by right-clicking the Dfs root and selecting *Replication Policy*. If you wish, you can have a different replication schedule for each day of the week.

Want to know more about Dfs? An abundance of information exists in the Windows 2000 Server Online Help, and you can also check Technet (www.Microsoft.com/technet) or Labmice (www.labmice.com) for additional articles on Dfs.

Encrypting File System (EFS)

Encrypting File System is a feature new to NTFS 5 volumes. A need for standardized strong encryption has existed not only for file protection, but also for protecting files that have been backed up to remote media. Some backup utilities provide their own native encryption algorithms. Windows 2000 EFS provides a solid and secure encryption algorithm that will outlast your backup application, meaning that your choice of a backup solution will not have to marry you to its native encryption algorithm.

EFS offers the following advantages:

- Uses 128-bit encryption for North American releases of Windows 2000
- Uses 40-bit encryption for international releases of Windows
- Uses the Data Encryption Standard X (DESX) algorithm
- Enables encryption and decryption to remain transparent to the user
- Requires a user's private key or an Encrypted Data Recovery Agent (administrator by default) to decrypt encrypted data
- Usually assigns the encryption attribute at the folder level

WARNING We have run into many people who believe that you can back up encrypted files and then decrypt them by restoring them to FAT volumes. This does not work. You will be able to open the file on a FAT volume after the restore, but its contents will be unrecognizable.

If you are wondering why you should encrypt at the folder level, it is because EFS works a little oddly with file-level encryption. When you encrypt a file, it remains encrypted until it is modified. Once modified, if its parent folder does not have the encrypted attribute, the file will lose its encrypted attribute and then can be opened by anyone. If you give the encrypted attribute to a folder, any file modified in the folder or added to the folder will acquire the encrypted attribute.

NOTE FRS does not support encrypted files. If you encrypt a file in a Dfs replica set, it will not replicate.

To encrypt a folder by using Windows Explorer:

1. In Windows Explorer, right-click the folder and select Properties.
2. Click the Advanced button at the bottom of the folder properties window.
3. Click the Encrypt Contents to Secure Data check box and click OK, as shown in Figure 3.13.

Figure 3.13: Encrypting files and folders using Windows Explorer

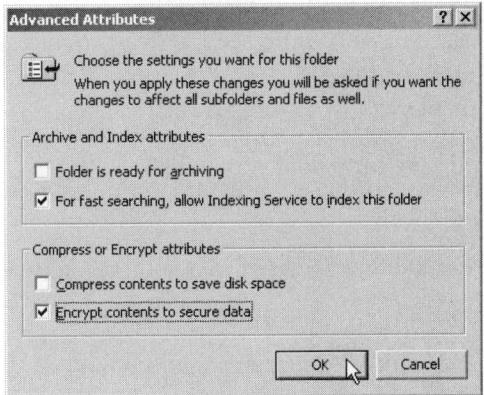

4. Click the OK button to close the folder properties window.
5. When prompted, choose whether you want the encrypted attribute applied just to the folder, or to its subfolders and files as well.

A folder, its files, and subfolders can be decrypted by clearing the folder's Encrypt Contents to Secure Data check box.

Using the Cipher Utility

Instead of using Windows Explorer to encrypt and decrypt files, you can use the `cipher` command to do so as well.

Here is the syntax for the `cipher` command:

`cipher /e [path to folder]` encrypts the folder specified in the path.

`cipher /d [path to folder]` decrypts the folder specified in the path.

There are many more switches available for use with `cipher`. Use `cipher /?` to see the syntax for all other switches.

Disk Quotas

Disk quotas can be used to impose disk space limits for each user in your organization. If you are getting tired of using your hardware as a storage vault for terabytes of MP3s, disk quotas might just be the answer for which you are looking.

If you want to set up disk quotas, you should consider the following rules:

- You cannot set quotas on individual folders or files (only at the volume level).
- Quotas are based on uncompressed file sizes; compressing a file does not give a user more space.
- Quotas set for a partition apply only to that partition.
- A partition must be formatted with NTFS.

To configure disk quotas:

1. From Windows Explorer, right-click a volume and select Properties.
2. Click the Quota tab.
3. Click the Enable Quota Management check box.
4. If you want to have users more than just warned when they exceed their quota limit, check the Deny Disk Space to Users Exceeding Quota Limit box.
5. Configure the maximum space and logging options, as shown in Figure 3.14.
6. If you need to customize disk quotas for specific users, click the Quota Entries button to do so. Otherwise, the quota settings will apply to all users.
7. Click the OK button to complete the quota configuration.

Figure 3.14: Disk quota configuration

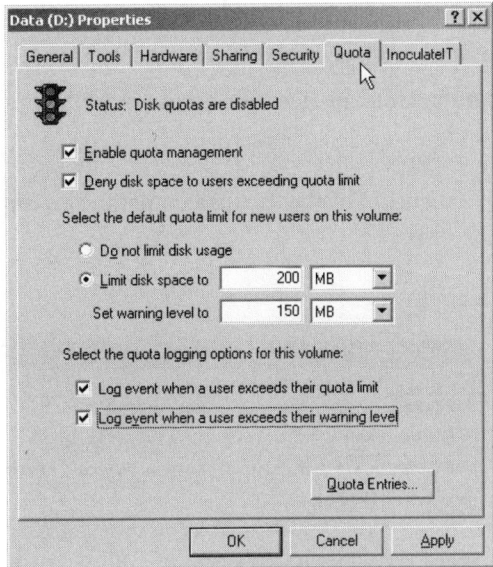

Monitoring Disk Usage with Diskuse

Diskuse is a command-line utility that is available with the Windows 2000 Server Resource Kit. With Diskuse, you can collect information on disk space usage on a user-by-user basis. The command can output usage statistics for a single user or for all users. Usage statistics can be output to the screen or to a text file.

The syntax is as follows:

    diskuse [path] [switches]

If you do not specify a path, the current folder is assumed. You can use switches to limit the command to a single user or to cause the output to be saved to a text file.

Here are the switches you can use:

/e:file writes all error messages and warnings to the file specified instead of displaying them onscreen.

/f: file outputs data to the filename specified.

/q indicates quiet mode; does not display any information on the screen. This switch is useless without the /f switch because you will run the command and wind up with no information.

/s scans current folder and all subfolders in the specified path.

/t outputs data in a table format. If the output is onscreen, the data is space-delimited. If the output is to a file, the data is comma-delimited.

/u:user scans and reports information only for the user specified.

/w outputs data in Unicode. Default output is ANSI.

Example

Figure 3.15 shows execution of the diskuse command to report on disk usage for the D drive and all subdirectories.

Figure 3.15: Diskuse execution

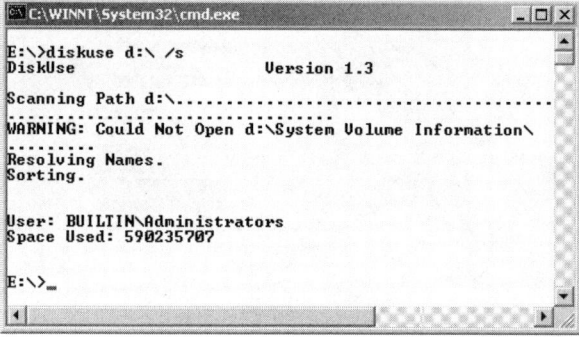

System State

The term *System State* refers to system-specific data that can be backed up and restored. The Windows 2000 System State includes the following:

- Boot and system files
- System File Protection catalog
- System File Protection files
- Performance Monitor configuration files
- Active Directory (if client is a domain controller)
- SYSVOL (if client is a domain controller)
- Certificate Server database (if client is a certificate server)
- Cluster database (if client is part of a cluster)
- Registry
- COM+ database

With NT, the Registry was often looked at as the lone necessary database for operating system recovery. In reality, many other services and databases needed to be synchronized with the Registry for stable operation. With this in mind, Microsoft devised the concept of the System State.

With Windows 2000, you cannot just back up the Registry using your backup software, even if that's all you want.

> **NOTE**   Registry backups are possible by running rdisk to create an Emergency Repair Disk. The backup files are stored in the %systemroot%\system32\Repair folder. Your backup software can back up and restore the Repair folder directly, but any live backups of the Registry can only happen as part of a System State backup.

If you want to back up any part of the System State, you must back up everything. The same rule applies for restores. If you want to restore only the Registry on a domain controller, you would have to restore the entire Active Directory database as well.

In some ways, the concept is solid. It is for your own protection, after all. Unfortunately, this feature has limited the backup and restore alternatives available for the Active Directory. For example, with NetWare many backup applications can restore single NDS object. To restore a single Active Directory object, you must restore the entire Active Directory database. For enterprise-level organizations, the time involved in this type of restore operation is often longer than the time that would be required to manually re-create the object. Microsoft is working with backup vendors to change some of its System State rules so that if you want to restore a single Active Directory object, such as a user account, you won't have to restore the entire System State to do so.

You should make sure you have plenty of free storage space to back up the System State as a complete unit. A typical System State backup will take a minimum of 150 to 250MB. Even if you are doing incremental backups of a computer each day, if the System State is defined in the backup job's content, you will back up every System State file, regardless of whether it has changed.

4

Working with Removable Storage Manager

In Chapter 3, "Windows 2000 Storage Enhancements," you were introduced to the many benefits of Removable Storage Manager (RSM) and Remote Storage Service (RSS). This chapter focuses on the implementation, configuration, and backup and recovery issues involving these two new features. The better you know how to work with RSM, the easier your life will be configuring and administering your storage devices.

Configuring RSM

Figure 4.1 shows the Removable Storage Manager Microsoft Management Console (MMC) snap-in. The snap-in enables you to perform several administrative tasks with media and storage devices, such as:

- Creating and managing media pools
- Inventorying a library
- Importing and exporting library media
- Enabling and disabling storage devices
- Cleaning drives
- Configuring libraries and drives

Figure 4.1: The RSM MMC snap-in administrative tool

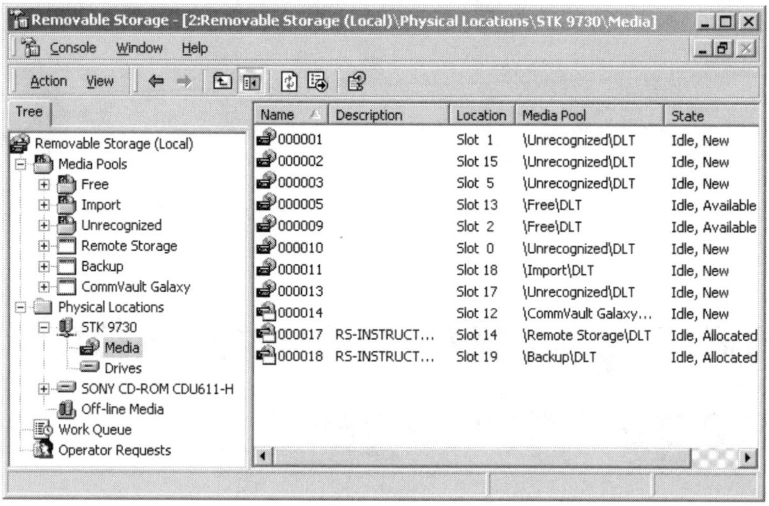

Media Pools

The first available configuration option is Media Pools. Before we get to the management aspects of media pools, let's first quickly define what they are. *A media pool* is exactly what its name implies: a pool, or a logical collection of media. Each pool is a logical bucket that is a means of organizing the media. Suppose you have three buckets of music cassette tapes: One has blank tapes, another has country music tapes, and the last contains rock 'n' roll tapes. All three buckets have tapes, but what set the buckets apart from each other is that the tapes in each bucket share some common attributes. This example illustrates the concept of a media pool.

Media pools provide an easy means to group media by their function.

Although every tape might physically be in the same library, it does not have to be in the same media pool. The media pool is used to set logical boundaries and is not restricted by physical configurations. The only true restriction placed on media pools is that they must contain the same media type. In other words, you cannot mix DLT and 8mm tapes within the same pool.

If you look back to Figure 4.1, you will see six media pools listed (under the Media Pools folder, on the left side of the screen). Three pools are represented by one icon, and the other three have a different representation. This is because RSM divides media pools into two classes: *system media pools* and *application media pools*. Table 4.1 describes the function of each system media pool. Application media pools are detailed in the upcoming subsection, "Application Media Pools."

Table 4.1: System Media Pools

System Media Pool	Description
Free	Group of media available for use by any application. When an application needs a blank medium, it can get one from the Free media pool. After an application takes a tape from the Free media pool, the tape is logically removed from the Free media pool and placed in the application's media pool.
Import	When media is added to a library and subsequently inventoried by RSM, it is placed in the Import pool if RSM recognizes its on-media identifier (OMID). Media that has been employed by applications using Microsoft Tape Format (MTF) will have a recognizable OMID and thus will be placed in the Import pool.
Unrecognized	Pool that contains two types of mediums: new mediums and mediums with an OMID that is not recognized by RSM. For example, say another application had used a tape prior to it being imported into a library controlled by RSM. If the application wrote its own proprietary OMID onto the tape, RSM will see the identifier but not recognize it. In this event, the tape will be placed in the Unrecognized media pool.

After media has been added to a library, you can drag and drop the new tapes to any pool you desire (as long as the media format is compatible). Typically, after importing tapes, you will highlight all the new tapes in the Unrecognized or Import pool and drag and drop them into the Free media pool.

> **WARNING** When tapes are moved to the Free media pool, any data on the tape will be destroyed, and RSM will mount and write a "free" label as the tape's OMID.

On-Media Identifiers (OMIDs)

Removable Storage Manager tracks tapes and disks by their *on-media identifier*—a two-part label we'll explain in a moment. To do this, RSM writes this identifier to the storage medium the first time it is inserted into a library. For read-only or write-once mediums, such as CD-Rs or WORM disks, RSM will not write an on-media identifier. Instead, it will use the volume and serial number already written to the disk as a means of identification.

So, what is an on-media identifier? As we've said, it's a two-part label. The first part of the identifier is the *label type*. This part identifies the tape format used to write data to the tape. RSM natively supports three tape formats: Microsoft Tape Format (MTF), HP OmniBack II, and Quarter-Inch Cartridge (QIC) 113. When tapes with some application's proprietary tape format are inserted into a library, those tapes are placed in the Unrecognized media pool.

The second part of the identifier is the *Media ID*. The Media ID is a code generated to provide a unique identity for each medium. Are they always unique? Not necessarily! RSM has an excellent way of handling duplicate Media IDs. Suppose you have a changer connected to a Windows 2000 Server that has two copies of Barry Manilow's *Greatest Hits* CD-ROM. No, Windows does not automatically eject these legacy CD-ROMs! This is what backward compatibility is all about. RSM will treat these CDs as equal and interchangeable. However, because each CD-ROM would have its own record in the RSM database, you can assign unique identifiers, such as a display name, to each CD-ROM. This way, you could disguise your secret need to listen to Barry Manilow while you work.

Application Media Pools

Application media pools are typically created automatically by applications that use RSM. Having each application work within its own media pool prevents applications from using each other's media. Typically, each application will have a single media pool displayed. However, it is possible for applications to share a common media pool. Also, some applications, such as Windows Backup, can utilize multiple media pools. For example, one pool can be dedicated for full backups, and another can be used for incremental backups. After media is used by an application, it is considered *allocated* by RSM and cannot be used by other applications. This method prevents an application, or an uninformed user, from "accidentally" placing a medium being used by one application in another application's pool.

Although they are typically created by applications, you can also manually create an application media pool.

To create a media pool, follow these steps:

1. From the RSM administrative console, right-click the Media Pools icon and select Create Media Pool, as shown in Figure 4.2.

2. You will then see the General tab of the Create a New Media Pool Properties dialog box (see Figure 4.3). This is where you will perform most of your pool configuration.

Figure 4.2: Creating a media pool

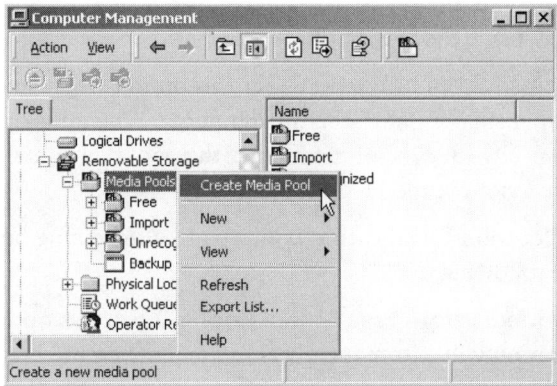

Figure 4.3: Creating a New Media Pool Properties dialog box

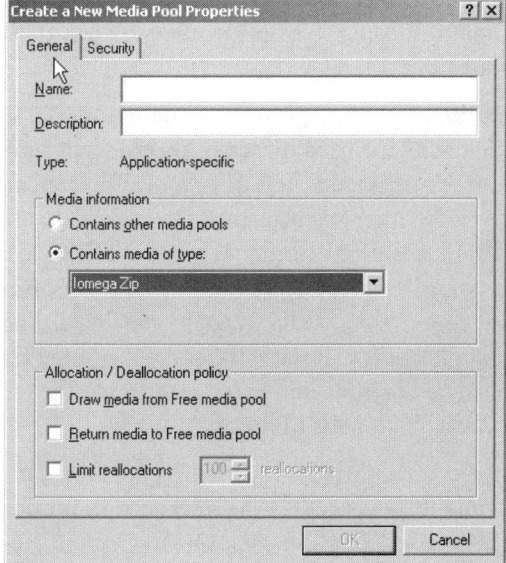

After you type a name and description for the new pool, you can choose the structure of the media pool in the Media Information portion of the window. The options are as follows:

Contains Other Media Pools   Select this option when you want to have other media pools contained in the pool you are creating. This is typically how applications create their own media pools. The first pool created is set to contain other media pools and is named after the application itself. After the first pool is created, then media-specific pools, such as DLT or CD-R, are created inside the new pool.

Contains Media of Type   Select this option when you want the pool to contain media but not other media pools. When this option is selected, you must specify the type of media that the pool will contain. Different media types cannot coexist in the same pool.

3. In the Allocation/Deallocation Policy part of the dialog box, you need to select from the following options:

    Draw Media from Free Media Pool   When this option is checked, the application will automatically take media from the Free pool when it is out of spare media.

    Return Media to Free Media Pool   Select this option when you want recycled media automatically returned to the Free media pool. When an application no longer needs the data on a particular medium, it can recycle the medium. Choosing this option allows other applications to use the pool's recycled media.

    Limit Reallocations   This option enables you to set the maximum number of times a medium is used by applications. Each time a medium is taken from the Free media pool, it is *allocated*. When an application no longer needs the medium and returns it to the Free pool, it is *deallocated* and can be used by another application. When it is taken again by another application, it is considered *reallocated*. Limiting reallocations enables you to place additional controls on media usage by placing a threshold on how many times an application will reuse the same medium. This technique enables you to place restrictions on media usage and thus remove overused or expired media from your libraries.

4. After you name and configure the media pool, you can then click the Security tab to configure its security (see the next section for details). After the security settings have been set, you can click OK to create the pool.

Media Pool Security

Figure 4.4 shows the media pool security settings. You should see that configuring security for a media pool is no different from configuring security for anything else, whether files, folders, or applications. Notice, however, that there are no inheritable permissions. To configure a user, group, or computer to use the media pool, you would simply click the Add button and then select the account object from the resulting list.

Figure 4.4: Media pool security

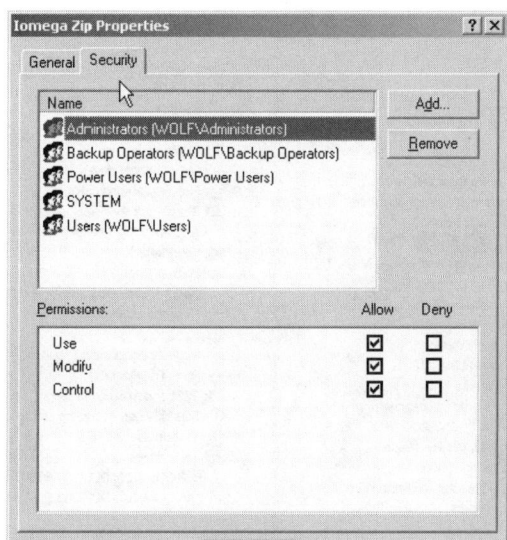

Table 4.2 explains the effect of each permission on media pool access and management.

Table 4.2: Media Pool Security

Action	Use	Modify	Control
Create media pools		X	
Delete media pools			X
Move media between pools		X	
Mount media	X		
Dismount media	X		

Physical Locations

The Physical Locations folder lists the physical devices that can currently be used by RSM. Although we are past the days of "plug and pray," do not just assume that you can plug your new library into the external SCSI connector of your new Windows 2000 Server and you will be up and running. Windows is not aware of every library and drive available. As you can see in Figure 4.5, Windows Device Manager sees the drives inside a library just fine but has no idea what type of library the drives reside in.

Figure 4.5: Unknown library in Device Manager

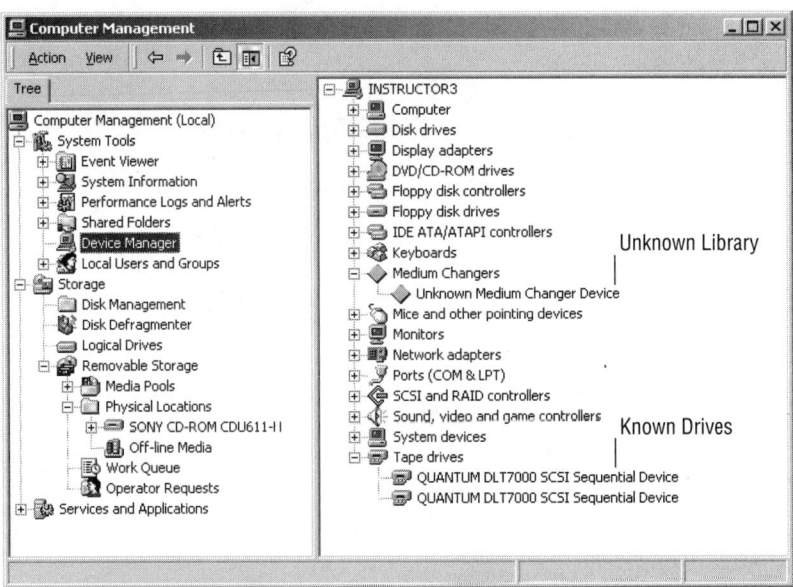

In this circumstance, RSM will not list either the library or the drives as physical locations for Removable Storage. This problem is something you will not normally notice. Unlike SCSI cards and other hardware, Windows does not tell you that it has found new hardware, nor does it automatically ask you for a driver. You might notice that no yellow question mark appears next to the medium changer. The yellow question mark is the typical symbol for an unknown device. When an unknown medium changer is listed, you have two courses of action: You can first try to run the rsmconfg.exe library configuration utility, or you can get the Windows 2000 driver from the library manufacturer.

Using the RSM Configuration Wizard (rsmconfg.exe)

The rsmconfg.exe utility is available with the Windows 2000 Server Resource Kit. Buying Windows and not getting the Resource Kit is like buying a car without air conditioning. You can get by without it, but your experience certainly is not as comfortable. The situation shown in Figure 4.5 is one ideal for use with the RSM Configuration Wizard, although its success is still not guaranteed. Windows can recognize two drives and also sees a medium changer. What Windows does not see is a relationship between the drives and the changer. This is where the wizard comes in. The wizard links any unmapped changer drive bays to a drive name. The wizard may not work for all changers, but it does provide an alternative to needing a specific Windows driver, especially if the library manufacturer has no plans to develop a Windows driver for the library.

To use `rsmconfg.exe`, you must first install the Windows 2000 Server Resource Kit. After installation, you need to check whether the wizard will work with your RSM configuration.

Check the `HKEY_LOCAL_MACHINE\System\CurrentControlSet\Services\NtmsSvc\Config` folder in the Registry. You should see a subkey listed for each changer. The changer that you are trying to configure should be listed as well, and you should see a correct value for that subkey's drivenumbers data. If the correct number of drives is listed in the Drivenumbers data field, you should then see a ??? entry for each unmapped drive bay. If your system meets these conditions, you will be able to use `rsmconfig.exe` to configure the medium changer.

To run `rsmconfg.exe`, do the following:

1. Make sure no stand-alone drives are loaded with media. The RSM Configuration Wizard sometimes has problems with loaded drives, even if those drives are not part of the library that you are trying to configure.
2. Make sure at least one medium (tape, disk, and so on) for each drive in the changer is loaded into the changer's slots (for a four-drive library, you would need four tapes loaded).
3. Click Start ➢ Run, type **rsmconfg**, and press Enter.
4. At the wizard welcome window, click Next.
5. Select the changer you want to configure from the list of changers that RSM failed to configure and click Next.
6. Let the wizard scan the medium changer to find slots with media, or manually tell the wizard which slots contain media. The wizard at this point will mount a medium into each drive in the changer.
7. The wizard will now scan all stand-alone drives attached to the system to see which ones are loaded. The loaded drives will be mapped to the drive bays for the medium changer, and the Windows Registry will be updated.
8. The changer is now configured. You can now exit the wizard or configure another medium changer.

> **NOTE** The RSM Configuration Wizard performs a manual hardware configuration of medium changers. This means that the changer is no longer autoconfigurable, and future hardware changes to the changer will not be detected by RSM.

The RSM Configuration Wizard is useful, but it has its limits. The best solution to configuring a changer to work with RSM is to update its driver to one that has the Windows 2000 driver extensions. This will enable the changer to remain autoconfigurable in the event that its hardware configuration ever changes.

Updating the Driver for a Library

You can update the medium changer driver by using Device Manager. The steps to update the driver are as follows:

1. Get the Windows 2000 driver from the manufacturer for your medium changer.
2. Right-click the medium changer object in Device Manager and select Properties.
3. Click the Driver tab and then click the Update Driver button.
4. When the Update Driver Wizard opens, click Next.
5. If Windows did not find the right driver the first time the system booted with the new device, it probably will not now, either. Click the Display a List of Known Drivers option and click Next.
6. Click the Have Disk button.
7. Type a pathname or browse to the path where the driver is located and click OK.
8. Select the appropriate model number for the library that the driver supports and click Next to complete the driver update.

After the proper driver is installed, you will then see the library and drives listed as physical devices in Removable Storage Manager. This is shown in Figure 4.6. At this time, RSM will immediately begin to perform an inventory of the library.

Figure 4.6: Proper library configuration

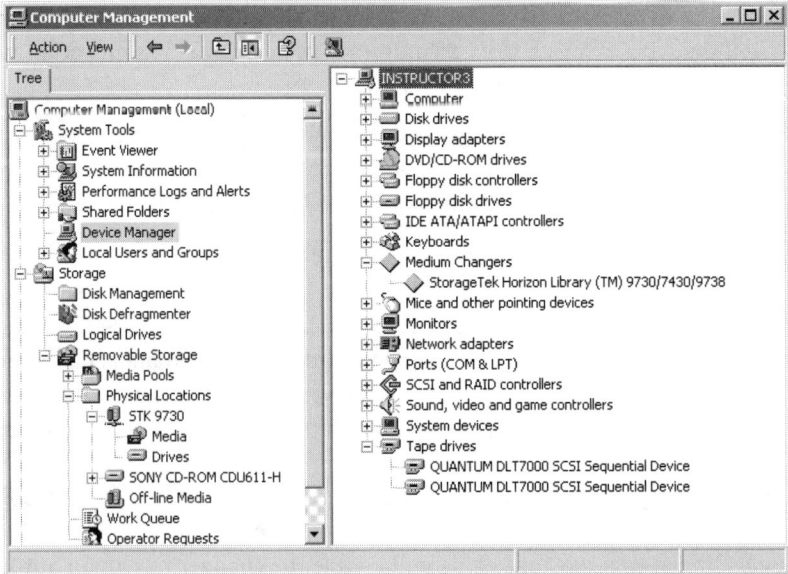

More Driver Problems

One other source of problems can exist for your library or drives. For devices to work with RSM, they must have the Windows 2000 driver extensions. If your library or drives are still using legacy NT drivers after an upgrade, or if they are using drivers from a third-party application, RSM will not recognize those devices. In that case, you can get the proper Windows 2000 driver from the manufacturer and follow the steps just outlined, or you can remove the old driver and let Windows try to detect its own updated driver for the device.

This second option can be done in four steps:

1. Uninstall the driver by right-clicking the device object in Device Manager and selecting Uninstall.

2. Determine the .inf file that is used as the driver for the device by checking the %Systemroot%\setupapi.log file. The file will list the device name along with its associated driver file.

3. Find the legacy driver in the %Systemroot%\Inf folder, and move the file to a temporary folder.

4. After the legacy driver is removed, return to Device Manager and right-click the Computer icon at the root of the Device Manager tree and select Scan for Hardware Changes. Device Manager should redetect the device and use the Windows 2000 native driver.

Now that you have seen the importance of device driver compatibility with RSM , you can look a little deeper at the physical configuration options available for RSM.

Library Configuration

Let's start looking at the configuration options by examining library properties. You can do this by right-clicking the library or medium changer and selecting Properties. Figure 4.7 displays the General medium-changer configuration options.

Under the General tab, you have the opportunity to configure the name and description of the medium changer. The State listed alerts you to the software state of the device.

Under the Inventory heading, you have three options:

Fast RSM creates an inventory of barcodes, if the library has a barcode reader. If the library does not have a barcode reader, during the Fast inventory RSM checks and lists each storage slot as either occupied or unoccupied.

Full During a Full inventory, RSM reads the OMID of each medium, in addition to checking its barcode or slot status. In reading the OMID, that means that RSM will physically mount each medium in the library into its drive, thus prolonging the inventory process.

None Choosing this setting will disable automatic inventories.

Figure 4.7: General medium-changer properties

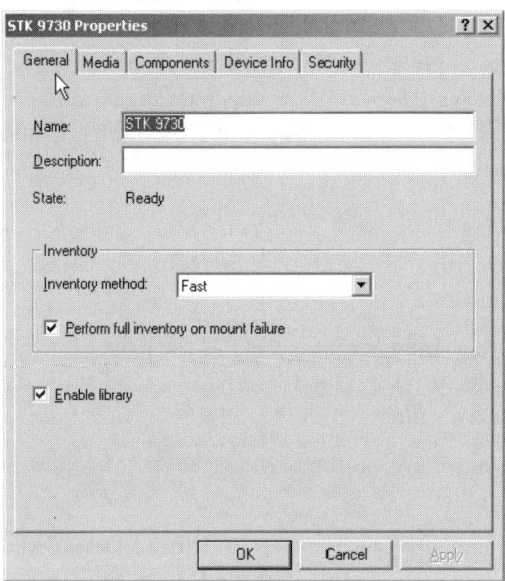

Although the Enable Library check box may seem pretty basic, this is actually an important consideration. If you are using backup or media migration software that docs not integrate with RSM, you have to tell RSM not to use the library. You can do this by clearing the Enable Library check box. Otherwise, the application will most likely run into resource contention with RSM and may not work with the storage device at all until it is disabled.

The Media tab (see Figure 4.8) enables you to view the media types in the library, as well as the media quantity. This tab provides a quick glance at how many tapes RSM sees as being in the library. The lower portion of the window enables you to see whether a cleaning tape is loaded in the library.

The Components tab of the library properties window provides basic information about the components contained in the library (see Figure 4.9). Under the Components tab, you can configure the time-out period that RSM will wait for the library door to close. After this time has passed, all RSM operations involving the library will fail. The Ports setting enables you to specify how long RSM will wait for you to add or remove media from the library's inject/eject port, or mail slot. After the time has elapsed, the media inject (import) or export operation will fail. Notice that you can also see how many drives are installed in the library and also whether RSM detects that a barcode reader is present.

Figure 4.8: Media properties of medium changer

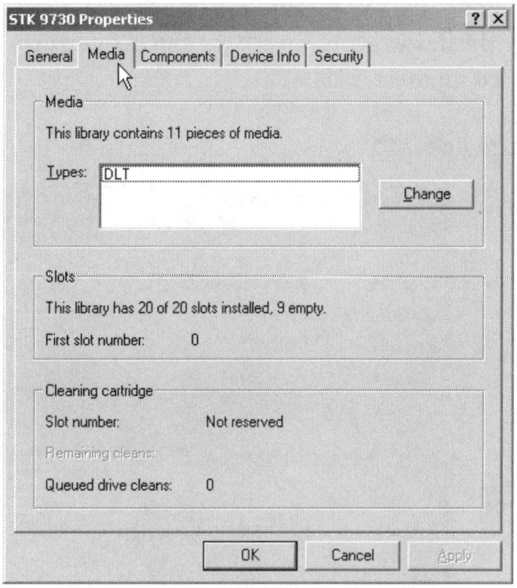

Figure 4.9: Library door and port time-out configuration

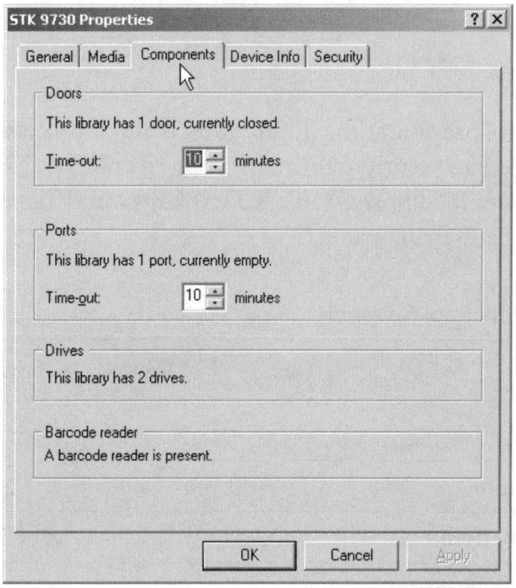

If you do not already know the type of medium changer that you have, you can find that information under the Device Info tab (see Figure 4.10). If you need to see the SCSI configuration for the device, you can see the Bus, Logical Unit Number (LUN), and Target ID displayed on this tab as well.

Figure 4.10: Library device info

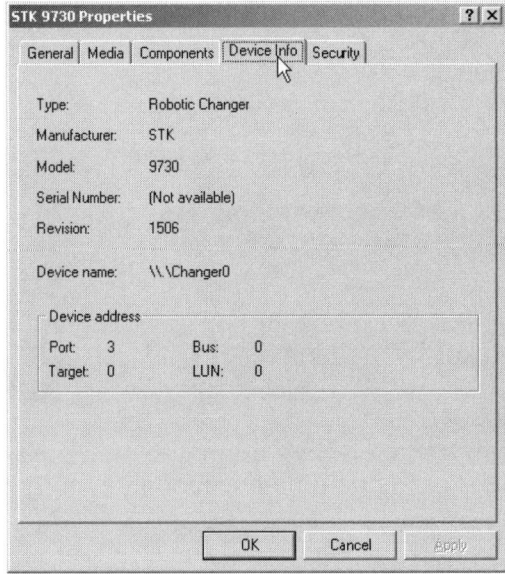

The security configuration at the library level is similar to what you saw earlier at the media pool level. The Security tab enables you to configure the users and user groups that can administer the library. Table 4.3 explains the effect of each security permission on library access and management.

Table 4.3: Media Pool Security

Action	Use	Modify	Control
Delete a library		X	
Inventory a library			X
Open the library door			X
Inject media into library			X

Continued on next page

Table 4.3 continued: Media Pool Security

Action	Use	Modify	Control
Export media from library			X
Insert/eject cleaner cartridge			X
Dismount a drive			X
Clean a drive			X

Drive Configuration

Now that you have seen what you can set at the library or medium-changer level, let's take a look at what drive configuration options you have (see Figure 4.11).

But first, we need to quickly mention the concept of *deferred dismounts*. Think for a minute about backup performance. Say you have several backups scheduled that will write data to the same tape. For example, you have written a script that uses Windows Backup to run three incremental backups of remote shares in sequence. Now imagine that the library dismounts the tape immediately after each backup completes. As soon as the next backup starts, the library has to remount the same tape. This process would waste several minutes of time, as well as resources. The time required for all your backups to complete would also be extended due to the mounting and dismounting of the tape. How do you prevent this? You can set the Deferred Dismount setting to prevent drives from automatically dismounting tapes after a backup or restore operation completes. Although you can manually set this value with RSM, other storage applications have the value hard-coded to a value such as 20 minutes.

Notice that the General tab also displays drive statistics for the drive. RSM does not track much drive information, but does show you the number of mounts and the date that the drive was last cleaned. Other applications track drive maintenance issues such as the read and write count, as well as the number of read and write errors. Although some applications will go so far as to tell you when to clean your drive, RSM will not. You should consult the drive manufacturer's website for information on thresholds of your drive as well as the prescribed cleaning interval.

The Device Information tab for drive configuration is similar to the library configuration. Although this tab has no configuration options, again you will be able to view the SCSI settings of the drive.

Figure 4.11: General drive properties

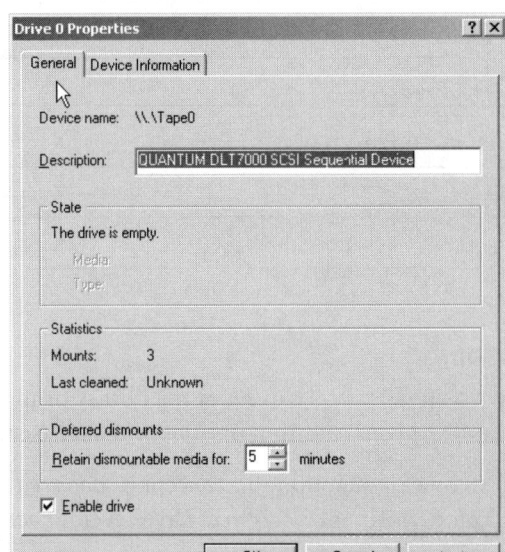

Work Queue

You should remember from Chapter 3, "Windows 2000 Storage Enhancements," that RSM is the engine that works with the physical devices. Jobs for RSM are tasks such as loading and unloading drives. After a drive is loaded, RSM does not handle the transfer of data to and from the drive. That is the responsibility of the application using the drive. With this in mind, to understand the work queue, you must understand how RSM operates.

RSM carries out tasks sequentially, in the order they are received. When you view RSM tasks, you will see that they are carried out one at a time. Keep in mind, however, that this does not prevent multiple drives from being used at the same time. For example, say you kicked off two backups at the same time. Each request for a drive mount would be sent to the work queue. RSM would mount a tape in each drive, starting with the first drive. After the first tape was mounted, then RSM would mount the second. After both tapes are mounted, the backup application controls the data flow to both drives, and thus both drives can be used simultaneously at that point.

The work queue is shown in Figure 4.12. As you can see, each RSM job is listed, as well as its status.

Figure 4.12: RSM work queue

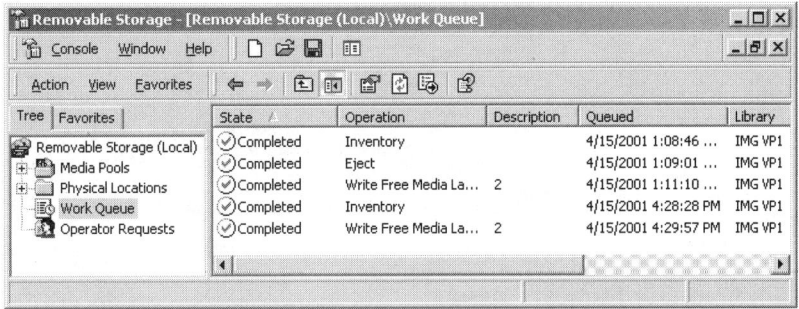

Operator Requests

The Operator Requests feature is another little-known feature of RSM. This feature is used by RSM and by applications that are RSM aware, such as RSS and Windows Backup. So, when do you need to use this feature? Say you have an application trying to use a tape that is not mounted in a stand-alone drive. Because the tape is not available, RSM will list the request as an operator request. At that point, you can manually mount the tape into the drive and then click to accept the request, or you can refuse the request. Table 4.4 lists the possible operator request actions you can take.

Table 4.4: Operator Request Actions

Request Status	Description
Submitted	An application or RSM has submitted a request for a manual action.
Completed	Either you manually told RSM, or it was detected by RSM, that the request was completed.
Refused	You have manually refused the request. The operation that initiated the request will either retry or fail.

After RSM initiates an operator request, a pop-up window will be displayed on the computer hosting the storage device where manual intervention is needed (see Figure 4.13).

At this point, the request will be listed in the Operator Requests queue, as shown in Figure 4.14. After RSM sees that you completed the action, such as inserting a tape into a stand-alone drive, the request will be listed as completed.

Figure 4.13: Operator request message

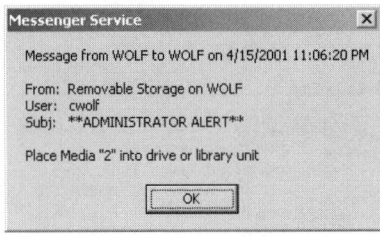

Figure 4.14: Operator requests queue

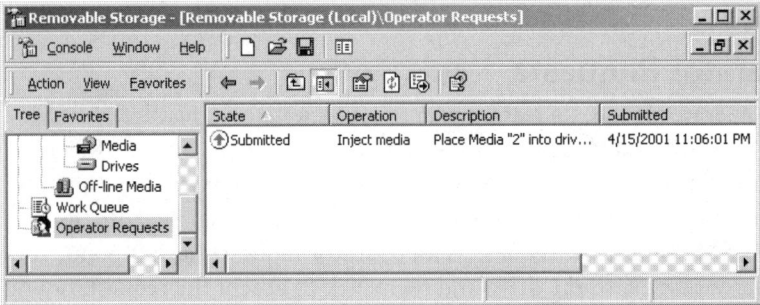

Now that you have seen all the configuration options available in the Removable Storage administrative console, let's take a look at the library and drive administration actions that you can perform.

Removable Storage Administration

Now that we've covered the basics of RSM, we will now look at its administrative features. In this section we will look at how to use RSM to:

- Inventory libraries
- Import and export media
- Work with cleaning media
- Configure Zip and Jazz drives for use with RSM
- Configure CD-ROM jukeboxes
- Run checks for RSM database integrity
- Back up and recover the RSM database
- Administer RSM from the command line

As you can see, RSM administration is pretty extensive, so let's get started.

Inventorying Libraries

When a library or medium changer is first configured for use with Removable Storage, RSM automatically performs an inventory of the library. Each time the library door is opened and closed, RSM will also automatically perform an inventory. If at any time you want a library inventoried, all you have to do is right-click the library and select Inventory.

When an inventory is performed, RSM will use only a single drive in the library to complete the inventory, regardless of how many free drives exist in the library. The use of a single drive is by design. As you already know, RSM will do only one task at a time, and working with a single drive fits right into that strategy. Also, Microsoft realizes that some drives will automatically eject a tape if it cannot be mounted. If RSM were trying to load another drive while the first drive was ejecting a tape, a chance exists that the library's robotic arm changer would run into the tape and cause possible damage to the library or tape.

Because RSM reads only the OMID off each tape during a full inventory, the tape reading process takes only a few seconds after the tape is mounted. With this in mind, very little time is lost by using only a single drive to perform the inventory.

Importing and Exporting Media

Adding and removing media from a library or changer is a simple process with RSM. To import media, you would right-click the library that you want to add media to and select Inject. This will launch the Inject Media Wizard, which will give you step-by-step directions on adding the media.

Exporting media is just as easy. To do this, you right-click the medium and select Eject. This will launch the Eject Media Wizard. Follow the steps presented by the wizard, and the media will be safely removed from the library.

Adding a Cleaning Cartridge to a Library

RSM cannot differentiate between a cleaning tape and a standard tape. To prevent confusion, you must explicitly notify RSM when you insert a cleaning tape into a library. This is done by reserving a slot for the tape with RSM. If the cleaning tape is injected into the library before a slot for it is reserved, you will see the following events in the Event Viewer:

```
Event ID: 7
Description: The device, \Device\Changer0, has a bad block
Event ID: 111
Description: RSM could not load media in drive…
```

Remember, when new media is injected into a library, RSM will try to mount each medium in order to read its OMID.

To prepare a library for the insertion of a cleaning tape, you must first run the Cleaner Management Wizard. This is done by right-clicking the library and selecting Cleaner Management. The wizard will then allow you to dedicate a slot for the cleaning tape. After this is finished, you can then import the tape into the library.

Cleaning a Library or Single Drive

Although RSM does not go so far as to tell you when to clean a library, it does make cleaning libraries easy. Cleaning libraries and drives with a cleaning tape is simple. To clean a library, first make sure that a cleaning medium has been imported into the library, and then right-click the library and select Cleaner Management. The wizard will take you through the steps of selecting which drives in the library you would like cleaned.

To clean a stand-alone drive:

1. Insert the cleaning tape into the drive. The drive will clean itself with the tape.
2. All you must do now is notify RSM that the drive has been cleaned. To do this, right-click the drive in the RSM console and select Mark as Clean, as shown in Figure 4.15.

Figure 4.15: Marking a stand-alone drive as cleaned

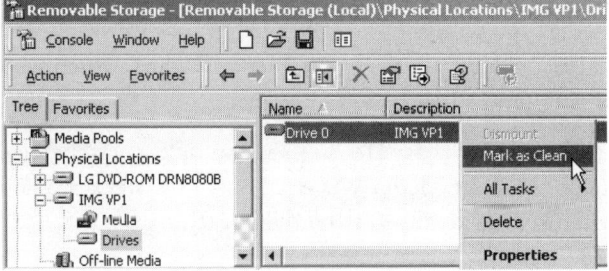

Configuring a Zip/Jaz Drive

When you install Windows 2000 on a system that has an ATAPI Iomega Zip or Jaz drive, RSM will not automatically be able to utilize the drive, even though the operating system will see the drive as a generic volume. For RSM to use the drive, you must download the drive's associated Windows 2000 driver from www.iomega.com. After the driver is installed, the Zip or Jaz drive will act as a stand-alone drive under the management of RSM.

This driver issue does not pertain to SCSI-attached Zip and Jaz drives.

Configuring a CD-ROM Jukebox

CD-ROM changers are handled much differently with Windows 2000 than they are with Windows NT. With NT, a separate drive letter is assigned for each piece of media the device was capable of handling. In other words, a 10-disk changer would use 10 drive letters. This type of format is not acceptable for modern changers that may hold 50 disks, or even considerably more. Therefore, with Windows 2000, a single drive letter is assigned for the entire changer.

The new setup has these advantages:

- With RSM integration, multiple applications can access the CD-ROM jukebox.
- RSM can handle extremely large CD-ROM jukeboxes.
- RSM tracks usage, media requests, and the device status.

But it also has a disadvantage:

- Disks must be manually mounted and dismounted into the single drive before you can access them.

By default, CD-ROMs contained in a changer are placed in the Import pool. You will also see the CD-ROMs listed in the CD changer's media pool. To mount a CD-ROM, you will have to manually right-click the CD-ROM in its media pool and select Mount. Once mounted, you can access the CD-ROM via the changer's assigned drive letter.

Using the RSM Database Integrity Checker (rsm_dbic.exe)

The RSM database maintains records of all media, drives, and changers that it supports. When this data becomes out of sync—for example, when a tape is associated with the wrong media pool or a library's inventory is inaccurate—operations involving RSM hardware components can outright fail. To find inconsistencies before they cause problems, you should regularly run integrity checks of the RSM database. When problems occur, such as erratic behavior of RSM-controlled devices or incorrect information displayed in the RSM administrative snap-in, you can run a database integrity check to verify that the RSM database is the source of the problems.

Like the RSM Configuration Wizard, the RSM Database Integrity Checker also comes with the Windows 2000 Server Resource Kit. Once installed, you can run the utility from the command prompt.

The syntax for the command is shown here:

```
Rsm_dbic [/v] [/p]
```
/v indicates verbose mode. This switch causes information to be displayed about RSM objects as they are being checked.

/p causes RSM to be paused while the integrity check is running and will then resume the RSM service after the check has finished.

> **WARNING** If the RSM service is running during a consistency check, it is possible that the database will be updated during the check, and this may cause an erroneous error to be reported. It is strongly recommended that you use the /p switch when you run `rsm_dbic`.

Figure 4.16 shows a sample execution of `rsm_dbic`.

Figure 4.16: Database Integrity Checker execution

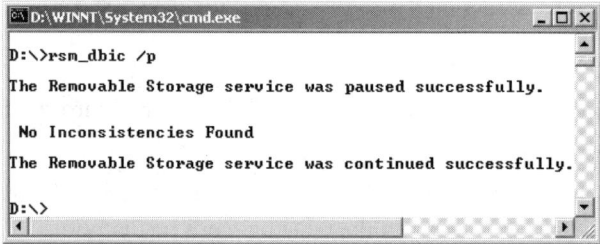

Using the RSM Database Utility (rsm_dbutil.exe)

Another helpful utility included with the Windows 2000 Server Resource Kit is the RSM Database Utility (`rsm_dbutil.exe`). Like the RSM Configuration Wizard, the RSM Database Utility is also a GUI-driven tool. The database tool is quite powerful, and enables you to perform the following tasks:

- Create a backup copy of the RSM database
- Change the location of the RSM database
- Search for objects in the RSM database based on their GUID
- Check for database integrity

Notice that you can check database integrity with RSM Database Utility instead of the RSM Database Integrity Checker (`rsm_dbic`). The difference between using the two utilities is that Database Integrity Checker is a command-line tool, whereas RSM Database Utility is GUI driven.

To run the RSM Database Utility, click Start ➢ Run, type **rsm_dbutil**, and press Enter. When the program executes, you will be brought to the Check Integrity tab. Notice that you still have the Verbose Output and Pause RSM options as you did when running `rsm_dbic` (see Figure 4.17). Other features that `rsm_dbutil` provides, however, are the ability to view the program output in Microsoft Internet Explorer or to select where to store the Integrity Checker results as a text file.

Figure 4.17: `rsm_dbutil` database integrity checks

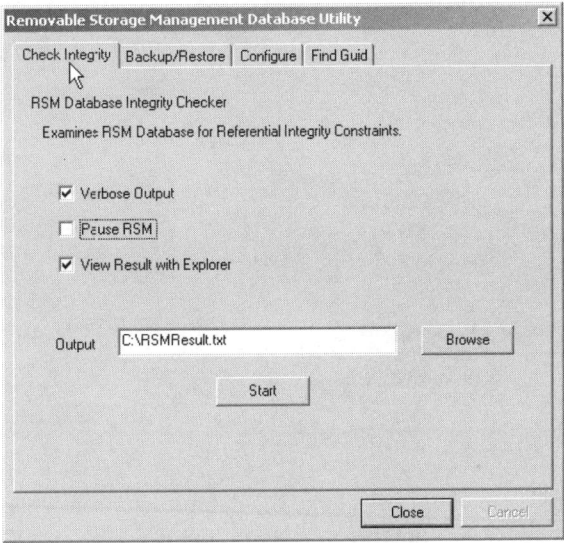

The Backup/Restore tab, shown in Figure 4.18, enables you to create a backup copy of the RSM database or to restore the RSM database from a previous backup. Most current backup utilities will back up the RSM database by using the Export NTMS Database API, which allows Removable Storage to export a consistent copy of the RSM database to the backup engine. The backup software can then write the exported file to the backup media. However, if your backup solution is not RSM aware, it may see the RSM database as an open file and skip it during the backup operation. Windows Backup is RSM aware and thus has no problems backing up the RSM database. You can ensure that a version of the RSM database is available to your backup program by using the RSM Database Utility to create a backup copy of the database prior to running the full backup. If you are not using other backup software, you can elect to back up the database to removable media such as a Zip disk and store the disk off-site.

When you click the Backup button, a folder called Export is created within the current RSM database folder. Two files are placed in the Export folder: `Ntmsdata` and `NtmsReg`. After you click Restore, the two files in the Export folder are used to overwrite the current `Ntmsdata` and `NtmsReg` files in the current RSM database folder.

Figure 4.18: `rsm_dbutil` Backup/Restore selection

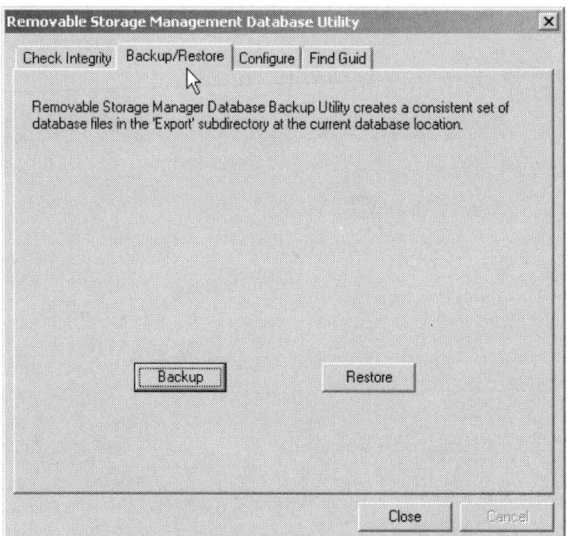

On the Configure tab, you can change the default location where the RSM database is stored. When you change the directory path, the Registry and RSM settings are automatically edited to reflect the next directory. This option is useful in the event you want additional fault tolerance for your RSM database as you decide to move it to a disk array such as a RAID 5 volume.

The Find GUID tab, shown in Figure 4.19, enables you to see the GUID of each object in the RSM database. Often, when an RSM-integrated application returns an error, the error message will return the GUID of the object that caused the problem. Normally, the GUID is of little use because you would not know the object that it represents. By using the Find GUID tab, you can cross-reference a GUID with its associated object and then determine which object is the cause of the error.

Performing RSM Database Backup and Recovery

Because the RSM database is usually live, or open during backups, your backup software may not be able to guarantee that your backup of the RSM database is good. In always preparing for the worst-case scenario, the sections that follow provide you with everything you need to know to confidently back up and recover the RSM database.

Figure 4.19: RSM GUID search utility

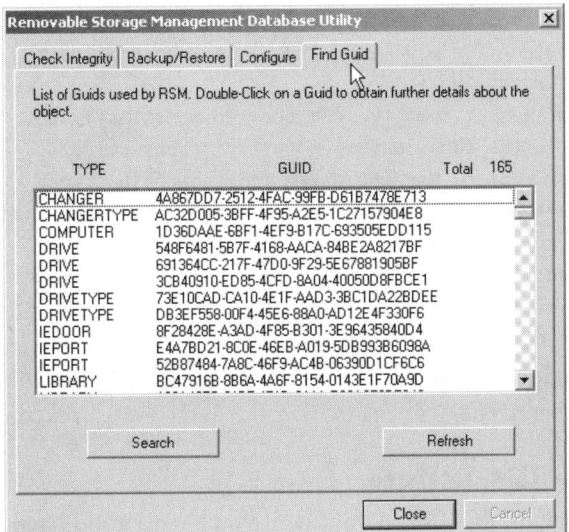

Backing Up the RSM Database

You have seen that backup and recovery of the RSM database can be performed by using the RSM Database Utility. However, this solution most likely will not integrate seamlessly with your current backup and recovery strategy. As you learned earlier, as long as your backup application uses the ExportNtmsDatabase API, it will have no problems backing up the RSM database. To do this, you just have to make sure that you select to back up the `WINNT\System32\Ntms` folder.

If your backup application does not use the ExportNtmsDatabase API, you will have a little more work to do. One alternative is to schedule or script the RSM service to stop before your backup and restart after the backup. You may want to schedule a separate small job just for the `WINNT\System32\Ntms` folder so that the RSM service is shut down only for a short time. The other alternative is to manually use the RSM Database Utility to make a backup copy of the RSM database files. You would do this before the scheduled backup.

Although stopping the RSM service in order to get a good copy of RSM data is an option, this cannot be done if RSM controls the media to which you want to back up. A solution would be to stop the RSM service, copy the RSM database directory contents to a unique folder on the local hard drive, and then restart the RSM service. Even if the original RSM files were skipped, your copied files would be backed up. The following small batch file will stop the RSM service, copy the RSM database directory to another folder, and then restart the RSM service. You could run the batch file in conjunction with another scripted backup operation.

RSM Database Copy Batch File

```
## File name: rsmbackup.bat
## This batch file will copy the RSM database files to
## the c:\rsmbackup folder.
## This will shut down the RSM service momentarily to
## complete the copy, and then restart the service.
## You may want to use the batch file in conjunction
## with another scripted backup to ensure the RSM database
## is backed up properly.
net stop ntmssvc
xcopy c:\winnt\system32\ntmsdata c:\rsmbackup /y
net start ntmssvc
```

If you use Windows Backup, you can use the switch /RS:yes to tell Backup to back up the RSM database. This will ensure that the database is backed up properly.

Restoring the RSM Database

As with backing up the RSM database, if you have a good backup solution, your backup product should do all that is necessary "behind the scenes" to restore the RSM database files. What if RSM controls your backup media? When your RSM database is backed up to a medium that is controlled by RSM, perform the following steps:

1. Stop the Removable Storage Service.

2. Delete (or rename with an .old extension) all the files in the Ntmsdata folder.

3. Run regedit to edit the HKEY_LOCAL_MACHINE\System\Current Control Set\Control\NTMS key. If the ImportDatabase REG_DWORD exists, change its value from 0 to **0x1**. If it does not exist, create it with a value of **0x1**.

4. Then start the Removable Storage service. RSM will think that it is running for the first time and will inventory the library.

5. You can then move the medium that holds the RSM data to the media pool that will be used in the restore operation. After the inventory, you should see all media in either the Unrecognized or Import media pools.

NOTE You may have to manually re-create the media pool or rerun the application that created the media pool. Consult your backup product's documentation for additional procedures.

6. Use your restore program to restore the RSM data.

7. Stop and restart the RSM service.

> **WARNING** After the RSM database has been restored and its service restarted, the RSM database might be out of sync. Any changes in configuration or media allocation that occurred after your last backup will not be reflected in the restored RSM database. You will need to manually make the changes necessary to update the RSM database.

Using the rsm.exe Command-Line Utility

When you have applications that are not RSM aware, scripting may provide a means for the application to work with RSM. The `rsm.exe` command comes installed with Windows 2000 and can be run in several formats. The utility can be used to allocate and deallocate media, create media pools, dismount media, eject media, mount media, and view media objects. We could explain every `rsm` command and option, but that would take about eight pages. Instead, you can find a complete listing of available command switches under Windows help, or you can type **rsm/?** from the command line.

Table 4.5 describes some of the available versions of the `rsm` command.

Table 4.5: Removable Storage Commands

Command	Function
rsm allocate	Enables you to allocate media to a media pool
rsm createpool	Creates a media pool
rsm deallocate	Deallocates (removes) media from a media pool
rsm deletepool	Deletes a specified application media pool
rsm dismount	Dismounts media from a drive
rsm eject	Ejects media from a drive
rsm ejectatapi	Ejects media from an ATAPI changer
rsm mount	Mounts media into a drive
rsm refresh	Causes RSM to poll a library, physical media, or all devices of a particular media type, and return their status
rsm view	Displays a list of media objects in a library, changer, drive, pool, and so on

Configuring RSS

With Windows 2000, RSM is the service that drives direct-attached removable media. Remote Storage Service utilizes RSM to access and utilize remote media. If you refer back to Figure 4.1, you will see that when installed, RSS automatically creates a media pool that is listed in RSM. Unlike RSM, RSS is not installed by default.

Installing RSS

Here are the steps for installing RSS:

1. From the Desktop, click Start ➢ Settings ➢ Control Panel. Click the Add/Remove Programs icon.
2. Now click Add/Remove Windows Components.
3. Check the Remote Storage check box and click Next.
4. If prompted, insert the Windows 2000 Server CD-ROM. When the installation completes, you will need to reboot the server.
5. After the server reboots, you can launch Remote Storage by clicking Start ➢ Programs ➢ Administrative Tools ➢ Remote Storage.

In Chapter 3, "Windows 200 Storage Enhancements," you learned that RSS is essentially an HSM application. The idea behind RSS is to free local disk space by migrating infrequently used files off your local storage to a direct-attached remote media device. When you configure RSS, you set three parameters:

Desired Free Space   Amount of local disk space you want to remain available.

Files Larger Than   Files must be larger than the value listed to qualify for migration.

Remote Storage Files Not Accessed In   Number of days files cannot have been accessed.

Say you have a file server than retains service contracts. Once stored, many of these contracts are not accessed again until the client's contract is up for renewal. You want to keep these documents available for users, but the high number of documents has your server running at near capacity. You decide to use RSS to migrate contracts that have not been accessed in the last six months to your two-drive Scalar 218 library. You configure RSS to migrate data from the D partition, where all the contracts are stored, setting the migration criteria for 20KB files that are older than 180 days. Files that are migrated will reside on a DLT tape, and they will retain the appearance of remaining on the server to the end users. Because your library has two drives, you can make additional copies of your remotely stored data for disaster recovery. Remote Storage Service is an easy-to-use and easy-to-configure service. Sound like something you can use? Read on!

Configuring Remote Storage Service for the First Time

The first time you open the Remote Storage Service administrative tool, you will be greeted with the Remote Storage Setup Wizard. After you get past the welcome window, you will be asked to select which volumes you would like Remote Storage to manage. After that, you can set the data migration parameters for the volume as shown in Figure 4.20.

Figure 4.20: RSS Volume settings

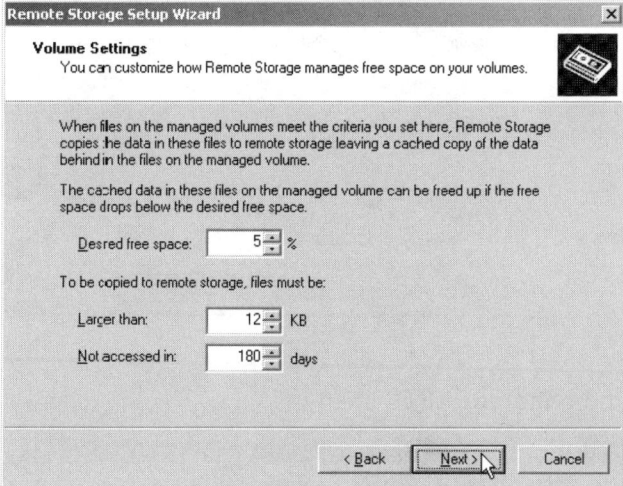

As you can see, you can set the desired free space for the volume and can set the parameters qualifying a file for migration. In the next window, you select the storage media for RSS to use for the volume's data, and you finish by configuring the copy schedule. At the final window, you set the time and frequency in which RSS will check for and migrate qualified files, as shown in Figure 4.21.

After you click OK to set the schedule, you have to click Next to proceed past the Schedule window. If your configuration information for RSS is correct, at that point you can click Finish to complete the configuration wizard.

Configuring RSS Volumes

Now that you have configured RSS to manage a volume, your work is not done. Many configuration options are available for the managed volume that were not shown in the configuration wizard. You may have directories that have old data you simply do not want to have migrated off the server's local hard drive. The answer to preventing data migration is simple: All you have to do is configure a filter that tells RSS not to even bother looking at that particular folder.

Figure 4.21: Remote Storage File Copy Scheduler

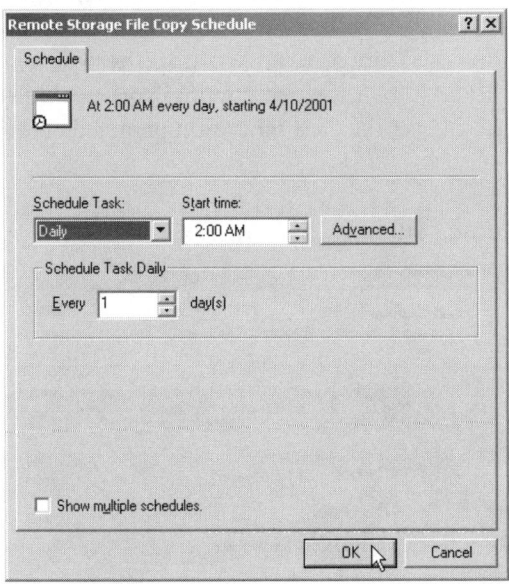

Figure 4.22: Remote Storage MMC snap-in

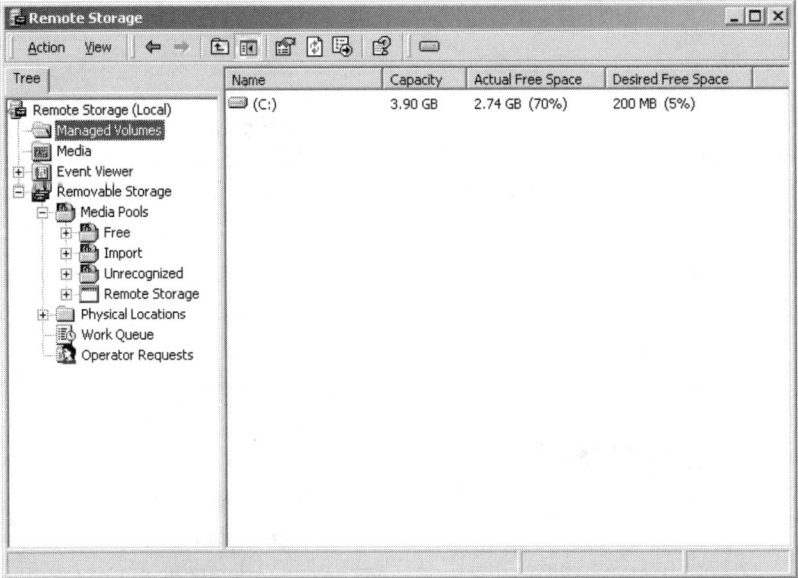

You can start your volume configuration by opening the RSS administrative tool (Start ➤ Programs ➤ Administrative Tools ➤ Remote Storage), which is shown in Figure 4.22.

With Managed Volumes selected, you will see a list of the volumes managed by RSS in the right pane of the window. To configure the RSS settings for a volume, right-click the drive and select Properties. Because much of the volume properties are self-explanatory, we will concentrate on the important stuff. The aspect of volume configuration that needs your attention is understanding how RSS filters data from being archived.

Figure 4.23 shows the Include/Exclude Rules tab of the Volume Properties window.

Figure 4.23: Include/Exclude Rules tab

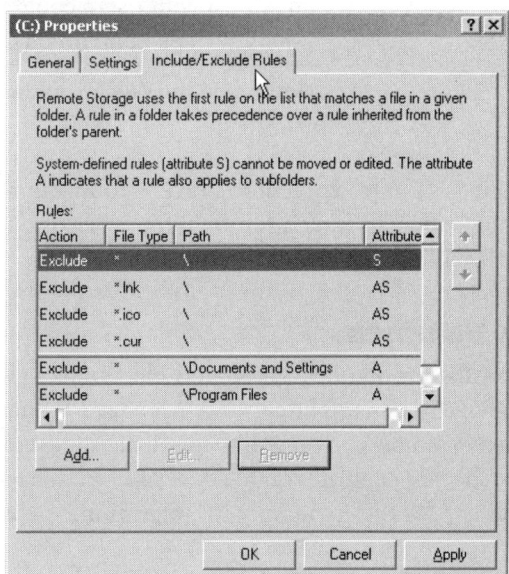

The first time you view this tab, you should notice that several files are filtered by default. Table 4.6 lists the default filters.

Table 4.6: Default RSS Filter Settings

Filter	Effect
`* with System Attribute`	No system files will be migrated.
`*.lnk`	No link files (shortcuts) will be migrated.

Continued on next page

Table 4.6 continued: Default RSS Filter Settings

Filter	Effect
`*.ico`	No icon files will be migrated. (Imagine each time your Desktop loads having to wait five minutes for your icons to be retrieved from a tape!)
`*.cur`	No cursor files will be migrated.
`*\Documents and Settings`	No files in the Documents and Settings folder will be migrated.
`*\Program Files`	No files in the Program Files folder will be migrated. Imagine if your users could not access important programs such as Solitaire on demand?
`*\WINNT`	Nothing in the WINNT folder will be migrated.

As you can see, RSS is "smart" enough to prevent you from having necessary OS files migrated to remote media. To filter additional file types or directories, click the Add button and then type in the filter parameters.

Adding New Volumes

After the initial configuration of RSS, you may elect to have RSS manage additional volumes. All you have to do is right-click the Managed Volumes folder, select New, and then click Managed Volume(s). You will then see the same configuration options shown earlier in Figure 4.20 that enabled you to set desired free space for the volume, and the minimum size and age for files to qualify for migration.

Configuring RSS Properties

Configuring properties at the RSS root enables you to set options that will affect all volumes managed by RSS. This configuration is done by right-clicking the Remote Storage icon and selecting Properties. By viewing properties, you can first see the amount of data, as well as the number of volumes managed by RSS (see Figure 4.24).

The Schedule tab enables you to edit the current RSS file migration schedule. This can also be done by using the Windows Task Scheduler, which is covered later in this chapter. Under the Recall Limit tab, you can limit the number of successful file recalls. A recall happens each time a user attempts to access a file that is physically contained in remote storage. The default recall limit is set to 60 recalls.

Figure 4.24: RSS General Properties

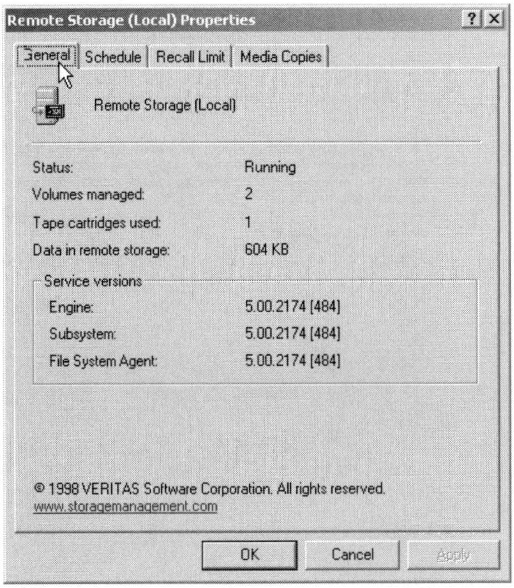

If you wish to protect your migrated files, you can have RSS maintain up to three additional copies of the remotely stored data. Copies are configured under the Media Copies tab. After setting a number for media copies, you can use the RSS console to synchronize your additional copies with the media master set, which contains the original versions of files that were migrated off a local system by Remote Storage. The process of syncing media copies will be covered shortly in the "Copying RSS Data" section. You can see the media copy settings in Figure 4.25.

Configuring RSS Media

The RSS media pool is automatically configured to take media from the Free media pool when it needs a new medium. If you click the Media folder in the RSS administrative console, you will see a list of media currently being used by RSS. To see a status of any medium, right-click the medium and select Properties.

The General tab in the Media Properties dialog box enables you to see the number and status of media copies that are associated with the selected medium. You can also see the amount of available and used space on the medium (see Figure 4.26).

Figure 4.25: Setting the number of media copies

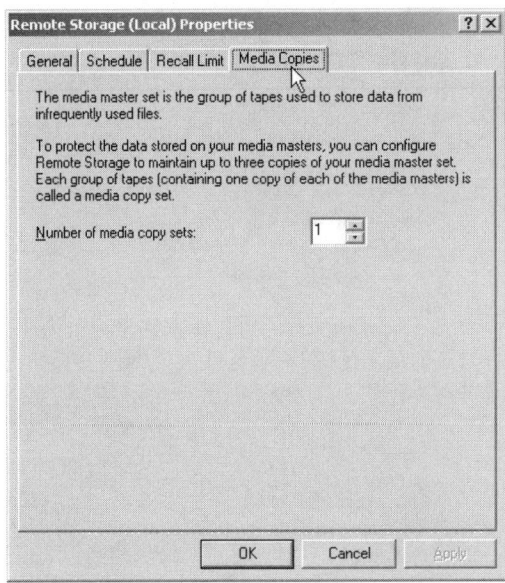

Figure 4.26: RSS Media Properties

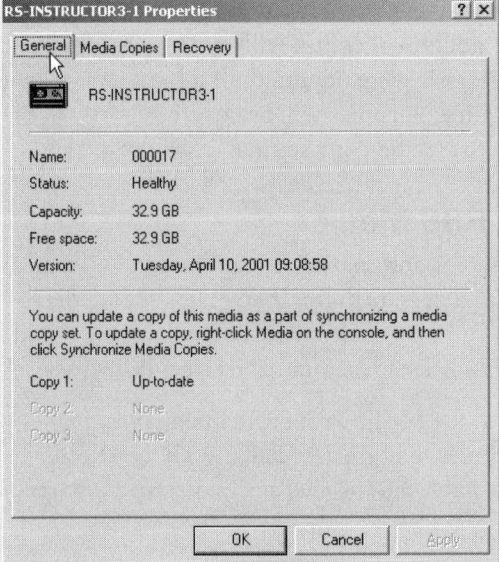

Figure 4.27: RSS Media Recovery options

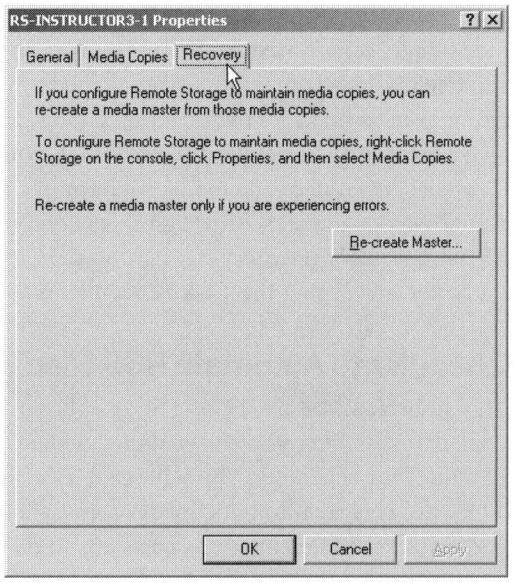

Under the Media Copies tab, you can delete any media copies that you no longer need available. This may be necessary if the active medium being used by a particular copy has become corrupted. The easiest course of action would be to delete the copy and then export the medium by using RSM. After that, you can create and synchronize a new media copy.

The Recovery tab is needed when the primary medium on which copies are based has become corrupted. As shown in Figure 4.27, you can click the Re-create Master button to create a new master copy from one of the existing copies. In doing this, you are essentially promoting a secondary copy to become the primary, or master, copy.

Now that you have seen the configuration options available for RSS, let's get into RSS administration.

Administering RSS

Administering RSS primarily consists of setting the data migration parameters. Once properly configured, RSS will almost manage itself. In this section, we look at how to configure RSS to operate automatically and seamlessly, while providing for insurance in the event that disaster strikes. Let's start with disaster recovery by looking at how to achieve backup redundancy for data migrated off a server by RSS.

Copying RSS Data

Although some backup solutions are "intelligent" enough to be able to back up data migrated to remote storage, others are not. If your backup product cannot follow the Remote Storage reparse points to the remote storage media, you will need to use the RSS administrative snap-in to make its own backup copies. After you have selected the number of copies you want of the original RSS media, all you have to do is tell RSS to synchronize media copies (right-click the media folder in the RSS administrative console and select Synchronize Media Copies). Although this is one way to make redundant copies of your RSS data, it is not the most efficient, in that you must manually perform the task. There is a better way: using the Task Scheduler, which you'll learn about next.

Using Task Scheduler to Automate RSS Media Copy Operations

The Task Scheduler can be accessed by clicking Start ≻ Programs ≻ Accessories ≻ System Tools ≻ Scheduled Tasks. After you perform one media copy synchronization, the job will be shown in the Task Scheduler. You will see it as a one-time job that has already been completed. One easy way to automatic media copy synchronization is to edit the previous job to repeat at a scheduled interval. The steps to do this are listed here:

1. From the Task Scheduler, find the synchronize media copy job that you had run. Right-click the job and select Properties. The job should be listed, as shown in Figure 4.28.

2. From the job Properties window, click the Schedule tab. Then click the New button. You can now enter the parameters for the job to run. Figure 4.29 shows a weekly media copy synchronization job scheduled to run every Monday and Sunday.

Figure 4.28: RSS jobs in Windows Task Scheduler

Figure 4.29: Changing RSS Media Copy schedule

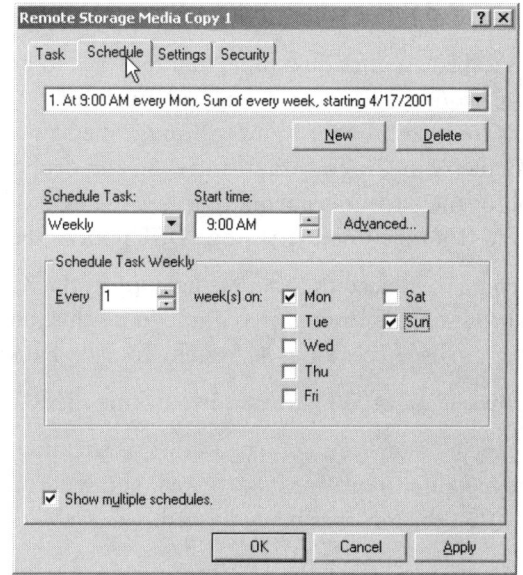

   3. After you configure the Schedule settings, click OK.

You should now see the new task parameters shown in the Task Scheduler. You can use the same steps to change the Remote Storage media migration schedule as well.

Browsing Remotely Stored Data

As you start to use RSS to migrate data to remotely stored media, you might want to know exactly what files you have migrated off a server. Later, you will see how to use a command-line utility to show file attributes indicating which files have been migrated off a server. However, that method is not as easy as the GUI-driven method that you are about to learn.

RSS uses Microsoft Tape Format (MTF) when it writes data to remote media. Because this is a standard format, you can browse and even restore remotely stored files by using any application that supports MTF. Remember, however, that the idea of RSS is to allow the RSS service to handle the media migration back and forth between a library and server. You should never have to use another application to restore RSS files.

> **TIP** When using Windows Backup to browse RSS migrated files, you should work with a secondary copy of RSS data. This way, your primary copy remains online and available in case RSS needs it to recall a file.

Using Windows Backup to Browse RSS-Migrated Files

To browse RSS-migrated files using Windows Backup, follow these steps:

1. For Backup to browse files on a tape, that tape has to be in one of Backup's media pools. From the Remote Storage administrative console, expand the Media Pools folder until your Remote Storage media pool is displayed. Click on your secondary media copy tape and drag and drop it into the Backup media pool for the respective media type (see Figure 4.30). In the illustration, a tape is moved from the Remote Storage DLT pool to the Backup DLT pool.

2. Now that you have placed the RSS media copy in the Backup pool, you can use Backup to browse the RSS-migrated data. To do this, open Backup by clicking Start ➣ Programs ➣ Accessories ➣ System Tools ➣ Backup.

3. You can browse data in MTF format by clicking the Restore tab.

4. Then select the medium you imported into the Backup media pool. After you click on the medium to browse its contents, you will receive a pop-up message alerting you that the media is being loaded.

Figure 4.30: Moving media from the RSS pool to the Backup pool

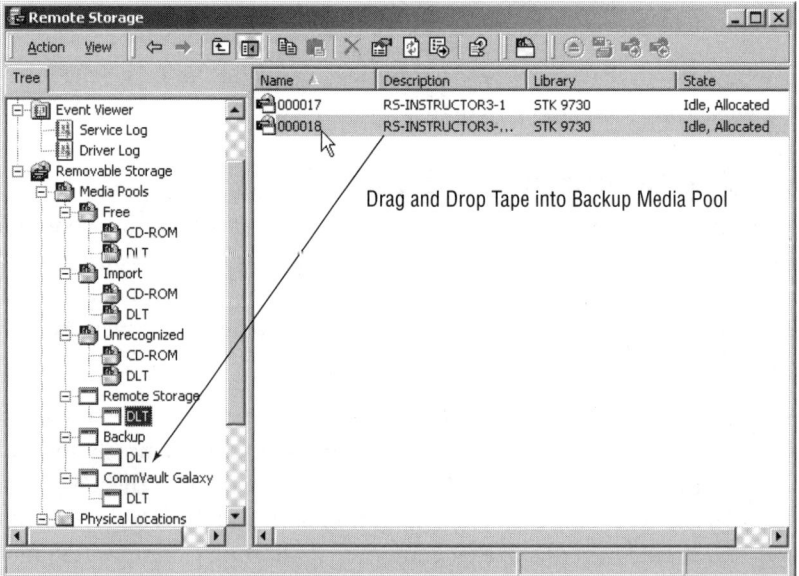

Figure 4.31: Using Windows Backup to browse RSS data

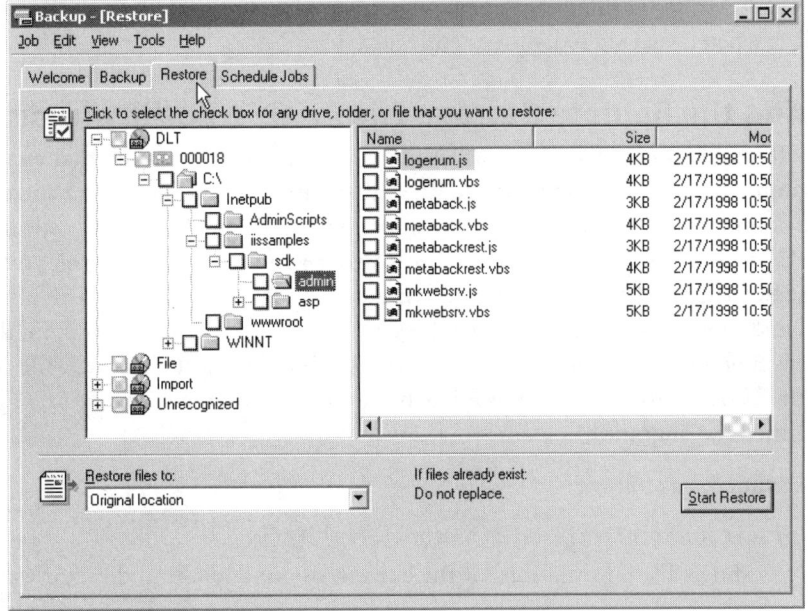

5. After the medium is loaded, you can then expand the directory tree to view the media contents, as shown in Figure 4.31. This will include all the files that RSS has migrated to the media.

6. After you are finished browsing the data, you can close Windows Backup.

7. Return to the Remote Storage administrative console and drag and drop the medium you had browsed back into the Remote Storage media pool.

Supporting Down-Level Client

You learned in Chapter 3, "Windows 2000 Storage Enhancements," that RSS will present a "Recall in Progress" message to users attempting to open remotely stored files. This message is displayed only when Windows 2000 clients and servers try to access the remotely stored file. Down-level clients, such as Windows NT 4 or Windows 95/98, will not receive any message when attempting to retrieve one of these files. If you were to look at remotely stored files by using Windows Explorer in NT 4 or Windows 95, you would not see the Archived icon that accompanies remotely stored files. That is because these down-level operating systems cannot understand the file attributes that accompany the reparse points associated with files migrated by RSS. Although down-level clients do not receive notification of files being recalled from remote storage, they still can open these files. Just understand that there will be some degree of latency that the user may not expect. The simple Microsoft solution would be to upgrade all clients to Windows 2000 Professional. Otherwise, you will have to make users aware of possible delays when retrieving old, infrequently accessed files.

Using the Remote Storage File Analysis Utility (rsdir.exe)

The Remote Storage File Analysis Utility is a command-line utility that enables you to examine the reparse points and see RSS information about files in the current directory and subdirectories from where the command was executed. This utility is included with the Windows 2000 Server Support Tools. After running the rsdir.exe, you will be able to see which files have been migrated or marked for migration, and can also see the logical and physical size of files. When files are migrated off a server by RSS, their physical size is much smaller than their logical size. When you run the utility, a file will have a status of *trunc*, for truncated, if it has been migrated, and a status of *Premigr* if it is qualified for migration.

The syntax is as follows:

rsdir [name of file or directory] [/s] [/f]

/s shows file information for the current folder and all subdirectories.

/f shows much more detailed file information, including the last recall time and the migration time.

When run with no file or folder specified, the command will return RSS data for all files in the current folder. Figure 4.32 shows sample rsdir output.

Figure 4.32: rsdir output

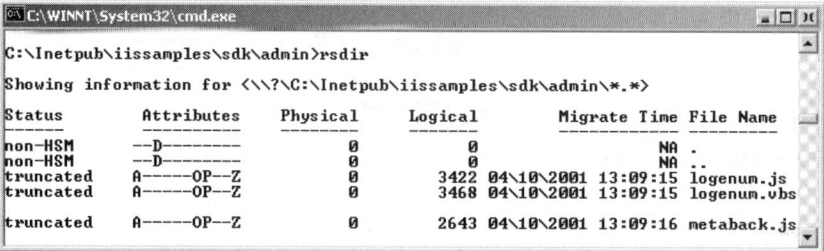

Using the Remote Storage Diagnostic Utility (rsdiag.exe)

The Remote Storage Diagnostic Utility also comes with the Windows 2000 Server Support Tools. This utility performs a check of the RSM databases and returns information on RSS-managed volumes, jobs, and media. In addition to displaying its results onscreen, the utility can also dump its output to a text file.

Here is the utility's syntax:

rsdiag [/c *jobname*] [/d filetype fullpath&filename] [/e errorcode] [/i] [/j [*jobname*]] [/m] [/r [/f]] [/s] [/t] [/v [drive letter]] [/x queuedrecall] [/w fullpath&filename]

/c <jobname> cancels the job you specify.

/d <filetype> <fullpath&filename> converts rsdiag information to a text file. The fullpath&filename is the full path to and name of the text file for the dump. The filetype parameter specifies the type of source file to export to text. The file type can be any of the following:

- -e: Engine database file
- -f: File System Agent database file
- -a: File System Agent collection file
- -n: Engine collection file
- -s: Subsystem collection

/e <errorcode> shows error information on HRESULT or WIN32 error codes. The error code can be entered in decimal or hexadecimal. The default code is decimal. If you use a Hex code, you must add **0x** to the beginning of the code number.

/i displays the version information for the RSS files.

/j [jobname] shows extended job information for the job you enter. If no job is specified, rsdiag will show job information for all jobs.

/m displays volumes available for RSS management.

/r [/f] displays the recalls that are currently queued on the RSS server's internal recall queue. Each recall will be shown by filename and logical size. With /f, additional information is shown, including the recall status, who initiated the recall, and the file offset on the media.

/s returns information about the physical storage media.

/t causes the trace Registry settings to be reread for the RSS, RSM, and FSA (File System Agent) services. This prevents the services from having to be reset.

/v [driveletter] without arguments displays volume information. With a drive letter supplied, displays extended information for the supplied volume.

/x <queuedrecall> cancels a specified recall in the RSS internal recall queue. Currently, queued recalls are shown by using the /r switch.

/w <fullpath&filename> shows the name of the storage medium that has the most recent version of the specified file. Also shows the data set of which the file is a member.

Figure 4.33: `rsdiag` Output

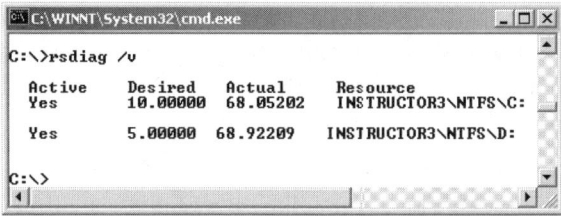

Backup and Recovery of the RSS Database

The RSS databases are jet databases that can be found in the WINNT\System32\Remotestorage\Engdb folder. RSS creates a backup of itself each time files are migrated to remote storage. The backup files are named with the .bak extension. With backups already in place, your backup software should have no problem backing up RSS data.

To restore the RSS database, do the following:

1. Stop the following services:
   - Remote Storage Engine
   - Remote Storage File
   - Remote Storage Media
2. Restore the Remote Storage folder and subdirectories to their original location.
3. Following the restore, move any files in the Remotestorage\Engdb folder to another folder. This is so you can successfully run the rstore.exe jet database recovery utility.
4. From the command prompt, type **Rstore %system root%\system32\RemoteStorage\engdb.bak**.
5. Restart the services you stopped in step 1.

RSS and Dfs

You have already read that RSS is limited to working with a direct-attached library. To many, this limitation would make the Windows 2000 HSM product, RSS, an unattractive solution. If you need to archive data from multiple servers, but have only a single library, one solution would be to have two Windows 2000 services, RSS and Dfs, work together. Dfs enables users to access files transparent to the files' actual physical location. This scheme fits in perfectly with utilizing RSS as your HSM tool. The only downside to this approach is that you have to use two services to fill this need, meaning additional overhead. Is this solution ideal for a distributed environment? Probably not. But if all you need is a local data management solution, this could work for you.

How It Works

On a file server, create an Archived shared folder and move infrequently accessed data to that folder. Instruct users of the change. Move the archived folder to the RSS server. Set the qualification settings (file size, not accessed in) appropriately. It is best if you dedicate an alternate volume, such as D, for RSS to manage. Make the file server a stand-alone Dfs root and create a link that points to where the archived share was moved to on the RSS server.

> **NOTE** Our solution of using stand-alone Dfs is ideal for environments where it is not practical to change your file share naming scheme, such as if applications access files by their share name. If this is not a consideration, you could implement domain-based Dfs, which would allow you to centrally manage Dfs shares and configuration replication for fault tolerance.

When users go to access the Archived directory on the file server, they will be automatically directed to the RSS server by Dfs. The redirection will happen without their knowledge. With Dfs, the physical location of the files will never be important. If your RSS server changes, all you have to do is change the Dfs link on the file server.

Figure 4.34: RSS-DFS network configuration

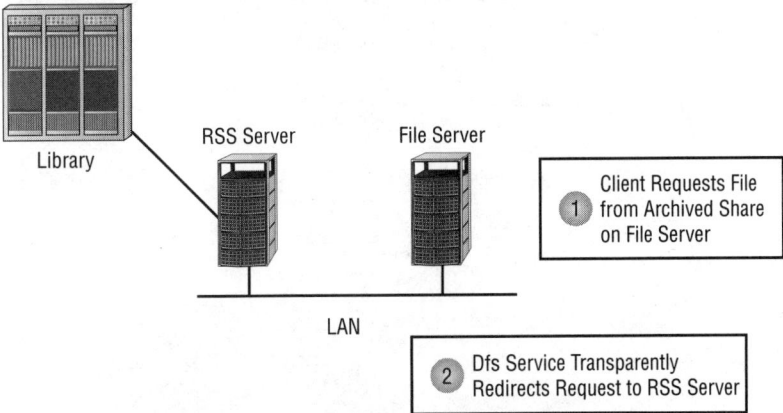

> **NOTE** Our solution involves an RSS-Dfs marriage to work as a small-scale HSM. If you need data archiving for a large-scale enterprise network, you should buy a more scalable product.

Configuring a Stand-Alone Dfs Server

To configure a stand-alone Dfs server, follow these steps:

1. Make sure the DFS Service is running on the server you wish to configure.

2. Open the Dfs administrative console by clicking Start ➢ Programs ➢ Administrative Tools ➢ Distributed File System.

3. Right-click Distributed File System in the console root and select New Dfs Root.

4. When the New Dfs Root Wizard opens, select Create a Stand-Alone Dfs Root and click Next.

5. Type the host name for the computer that will host the Dfs root and click Next. This should be the name of the server you are configuring Dfs on.

6. You now must specify the folder that will be used as the network share by users trying to access the Dfs data. If you wish, you can use an existing share or you can create a new one. After you enter the folder path, click Next, as shown in Figure 4.35. If you entered a path to a new folder, the wizard will ask if you want the folder created. Click the Yes button.

Figure 4.35: Creating a new Dfs network share

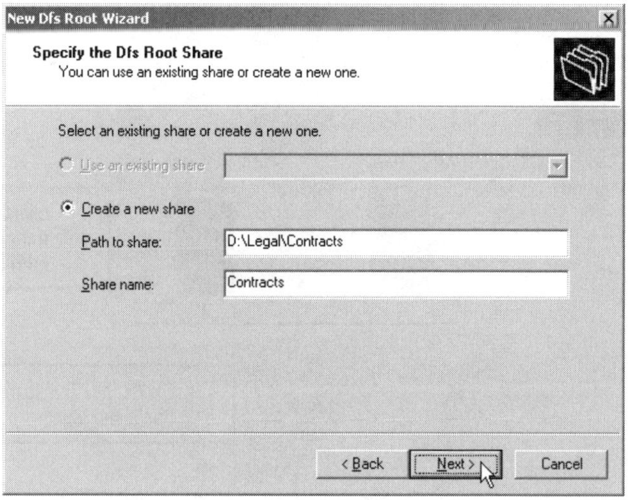

7. You should now see the folder name listed as the share name for the Dfs root. Click the Next button.

8. Verify that the configuration information you entered is correct and click Finish to close the wizard.

9. You should now see the Dfs root you created in the console. Right-click the root and select New Dfs Link.

10. In the Create a New Dfs Link dialog box, shown in Figure 4.36, type a link name. The link name will appear as a subfolder of the folder that you shared when creating the Dfs root. Then enter the path to the network share you want the link to point to. This is where users will be transparently directed when they click the link name.

Figure 4.36: Creating a new Dfs link

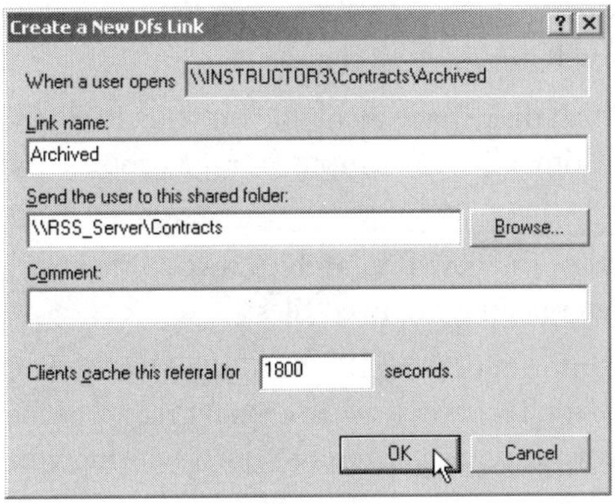

11. Browse the network to make sure Dfs is handling your link properly. When you click on the Dfs root share you created, you should see that link listed as a subfolder. This is shown in Figure 4.37.

12. Move all files from the previous network share to the new share created on the RSS server. With Dfs configured properly, the physical movement of these files will be completely transparent to the end user.

Figure 4.37: Verifying the Dfs link

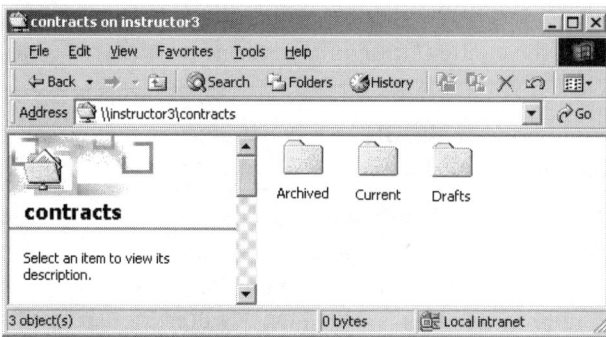

Finally, here are some tips for configuring a stand-alone Dfs server:

- Have Dfs use a share that users already access; this way, their habits and shortcuts will not have to change.
- To keep local disk space available on your RSS server, use the RSS console to initiate a Copy Files to Remote Storage process immediately after you set up the new Dfs link.
- Alert users of the new RSS architecture so they will be aware of the small delay when opening archived files.
- For more information on Dfs, read the *Step-by-Step Guide to Distributed File System* at TechNet (www.microsoft.com/technet). Use "Dfs Step-by-Step Guide" as your search criteria to quickly bring you to the reference.

5

SCSI Solutions

Imagine looking at a desk with two books that completely revolve around SCSI. One happens to have a little more than 100 pages, and the other weighs in at about 400. Which would you go for?

Now, most likely if you chose the first one, it's because you are new to SCSI, especially as it relates to storage. Perhaps you're familiar with the more commonly used connectors for a desktop system, Integrated Disk Electronics (IDE). SCSI may be a term you hoped never to come across as you passed your Microsoft Engineer exams, and 95 percent of the time, you didn't. But storage is for the big boys, and SCSI knowledge is a cornerstone concept for storage.

If you chose the larger book, it's likely because you are already SCSI proficient and would like to reach out for the next level, perhaps even the developer level. Whichever you would have chosen is fine—the key focus is that in one fashion or another you need to learn about SCSI if you're going to be in the storage game, regardless of whether or not your operating system is Windows 2000.

We recommend choosing both books. Specifically, we recommend *Making SCSI Work: A Practical Guide* by the Paralan staff. This is an easy-to-read guide that Paralan has graciously allowed us to pull information from in putting this chapter together. Paralan realized there was a lack of basic SCSI knowledge among engineers and found this book to be a way of rounding out the edges of SCSI knowledge (as well as assisting them to choose the Paralan product line that includes SCSI converters, extenders, testers, and so on). The second book we recommend is

The Book of SCSI 2nd Edition: I/O for the New Millennium by Gary Field and Peter Ridge et al., published by No Starch Press, Inc. This book comes with a CD-ROM that includes SCSI diagnostic tools, and it goes through the basics of SCSI, troubleshooting techniques, and even into ASPI programming. An additional resource is Gary Field's SCSI site, www.scsifaq.org.

So, sit tight. We are going to start at the beginning, give the SCSI life review, the terminology trail, and, finally, the troubleshooting techniques. Are you wondering how we're going to do it in a single chapter? Simple—we are going to focus primarily on storage, whereas SCSI encompasses a great deal more. In addition, we will leave out varying technologies that are covered later in this book, such as RAID. Finally, we're going to cut out all the boring stuff!

What Is SCSI?

SCSI stands for Small Computer Systems Interface. It has been and will continue to be one of the most flexible and powerful means of communicating information between peripherals and computers. Granted, there are a number of irons in the fire in relation to SCSI competitors, but the SCSI interface still holds the primary edge of the market. With the future stabilization of *iSCSI* (SCSI through IP), the life span of SCSI appears endless.

A History of Evolution: From SASI to SCSI-3

SCSI was developed in 1979 by a disk drive manufacturer named Shugart. Shugart was in the process of developing disk drives that would use a newer universal interface. Drives at that time used head/cylinder/sector addressing, but Shugart was looking for a way to use logical block addressing and an 8-bit data transfer that would work in parallel, as opposed to the serial transfer at the time. The interface was originally called Shugart Associates Systems Interface, or SASI for short.

Great. How does this help you? Well, the work on SASI produced one of the first small-scale "intelligent" hard disk interfaces for smaller systems. Previously, every device you used within a computer had its own interface. For example, a tape drive required a different interface card than a hard drive. Even worse, hard disks from different vendors came with different flavors of the same interface. Incompatibility doesn't begin to describe it.

A few years after its development, Shugart teamed up with NCR and presented SASI to the American National Standards Institute (ANSI) review board. The board accepted it as a project under the SCSI title. SCSI has helped to end the incompatibility nightmare. SCSI, as an "intelligent" interface, allows for a single interface that enables many devices to be attached to it. Now, if you need to add a hard drive to your SCSI bus, you grab a SCSI hard drive, add a SCSI cable, and hook it up. You may have to set a few jumpers and read over basic configuration rules, but you won't spend forever. Then, if you have additional pieces to connect to your adapter's bus, like a CD-ROM drive or a scanner, just hook those up, too, and your computer will use them.

Wow, that's easy! Really? No. Sure, it is better than the past, but there can be a good deal of trouble here for many engineers, especially in relation to storage. Part of the reason for difficulties with SCSI relates to a lack of knowledge regarding how devices should be connected, using proper termination, cable length limits, and so on. These are major troubleshooting issues that are often avoidable through education. But let's stay focused on the history lesson for a moment.

SCSI got the approval from ANSI in 1986 and was then referred to as *SCSI-1*. SCSI-1 defined the capabilities of the SCSI bus, which enabled up to eight devices to communicate along a single cable through parallel communication. The speed of SCSI-1 wasn't earth shattering at 5MBps, but the flexibility of SCSI enabled developers to see future speeds and to continue inventing. SCSI-1, while solving one type of compatibility issue, created another because the set of commands initially released were limited in abilities. This caused a lot of vendor-specific extensions, which resulted in incompatibilities.

In 1985, a larger command set for hard disks was established called Common Command Set (CCS). This allowed for fewer incompatibility issues with disks; the command set allowed control of a wide variety of physical and logical parameters to suit almost every physical disk.

In 1986, work on SCSI-2 began, which included a CCS for all device types and some optional hardware extensions. Fast synchronous transfers and Wide SCSI were also introduced. All these extensions even allowed compatibility with older devices. Final approval for SCSI-2 came in 1994, which is somewhat humorous because practically all devices developed in the '90s prior to the approval were already compliant thanks to the draft proposed in 1989.

Today, development of SCSI continues. A new committee has been formed to work on SCSI-3 that attempts to break up the standard into a more layered format, in line with the SCSI Architectural Model. Through a modular approach to the formation of this standard, the various parallel interface alternatives have found some room for standardization, and there are competing serial interfaces in development as well, including Fibre Channel, FireWire (IEEE 1394), and Serial Storage Architecture (SSA).

Now, this little history lesson is just the tip of the iceberg in relation to all the changes and the developments from one standard to another, but you get the general idea that SCSI is an evolving standard that continues to grow and will continue to grow for some time. Now that we have that established, let's consider the real technical side.

SCSI Terminology

A SCSI device can be either the initiator or the target of an operation. The *initiator*, as its name suggests, initiates the operation. It accomplishes this by sending out a SCSI command. That command is directed toward the target. The *target* will attempt to perform the task that was requested by the initiator.

So, to begin with, the initiator has control over the SCSI bus. But once the target is selected, it then controls the bus during the command transfer, the command execution, and the data transfer. Figure 5.1 illustrates the initiator and target concept.

Figure 5.1: Initiator and targets

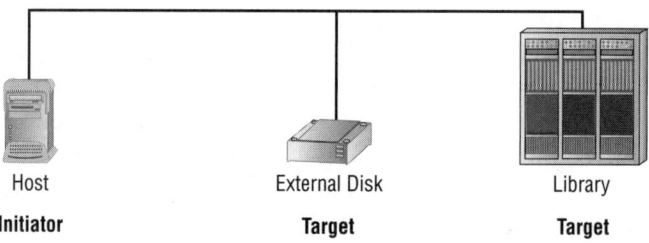

Now, the target's control over the bus could become a problem. Let's say an initiator makes a request for a tape drive to rewind the tape. This could take some time. If the target retains control over the bus during that time, no other requests will be handled on the bus. Therefore, one of the key functions of the target is to release use of the bus while it continues to handle the command request. This disconnect/reconnect feature is one of the most important differences between IDE and SCSI.

What Exactly Is the SCSI Bus?

The *SCSI bus* is a device-independent, system-level, peripheral interface. Great. What does this mean in English? You actually already know; the meaning is just being hidden behind large words. *Device-independent* means you can attach different types of devices (hard disks, scanners, and so on) from different vendors on the same bus. The fact that it is *system-level* or is a *system-level bus* is because, as opposed to just an interface or connection, SCSI has intelligent controllers on each SCSI device working together to manage the flow of information on the channel, putting the bus on the system level. Although it is more than an interface, we can still call it a *peripheral interface*, which means it is the connection point between the system and the peripherals (such as your CD-ROM or SCSI scanner). An extensive set of parameters, along with standard commands, enables a computer to determine exactly what peripherals exist on the bus and to use them accordingly.

All devices of a given device type understand the same set of commands. The differences in the capabilities of the different devices are defined by a set of parameters, which the host can query. But, as a system-level interface (which we just talked about), SCSI goes further. SCSI puts the device-specific intelligence in each device. A `FORMAT UNIT` command causes a hard disk to format itself. While doing so, the host can process other tasks. Once finished, the hard disk will notify the host.

A lot of hardware-dependent information, which is not vital to the host, is hidden from the host. Good examples are hard disks; instead of having to address information on the disk the traditional way by giving its cylinder, head, and sector number, a SCSI disk requires only a logical block number. This offloads a lot of calculation work from the host. Because each disk model is different, the disk itself knows best how to store information in a way that results in the lowest possible latencies.

A typical SCSI configuration consists of a host and at least one device connected to a SCSI bus. A SCSI bus cannot have branches without some kind of SCSI expander. The bus cable is daisy-chained from one device to the next. Both physical ends of the SCSI bus must be terminated with a SCSI terminator. This may be done by enabling termination on the device (if it allows for internal termination) or by installing a separate SCSI terminator.

> **NOTE** A *daisy chain* describes the way SCSI devices are connected, beginning at one end of the cable and continuing from device to device until it reaches the end, which is usually the SCSI adapter. It's this entire daisy chain that makes up the SCSI bus.

So, even though several physical components make up a SCSI bus, such as the cables, the terminators, the Host Bus Adapter (HBA) card, and the devices, the bus is not a physical piece that you can touch. Now, this is the first time we've used the term *HBA* to define the card. This is the actual card that needs to be installed in a system to provide communication between the system and the devices along the bus.

So you might be wondering, how many devices can I connect to the bus? Good question, because if you are familiar with IDE, you usually have two IDE ports that allow two devices to be connected to each integrated adapter. With SCSI, the number of devices you implement will depend on the flavor of SCSI you're using.

Narrow and Wide Buses

There are two types of SCSI buses: Narrow and Wide. Each allows a different number of devices to be attached. Because all devices on the bus are daisy-chained together, all the devices, including the host adapter card itself, will need a unique SCSI ID. The IDs can go up to only the number of devices a particular bus can support.

A Narrow SCSI bus has an 8-bit data path and can support up to eight devices, ranging from 0 to 7. A 16-bit Wide SCSI bus can handle 16 devices, ranging from 0 to 15. And a 32-bit Wide SCSI bus can allow for 32 devices, ranging from 0 to 31, although most SCSI experts would agree that you're not likely to encounter many devices using 32-bit Wide SCSI.

SCSI IDs and LUNs

So you have a Narrow SCSI bus configured with eight devices, including the adapter card. How will the system know which device it's working with on the bus? Well, as we've said, each SCSI device must have a unique address called a *SCSI ID*. Consider these IDs like homes on a block. Each house is on the same street, but each needs a unique address so people can find the home they are looking for.

You can set these IDs on the devices through the use of a switch, jumpers, or even a wheel. The wheel may seem strange, but it's actually a lot easier than jumpers. I had a SCSI scanner that the manual indicated needed to be on SCSI ID 2. The wheel in the back of the scanner could easily be changed with a screwdriver. I looked, and it was on 7, which is where I had my host adapter. I played with the setup for about three hours before I realized the problem, followed the manual, and set the wheel to 2. (This illustrates the necessity of following your manuals for your IDs.)

So the SCSI IDs need to be unique, and they need to fall within the constraints of your particular bus type (narrow or Wide), whether allowing for 8 or 16 devices on the bus. Figure 5.2 provides a visible representation of ID assignments.

Figure 5.2: SCSI IDs

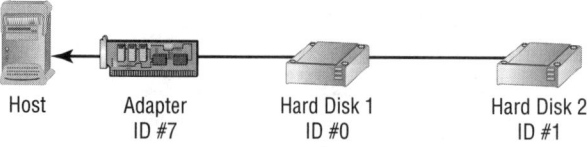

It's important to also understand the priority assignments that come into play with SCSI IDs. These IDs have real meaning on the bus. When two devices try to use the bus at the same time, the one with the higher ID gets access. That's why the host adapter usually gets an ID of 7 because it is the most important device.

You might be tempted by the concept of priority to place your hard disk's ID at 6, right after the host adapter in terms of necessity. Doing this is not always the best idea, especially if you're going to be using a CD-ROM on the same bus. It's usually recommended to put your slower devices, such as hard disks, at the lower IDs, and your faster (less used) devices, such as CD recorders and streaming tape drives, at the higher IDs. The faster devices fail to operate properly if their data stream is interrupted, which would be the case with the amount of hard disk activity that could cut into the bus.

So, is that it? Eight or 16 devices? This is where LUNs come into play. A SCSI target might have (at times) several physical peripheral devices connected. In this case, they would appear as logical units with their unique logical unit number (LUN) under the SCSI ID of the SCSI device. LUNs are mostly used with devices that would require more than a single address location, such as a library with multiple disk drives or a RAID array. LUNs can be used to address the drives in a CD tower or all elements of a library unit using a single SCSI ID.

If we go back to our street address analogy, just imagine that the block has an apartment complex with eight apartments. All have the same street address but a unique apartment number added to the address. LUNs work the same way. Every device with a SCSI ID can have up to eight LUNs (64 under SCSI-3 standards), also numbered from 0. This is how RAID systems handle multiple drives under a single drive case. The system gets a single SCSI ID and uses multiple LUNs.

> **NOTE** We'll consider RAID systems in greater detail in Chapter 8, "RAID Technology."

Well, now what? Ah, there is more terminology to learn. Now we need to discuss SCSI interfaces, cable types, and termination.

The Parallel SCSI Interface

The primary SCSI interface today is parallel. This may change in the future as serial interface alternatives mentioned earlier merge into the SCSI-3 specifications. For now we'll concentrate on the types of parallel interfaces that SCSI has.

SE, HVD, LVD

Parallel SCSI has three major interface alternatives, which are not electrically compatible: single-ended (SE), differential (or high-voltage differential: HVD), and low-voltage differential (LVD). LVD single-ended and LVD are somewhat compatible when the devices use multimode drivers (LVD/SE), which almost all do.

You might be wondering what is meant by *electrically compatible*. For one thing, SE and HVD use different electrical voltage levels, with HVD using the higher voltage, or more robust voltage. Also, HVD uses two wires per signal, a positive and an inverted. These changes allow HVD to go farther distances, which makes sense because it was designed for external use. LVD uses the lower voltage (like SE) but can use longer distances. So, without being an electrical engineer, you can see the problems with compatibility that are involved between the different types.

Single-Ended

Single-ended SCSI is the most common. Its original purpose was internal (for buses inside a computer cabinet), although modern use includes external connectivity as long as the distance limitations are respected. Single-ended SCSI has a limitation of 6 meters in length per segment. (Some versions of SCSI, such as Fast SCSI and Ultra SCSI, require even shorter distances.) Now, for those of you who don't do the whole meters/feet conversion in your head, let's just say that a single meter is about 3 feet or a yard (really 3.28 feet to be more precise). So when you hear 6 meters, you can think 18 feet. Now, that isn't too bad, unless you have a tape library in the server room that happens to be 100 feet from a server that you'd like to connect to one of the drives.

On a single-ended bus, the devices signal each other through one wire (and a ground reference). It's a cheaper way to go and great for shorter distances. What happens if you go longer than you should on a single-ended cable? Well, just like distance limitation in networking, you might encounter signal loss or noise problems. It's like an arrow shot from a bow. The arrow can go only so far and then it eventually lowers into the ground.

Now, you can extend beyond these limitations by using expanders that you can purchase and implement. *Expanders* are electronic units that enhance or convert the physical characteristics of a parallel SCSI bus. SCSI converters, extenders, regenerators, and switches are examples of expanders. They are not SCSI devices because they do not have a SCSI ID and are not visible to the system software.

> **NOTE** You can find out more about specific expanders that companies provide by searching the Internet for *SCSI expanders*. For one point of reference, you can check www.paralan.com to see some of the Paralan product line of SCSI expanders.

Differential

Defined in the SCSI-1 specification, differential was offered as an alternate to single-ended. Remember, single-ended was designed for use within a computer cabinet, so differential was for external use. Differential, as mentioned earlier, is electrically incompatible with SE because it uses a higher voltage and this allows for farther distances. Instead of a single wire, it uses two wires per signal. Due to the high power requirements for differential, the differential drivers cannot be integrated into the protocol chip of the devices, which increases the overall cost of differential applications.

On average, differential (being more expensive) is not used as often as single-ended if you look at the entire SCSI world. However, from the perspective of storage devices, differential is used quite a bit for tape libraries and RAID systems because of the distance opportunities available.

One point we don't want to fail to mention is that differential bus segments can be up to 25 meters in length (again for those of us on the U.S. side of the "pond," that is about 80 feet). Another good quality of differential is that it is less sensitive to electrical noise than single-ended SCSI. In short, it can handle the noise better because two wires are used and equally affected by the noise, which cancels out the noise.

Before we get into LVD, we just want to mention that due to the advent of low-voltage differential, the term *differential* needs to be clarified when referring to an interface. Therefore, differential is also called *high-voltage differential* (HVD) due to its need for higher voltage.

Low-Voltage Differential

You can see the driving force behind a good deal of the technology so far. With single-ended, there were cable limitations. As speed increases in SCSI, the cable lengths get shorter. That drove the differential (HVD) move. But then, because differential was so expensive and required such a high amount of power that bus drivers couldn't be integrated into the SCSI protocol chips, a combining of technologies was needed: an interface with the capability to handle longer distances but with a lower power requirement that would allow the bus drivers to be integrated into device chips. *Low-voltage differential* was born.

Like HVD, LVD is less susceptible to electric interference. LVD can also go farther than SE at higher data rates. What is the difference between HVD and LVD besides the voltage? Well, an LVD bus can be only 12 meters (40 feet). This is true for all types (like Ultra-2) that currently support LVD, regardless of their speed rates. Another difference (and benefit) of LVD is its capability to work with single-ended devices. LVD is not directly compatible with single-ended, but LVD devices have the capability to use multi-mode drivers that automatically detect the type of bus used and to switch into the appropriate mode of operation. This will enable you to use an LVD/SE device on a single-ended bus without having to set any switches or jumpers. Therefore, LVD has been introduced gradually, without the loss of current investments in single-ended devices.

> **TIP** The advantages of LVD are lost when an LVD/SE device is used in a single-ended bus. Actually, as soon as one single-ended device is connected to an LVD/SE bus, the whole bus switches to single-ended mode with all its limitations. That may cause unexpected limitations to your bus.

SE, HVD, LVD Confusion

Single-ended, HVD, and LVD use exactly the same connectors. This can really cause confusion. Therefore, each interface alternative has its own logo, as shown in Figure 5.3. The trick is to get manufacturers to put this logo on all their devices.

Figure 5.3: SCSI interface logos

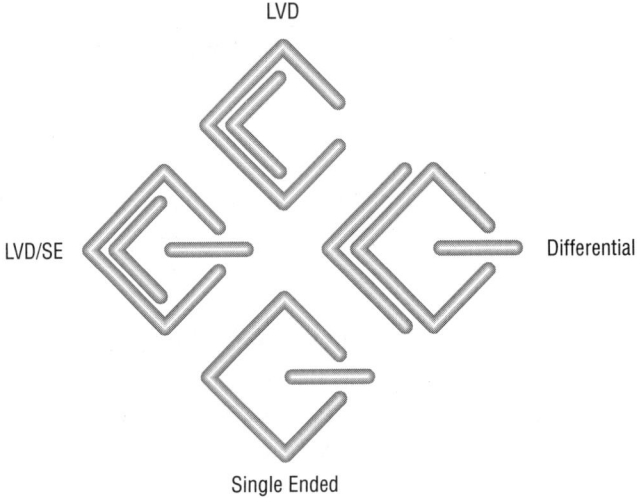

I wrestled with an ADIC Scalar 218 library for days because the termination wasn't clear on it, and I had terminators that appeared to be differential but turned out to be single-ended. I kept swapping out terminators and running around the building looking for people who guaranteed me that they had a differential terminator (they were wrong!). Finally this hardware guru, Edwin, said, "Oh yeah, first you need a converter from Centronics to 68-pin and then you can use a 68-pin differential terminator" (which I happened to have plenty of). He was right, but the point is that you need to know what types of SCSI interfaces you're working with. Read the documentation (although I must say in my defense that I didn't have the documentation).

If there is no logo, it's usually safe to assume that it's single-ended SCSI. Connecting a single-ended device to a differential bus or vice versa won't work but it shouldn't damage a device that is built properly.

Is there a better way to determine whether you have single-ended or differential? Sure. You need to perform an ohmmeter test. Make sure the power to the computer is turned off. Pull the cable connector off the host's SCSI port and measure the resistance between pins 2 and 24 on high-density or Centronics-type 50-pin connectors, or between pins 2 and 33 on 68-pin connectors. If the resistance is a few tenths of an ohm or less, it is a single-ended SCSI port. If it is more than a few tenths of an ohm (probably something over 1 ohm), it is a differential SCSI port.

Termination

Termination is an electrical circuit at the end of a cable designed to prevent the reflection of signals. Termination is one of the most critical parts to SCSI. As the preceding story told, without proper termination of the proper interface type, your devices will not work. In addition, both ends of a SCSI bus need to be terminated. This might sound simple, but rest assured that it isn't. In fact, termination issues are the cause of most SCSI problems in the real world.

A SCSI bus must be terminated on both physical ends. SCSI terminators on the single-ended bus also pull up the signal to its inactive level. Terminators are different for single-ended, differential, and LVD.

Single-Ended Termination

Single-ended termination, for example, has a twofold purpose. First, the terminators pull up the signal to the idle level to enable the devices to pull them down to the active state. Second, they suppress the signal reflections that would otherwise occur at the end of a transmission line.

Single-ended SCSI has two kinds of terminators: passive and active. The differences between them relate to quality and price.

SCSI-1 used passive termination schemes, which involves the use of a resistor that will hold the signal line at 3 volts.

> **WARNING** Some devices have built-in terminators. You might accidentally place these in the middle of your bus without removing the terminator. This would cause problems, so make sure that no devices in the middle of the bus are terminated, especially the HBA card when you are using internal and external devices attached on the same bus.

> **WARNING** Be aware that many older peripheral devices use passive terminators for on-board termination. In such situations, you should disable the device's terminators and use an active terminator external to the device.

Active termination will use a voltage regulator, as opposed to a resister, which will pull up the signal. The result is a much cleaner signal than passive provides.

> **NOTE** To determine whether active or passive is in use, you can check whether the terminators are changeable through jumpers or software. That would usually indicate active termination.

The Paralan guide on the subject *Making SCSI Work* summarizes the whole picture on termination with the following: "The exclusive use of active terminators in a single-ended system is strongly recommended. You should even check whether the internal terminators on your last peripheral and on the host adapter are active. If not, you should remove them and install active terminators directly onto the internal cable. If there is no additional connector on your internal cable, you can use a pass-though terminator, which has a male and a female connector and plugs directly on the last device on the bus. Pay attention to any cabling after the pass-through terminator, as it will form a stub. This stub must be shorter than 10cm (4 inches) in single-ended systems."

Differential Terminators

The differential SCSI bus, much like all SCSI alternatives, requires termination on both physical ends. A differential terminator is a simple resister network and this makes it passive. The need for active termination in differential is eliminated.

LVD Termination

Similar to differential termination, LVD requires termination on both physical ends. An LVD terminator will use a 1.25 volt source and also uses resistors. In the case of a mixed LVD/SE environment, some LVD/SE terminators will use a chip that has an auto-sense that allows it to switch from LVD to SE when needed.

Internal, External, and Mixed Termination

So, now that you have an understanding of the types of termination, it's important to consider the places to put termination.

For internal device termination, you need to make sure your host adapter is terminated and then make sure that the last device on your bus is terminated. If you don't have a device attached to the last connector of your bus, then make sure you get a terminator and attach it to close off the other end with termination.

> **NOTE** Modern host adapters can be terminated through jumpers or through the on-board SCSI BIOS settings. Depending on your card, you have an opportunity on boot to hit control keys and configure your SCSI BIOS. In some cases, this is really helpful because you can reset your SCSI IDs automatically through the BIOS settings.

For external device termination, you again need to ensure that the HBA is terminated in the same fashion as mentioned above. With external devices you need to either terminate the device internally or attach a terminator to the last device in your daisy chain of devices. Figure 5.4 shows a representation of an external tape library with two drives attached to a server. Notice that the server's HBA is internally terminated, and the library drives are daisy-chained together and then terminated on the second drive.

Figure 5.4: External termination

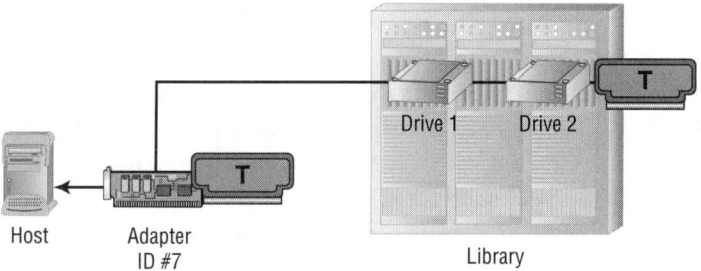

When you are using your HBA to handle a combination of both internal and external termination, you want to terminate both ends only. For example, if you have an HBA connected internally to a hard drive, but externally it's connected to your SCSI library, then you are using two different types of termination. This means that you disable the termination on the HBA and make sure that the last internal and the last external device is terminated on the bus. Figure 5.5 shows a representation of an internal SCSI hard drive terminated and an external library terminated, while the HBA is left unterminated.

Figure 5.5: Mixed internal/external termination

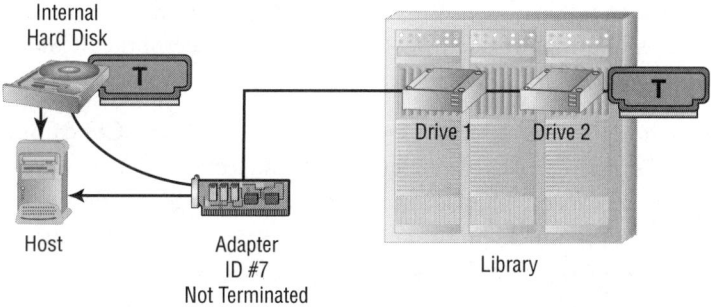

More about termination will be included in the "Troubleshooting SCSI" section, including information on the TERMPWR line.

> **NOTE** TERMPWR (Term Power) is the operating power for the SCSI terminators and is supplied through the TERMPWR line of the SCSI cable. The host adapter must provide it, but if other devices also provide termination power, it prevents voltage loss on long cables. If terminators are not powered, the parallel SCSI bus cannot work.

Cables

First off, don't buy cheap cables. Using a good quality SCSI cable is the key to building reliable SCSI bus subsystems. Research done by Paralan indicates that "90 percent of the problems encountered with a new installation of external SCSI devices have been associated with the SCSI cables used in the installation." And anyone who has worked with SCSI cables can easily verify that next to termination, this is your key troubleshooting concern. (Some may argue that this is first, and termination second, but "they" didn't spend three days with us playing around with terminators.)

Cable troubles are not always easy to diagnose. In some cases your system will not work at all, other times you'll have sporadic difficulties with it. You might blame every last possible thing (devices themselves or incorrect drivers) when the real problem could simply be your cables. The money you thought you saved has just been wasted anyway.

So how do you know you're dealing with cheap cables? The cheapest external cables have only 25 wires connected. These cables don't work with differential SCSI at all because differential requires a pair of wires for each signal. They also exhibit problems with high-speed, single-ended SCSI because they carry only a few ground lines.

The best type of SCSI cable uses 25 twisted pairs of conductors for Narrow SCSI and 34 twisted pairs for Wide SCSI. And they need to meet all the SCSI standards for impedance and need to be properly wired to their connectors.

Cable length is also an important factor to consider. With SCSI cabling, shorter is better. You see, signals on a cable are created with electricity. And they lose energy as they travel farther distances. This becomes difficult for the SCSI adapter to interpret if the signal degrades too much. So the shorter your cables, regardless of the distance you are allowed, the more optimized your SCSI bus will be.

If you happen to have to go long distances with your cables, you can, as mentioned earlier, get repeaters called *expanders* to strengthen SCSI signals and extend the length of your bus.

Stubs

You might hear the term *stub* in reference to SCSI cables. These are unterminated ends on a SCSI cable. Now, you've already learned that branches are not allowed on a SCSI bus. Everything must be terminated, right? Well, in reality, there will always be short branches, which are stubs. With most SCSI devices having a single connector, the actual connection between the device connector and the chip itself is considered a stub. Another king of stub is created when you use a pass-through terminator so that you have termination but then a little bit of cabling is coming from that to the device. You might be asking, "Doesn't a stub cause signal reflections?" Yes. The SCSI specification allows a stub length of 10cm for single-ended and 20cm for differential SCSI. Longer than that, and you'll have the same problems as with an unterminated system.

For a smarter way to branch off a SCSI bus, use an expander, which doesn't form a stub, but rather a new SCSI bus segment.

Internal and External Cables

We want to add a quick note here on the physical appearance of your cables. The internal cables look just like any other ribbon cables within your systems (although some are flat ribbon, while differential uses twisted-pair ribbon). One edge has a colored stripe, which shows you the first wire of the group, and you plug the connectors into your internal devices. One difference from your IDE cables is that rather than only two connectors, you will have eight, with one for your adapter card. Keep in mind that the last connector will need to be terminated or connected to a device that is terminated.

External cables are round and thick and somewhat difficult to work with at times. This may be one reason why you'd try to opt for longer cables, because it makes it easier to be neat with these. But fight that urge, because, again, shorter is better.

There are two types of common external cables: cables with 50 wires (for narrow and Fast SCSI) and cables with 68 wires for 16-bit Wide and Fast Wide SCSI-3. The cables all look pretty much the same; it's the connectors you can use to determine what you're working with.

External SCSI Connectors

Connectors are what allow you to connect to the SCSI card's external port and the device's external port. External connectors come in four flavors, although in reality only two types are important:

> **50-pin Connectors** These are used with Narrow SCSI (8-bit). There are two types. Most external SCSI-1 devices use the Centronics version, and SCSI-2 devices have the high-density connectors.

> **68-pin Connectors** These are used with Wide SCSI because these cables are designed to handle some of the extra concerns with Wide SCSI, for example, additional data bits and such.

We could write a whole chapter on connectors but we'll leave it at this. If you'd like to find out more, the Paralan guide provides an appendix that takes you through each and every connector available currently and in the near future. Gary Field's book includes an appendix that provides additional connector information as well. Or you can research SCSI connectors on the Internet to learn all the ins and outs. For some good leads, try www.scsischool.com and www.scsita.org/aboutscsi/Pictures.html. The main point to remember is that you need the right cables to connect to the right devices, and then those cables need to have the right connectors.

You can purchase connector converters. These can be your best friends sometimes, for example, when you have a Centronics SCSI device that needs to be connected to a high-density cable. However, if at all possible, it's best not to work with converters because SCSI electronics are tricky enough as it is without adding extra pieces into the mix.

SCSI Speeds

You know, we've been throwing out terms here without defining each and every one, and that is because with SCSI there just is no way to define every last piece before explaining how they work together. For example, we've mentioned Fast SCSI and Ultra SCSI and Wide SCSI. What are these terms? And what speeds can SCSI handle?

It is important to understand that the speed options apply only to data transfers. Everything else, including the command transfer and the exchange of messages, uses the asynchronous transfer mode. So when two devices start talking to each other, they asynchronously exchange a sequence of messages. If the initiator is capable of doing synchronous transfer, it requests to do so, including the maximum speed it is capable of handling. The target responds and agrees on the initiator's speed if it is capable of supporting it. Otherwise, it simply returns its own maximum speed, and the initiator will have to reset itself to the lower speed. This negotiation is carried on with each peripheral device.

SCSI-1 included only two options, asynchronous and synchronous SCSI, but others developed over time, such as Fast, Ultra, Ultra-2, and Ultra-3.

Here are their definitions:

> **Asynchronous** This type of transfer has no connection to fixed clock rates. Instead a pair or signals are used performing what is termed a request/acknowledge handshake (which makes sense because the signals are called the request and the acknowledge signals). This process actually degrades on longer cables. Modern asynchronous can perform about 5 megatransfers per second.

> **NOTE** Because SCSI uses the different bus widths of 8, 16, or 32 bits, the speed of the transmission is often given in *megatransfers per second*. So the Ultra SCSI speed of 20 megatransfers/sec is 20MBps for narrow, 40MBps for 16-bit wide, and 80MBps for 32-bit Wide SCSI.

Synchronous Uses the same request/acknowledge handshake but uses a fixed timing. The logistics of how it all works is research work for you, but the speed is important and synchronous transfer was limited in SCSI-1 to handle 5 megatransfers per second. (That's 5MBps for narrow, and 10MBps for Wide SCSI).

Fast SCSI Defined in SCSI-2. Fast SCSI can handle 10 megatransfers per second. The higher speed brought some limitations that were mentioned earlier in regard to single-ended SCSI, which is lowered now to 3 meters of length, rather than the standard 6 meters. Passive terminators are no longer recommended with Fast SCSI. Differential SCSI was unaffected, though, and can still be used at distances of more than 25 meters.

Ultra SCSI Defined in SCSI-3. Doubles the speed again to 20 megatransfers per second. The same restrictions apply on single-ended as they did for Fast SCSI. In addition, on single-ended SCSI, it's recommended that you use four or fewer devices on a bus. If you go over this limit, then it's recommended that you keep the distance between devices down to 1.5 meters. With Ultra SCSI, it's an absolute must that you use high-quality cables and terminators.

Ultra-2 and U160/m Speed is doubling in our preceding examples, so we'd expect that to continue. Ultra-2 can handle 40 megatransfers/sec and U160/m can handle 80 megatransfers/sec. Single-ended cannot be used for Ultra-2 and beyond; that's where LVD comes into its own.

So, as a quick and easy reference, take a look at Table 5.1.

Table 5.1: SCSI Speed Options

Type	Narrow	Wide
Synchronous	5MBps	10MBps
Fast	10MBps	20MBps
Ultra	20MBps	40MBps
Ultra-2	40MBps	80MBps
U160/m	N/A	160MBps

Terminology Summary

Now, there is really no need to redefine each of the terms in this chapter, but by this point you should have a pretty good view of the major terminology. One of the biggest problems noted, though, is a way of putting it all together. Let's see if we can do that now.

Let's walk through a real-world type of situation. Say you have some supplies on hand: an adapter card, drivers for the card, cables of all types, terminators, a tape library with two drives, and a server to put them all together with.

So, the library and its drives support an 8-bit bus and use single-ended interfaces. This would be a narrow bus, as opposed to a 16-bit Wide bus. The fact that it's single-ended, rather than differential or LVD, is also important, especially when you go looking for a terminator for the library. You are working with Ultra SCSI cabling, which mandates an active terminator for your library's second drive. You've installed the card and terminated it as well, through the BIOS program for the SCSI BIOS. You make a note that if you decide to install internal devices such as a SCSI CD-ROM or hard disk to your bus, you will have to terminate those devices and unterminate the HBA card. You boot up your Windows 2000 system (because that is the focus of this book) and you ensure that the proper drivers are installed. When you go into the Device Manager screen, you should see the results shown in Figure 5.6. You are a SCSI wiz.

Figure 5.6: SCSI devices appearing in Windows 2000 Device Manager

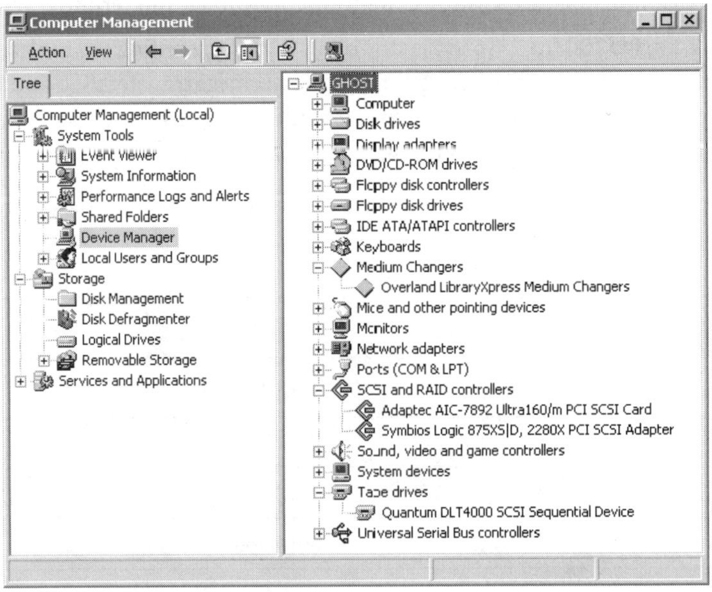

Two questions: Did you understand all those terms and their counter terms? If not, then reread the first part of this chapter. If you did, then here is the next question: What if you put it all together, follow all the rules, and it doesn't work? Well, welcome to the club.

Troubleshooting SCSI

There is a price to pay for everything. With SCSI, you get some tremendous benefit at the price of some real aggravation. Funny thing is that most of the aggravation is self-inflicted. You can prevent a lot of your own heartache by following a few simple rules (sometimes).

Now there are literally whole books that cover SCSI troubleshooting. Our primary concern relates to storage, but even providing every last piece of storage-related advice would take forever. So here is the most important troubleshooting tip for all of storage: be patient.

Sounds silly? Sounds like a given, right? Then you've never worked with SCSI before. Try spending hours changing cables, changing terminators, blaming tape libraries, and see if you still know what SCSI patience is. It is the highest form of patience you can achieve.

Now, in case you want some actual technical troubleshooting, here is a list of points that Paralan included in their guide and has allowed us to reprint here for you.

Troubleshooting the Parallel SCSI Interface *by Paralan*

When a parallel SCSI bus has problems, the symptoms may vary widely. The easiest problems are the ones where the whole bus or a specific device won't work at all. More difficult to diagnose are sporadic errors, as when a device is sometimes not found on power-up or sporadic read or write errors. The steps to take to diagnose a problem are always the same and they can't be overemphasized: always check the basics first. In many cases, basic configuration mistakes show up only after some time, under specific circumstances, or after modifying an installation.

Step 1: Check the Basics—Visual Inspection

Are all the cables seated properly? Check for broken or bent pins, especially on high-density connectors and on internal connectors. Also, check that the connectors are seated properly and that any latches and/or screws are tightened down.

Are the two ends of each bus segment terminated? Termination may be by external terminators or terminators on the device. On modern host adapters, you can disable the terminators via BIOS setup. Check it. A single-ended bus without terminators doesn't work at all. With one terminator a short bus may work, possibly with sporadic errors.

Continued on next page

Have the terminators in all devices in the middle of the bus been removed/disabled? Three and more terminators on a bus may work, but they will likely cause sporadic errors. Some newer devices allow one to enable/disable the terminator with a switch or jumper. On older devices they must be removed from their sockets.

Is TERMPWR present? Every external terminator needs TERMPWR, the +5 volt supply on pin 26 of the single-ended A cable. A terminator with LED will display the presence of TERMPWR, or you can use a multimeter to check it.

Is the bus length within the limits? The limit for a single-ended "slow" SCSI is 6m (20 feet), for fast SCSI 3m (10 feet) is recommended, and Ultra SCSI supports 3m (10 feet) with up to four devices and 1.5m (5 feet) with more than four devices.

Are there any stubs or branches on the cable? Branches are not allowed without an expander. Unterminated ends (stubs) can be only 0.1 m (4 inches) long for single-ended or 0.2 m (8 inches) for differential SCSI.

Did you write down the ID of every device? There must be no duplicated IDs on the bus. If you use wide devices on a narrow bus, the IDs must be from 0 to 7. If you use narrow devices on a wide bus, we recommend that you assign an ID from this range to all devices.

Step 2: Remove or Replace Components

Remove one peripheral at a time to find out whether something changes. Note that if removing a peripheral cures the problem, this does not necessarily mean that this peripheral is faulty. If you can, replace it to find out whether it really caused the problem. Otherwise, continue with the other steps. Faulty terminators or cables may also cause problems that disappear when you remove a device.

If you use passive terminators on a single-ended bus, replace them with active ones. We strongly recommend active terminators for every purpose. They are optional with slow SCSI, recommended for Fast SCSI, and mandatory for Ultra SCSI.

Replace the terminators, one at a time, with another brand if you can. Faulty terminators can cause all kinds of problems. Some brands of single-ended active termination chips are better than others, so try a different brand if you can.

If you use an external round cable, temporarily replace it with a ribbon cable. Bad or poor-quality external cables are a major source of problems. The faster the bus and the longer the cable lengths, the worse the problems. To find out, you can remove the covers of all cabinets and use a flat ribbon cable to connect all peripherals. Electrically, this is about as good as it can be.

If the cable length is close to the limit, try an expander. An expander is a very useful tool to isolate problems. First, it extends the allowable bus length, and second, you can move it to different places in your configuration to determine where the problem shows up.

Continued on next page

Vary the transmission rate of the SCSI bus. There are times when a system that is failing might function when the system is slowed down. This will give you some clues as to where to look and allow other operations of the system to be tested, until the problem can be resolved. Cables, cable lengths, and terminators become more critical as the speed of the system is increased, and may be a reason why the system does not function at faster transfer rates.

Step 3: Use a SCSI Bus Analyzer to Determine What's Going On

At this stage, you may have to get an external consultant with an appropriate tool such as a SCSI bus analyzer or a logic analyzer. Problems that can be investigated include:

- One of the signal lines is hanging. You can check this also with a SCSI bus analyzer or an oscilloscope.
- There may be problems with negotiating synchronous or wide transfer.
- A device may start a target-initiated action, and the host adapter may not like it.
- A device may reject a command.
- There may be excessive parity errors.

Step 4: Optimize Performance of Your SCSI Bus

What if you feel the performance doesn't live up to your expectations? Check your expectations. Many manufacturers advertise the burst rate at which their peripheral transfers over the SCSI bus. This may be much higher than the sustained data rate, the rate at which the peripheral reads or writes the medium. Example: A DAT drive without data compression might be capable of transferring at 10MBps on the SCSI bus. The sustained data rate, however is only 150KBps. When you measure the performance of an application, you will not be much faster than the sustained data rate.

Do old devices hog the bus? You might still own devices that are not capable of disconnecting to free the bus during lengthy operations. Or they might have the disconnect feature as a jumper selectable option—and it might be disabled. But even devices that do disconnect can be good or bad citizens on the bus. Example: A disk might disconnect when a seek is necessary (5–40 ms), when the sector is rotationally too far from the head (2–17 ms), or always after a command was received for the time that the command processes (1ms). (You can see the difference in times here and how this would affect the bus, even with devices that are compliant.)

Does your bus suffer from asynchronous degradation? The longer the cable length, the slower the asynchronous transfers. Remember that command and message transfers are always asynchronous.

—Source: *Making SCSI Work: A Practical Guide*. By The Paralan Staff.

And that solves everything right? Not quite. In real-world SCSI implementations, don't be surprised if things don't always go according to the standards. Let's go into the trenches with an engineer who can attest to the unpredictable ways of SCSI.

In the Trenches with Jim Power

I was installing CommVault Galaxy Storage Management software at a Lucent Technologies manufacturing facility in Columbus, Ohio. The configuration was to back up several NT servers along with a NetApp filer. The NetApp filer would utilize NDMP commands to back up to direct attached drives inside the StorageTek 9710 tape library.

When I arrived on site, I configured the SCSI chain in the following manner: the Galaxy media manager server was connected to the arm controller bus of the StorageTek 9710, which was daisy-chained to drives 1 and 2 and terminated at drive 2. The NetApp filer was connected to drive 3 and daisy-chained to drive 4 and terminated. The Galaxy media manager server was running Windows 2000, the tape drives were recognized, and the drivers were loaded and started. The NetApp filer saw drives 3 and 4 and assigned the proper names to them. This was the proper configuration as documented in the installation guides (shown here).

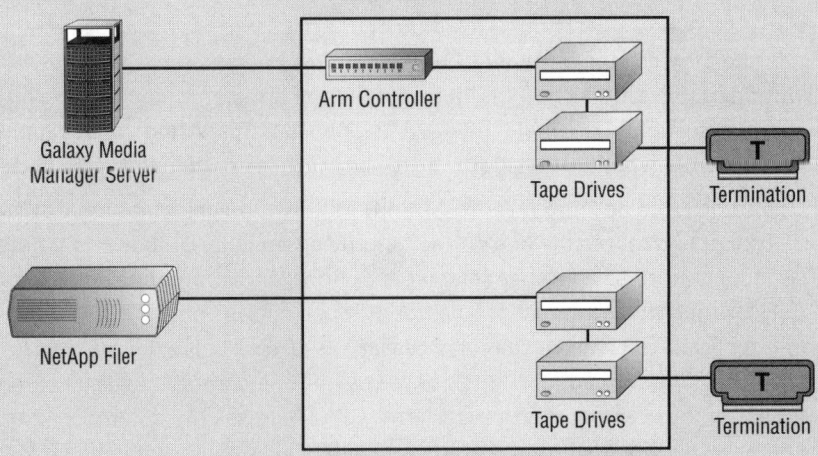

The Galaxy software provides a utility to validate whether it can write to a drive. Drives 1 and 2 validated successfully; however, it could only mount tapes in drives

Continued on next page

3 and 4, not validate them. Because the drives were not physically connected to the Galaxy media manager server, I had limited troubleshooting tools available to me. After switching cables and terminators, I discovered a bad terminator on drive 4 and replaced it. Galaxy still could not validate the drives. Everything else looked fine, so I called StorageTek to check the drives. StorageTek discovered drive 3 was bad and replaced it. Galaxy still could not validate.

I decided to try more cable switching to see whether any cables were bad or pins bent. Everything seemed fine. On a whim, I swapped the cable coming out of the NetApp filer from drive 3 and connected it to drive 4 and daisy-chained drive 4 to drive 3 and terminated drive 3. I then reassigned the drive names in the NetApp filer to coincide with the physical setup. I still could not validate. When I reset the NetApp filer to its original configuration, both drives validated successfully and I was able to back up to all four drives without a problem. (See Figure 5.7.)

Figure 5.7: The solution that worked

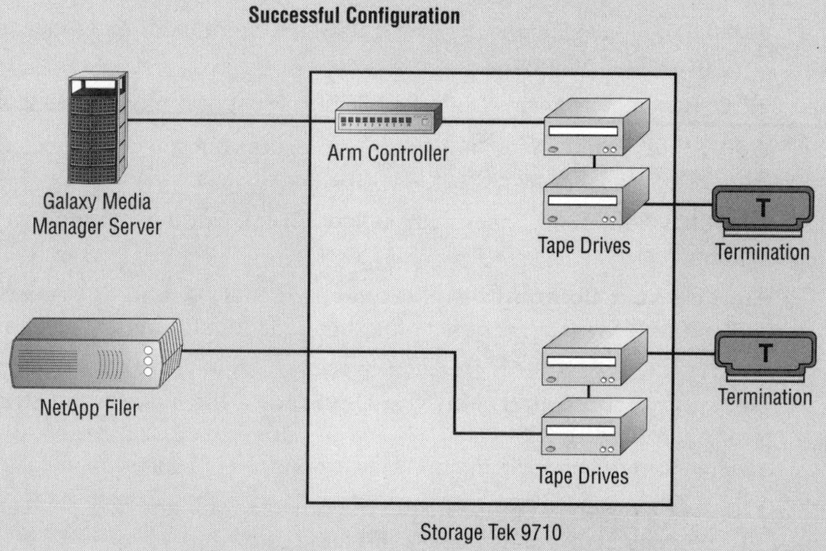

Successful Configuration

To satisfy my own curiosity, I put the cables back to the way they were originally set up and reset the filer. Galaxy could not validate. The only configuration that worked was drive 4 daisy-chaining to drive 3 and terminating, with the filer seeing the setup this way. It was bizarre to say the least.

You can see from Jim's experience, which spanned the course of several days of troubleshooting, that sometimes even equipment right out the box can be problematic from a standard troubleshooting view and sometimes downright impossible. Again, patience and a bit of creativity are needed at times.

> **SCSI Troubleshooting Tips from Gary Field**
>
> The following is an attempt to condense 15 years of SCSI tinkering and troubleshooting down to just the most important concepts and tips:
>
> **Don't Get Hung Up on the Terminology**   Don't believe half of what you see in catalog ads.
>
> Go to www.scsita.org or www.scsifaq.org.
>
> **Learn the Names of the Various Common Connectors**   You'll need to know what to ask for when connecting your devices:
>
> **Centronics50** (not as popular as it once was): Older external devices.
>
> **HD50** (sometimes incorrectly called SCSI2): Common for external connection on narrow host adapters.
>
> **HD68** (sometimes incorrectly called SCSI3): Most new drives have these.
>
> **SCA/SCA-2**: Intended for "hot-swap" enclosures but can be connected to a 68-pin cable with a proper SCA adapter (be sure it says it's LVD compatible).
>
> **VHDCI68** (sometimes incorrectly called SCSI5): Not too common yet, but it's coming fast.
>
> **Don't Sweat Compatibility between SCSI-1, -2 and -3**   A newer drive will almost always work on an older host adapter. It's mostly just a matter of having the right cables and adapters.
>
> **Terminate the Cable, Not the Devices**   This makes it much easier to rearrange or add devices later. Newer disk drives (LVD, U2W, U3W, SCA) don't even have terminators in them. This was done to help push you in this direction.
>
> **Go One Step at a Time**   Install the host adapter and one device, and get that working before connecting everything to the bus.

Final Thoughts

Troubleshooting is an art, and the key is patience. Some final words of wisdom:

- If possible, keep extra cables and terminators of different types handy. In our experience, this has proved to be invaluable. (Keep tabs on who borrows from you and whom you borrow from, because you could lose your equipment for being kind to an engineer in need.)

- You might want to pick up some troubleshooting equipment (such as an oscilloscope and a multimeter) if working with SCSI is going to be a standard practice for you.

- Read the manuals to your devices. Make sure you're following proper specifications. Ensure that you meet SCSI specifications, too.

- Make sure you document every problem you encounter. Recording your problem, recording the devices your adapter can see on boot, and recording the SCSI IDs in use will come in handy when you're troubleshooting.

- Ensure that you are using the latest drivers. One problem with regard to Windows 2000 is that it is Plug and Play. That is a wonderfully positive thing; however, it also means that a driver is found for your adapter and devices. These drivers could be older than the ones that came with your device or the ones that come from the vendor's site. Check with the vendor to make sure you are using the correct driver.

Now that you have a handle on SCSI solutions, it's time to combine your knowledge of SCSI with some serial options that are being defined, such as Fibre Channel. In fact, next we're going to pool our SCSI knowledge in with Fibre Channel to enter the world of storage area networks (SANs).

6

Storage Area Networks (SANs)

More has been written about Storage Area Networks (SANs) than has been implemented. You can find all sorts of administrative information that gives details on the developmental side of SAN concepts, such as the angle light pulses over Fibre Channel within SAN technology. This conceptual knowledge may be interesting to you if you're a SAN architect, but to design and implement SANs from a field perspective—or even from a pre-sales engineering perspective—you need a more rounded viewpoint of the story, one that encompasses specifications and real-world implementation.

SANs are high-speed, dedicated networks that join together any combination of storage devices (RAID arrays, tape or optical libraries, JBODs, all defined in Chapter 2) to the frontend production servers (see Figure 6.1). SANs enhance backup and restore performance and ease congestion on an enterprise's Local Area Network (LAN), freeing it for normal business activities and communication.

Figure 6.1: A simple SAN

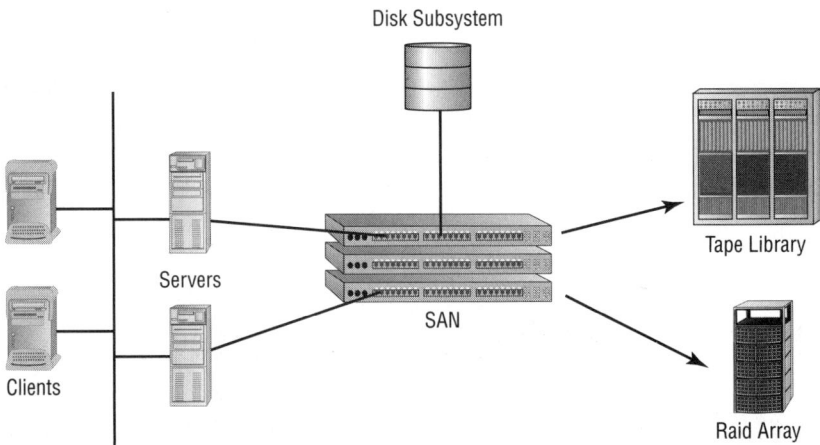

As you can see, the servers are connected to the clients via Ethernet, and the SAN-side connection is usually handled through Fibre Channel, a network standard discussed in the "Understanding Fibre Channel" section.

We say *usually* because the physical connectivity is actually separate from the SAN. However, it was through the advent of Fibre Channel that SANs have been possible and have succeeded in the marketplace. SCSI (discussed in the previous chapter), however, continues to be the leading connector between the storage devices and the Fibre Channel network. This is because storage devices are primarily designed with SCSI connectors (however, some modern devices are beginning to enter the Fibre Channel world, such as EMC's FC 4700).

The Benefits of a SAN Solution

One of the many benefits of a SAN is that it works toward eliminating server input/output (I/O) bottlenecks. Because the storage-related I/O is offloaded to the SAN devices, the servers are given back that needed bandwidth for server-side applications, which certainly lightens the overall load of the server. The server is not completely out of the picture with SAN solutions, though. The server monitors and manages your storage devices.

Another benefit to SANs is that storage can be added to your organization without adding additional servers. The storage can be added to your SAN storage "pool" and managed by your servers, rather than adding to the number of servers within your organization. Essentially, this makes it easier for you to manage your data because now your data is added to one centralized location and is managed from that location. In using the term *managed*, we mean backed up and restored and structured for permissions and quotas—in effect, all aspects are now at your fingertips. This makes it easier to manage and also lowers the Total Cost of Ownership (TCO) for your business.

Storage TCO, along with Return on Investment (ROI), is a driving force for SAN technology considering the growth that companies are seeing with their storage needs in relation to the cost of purchasing and managing that storage. It has been determined that the number of administrators (and the stress upon those administrators) can be reduced by moving toward centralized storage through a SAN.

SANs also provide a reasonable way to develop storage plans. Most storage is implemented on a by-server need basis. When a server is running out of space, additional disks are implemented, an array is added, or data is moved around to make room. Libraries and stand-alone drives are purchased and spread throughout an organization to allow for backup of that data. A SAN allows for that data to be centrally located and scaled and centrally backed up.

Another key benefit involves the ability of your storage solution to be scalable and transparently implemented. In other words, with a SAN solution you can add to your storage without your users being affected or even aware of your changes. The changes are transparent and allow for a 24/7/365 solution.

The primary benefit of a SAN environment for administrators is a developing concept called *virtualization*.

> **NOTE** Virtualization (in its purest form) is a developing concept discussed in greater detail in Chapter 14, "The Future of Storage." The basic idea of virtualization is that the physical boundaries of storage are lifted from off the servers. Devices are pooled together for all servers connected to the SAN to utilize. In addition, virtualization relates to the way data-management software handles the physical storage devices (RAID arrays, libraries, and so on) within your SAN environment.

The big question is "How does a SAN provide these benefits?" The key to understanding the answer lies in the current SAN components, including their (usually) Fibre Channel architecture. Let's now look at the Fibre Channel standards.

Understanding Fibre Channel

For those of you who are new to Fibre Channel, you might be thinking, "Hey, isn't it spelled *Fiber*?" Not quite; however, you are not alone in that belief. *Fiber optics* is not the same as *Fibre Channel*. Fibre Channel (FC) is a set of standards that involves physical cabling (which can include copper FC cables and fiber-optic FC cables) and standards (which relate to types of command sets that can flow within the physical cabling between devices that also adhere to the FC standards).

FC is a network standard that defines connectivity requirements, distance limitations, and protocol multiplexing. The American National Standards Institute (ANSI) approved it in 1994. According to the Fibre Channel Industry Association (FCIA) at www.fibrechannel.org, some of the standards for FC include the following:

- Performance from 266 megabits per second to more than 4 gigabits per second
- Support for distances that reach up to 10 kilometers
- Small-sized connectors and broad availability through standard components
- Support for high-bandwidth utilization and multiple cost/performance levels based upon need and financial status
- Ability to carry multiple existing interface command sets, including Internet Protocol (IP), SCSI, Intelligent Peripheral Interface (IPI), High-Performance Parallel Interface (HIPPI-FP), and audio/video

One of the large advantages of FC is that it is a standards-based solution. With FC, you have a solution that can grow outside of the single-provider scenario. Basically, you don't have to purchase products from a single vendor if all vendors are using the same standard. This allows for less worry over the competition on which standard will succeed and what products it will interact with; rather, the time can be spent working on the product's abilities instead. Although FC can provide many benefits in the future of networking, including CAD/CAE, audio/video implementations, real-time collaboration, and so on, our primary focus relates to enterprise storage. So how do you benefit from FC in this way?

Benefits of Fibre Channel

Keeping in mind what you learned about SCSI in Chapter 5, "SCSI Solutions," do you notice any flaws with SCSI technology? When considering distance limitations and speed limitations, not to mention the number of devices that SCSI can handle per system and the direct attached requirements that appear to come with SCSI devices, it makes you want a little more flexibility in your storage planning. This is where the Fibre Channel standards triumph.

FC SANs allow for hundreds of devices (depending on the chosen topology), which makes the data available to all connected devices across the network. Distance limitations are overcome when you consider that the distance of a SCSI device from its connected server is much shorter than the possible 10km distances of FC. FC doesn't require termination, which is one of the trouble spots for device connectivity in SCSI. FC is *hot-pluggable*, which means you can attach it to the network while it's active. FC also moves at faster speeds than SCSI. And finally, FC handles auto addressing, which in SCSI is done through ID addresses of the devices on the cable that often requires good documentation of the adapter, the target ID, and the Logical Unit Number (LUN).

> **NOTE** Is FC the only reasonable SAN solution? What about Gigabit Ethernet? Some wonder if the introduction of Gigabit Ethernet will remove the speed advantage of FC. This is true; Gigabit Ethernet creates a more level playing field in terms of speed. And, remember: SANs do not need FC to be considered authentic. With Gigabit Ethernet, however, there are still limitations due to the use of SCSI devices. So, in addition to Gigabit Ethernet, a new technology called iSCSI is being developed that will allow SCSI commands to be sent over Ethernet (similar to the way FC allows for this). ISCSI is discussed in greater detail in Chapter 14, "The Future of Storage."

Currently, Fibre Channel is the best solution to SAN implementation. This doesn't eliminate the need for SCSI, though. Most storage devices are still connected via SCSI interfaces. Later in the "Exploring SAN Components" section, we will discuss some of the devices necessary to connect a library using SCSI connectors to an FC SAN.

The Two Flavors of Fibre Channel

As mentioned at the outset, FC can be implemented in copper or optical form.

Fiber-optic cabling has an advantage over copper because, for one thing, the electrical interference over fiber optics is nonexistent. The down side to fiber optics is the cost. Compared to copper implementations of FC, the cost might seem astronomical. That's why it's important to know your needs and your budget in relation to the technology you purchase. Don't assume you must buy optical cabling when copper would be the best choice.

Copper is usually referred to as either *intracabinet* or *intercabinet*. Intracabinet implies all connections being within a single enclosure (such as within a rack) and allows for distances of about 13 meters. Intercabinet implies longer distances for a maximum of 30 meters and requires active components that allow for the extended distance of signals over the copper. Copper connectors were initially DB-9 connectors, but these are out of date. The new standard connector is HSSDC type, which is flat-looking, like a USB connector.

> **NOTE** Speeds of up to 100MB can run on both copper and fiber cabling, but faster speeds require fiber optics.

Optical cables are referred to in terms of *mode*. Modes relate to the frequencies of light waves. For example, a single-mode fiber (9 micron) cable can carry optical light farther and faster (currently 10km at gigabit speed.) A multimode cable can be broken down into two forms (62.5 micron and 50 micron). The 62.5 micron can handle 175-meter distances, and the 50 micron can handle 500-meter distances. So, even if you didn't know what a micron was, you'd get the hint that the smaller the micron, the longer the distance. The SC connector is used for fiber optics.

The term *micron* relates to the core of the cable and the size of that core. A micron is a millionth of a meter. In Figure 6.2, notice the micron core and the micron cladding.

Figure 6.2: A 62.5/125 micron multimode cable

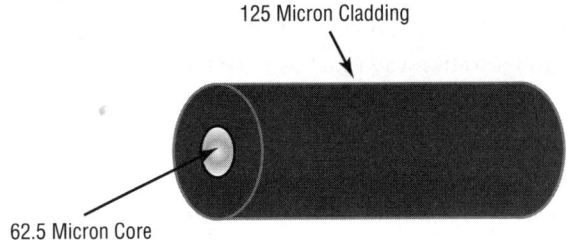

Because fiber is not an electrical conductor, it can be used where electrical isolation is required—for example, in areas where electrical sparks are dangerous (such as chemical plants) or areas where security is essential—because fiber is difficult to tap into and read. From the perspective of storage, though, it's a trade-off between the price and the need for distance and low Electromagnetic Interference (EMI).

You may be wondering why the smaller core allows for greater distances with optical cabling. In copper cables, the larger the core, the less resistance you get on the cable, the more current is allowed, and the farther the distance. With optical, however, the situation is different. Light travels along the cable through a process called Total Internal Reflection (TIR), which involves two different types of glass that have different refractive indexes. In plain English, the light wave will bounce back and forth within the tunnel. If the tunnel (or core) is larger, then in multimode fiber the signals will bounce back and forth along the cable in a variety of angles and at different speeds. The result is a scattering effect that slows the signal and reduces its distance capabilities. The smaller core is single-mode fiber, meaning there is only one mode of propagation, allowing for higher bandwidth and greater distances.

> **WARNING** Do not bend your fiber-optic cable beyond a three-inch limit. These cables are expensive and easily breakable; bending could harm the tiny glass filaments inside.

Another factor to consider when working with copper or optical FC cables is that the cable is only one piece of the puzzle. The cables plug into transceivers, which also must be designed for copper or optical. Again, costs are involved in your choices, with optical being the much more expensive of the two.

Now, before we move forward into SAN topologies with FC and SAN components, let's discuss a few FC details.

Fibre Channel Specifications

Fibre Channel as a communications protocol is developed in a layered model (similar to the OSI model) that breaks the functionality of it into five layers: FC-0, FC-1, FC-2, FC-3, and FC-4. Table 6.1 describes each layer.

Table 6.1: Fibre Channel Layers

Layer	Description
FC-0	Handles signaling, media specifications, and Receiver/Transmitter specifications. This layer will define the physical interface as either optical or copper.
FC-1	8B/10B character encoding for transport and link maintenance controls.
FC-2	Handles breakdown and reassembly of data through frames. This layer defines the frame format, sequence and exchange management, flow control, classes of service (which will be discussed shortly), login/logout, and topology information.
FC-3	Under development for common services for multiple ports on one node.
FC-4	Considered the top of the layers and is called an Upper Layer Protocol (ULP). The interface mapping between FC and SCSI, IP, HIPPI, ATM-AAL5, IPI-3, and so on.

To make it easier to understand the various layers, you might liken FC to the OSI model with FC-0 and 1 being similar to the Physical layer. FC-2 is like the Data Link layer. FC-3 is not really definable by a layer considering it is still in development. FC-4 might be considered to be similar to the Network and Transport layers, with the protocols being mapped toward FC.

For more information on these standard classes, visit the ANSI website at www.ansi.org.

> **NOTE** FC defines various ports. Any port on a node, such as a disk or computer, is called an N_port. A port on a Fabric is called an F_port. A port that has Arbitrated Loop capabilities is called an L_port. You can combine these to make up NL_ports or FL_ports. A port that connects switches is an E_port.

FC architecture also defines communication strategies called *classes of service*. There are six classes, but Class 5 has been dropped. Table 6.2 lists the classes.

Table 6.2: FC Classes of Service

Class	Definition
Class 1	A dedicated connection between two N_ports. Once connected and established, the two ports can communicate using the full bandwidth of the connection. Only end-to-end flow control is used in this class. This class should really be used for data that needs to be continuous and timely. There is acknowledgment of frame delivery with Class 1 communication.
Class 2	This is connectionless although acknowledgment of frame delivery is included. Both buffer-to-buffer and end-to-end flow control are used in this class.
Class 3	This goes to the next level with connectionless communication with no acknowledgment. This class only uses buffer-to-buffer flow control and is the selection for SCSI communication.
Class 4	Used within a Fabric topology (defined shortly). This provides fractional bandwidth allocation through a fabric that connects two N_ports.
Class 5	Involved isochronous, just-in-time service, but it hasn't developed and is considered scrapped.
Class 6	Provides multicast services. Allows N_ports to set up connections between the sending server and the destination N_ports. End-to-end flow control is used between the N_ports and the multicast server.

Flow control handles the problem of sending and receiving frames in a controlled manner. FC addresses the issues of flow control by allowing devices to send data only when they are ready and only after they've logged on to each other. During the logon process a definition of credit is determined. This involves the number of frames a device can receive at a time. This prevents devices from being overwhelmed with too many frames.

Flow control can be considered one of two types: Buffer-to-Buffer and End-to-End. Buffer-to-Buffer deals with individual links between FC ports. Credit values are set on each port when the connection is made. End-to-End flow control doesn't concern itself with individual links and uses acknowledgments to monitor credit levels.

Now that we've explored some of the different architectural considerations of FC and the different media available for implementation of FC, it's important for you to understand the transceiver, which is connected to the host bus adapter cards used for connecting these cables to the systems or components. These have evolved over the short time FC has been in existence. It would be good to be familiar with both types for backward compatibility.

Gigabaud Link Module (GLM)

One of the first types of transceivers is a Gigabaud Link Module (GLM). These are modules that are latched onto the Host Bus Adapter (HBA) circuit board and require the system (either the computer, the hub, the switch, or the bridge) to be powered down to perform maintenance. The GLM format has been replaced with a more flexible solution.

Gigabit Interface Converter (GBIC)

The Gigabit Interface Converter (GBIC) form factor has taken the lead for developers in the industry. GBICs are hot-swappable and allow for both copper and optical formats. The optical format is designed for SC connectors, and the copper format is designed for HSSDC connectors.

The following is a list of GBIC types and distances:

- Passive Copper (less than 10m)
- Active Copper (less than 25m)
- Short-wave (multi-mode) optical (less than 500m)
- Long-wave (single-mode) optical (1–10km)

Our next consideration, however, relates more to the implementation of FC SANs in topology.

Understanding Fibre Channel Topologies

Fibre Channel architecture has developed three topology options for connecting devices physically: Point-to-Point, Arbitrated Loop, and Fabrics (also called *switched fabric*).

Point-to-Point

Point-to-Point is the simplest topology and the easiest to explain. There are two devices in a point-to-point FC connection. The Gigabit Linking Modules (GLMs) or Gigabit Interface Converters (GBICs) are connected back to back, as shown in Figure 6.3.

Figure 6.3: The Point-to-Point topology

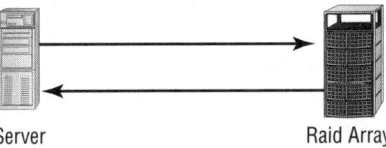

Within the Point-to-Point topology the two devices are usually a server and a storage device or RAID array. Transmit and receive connections are reversed so that the transmit connection of the server is linked to the receive connection of the device and vice versa. The Point-to-Point connection is a high-speed, dedicated connection.

Now, Point-to-Point is great for that simple SAN configuration, but what about when you need to grow? The next level involves a new topology.

Arbitrated Loop

Arbitrated Loops allow for additional devices within the SAN up to 127 in total over a single 100Mbps loop. The devices are connected in a closed logical loop, as shown in Figure 6.4. The term *arbitrated* is used to define one connection (between two devices) at a time. To allow for multiple connections, the devices need to negotiate with each other.

Keep in mind that an Arbitrated Loop is a shared transport. In other words, if you are working with 100Mbps and you have 100 active connections on that loop, then you are sharing the 100Mbps down to 1Mbps per active connection. The reality, however, is that SANs generally don't have that many active connections at one time. More often, a handful of active connections occur at one time, which allows an Arbitrated Loop to remain a worthwhile technology with good speeds.

Figure 6.4: The Arbitrated Loop topology (logically)

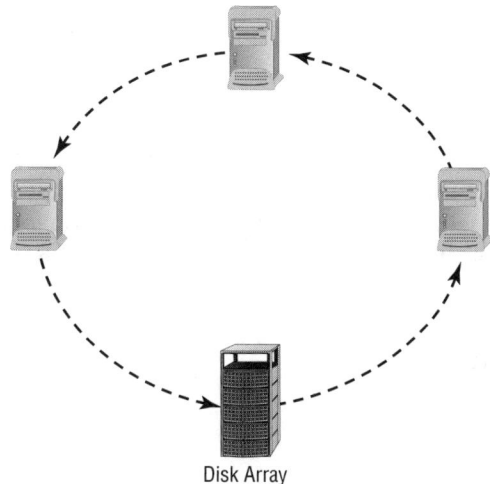
Disk Array

Within the loop, each of the device's transmit ports are linked to the next device's receive port. From a physical perspective (shown in Figure 6.5) there is an Arbitrated Loop hub that allows the loop to function by opening and closing Port Bypass Circuits (PBCs). If a device fails or if it is disconnected, the hub senses there is a problem and closes the port.

Figure 6.5: The Arbitrated Loop topology (physically)

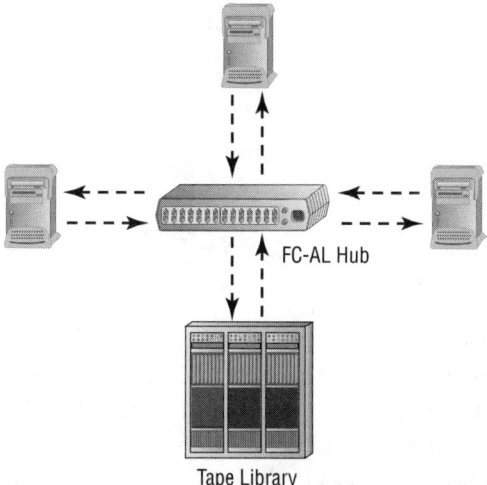
FC-AL Hub

Tape Library

Currently, Arbitrated Loops are the most widely implemented topology, although Fabrics are close behind.

Fabrics

The topology considered the most powerful of the three involves the use of fabric switches in the design. Of course, these switches are not cheap, and so the Fabric topology is more costly than the others. One of the key strengths is that each port can achieve 100MBps with the ability of handling 16 million logical devices per fabric. So, imagine the full speed of a Point-to-Point connection with the ability to have millions of devices. That can't be cheap. Consider the example of a Switched Fabric in Figure 6.6.

Figure 6.6: A Switched Fabric

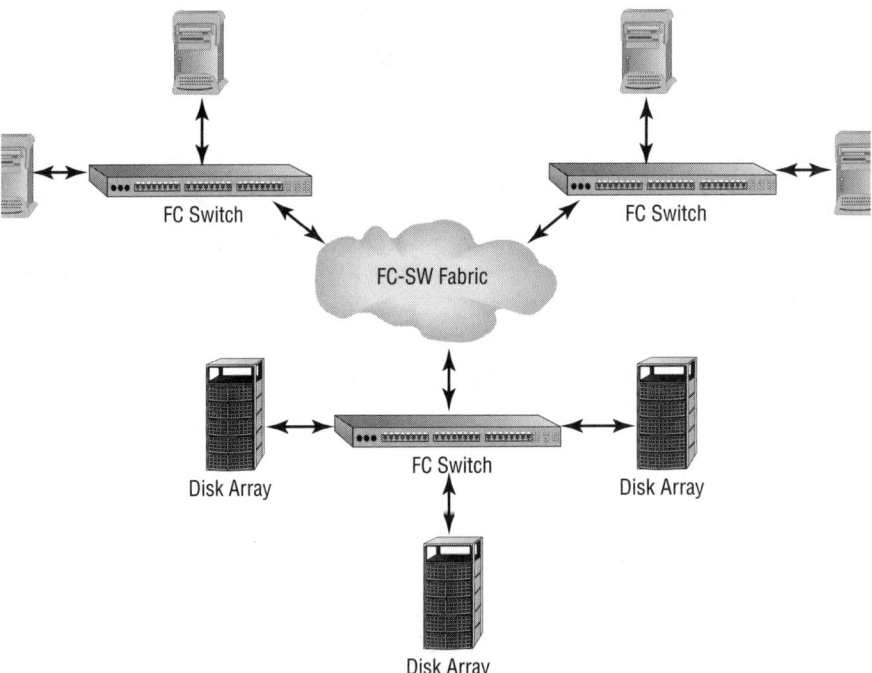

Fabrics may be familiar to us when considering the similarity to telecommunication/networking devices that implement switching. Take your phone system, for example. You make a call by supplying a phone number that might be likened to an address (fabric address, which can allow for millions of different connector addresses). The switch makes the connection and locks in the bandwidth needed for that connection between the two devices (in this case, phones) until the call is closed and the devices terminate the connection. Although two people are talking, the system is not locked down for other communication; rather, others can communicate at the same time.

> **TIP** If you need more detailed information on the inner workings of SANs, consider the book *Designing Storage Area Networks* by Tom Clark. It's an excellent resource.

Exploring SAN Components

SAN technology goes beyond some fancy topologies with standards for communication and beyond the cables and the connectors; it encompasses an entire new phase of network devices. Some of these devices have already been mentioned, but let's review them (see Table 6.3).

Table 6.3: SAN Components

Component	Description
GBICs	The transceiver attached to both the HBAs and the devices to allow the cable to be plugged in.
Host Bus Adapter (HBA)	Each computer attached to an FC network needs a special adapter, an HBA, that can send and receive signals across FC cables. With storage, HBAs perform the addressing function between the FC and the SCSI addressing.
Bridge, Router, or Gateway	These pieces of equipment translate Fibre signals to signals that can be understood by SCSI devices (Fibre-to-SCSI communications) and vice versa. A gateway can also communicate between an FC network and native Fibre devices (Fibre-to-Fibre communications). Bridges, routers, and gateways are used to connect servers and storage devices to the SAN.
Hub	In a Fibre Channel Arbitrated Loop (FC-AL) (described previously), the hub is the center of the network to which servers and storage devices are connected.
Switch	In the more complex network environment of Switched Fibre, the switch is the center of the fabric network. Servers and storage devices are connected to the switch, which is more intelligent and has more bandwidth allocation capabilities than a hub.

> **NOTE** There are devices used to bridge the gap between SCSI devices and FC devices. These are bridges, as mentioned in Table 6.3. However, they also perform a routing function and are called *routers*. So, the debate rages over what to call them. We suggest *brouter*. Many thought this was gone from their vocabularies, but it's the only way to express both capabilities of these devices.

The common question asked in relation to this equipment is, "What company makes the best of it?" That is a difficult one to answer. Sometimes even companies that you think are great are really "OEMing" the device from another company. An Original Equipment Manufacturer (OEM) builds products that it sells under its own company name and brand, but in reality it uses product components from other companies. To find the answers you'll have to do the research on a vendor-by-vendor basis. However, one company that has stayed in the shadows for quite some time is Brocade Systems, which we've chosen to highlight in this chapter. They have the lion's share of the market and only sell through other vendors.

The Brocade Perspective: Protecting Your Data

Brocade Communication Systems (founded in 1995) is the worldwide leader in enterprise SAN solutions; more than 90 percent of networked SANs are built on Brocade infrastructures.

> **NOTE** The material to follow was developed by Cyndie Behrens, a public speaker for Brocade.

Brocade does not sell directly to consumers, but instead it partners with leading server, storage, integrator, and application developers. Brocade has also been developing SAN switching technology for quite a while.

Brocade sees storage management issues in three categories:

Accessing Data   Administrators are struggling with providing reliable, high-speed access to data. Data is the life-blood of any organization, and providing fast access with integrity is a mission-critical application.

Managing Data   Typically, when you talk about managing data you're talking about keeping track of how much you have, who (or what application) is using it, and how efficiently it is being used. If you asked an administrator in the mainframe community how much storage they have, they can tell you down to the MB how much they have, how much each application is using, and how much is not being utilized. The result typically shows high utilization rates of about 80 percent. However, if you ask the same question of the distributed community of Unix and NT administrators, often administrators are struggling with keeping track of how many servers they have and may often quote storage capacities in wide ranges, such as 1–10TB of storage. Storage utilization in these environments is close to 50 percent or less. SANs allow administrators to more efficiently utilize and grow their storage resources.

Protecting Data   Protecting data means more than just the typical backup and recovery of data. It means providing high-availability environments that enable administrators to protect themselves against all types of failures. It means providing continued application access to data with the least interruption of service. Administrators must protect themselves from hardware, software, and physical (fire, flood, earthquake, terrorism) failures, as well as from the most common type of failure: user error. In fact, user error accounts for approximately 50 percent of all interruptions of service to applications.

SAN Benefits

The customer savings through deploying SANs are measurable. The savings typically fall into two categories: reduction in capital expenditures and reduction in personnel costs. SANs help administrators better utilize server, storage, and TCP/IP network resources and, therefore, they can reduce capital investments. SANs also can reduce the amount of personnel required to manage storage. Administrative staff can more easily manage more and more storage with the same or less staff. A study by ITCentrix showed that management costs in decentralized, non-SAN environments amount to 60 percent of the total cost of storage, and SAN-architeched solutions only resulted in 10–15 percent of management costs out of the total cost of the storage. Data management costs 5–7 times the initial acquisition cost, according to the Gartner Group (www3.gartner.com).

The key SAN applications being deployed that solve the storage management–related issues are often called the "killer" SAN apps. They are actually only the first wave of SAN applications. They include new ways of performing backup and recovery, often referred to as LAN-free and server-free backup and recovery. The trend is back to a centralization of server and storage resources so that administrators can more easily manage, scale, and utilize the resources. New ways of implementing high-availability clustering are enabled by SANs. Instead of dedicated failover servers that sit idle waiting for another server to fail, multiple servers can now all share storage and any of the servers can pick up a failing server's workload. The fourth key SAN application is new ways to provide disaster tolerance, disaster recovery, and business continuance for administrators. Just the simple ability to have disk and tape being remote from the hosts, from meters, to tens of kilometers (kms), to hundreds or thousands of kilometers opens up all new possibilities for electronic tape vaulting, offsite data, and remote mirrors of data.

Brocade supports native FC performance up to 120kms, and it also allow FC to flow over ATM and IP networks for thousands of kms. Different applications are typically used for these different distances. For example, all SAN applications (disk mirroring, data replication, remote clustering, electronic tape vaulting, remote disk access) work over distances up to 120kms because there is no performance implication. For longer distances with using ATM or IP, a company might deploy asynchronous disk mirroring or replication or electronic tape vaulting.

Scalability

Let's consider the ability of SANs to scale for a moment. Scalability means how large you can grow, or how many hosts and storage devices you can support in the network. It's not as important how many you support on any particular switch. Providing an overall solution for administrators supporting their current and future connectivity requirements is what counts. What is also just as important is the ability to grow into large-size SANs in incremental steps, what is called a *pay-as-you-grow* strategy.

Administrators (or customers) don't throw out their entire existing I/O infrastructure in one fell swoop and change everything to SANs all at the same time. What typically occurs is that administrators pick their biggest pain point and attack that first. Not only does this save in the overall cost of your deployment, but logically it makes sense to administrators to grow in incremental steps whenever you deploy a new technology and architecture. It lowers the risk administrators may feel when they deploy new technologies.

Scalability also entails being able to grow nondisruptively. Administrators want to scale their environment without affecting the operations of the environment already in place. With a SAN, you can plan from the outset to implement a design that allows you to grow without redesigning the topology.

The switches can automatically recognize the addition of new switches to the fabric and even pass along certain fabric-wide information, such as the addressing and zoning information.

Another term for nondisruptive growth might be dynamic scalability. The ability to keep your existing fabric and grow by adding more switches instead of only growing by replacing an existing switch with a bigger switch (forklift upgrade). Forklift upgrades are inherently a disruptive upgrade.

Availability

Availability is achieved through a resilient network. It is all about end-to-end availability. High availability means that an application has continued access to its data. It is not about how long a particular component in a switch stays running. It doesn't matter if a GBIC, a link, or a switch fails, as long as you design your environment so that the application still can get to the data even with those failures. In fact, these failures shouldn't affect your availability numbers because from the application's perspective, there wasn't a failure!

Many types of failures can affect application access to data. High availability means protecting against all types of failures, such as the ones mentioned earlier. To protect against user error, you would want to design a SAN that requires little human input. You'd want the SAN to be auto-configuring and auto-reconfiguring. You would want to be able to add a switch to a SAN and have the existing SAN automatically recognize that this was a switch that was added and educate the new switch on the rest of the SAN design (such as the zoning information). Brocade networks are auto-configuring and reconfiguring. They self-learn the topology nondisruptively. The more manual steps in any process, the higher the likelihood for human error. Automating as much as possible and designing your SAN with certain topologies (such as with a dual fabric) will go a long way to minimizing the likelihood that human error will affect application availability to data.

High availability means being able to heal thyself without user intervention or even perhaps without host server intervention. If a route between a host and its storage is unavailable, Brocade will simply reroute to the next lowest cost route. The unavailability of the original route did not affect application availability to its data. In fact, the Brocade switches may automatically perform the rerouting without the host servers even knowing that this took place. It is that quick and painless, and it is all about SAN fabric design and putting resiliency and intelligence into your network.

High availability is all about designing no single-points-of-failure in the network, so that no matter what type of failure occurs, the application still can get to its data.

Figure 6.7 shows an example of this type of resiliency.

Figure 6.7: A dual fabric arrangement

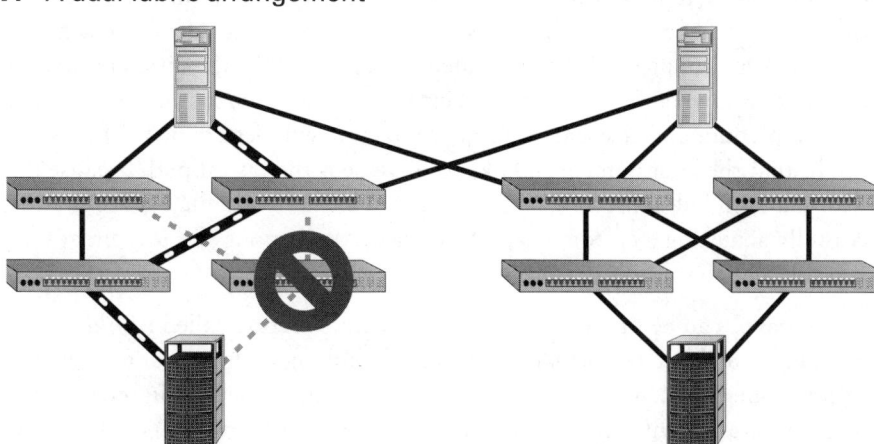

Performance

High performance (*throughput*) is a key requirement to building large-sized SANs. Administrators are putting networks between their hosts and their storage and need to feel assured that the host will have high-speed access to its storage. So, the first requirement is for the network to pick a high-throughput route to get to data.

Brocade has intelligent routing algorithms based on both a hop count and a cost analysis. The ANSI T11 committee has just approved Brocade's routing algorithm, Fabric Shorted Path First (FSPF), as the new FC interoperability routing standard. FSPF may sound familiar to those with a TCP/IP networking background, because it is based on Open Shortest Path First (OSPF), the routing intelligence from traditional networking.

So how does FSPF work? In most SAN environments today, each FC link is 1 gigabit (Gb) per second, so the primary determining factor for the fastest path is actually the least number of links you have to traverse, also sometimes referred to as the shortest *hop count*. A hop is when you send data from one switch to another switch, so if the data traverses two switches to get to the storage, then it is called *1 hop*. Brocade supports 7 hops between a host and its storage.

With some of the more recent Brocade Fabric OS versions, an administrator can fool the routing protocol into thinking one link is slower (or faster) than another link, even though technically today the link might be 1Gb/second. An administrator might do this to force a certain path, but in general this is not a recommended approach. However, as new technology is introduced, such as now that Silkworm 3800 switches with 2Gb/second links are available, customers may want to protect their current SAN fabric investment and build nondisruptively with 2Gb/second links—providing a mixed 1Gb/2Gb environment. Often 2Gb switches and links are deployed in the core of the fabric while the 1Gb switches and links are deployed at the edge of the fabric. So now in a mixed 1Gb/2Gb environment, the routing algorithms must take the different link speeds into consideration when figuring out the best route. With a mixed-link speed environment, both hop-count and cost-basis (weighting factor) will determine the fastest path. It may not be that the least number of links to traverse is the fastest path because the bandwidth of each link must now be considered. This network intelligence is critical to successfully achieving a customer's performance expectations and it is already built into Brocade's FSPF routing algorithms.

Performance can be significantly enhanced with a feature called *trunking*, which provides up to 8Gb/sec performance by logically linking up to four inter-switch links (ISLs) into a single trunk. Workload is balanced across all of the ISLs in the trunk, with each incoming frame sent across the first available ISL in the trunk. As a result, the entire fabric is utilized more efficiently.

Security

Security is also a key requirement of building a successful enterprise-level SAN. Typically the first topic people talk about when it comes to switches and security is zoning, although security actually means many more things than just zoning, such as what users have access to the management consoles, how switches authenticate themselves to other switches, and so on.

SAN Zoning

The reason zoning is so important is that although we often talk about SANs as enabling any host to connect to any server, this is not what most administrators want to do. They don't want any-to-any connectivity; they often want controlled access to resources. For example, they want a Unix server to have access to its own storage, and an NT server to have access to its storage, or they want time-based access to resources. For example, they want this group of servers to have access to the tape library from 5 P.M. to midnight, and some other servers to have access to the tape library from midnight to 5 A.M. So, zoning is all about controlled access to resources.

Brocade provides industry-leading security with flexible, granular zoning. They provide both hardware and software enforced zoning. Hardware zoning means that the access control is controlled by the ASIC. In other words, the switch acts like a firewall—actually blocking data from flowing to where it shouldn't. Software zoning means that the name server, or database, in the switch is controlling the access. The problem is that with only software zoning, NT/2000 machines, for example, when they reboot, may go dialing for storage and have access to storage that you didn't want them to, or they can disrupt a Unix server in the network by continually trying to talk to its HBAs. The only way to prevent this is with hardware zoning.

It is critical to provide hardware zoning and to allow both hardware and software zones to be overlapping zones. That is, a storage device, for example, must be able to be in more than one zone. Maybe a storage array or tape library is being shared between many different servers. So this array or library must be able to participate in multiple zones simultaneously, that is, be in overlapping zones. Figure 6.8 shows some zoning examples.

Zoning must also be highly scalable. Brocade provides an unlimited number of zones. Some competitors limit the number of zones to something as small as 16 zones. This would not be an enterprise-class zoning distinction.

Figure 6.8: Zoning

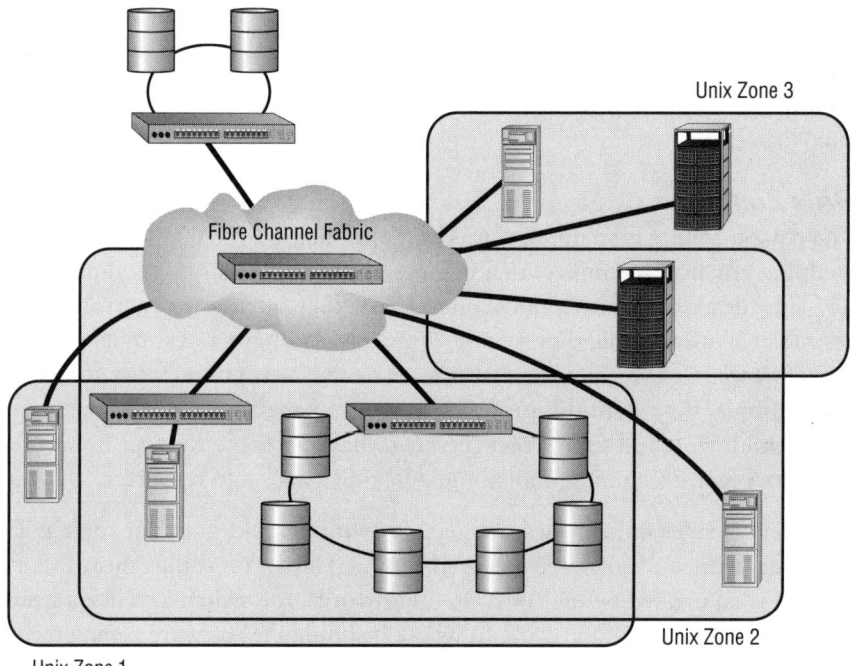

Secure Fabric OS
Secure Fabric OS takes security to a whole new level. It is a comprehensive, policy-based security solution based on proven, standards-based mechanism. Many of the features that LAN/WAN security experts are familiar with are now available in SANs. Secure Fabric OS provides secure access to management interfaces, switch-to-switch security, secure access points to the network, and the concept of trusted switches to control your policy-based security solution.

The Brocade Family
Brocade offers three families of switches that you can use as building-block components in designing your networks. The first two families are entry-level switches. The main intent of the entry-level switches is to provide a lower-cost entry into the SAN market for customers who may be considering hubs but who could use the fabric functionality (see Figure 6.9).

Figure 6.9: The Brocade family

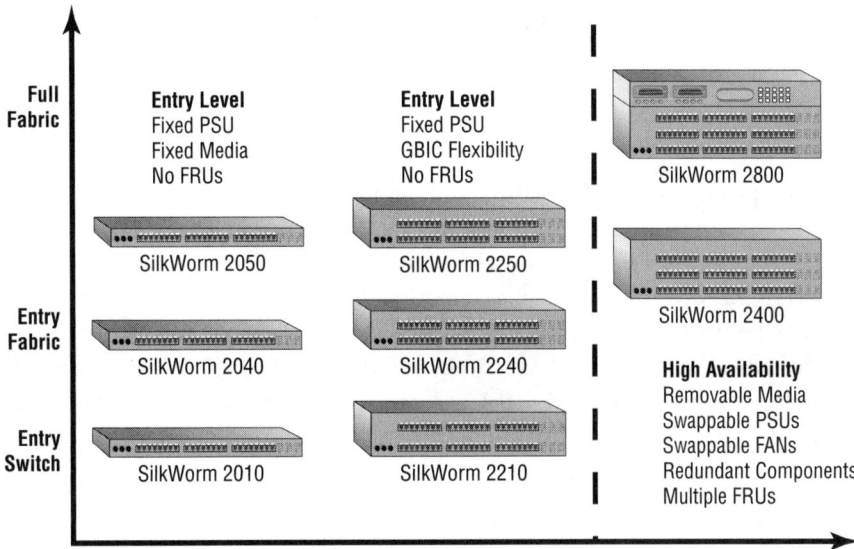

The first entry-level family is the 8-switch family: the 2010, 2040, and 2050. The main way the entry-level models are different from the Brocade flagship line (the 2400 and 2800) is "sheet-metal." There is less redundancy built into the entry models. They are designed to be single-field replaceable units (FRUs). So, if anything fails, the entire switch is swapped out and replaced. There is a single, fixed power supply, and on the 8-port models, fixed media. Seven ports are fixed, short wavelength ports, and one port is a GBIC (which actually would be a FRU). The GBIC allows for any type of connection: copper, SWL, or LWL. The 2010 is an entry switch or a *loop* switch, the 2040 is an entry fabric, and the 2050 is a full fabric. All models have the same ASICs and software. What differs is the software that is enabled:

- The 2010 only supports loop devices.
- The 2040 supports all of the functions we have been talking about, but only for a small-sized fabric of two switches. Brocade doesn't allow more than two 2040s to be connected into a fabric.
- The 2050 has all of the Brocade function; nothing is disabled.

So, a customer can start with either the 2010 or 2040, and with a simple license key can upgrade to the 2050 and get the full fabric functionality. The customer can also just start with the 2050. One important point is that you don't upgrade from 2010 to 2040 to 2050. You only upgrade from either the 2010 or the 2040 to the 2050.

The second family is the 16-port entry-level family, which is the same concept as the 8-port family. The only difference is there is no fixed media. All ports are GBICs, capable of supporting any type of connection. The models are the 2210, 2240, and 2250.

The flagship line consists of the 2400 and 2800. The 2400 is 8 ports, and the 2800 is 16 ports. These models offer more redundancy, such as dual hot-swappable power supplies, hot-swappable cooling elements (fans), and other redundant components.

Another product is the Silkworm 6400, an integrated fabric that offers 64 user ports (ports that can be used for host and storage attachment). The 6400 is a pre-built fabric designed as another network building block. Some of the networking tasks, such as connecting ISLs between switches, are already done for you, so the device goes in more quickly. Because some of the grunt work has been done for you already, it's a packaged, integrated solution. This is a way to get 64 ports in a small 14U enclosure (192 ports, or three 6400s in a standard rack), at less than 50 percent of the cost of comparable products. This is a high-density, low–floor space solution.

What's important is that the 6400 has all of the Brocade networking functionality. It is not necessarily intended to be a stand-alone unit, but instead to be another component in the network attaching to other 6400s, or any of the other Brocade switches, such as the 2400 and 2800.

The Silkworm 3800 Enterprise Fabric Switch is the first in a family of 2Gb products, and it is fully forward and backward compatible with the entire Silkworm family. This 16-port switch is the first switch based on the third-generation Application Specific Integrated Circuit (ASIC) that delivers advanced fabric services needed for enterprise storage applications. These advanced services include trunking and content-based analysis using Brocade's new frame filtering capability. Frame filtering enables advanced zoning and new end-to-end performance monitoring.

> **NOTE** The Silkworm 12000 is Brocade's first modular, multiprotocol core fabric switch designed to support next-generation storage appliances. It has a 64-port and a 128-port configuration. It is designed to support both IP and Infini-Band networks. It is designed for 1Gbps, 2Gbps, and 10Gbps FC solutions.

For more information on Brocade products, go to www.brocade.com.

Vendor Options

Brocade is certainly a giant in the industry of SAN switches, which are a core component to any SAN once you get past the decisions of copper/optical cabling/GBIC/HBAs.

However, it would be unfair to mention only one vendor without at least trying to incorporate a few others, such as Vixel and Gadzoox.

Vixel

Vixel Corp (www.vixel.com) has a line of FC switches, called the 9000 series, which launched with a 2Gbps speed. These switches (the 9100, 9200, and 9300-HA for high availability) provide data-throughput rates of 400MB/second at each port. They support up to 32 switches and 7 hops in multi-level solutions.

Gadzoox

Gadzoox Networks (www.gadzoox.com) is another provider of storage solutions. They have a 2Gb switch called the Slingshot that uses the FSPF routing protocol defined through Brocade. This will allow switches from different vendors to work together. The Slingshot includes 18 auto-sensing ports for loop and fabric, speed negotiations between 1Gb and 2Gb on a port basis, and a host of other highlights.

Additional Details for SANs

Of course, SAN technology discussions can range into all sorts of management solutions and beliefs on future implementation. Currently, because of the price of FC, many are waiting for the technology to mature and the competition to flare, (hence bringing prices down) before building a SAN. Two topics we'll discuss are Dynamic drive sharing and SAN appliances.

Dynamic Drive Sharing

Dynamic drive sharing is one of the benefits of SAN that is not waiting in the wings for future development. Many data-management architectures use the concept of a three-piece solution. One server acts as a control center for data management and job control. Other servers maintain connections to the stand-alone drives, libraries, RAID arrays, and so on, although the connection can be literally through a SCSI connection or through a SAN connection. The systems requiring backup will hold the third portion, an agent of some sort that will control the backup of your Exchange, your SQL, Oracle, or any client system you're looking to back up. Traditionally, the architecture works in such a way that the control server directs the data from the client to go through the media server to the backup media.

Under arrangements without SANs, you could perform a function called *library sharing*. Let's say you have a library with four drives. You can physically connect four servers up to that library through SCSI connections. One server would control the arm changer and a drive, and the other three servers would control a drive of their own.

What does this mean for you? Well, if you can allow four backup jobs to kick off of the same library. All four drives would be used equally, which is already a positive point for the lifetime of those drives. Often, the first drive in a library is overworked while the others lay stagnant. The down side is that if you have multiple jobs going through, your media servers can only use the drive they are associated with, so those jobs may be waiting to go to tape while another drive has finished its job and is waiting. Because of the direct SCSI connection, the waiting drive will not be able to help the other media server.

This option is a nice way to split up the use of a library, but with SAN configurations you can go even further than this. You can actually share drives between your media servers. If the library is connected to the SAN and your media controlling servers are also connected to the SAN, then all media agents will see the library as individually belonging to them. Through data-management software configuration you have the ability to allocate those drives to all media servers.

What does this mean for you? It means you can prevent the scenario mentioned previously with library sharing. If multiple jobs are kicked off, all of the drives can be put to use; then if one drive becomes available, that drive will be put to work by any media server that needs it. Dynamic drive sharing allows your library to truly be used equally and to handle more work within an ever-decreasing backup window.

SAN Appliances

Usually, the term *appliance* is synonymous with Network Attached Storage (NAS). However, because of the complexity involved with SAN configuration and the increasing talk of virtualization products, hardware and software efforts have been combined to develop SAN appliances.

These appliances are not new; in fact, some companies have been shipping them for more than a year.

There are two different types of SAN appliance: *symmetric* and *asymmetric*. Asymmetric appliances allow for independence between the management functionality and the data transfers themselves. This allows for external management of the storage data (called *out-of-band*). Symmetric appliances, however, perform *in-band* management of data. In this case, the appliance is positioned directly between the servers and the storage devices on the SAN.

How do you benefit from these appliances? Well, considering the concept of an appliance, you have an easier implementation. This reduces time to implement and administer, thus lowering TCO. In addition, there is an ability to provide centralized management through SAN appliances without using the common, vendor-specific management that usually locks many into their current situation.

There are several other key features to consider in relation to SAN appliances, such as:

- Snapshot capabilities (just like NAS)
- Three-way mirroring (again, similar to NAS)
- Booting from the SAN through the FC array
- Remote mirroring
- Additional security

For more information on these types of appliances, consider trying one of the vendors, such as Dell (www.dell.com).

So Much to Learn...

So little time, right? At the outset of the chapter we mentioned that more has been written about SANs than has been implemented. This is woefully true. SANs are expensive and currently difficult to set up. One of the best engineers in the field of storage, Joe Masi, did quite a bit of SAN configuration for Verizon. His experience was a combination of uneducated administrators and finicky equipment.

SAN technology is still in its early stages, and people are unaware of how it does and does not work. The equipment, if functioning improperly, leaves you walking in circles trying to find the solution. Joe spent days only to find that a drive on the library was bad, a new SCSI cable was worthless, and every day after he got things somewhat working, the in-house administrators would start moving things around, confusing the SAN's bridge tables.

Why all this discouragement now, when this has been such a positive chapter? Because we don't want to give you the impression that everything works great all the time. The technology is improving and stabilizing, but you will still need patience and a great deal of knowledge to handle SAN implementation successfully.

Network Attached Storage (NAS)

If we had a nickel for every time somebody asked us, "What's NAS?" we'd have, well...we'd have about a dollar or so. This indicates two things: First, Networked Attached Storage (NAS) and NAS-related products are still in development (with Microsoft releasing products in early 2001). Second, administrators, even in the field of storage, are still unaware of technologies that are replacing direct-attached storage solutions, such as NAS and Storage Area Networks (SANs), covered in Chapter 6.

On first glance, you might think NAS is similar to SAN. But the two are completely different, as you will see in this chapter. In addition to pointing out the differences, we'll also dispel the myth that these two technologies are in competition with each other.

So, let's kick things off with a basic description of NAS technology and review the benefits gained by utilizing it.

What Is NAS?

NAS was designed to separate your storage resources from your application servers. Think about it: How much of an improvement could be gained by getting rid of the high overhead, the complex operating system structure (which causes a greater possibility of failure), and the overwhelming total cost of ownership (TCO) involved in handling your storage? We've heard for years about a need for thin-client workstations. What about thin-client *servers*—a box without so much overhead and high maintenance? That is where a NAS appliance comes into the picture.

The concept of a household appliance is really appropriate to understanding NAS appliances. For example, think of a toaster. Not much work is involved in making toast in a toaster. You pop the bread in, push the lever down, set it to light or dark, and you're all done. A NAS appliance is easy to use, as well. It connects directly to the Local Area Network (LAN) and uses network protocols (TCP/IP or IPX) with industry-standard protocols such as CIFS and NFS (described later) for file sharing.

NAS appliances are dedicated to serving files, allowing both Unix- and Windows-based systems (in addition to other systems, such as NetWare) to share these files. As a result of their singular goal, these appliances accomplish the following:

High Performance Because of an operating system and hardware platform that are tailored toward a singular function

Low Overhead Less to worry about in installation and maintenance

Greater Reliability A streamlined operating system that makes failure less likely

Low Cost and Maintenance Lowers the total cost of ownership, although certain NAS implementations require greater costs initially

In comparison to a general-purpose server (such as a Windows 2000 File and Print Server), these appliances are a dream come true. A Windows 2000 Server handling file services would contain millions of lines of code (some say six million) to accomplish what a NAS appliance can streamline into a fraction of that. In addition, NAS appliances are much simpler to administer through web-based tools, Telnet, or serial cables directly attached to the appliance for the initial configuration setup.

Another key reason for using NAS appliances is installation time. Setup times for a Windows 2000 Server have been estimated at several hours. To set up a NAS appliance, you're looking at a matter of minutes. Connect the *filer* (which is another term for NAS appliance) to the network, ensure that you have power (in some cases, redundant power is supplied for fault tolerance), establish a few settings—such as the Internet Protocol (IP) address, the address of the Domain Name System server, the host name, and so on—and you're up and running. If you have a problem with the appliance, you use a web browser (now that the IP address is configured) and take advantage of the web-based interface that enables you to manage the appliance. We'll get a chance to discuss this type of setup for one of the more common and reliable NAS appliances produced by Network Appliance (www.netapp.com); see the "NAS by Network Appliance" section.

Another major benefit of NAS is the support it provides for multiple client file systems. Many organizations are still using both Windows and Unix, leaving the network administrators to deal with two different environments. In this mixed-storage scenario with two environments, a dedicated server is required for each protocol. If engineering is using a CAD application with the Unix File System (UFS) and the rest of an organization is using Windows Office applications with the NT File System (NTFS), the network administrators must support two independent file server types. NAS appliances are different in this respect; they support multiple operating environments, and most allow file sharing on the same appliance. This provides a great deal of flexibility for customers using different platforms.

Some of you might be thinking, "Why would I need a NAS appliance when disk drives have gotten so cheap lately?" You might be adding up your numbers incorrectly. True, you can buy hard disk storage at a low cost per megabyte, but there is a good deal of administrative overhead involved that adds to your TCO. The cost of storage changes (including administrative overhead) from one report to the next and from one month to the next. One report could state $3.50 per megabyte each year. So, your goal in lowering TCO is to reduce overall storage costs beyond the standard storage rates. In considering NAS solutions, you'll want to consider NAS vendors' numerics for the yearly support of storage and weigh that against the initial cost. Greg Dahl, vice president of marketing and business development for Tricord Systems (www.tricord.com), says this: "The actual cost of NAS and most server-based storage is about the same—ranging from 2 cents per megabyte to more than 30 cents per megabyte. Once both solutions are purchased and installed, they offer similar functionality. The real difference comes in configuring, deploying, and managing the storage."

Cost, though, should not be considered from the perspective of what is spent on the storage system itself. Claims have been made that 80 percent of the total cost of storage is centered around storage management, which can include the time involved by a skilled staff to keep storage systems running smoothly.

So, NAS may not lower your initial upfront money per megabyte, but it will lower your administrative costs over time. One less administrative salary to maintain your data will make up for that hefty initial investment for your appliance.

Before we start sounding like a commercial for NAS, we want to set the record straight early on: NAS is great, but that doesn't mean every vendor's implementation will measure up. Cars are great, but would you consider all cars to be the same? Options differ, as do prices of appliances. Your needs may vary, too. Not everyone needs a minivan, and not everyone can drive a Porsche. The same can be said about NAS appliances. You need to consider your short-term needs, your long-term needs, and your budget before you determine that NAS is the solution for you. Some companies have opted to continue with current solutions of sharing drives from existing servers after they considered the low price of magnetic storage in relation to some of the NAS solutions available.

Before going into greater detail on NAS solutions, let's discuss a common topic among storage engineers: the relevancy of NAS in a market that has been heavily developing SANs.

NAS vs. SAN

NAS and SAN are *not* competitive technologies; they handle different needs. In a mixed environment of Unix and NT, the data needs to be accessed by customers with disparate operating systems, but because the file structure is platform specific, there are a great deal of interoperability problems. NAS solves the problem by enabling you to use common file protocols on large disk arrays directly attached to your existing Ethernet LAN, as shown in Figure 7.1.

Figure 7.1: The NAS appliance serves a specific purpose.

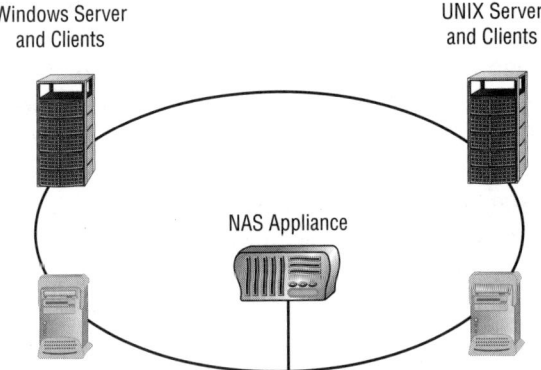

The result is a cross-platform environment that allows access to storage regardless of operating system. On top of that, depending on the amount of money being spent and the vendor providing the NAS appliance, this solution also gives you a place to store terabytes (TB) of data.

Think about this scenario: You have a company whose primary focus involves web serving. Its strength is in its web pages and streaming content. In addition, the company uses backend SQL servers that handle transactions tied to those web pages. LAN traffic is already at its peak. A SAN configuration using Fibre Channel on the backend database servers will allow for your database backups, and a NAS arrangement on the frontend will provide the file-sharing capabilities that web services require. The combination of both technologies creates an attractive solution.

There are some similarities in the benefits that SAN and NAS provide, which may be at the heart of the perceived controversy of which will win the market. NAS makes a file system on the other side of a LAN appear as if it's locally attached. A SAN makes a device on the other side of the SAN appear as if it's locally attached. Figure 7.2 shows the NAS and SAN similarities.

Figure 7.2: NAS and SAN similarities

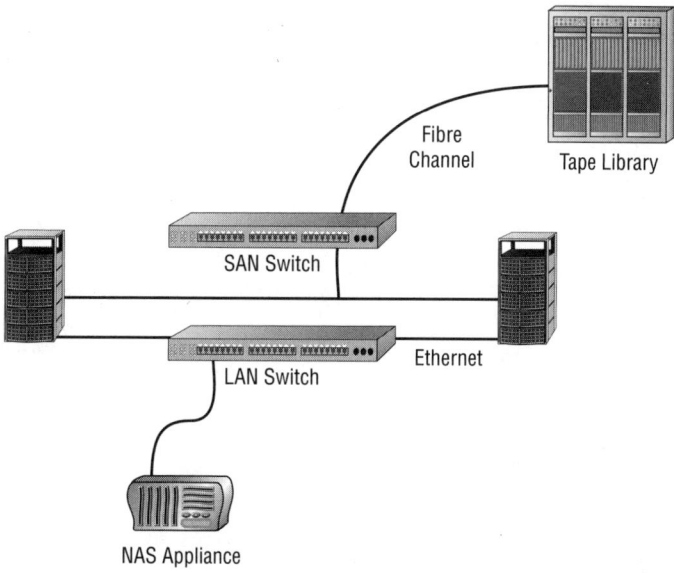

Both NAS and SAN offer a solution that changes the nature of direct-attached storage by moving it to the network. The use of differing technologies to accomplish this task causes one to ask the question, "Which is better or faster?" Obviously, the SAN implementation, with Fibre Channel optimizations on a dedicated network, would move data faster under current Ethernet speeds. However, Gigabit Ethernet or iSCSI may create a level playing field in terms of speed.

Table 7.1 compares the two.

Table 7.1: NAS vs. SAN

	NAS	SAN
Network Infrastructure	TCP/IP or IPX used over Ethernet or Fast Ethernet. Also possible through Token Ring, FDDI and ATM.	Fibre Channel.
Protocols Used	Standard file-sharing protocols: SMB/CIFS, NFS, and so on.	Raw data requests directly to disk drive.
Getting Started	Some implementations would not be considered cheap on initial cost, but their installation is fast and their maintenance is easier.	Difficult (as you saw in the previous chapter) and expensive.
Ready for Production	Longer existence, utilizing industry standards.	Still in early development stages. Currently, problems arise with implementation.

Later in this chapter, the "NAS and the Future" section discusses issues that may continue the debate on NAS vs. SAN implementations.

NFS and CIFS

Network File System (NFS) and Common Internet File System (CIFS, pronounced *sifs*) are resource-sharing protocols that enable you to remotely access file systems. They stem from two different sides of the technological spectrum, one being Unix and the other being Windows. However, they share the goal of accessing shared files for their respective systems.

Understanding Network File System (NFS)

Sun Microsystems introduced NFS in 1985. NFS was designed to provide remote file access to the Unix File System (UFS) in such a way as to enable the client to feel as if those files are local.

Since its introduction, NFS has become the most widely used remote file access protocol primarily because of its ability to maintain *stateless* connections. In other words, NFS has no real awareness of the connection state between the client and the server. This term usually describes the ability NFS has of stressing error recovery solutions for files rather than file locking, which CIFS uses. Because file locking is not an issue with NFS, the server using NFS can reboot without the clients being aware of a problem if services become available again quickly enough. This is very different from CIFS.

NFS was originally implemented only on Unix-based systems, but various implementations are now possible for any platform in use. The only drawback to these non-Unix implementations is that NFS will not emulate the client's local file access.

Understanding Common Internet File System (CIFS)

This protocol for remote file access was originally termed Server Message Block (SMB) by Microsoft and Intel back in the early '80s. SMB was developed to allow Windows platforms network access to UFS. In 1996 Microsoft introduced CIFS as its NTFS version of SMB.

CIFS is an open standard that Microsoft wants to be the standard for all remote file system access. CIFS provides remote file system access (similar to that of NFS) to NTFS (the NT file system) along with other Microsoft-supported file systems depending on the operating system you're working with (such as FAT, FAT32, CDFS, HPFS in NT 4, and so on). One of the limitations of CIFS is its need for locking, which requires a continuous connection. Reboots are therefore a problem to users who did not disconnect their connections prior to servers being shut down or rebooted. The user's system will continue to think it is connected and cause tremendous delays, and even lockups, if the user attempts to access remote files that are no longer available. It's because of this need to maintain the session between client and server that CIFS is considered a *stateful* protocol, rather than stateless.

The big question is this: How does knowing NFS and CIFS help you implement and administer storage network solutions? First, it gives you the vocabulary you need when a marketer weaves yarns of NFS and CIFS support options. Second, if you do work in a heterogeneous (mixed) environment of Unix and Windows platforms, then you understand the need to provide a mixed collection of accessible storage. NAS appliances, in some cases, offer the ability to use both file systems (UFS and NTFS) and also allow for both methods of access (NFS or CIFS) or even a mixed method of either in some cases. One great example of this type of access is the Network Appliance filer, produced by Network Appliance (www.netapp.com). We cover this product line and go through a step-by-step installation of a Network Appliance filer later on in "Implementing Your Network Appliance Filer." For now, you're ready for the next step in NAS development: NDMP.

What Is NDMP?

The backup and recovery of a NAS appliance is no easy task. If we're talking about a real NAS filer, then we're looking at a device that has a limited operating system rather than a general-purpose operating system. The operating system for the appliance wouldn't usually include backup software, which would probably have more lines of code than the appliance operating system itself.

So, how do we back up these appliances that are supporting huge amounts of data, some in the terabyte level? One possible solution includes over-the-LAN backup, but with such a high level of data pulled through your network pipe, a more workable solution is Network Data Management Protocol (NDMP).

NDMP Arrives

In 1996 Network Appliance and Intelliguard (which was later acquired by Legato) tried to solve the backup/recovery problem with NAS appliances. The standard protocol they came up with was NDMP. It is an open standard that allows for enterprise-wide backups for heterogeneous NAS appliances. *Heterogeneous* means varied or mixed, which indicates support for multiple file types and file access types, such as NFS and CIFS.

NDMP source code is openly published for everyone to use and to make recommendations for improvements. This even takes into consideration future implementations of NAS appliances. If future NAS appliances are NDMP-compliant, then software developers who have developed NDMP solutions for backup and recovery will have an easier time porting these devices.

How Does NDMP Work?

NDMP acts like a mediator between the client and the server. The current practice for storage management vendors is to adapt their software to meet the needs of the other vendors. Depending on the architecture of the operating system, the storage management vendor will need to adjust their products. So, if you have two distinct NAS appliances using two distinct operating systems, the vendor would need to develop two distinct solutions. Then they'd have to test those solutions in every possible circumstance, with various applications that need backup/recovery solutions and with every possible library and stand-alone drive. Quite a challenge!

NDMP, as an embedded protocol, separates the data path and the control path, so network data can be backed up locally yet managed from a central location, as shown in Figure 7.3.

Figure 7.3: The separation between paths

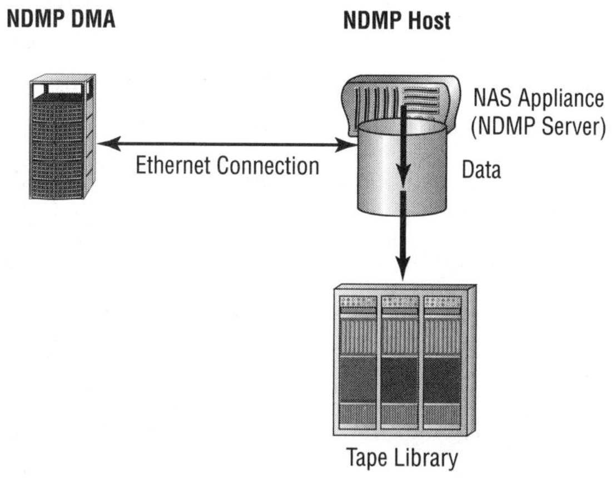

NDMP DMA — Ethernet Connection — NDMP Host / NAS Appliance (NDMP Server) — Data — Tape Library

Some of the terminology in Figure 7.3 is best described using the NDMP specification:

Network Data Management Protocol (NDMP)   An open protocol for enterprise-wide, network-based data management such as backup and recovery. NDMP is a control protocol, used to control the NDMP services participating in the session. NDMP does not carry the payload data; the data is transmitted over a separate connection using any protocol.

Data Management Application (DMA)   The DMA that controls the NDMP session. In NDMP there is a master-slave relationship: The DMA is the session master, and the NDMP services are the slaves. In NDMP versions 1, 2, and 3, the term *NDMP client* was used instead of the DMA.

NDMP Host   The host computer system that executes the NDMP server application. Data is backed up from the NDMP host to a local tape drive or to a backup device on a remote NDMP host.

NDMP Service   The state machine on the NDMP host accessed with the Internet protocol and controlled using the NDMP protocol. This term is used independently of implementation. There are three types of NDMP services: Data Service, Tape Service, and SCSI Service.

NDMP Server   An instance of one or more distinct NDMP services controlled by a single NDMP control connection. Thus a data/tape/SCSI server is an NDMP server providing a data/tape/SCSI service.

These definitions are subject to change as finalized revisions are implemented on the draft; they are provided here merely for instructional purposes on the functionality of NDMP. For more information on NDMP, visit www.ndmp.org.

There are three portions to the process of NDMP backup. There is a backup device, such as a stand-alone drive or tape library. There is the NAS appliance itself, which is a holding point for data (under a file system format and being accessed by a file system access protocol). And there is an intermediary control point located off to the side as a DMA or client that will direct NDMP commands toward the filer.

During the backup, the software control point (the DMA) will control what is being backed up and will manage the database (or catalogue, or index, whichever term is comfortable to you) of the data that has been backed up and where it's located.

System and backup software vendors use their knowledge of NDMP and add a small amount of code to their software, rather than an entire data manager that would take up too much room and make the appliance vendor specific, rather than open for all. Once an appliance is NDMP-compliant, the appliance is ready for backup through an over-the-network set of commands sent to the filer.

The real strength of NDMP is the standard access approach to backup. The same backup of the same NAS operating system to the same library by two distinct software vendors will use different calls and different data flow management. However, if vendors use NDMP, then they will be using common interfaces for common data flow architecture, regardless of the backup software, the NAS hardware platform, or the backup device being used.

Now, why would companies want that? Proprietary solutions are the key to success, aren't they? If everybody worked with everybody, how would companies make money? When you get to the "Windows-Powered NAS" section later, you'll see Microsoft's answer. Let's first consider the benefits to utilizing NDMP, especially from a vendor's perspective.

Compliance Benefits

Software/hardware vendors realize that the implementation of the NDMP standards will eliminate their cornering the NAS market. They also know that without some uniformity, people will pass up the NAS environment in favor of something more flexible and open.

Without some interoperability among all of these different vendors (the operating system, the backup software, and the tape solution), companies force people to find a different solution, even if it costs more.

So, these are some of the benefits of NDMP compliance:

- Product timeliness is shorter. Without NDMP, the backup software companies need to spend more time worrying about compatibility.

- Plug and play becomes a reality, right up to the backup solution being in place and functional. And for appliance manufacturers, this doesn't involve a tremendous amount of added coding.
- The vendor can spend more time worrying about improving the graphical side to the product and marketing the product, rather than testing every last piece of equipment.

NDMP has so far been popular with various backup vendors, NAS vendors, tape library manufacturers, and others. Some of these software vendors include CommVault Systems, Mirapoint, Quantum|ATL, Spectra Logic, Tivoli, and Veritas (see Table 7.2).

Table 7.2: NDMP-Enabled Solutions by Vendor

Company	Solution	Product Type
CommVault	Galaxy	Backup software
Legato	NetWorker	Backup software
Veritas	NetBackup	Backup software
Quadratec	TimeNavigator for NDMP	Backup software
EMC	Celerra, IP/FC 4700	NAS appliances
Network Appliance	F85, F7xx, F8xx filers	NAS appliances
VA Linux	9205 NAS	NAS appliance
Land-5	IceNAS	Operating system
Network Appliance	Data ONTAP	Operating system

This is only a partial list of well-known solutions in the field. For a full list of solutions, visit www.ndmp.org/products/index.shtml. So, NDMP is synonymous with NAS, right? Well, that was the hope, and to most experts, the answer would be "yes." Before moving into that arena, let's look at where NDMP is in the standardization process.

NDMP Version 4

In the early part of the year 2000, NDMP versions 2 and 3 were equally deployed. There were various issues that needed to be resolved within the specifications, as with any developing set of standards. In April 2000 the Storage Network Industry Association (SNIA) formed a subgroup of the SNIA Backup Working group. Its goal was to handle the deficiencies that currently exist in NDMP. This has been a larger undertaking than was once expected. What began as a cleanup project turned into a full overhaul. This new NDMP group decided to move beyond the refinement process and submit NDMP version 4 to the Internet Engineering Task Force (IETF) to obtain standardization approval. With standardization of NDMP also comes greater notice from vendor interoperability and implementation.

If you would like to read more about NDMP, then visit the website at www.ndmp.org. The site will link you to every article and reference to NDMP and NAS you could ever hope for, including vendor information and case studies.

NDMP Version 5

There are plans in place to move toward NDMP version 5 and beyond. The good news is that these plans for continued revisions of NDMP once again show how NDMP is continuing to be a valid player in the storage industry. Some would call it the *de facto* standard for data management because of the ease of use for all vendors involved.

So, now that we've covered NAS, CIFS, NFS, and NDMP, let's move into the primary backup solutions for NAS appliances.

Backup Strategies for NAS

Captured storage (or storage inside of a server) and direct-attached storage (such as RAID arrays connected to servers) have their limitations in terms of scalability, but most administrators are comfortable with the way in which these storage structures are backed up. They've been handling it for years. What about NAS? Sure, it's less management intensive than the other two options, but NAS still has difficulty in providing protection for all those bytes of data.

The backup solutions for NAS are connected to both NDMP and the ability of various software companies to implement the different backup types that NDMP can handle.

Currently, the main options for backing up a NAS appliance include:

- Backing up over the LAN (without NDMP)
- Backing up from the filer to a locally attached tape drive/library (LAN free)
- Backing up from a filer to another filer (three-way)
- Backing up from filer to a server
- Backing up from a server to a filer

Let's visualize these options and see why you need to consider your options before buying the software.

Backing Up over the LAN (without NDMP)

Depending on your needs and budget, backing up over a LAN is a somewhat reasonable solution for your appliance backups. To accomplish this task you use either NFS or CIFS to pull the data from the filer through the LAN to be written to the backup media, as shown in Figure 7.4.

Figure 7.4: Mounting/mapping to the filer and backing up over the LAN

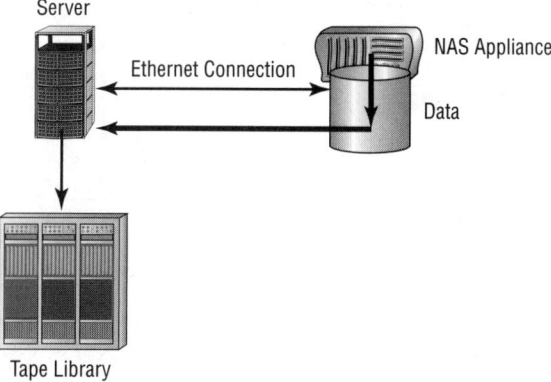

This solution is your only choice if your NAS appliance doesn't support NDMP and if you can't implement your solution on the appliance; however, there are two key problems with this solution.

Metadata (which is your security attributes, access control lists, and such) can be lost within this kind of backup, so check with your backup software vendor to ensure a workaround. One workaround that vendors have attempted is to port their agents to the appliance itself, which enables the metadata to be backed up, but this is not always a possibility.

Another problem with this solution involves the tremendous amount of LAN traffic that begins to build up as you add filers and your data increases. You can combat this with high-speed switches, or you might even try to create a secondary Ethernet network for your NAS backups—not a Fibre Channel SAN, but a cost-effective (ahem...cheap) solution to your problem.

Backing Up the Filer to a Locally Attached Library

By backing up the filer to a locally attached library, we use NDMP to send commands from a control system to the NAS appliance, as shown in Figure 7.5. The appliance has a tape device directly attached, and data from the filer is sent through either SCSI or Fibre Channel directly to the library.

Figure 7.5: Back up your appliance to a locally attached library.

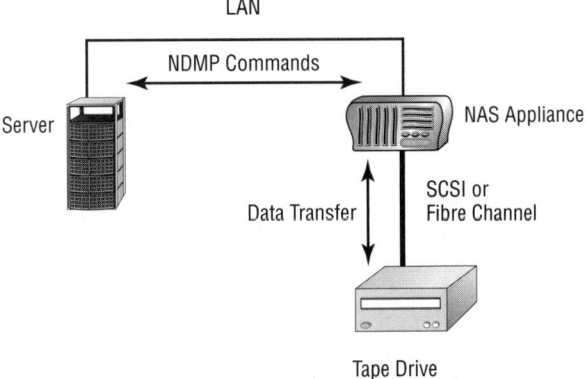

Now, this solution is somewhat flexible. It's considered *LAN-free* because the backup data path does not traverse the LAN. The flexibility comes in where you can attach one or more stand-alone drives to each filer, or you can take a library with multiple drives and attach each drive to a different filer. If SCSI distance limitations come into play, you might consider SAN Fibre Channel connections to a backup media library.

Backing Up from One Filer to Another (Three-Way)

This solution allows for one filer with a library attached to perform backups for other filers across the network, as shown in Figure 7.6. Now, this solution doesn't allow for a complete LAN-free operation, but it saves you money on libraries for every filer in your enterprise.

This solution is not recommended for large filers that will be sending a great deal of information over your LAN, even if you create a secondary backup LAN. This is a great solution for those smaller-sized filers. Stay with direct-attached SCSI drives for your larger filers to keep their traffic off the network.

Figure 7.6: Three-way backup

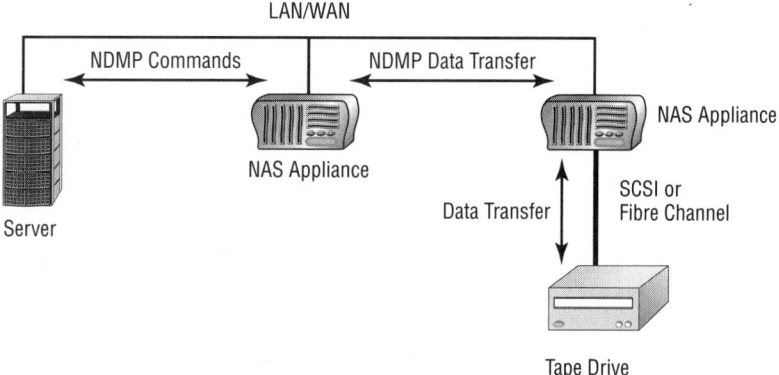

Backing Up from the Filer to the Server

This sounds like the first solution, right? It's a bit different. Once again, the tape drives are connected to the server, and the filers are sending their traffic over the network. However, rather than using mounted/mapped shares, you can use NDMP while CIFS and NFS remain out of the equation. You have the opportunity to back up all your clients and servers to one centrally managed location. The only dilemma is that you would need to install an NDMP Server application on the server to which you're backing up.

Backing Up from the Server to the Filer

This scenario also provides an enterprise solution. You want to alleviate pressure from the servers, right? How about alleviating the backup all together? In this option you attach the library to the appliance and then use NDMP to back up not the server but an NDMP client.

Who Supports What?

The last two options—backing up from the filer to the server and backing up from the server to the filer—are not as popular as the others. In fact, in most cases they're not supported.

Only Legato's BudTool and Workstation Solutions' Quick Restore supports all five backup options. But Veritas NetBackup, CommVault's Galaxy, SyncSort's Backup Express, and Quadratec's Time Navigator can support backing up over the LAN with mounted/mapped exports/shares, the LAN-free, and the three-way backups. (Competition being what it is, these companies may have solutions for the additional backup types for NAS by the time of this printing.)

> **NOTE** Terminology differs depending on the operating system. Unix mounts *exports*, and Windows uses *mapped shares*.

Research a vendor's abilities before spending money on a solution that may not meet your envisioned needs. Your data is too valuable to leave to chance. If NAS through NDMP is your solution, then your backup solution should complement your choice.

NAS: The Microsoft Way

Does it seem a bit strange that NAS and Microsoft would go together? Well, in early 2001 Microsoft entered the NAS game, teaming up with some heavy players to move quickly into the market. This section covers an overview of what Microsoft is offering and what their partners are putting on the market.

> **NOTE** If you want more information about Microsoft and NAS, go to www.microsoft.com/windows/powered/nas/default.asp.

Windows-Powered NAS?

You may have thought that an appliance must come with a light operating system such as a proprietary one, such as ONTAP by Network Appliance, or a toned-down version of Linux. Well, most of us thought the same thing, but Microsoft makes the rules. Windows-powered NAS is pretty cool actually.

So, how does it work?

A NAS appliance utilizing Windows-powered NAS is manufactured by a vendor that strikes a deal with Microsoft. If you'd like a current list, visit the Microsoft site (www.microsoft.com/windows/powered/nas/default.asp). In fact, Microsoft has directions and a tool called the Server Appliance Kit (SAK) that makes it easy to build server appliances with Windows 2000.

Microsoft allows Windows 2000 to be installed on the device so that it can take advantage of the file-serving features (as well as all of the great Windows 2000 features for handling files such as EFS). So, is this really NAS, as the definition has come to be known, or is it just a Windows 2000 Server? It is NAS; let's explain why.

Microsoft terms these appliances *Windows-powered* because manufacturers creating these appliances take the Windows 2000 operating system and just turn off services that are not going to be used. Then they go ahead and install the operating system on the box they create. Then they add their personalized web interface (or use the one Microsoft has created for these appliances) to the appliance. You now have a NAS appliance that can be plugged into the network and up and running quickly without a great deal of overhead. But let's look more closely at what Microsoft is allowing here.

Microsoft claims several key features of NAS appliances running Windows 2000:

- Easy implementation
- Windows 2000 proven abilities
- Easy administration
- Interoperability with Active Directory

There are other features, but these are the main ones. As we break these down, you might just find you like this as a possibility, even if you're a die-hard NAS administrator who gets nauseous at the thought of an operating system with millions of lines of code running on anything called *NAS*.

Easy Implementation

Plug it in, turn it on, and it works. It doesn't get much simpler than that with any Microsoft product. OK, there have to be some configuration issues, right? What about the IP address and machine name? That is true. The hardware and software are installed and preconfigured to allow only for file sharing. In fact, Microsoft makes it clear these appliances will not support any features other than file sharing. They cannot become Domain Controllers, DNS servers, or DHCP servers. They have one job only. So, the configuration is easy from that standpoint. To configure it during deployment, you would use a browser-based configuration where you would only need to know the machine name and an IP addressing scheme for the filer. There are claims that you can have the box running in 15 minutes or less, which is what NAS is all about, right?

Along with easy implementation, Windows-powered NAS supports both Windows and non-Windows (in other words, Unix or Unix-based) clients.

Windows 2000 Proven Abilities

Windows 2000 has proven itself to be a tremendous improvement over its predecessors in terms of reliability and scalability, not to mention its subset of integrated features. Even the remote storage solutions covered in Chapter 4, "Working with Removable Storage Manager," are phenomenal enhancements.

However, one reliability concern is the need for frequent reboots—something for which Windows is notorious. Other NAS appliances have already proven that when they come up, they stay up. Remember that the version of Windows that is incorporated into the NAS appliance is a locked-down version that will not require a great deal of administration or maintenance downtime because these services are proven as reliable. Applications that may interfere with this process of uptime are also disallowed under the agreement with Microsoft. Neither the user nor the information technology (IT) departments can install additional software on the filer.

Windows 2000 supports hot-plug drives, RAID, and clustering. All of these are still allowed in Windows-powered appliances. Also included in Windows 2000 is driver signing and Distributed File System (Dfs) and Encrypted File System (EFS). Of course, the more that is supported, the bigger the need for a well-trained management staff who understands these features and the higher your TCO. It's a catch-22.

And all of the great RSM and RSS features that you learned about in Chapter 4 are also included. They create bigger staff needs, but again, greater product features.

Easy Administration

Microsoft NAS appliances can be handled through Web-Based Enterprise Management (WBEM), which is a combination of Windows Management Instrumentation (WMI) and Component Object Model (COM) technologies. The goal is what they term a *headless* setup. Meaning, you don't have to be sitting at the box to implement or administrate it.

You can also administer the appliance through the Microsoft Management Console (MMC) or even through a terminal services session.

Interoperability with Active Directory

The NAS appliance can become an object within Active Directory, which allows you to manage it through your Active Directory tools as you would any other file server. This includes security features of Windows 2000 Active Directory and even Group Policies.

Also, support for Kerberos is included (which is an industry-supported form of security developed through MIT that Microsoft has incorporated within Windows 2000 Active Directory).

What's Wrong with This Picture?

When Microsoft first hit the market with its Windows for Workgroups, they weren't ready with an enterprise solution and they knew that. Even with NT 4.0 they were just beginning to formulate larger-scale solutions. Well, Windows-powered NAS appliances come with a unique pitch.

Not only does Microsoft omit NDMP (an open standard protocol that would make it possible for any developer to work with backup solutions), but it doesn't even mention it in the documentation. Doesn't Microsoft know it would be a question people would ask?

Well, we went looking for the answer. We called Microsoft, Dell, Maxtor, Veritas, and so on looking for solutions. The support personnel we spoke with attempted to convey the answer but weren't quite sure what the answer was.

Our main question was this: What does a Window-powered appliance use to perform direct-attached backups to a library connected through the device's built-in SCSI port?

The final answer: There was not much of a difference between a regular server with a built-in SCSI adapter needing to back up data and one of these Microsoft Powered NAS appliances. Those companies that Microsoft has approved, such as Veritas, have a light version of their volume managers (the light Backup Exec application) pre-installed, and that eliminates the need for NDMP because, remember, one reason for the protocol standards were to prevent the need for more lines of code on NAS filers. Windows 2000 is filled with code, so what's a little more?

So, controlling the backup is easy without the need to install additional software. In addition, other backup companies that already work with Windows 2000 are allowed to install their managers on the appliance. This makes for a great solution all around. Even though initially we considered the lack of NDMP to be a limitation, the reality is that Microsoft doesn't need it, and the backup software vendors don't either. If your software works on Windows, then it will work on these server appliances.

Now, if you happen to be a lover of NDMP, then another option you have is to install NDMP server software (you can find, or create, your own) and back up with NDMP through that.

There are plenty of devices available, and we'll cover the configuration of one of the major players of NDMP-compliant NAS filers: Network Appliance.

NAS by Network Appliance

Network Appliance filers are a proven, reliable product. They come in various shapes, sizes, and colors, and they must weigh a ton (definitely a two-person job if you plan on carrying one of these). But, starting at $50,000 on certain models (close to the price of a new Porsche), you would expect a little more weight to the package.

Network Appliance's product line includes some flexible solutions that require some forethought before choosing. For example, the Network Appliance 840c is enhanced in its design for multiple processors in an active/active clustered failover. The 840c scales up to 12TB of network-accessible data. The regular 840 scales up to 6TB. The other filers scale down from this point with the 820c supporting 6TB in cluster, the 820 supporting 3TB, the F760 supporting 3TB (6TB in cluster), the F740 supporting 1TB, and the F85 scaling up to 648GB.

> **NOTE** Do not put your Exchange database files on NAS network drives. Although Performance Optimizer doesn't allow you to do this, you can edit the Registry or Active Directory to allow for the file paths to be forced. We aren't saying that it won't work, just that Microsoft will not support it if you do this. One of the reasons for the lack of support is that Exchange requires a good deal of input/output (I/O)—as any high-performance database program would. Putting your Exchange database files on your NAS server may create I/O timeouts and reliability issues. For further information on this problem, go to Microsoft's TechNet website at www.microsoft.com/technet and search for "Q288212" within the Knowledge Base.

Each of these offers differing size and price solutions, but they all provide the easy-to-manage ONTAP operating system. Let's consider a few other key points to Network Appliance filers before we walk through a configuration of one.

Network Appliance filers include software by Network Appliance called SnapMirror and SnapRestore as part of the ONTAP operating system. This software includes the Snapshot function, which will store up to 31 read-only versions of a filer's volumes. The ability to perform these snapshots is great, but what's even better is the ability to do it online with minimal disk time. Now, the benefit here is that files that have been lost can be retrieved from the snapshot without restoring the entire snapshot.

SnapMirror allows you to use the Snapshot feature and send it across your LAN or Wide Area Network (WAN) to another Network Appliance filer. This is great for disaster recovery purposes but also for backing up the filer as a form of backup/recovery solution and for testing various scenarios without using your production environment. Another great feature to SnapMirror is the ability it has to send incremental updates throughout the day to ensure an up-to-date picture.

SnapRestore, using the Snapshot feature of the ONTAP operating system, will allow you the opportunity to restore volumes that have become corrupt or infected by virus. It resembles technology that you may have worked with before such as the ability to create an image that can restore the entire structure back in minutes instead of hours.

Snapshots 101

Snapshots add a fourth dimension (time) to a file system's content. The Network Appliance file system (WAFL) can "freeze frame" itself at any point in time and make the frozen versions of the file system available via "special" subdirectories that appear in the active file system. These frozen frames are called *snapshots* and, depending on the filer and the ONTAP version your filer is using, that will determine the number of snapshots that can be made. The point is that you not only have the ability to restore the snapshot, but individual files within the shot can be restored. In fact, restoring a file from a snapshot appears to be as easy as connecting to a filer's snapshot directory and locating the subdirectory that holds the last snapshot, whether it is hourly, weekly, or daily (which is found under the nightly subdirectory). To recover a deleted file or folder, the user simply drags the file from the snapshot directory and copies it to their home directory.

The concern is that these snapshots would utilize a tremendous amount of disk space. Each snapshot appears to the user as though it is a read-only copy of the active file system, independently maintained on a separate area of the filer's disks. This is not how Snapshots work, and actually, the snapshots usually require only a tiny amount of disk space. How is that possible?

Snapshots work at the block level. With any file system, each user-visible file and directory is composed of some set of blocks on the physical media. WAFL is the same in this respect. When an initial snapshot is taken, the snapshot uses the same set of disk blocks that make up the file in the active file system. The snapshot contains pointers that lead off to the original disk block location, which is why the snapshot doesn't take much space. The trick comes in when a change is made. If a document is changed, the portion of that document that resides on a particular disk block is the only portion that is changed. With a file system that supports snapshots, rather than change the original disk block, a new block is used and given a different name. See Figure 7.7 for an illustration.

Figure 7.7: How Snapshot works

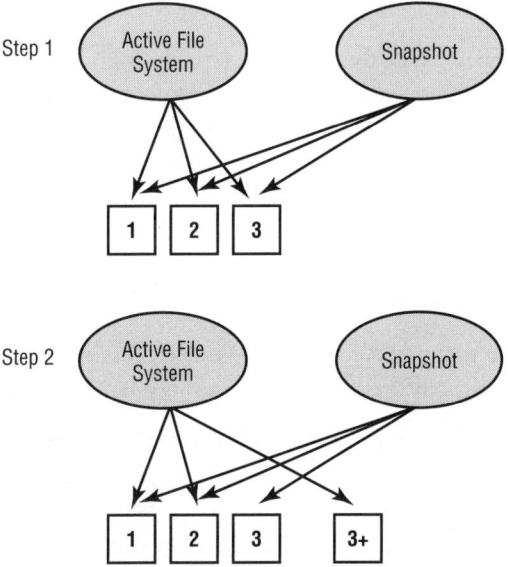

Now, the new block is part of the active file, and the older block is still in existence and part of the former snapshot pointer. So, in reality, the snapshots begin to use disk space when files change and blocks increase, rather than overwriting the existing block.

Using Snapshots

An administrator can kick off a snapshot whenever they feel inclined, but the nice feature for Snapshots is the scheduler, SnapSchedule. This enables administrators to define hourly or *intraday* shots, nightly, and weekly shots. Network Appliance filers come with an administrative guide that explains how to work with the SnapSchedule application.

Snapshots have a tremendous impact on backup, restore, and archive operations. There are so many factors to consider when trying to put a disaster recovery process in place for your organization. For example, what is your window for backup, how do you verify the integrity of your backup data, and how fast can you back up your data? These are all important considerations, and the more businesses that move toward 24/7 working scenarios, the shorter those windows become. And then, what is to say that after a backup has completed, a user doesn't change the file? The snapshot technology, implemented within Network Appliance tools, such as SnapMirror and SnapRestore, can resolve a good deal of these problems. They take seconds to do and facilitate your need to have 24/7/365 uptime.

Snapshots are not only a scheduled feature but are also used by tape backup software that uses the "dump" command through NDMP-compliant backups. These backups will grab backup data from the Snapshot copy, which eliminates the need for the file system to be taken offline or for you to worry about open files.

A variety of strategies can be used between snapshots and tape backups, depending on your needs. For example, you might use snapshot technology for daily online backups and then use tape backups on the weekend. This ensures the weekly backup and allows users to recover their files in the case of an error. In addition, let's say you have several filers in your organization. If certain units have more critical data, then those filers can perform intraday snapshot copies. Another possibility is to use the SnapMirror application to copy your snapshots to another filer for fault tolerance. For a great article that includes case studies of snapshot utilization within various companies, go to www.netapp.com/tech_library/3066.html.

One final positive point to Network Appliance filers that we haven't mentioned is their ability to add additional shelves of disks that are hardware RAID swappable disks.

Now let's go through the preparation involved in putting one of these filers up on the network.

Implementing Your Network Appliance Filer

Now, wait a minute, don't you merely plug in a filer, it works, and that's it? Not quite. You should still know how to access the filer, set it up, create volumes and QTrees, and so on. We will talk you through some of this, so don't worry. If your company happened to purchase one (or more) filers, it comes with a great set of instruction manuals. And, remember, the ONTAP operating system is not filled with a billion lines of code. There is only so much you can do, and most of it is from a web-based administration screen.

For remote administration, there are several ways to get into the Network Appliance box; we will show you a few of them and go through a couple of commands. The following methods can be used to administer a Network Appliance filer:

- SNMP
- Telnet
- HTTP
- HyperTerminal connection

NOTE In using a HyperTerminal connection, make sure you can use the serial port in the back of your Network Appliance filer titled *CONSOLE*. Connect your RS-232 Cable (Null Model cable) into this port. Do not use the connection point called *DIAGNOSTIC,* which is for the Network Appliance techs to play with.

To get a look at the backup options of a Network Appliance filer, consider Figure 7.8, which shows you the redundant power supply connections.

Using HyperTerminal

Although there are several options, we will be walking through the initial configuration using HyperTerminal. Once your cable is connected to the proper serial port, then establish your HyperTerminal settings. Choose 9600 Baud, with 8 data bits and XON/XOFF flow control.

You may be wondering why you need to use HyperTerminal. One of the reasons why you may need to begin with HyperTerminal is that you may need to change the IP address of the filer to work with your domain and subnet. This is done through the serial connection by typing in the command Setup and then answering a series of questions or, in some cases, leaving the default answers.

Once you are sure that the filer is set up and on the network through HyperTerminal, test it by pinging the box by its IP address. Depending on your name resolution, you want to ensure that you can ping it by name, so you may have to create a manual entry for the filer.

Figure 7.8: The rear of a Network Appliance filer

For a look inside the filer, see Figure 7.9.

Figure 7.9: The internals of a Network Appliance filer

To ensure that you are connecting to the correct port, Figure 7.10 shows you the ones in use.

Figure 7.10: The various serial ports on the back of the filer

Once you are able to connect and the filer is functioning on your TCP/IP network, you will now have the option of using either a command-line administration method or a web-based method. A web interface is usually easier to work with and requires less command-line memorization.

Remember to Verify

It is now time to verify that the NDMP service is enabled and running on the filer. Use the web-based administration interface to turn on the NDMP service, or run the ndmpd on command from the filer console or Telnet session. Note that if you use the command-line method, the service will be disabled again upon reboot, unless you use the commands into a script the filer runs upon boot. To keep ndmpd permanently enabled, you must add the ndmpd on command to the end of the system startup script in /etc/rc. The web-based interface will do this for you automatically.

The Web-Based Interface

To access the web-based interface, you need to open Internet Explorer and type in the IP address (or, with DNS resolution, the name of the filer) of the filer with a forward slash and then **na_admin**. For example:

    http://192.1.1.1/na_admin

This will take you to the screen shown in Figure 7.11.

Figure 7.11: The IE entry screen for administration

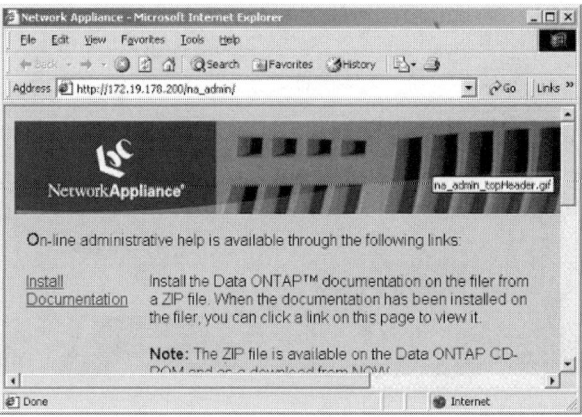

From within this screen you would scroll down and choose the hyperlink that allows you to administer the filer. Before being allowed access to the inner courtyard of the filer's administration tools, you would be faced with a password screen. After entering your information, hit OK. You will then be taken into the screen shown in Figure 7.12.

Once inside the administrative interface, you can navigate your way down to the NDMP option and expand it. Then select the Enable/Disable option, as shown in Figure 7.13.

Keep in mind that the choice is up to you as to whether you use NDMP. There is no hard and fast rule, but if you want to take advantage of these features, then you'll have to turn it on. Now, this is an option that isn't configured straight out of the box, so you need to take a second to configure it.

Figure 7.12: The Network Appliance filer's administration interface

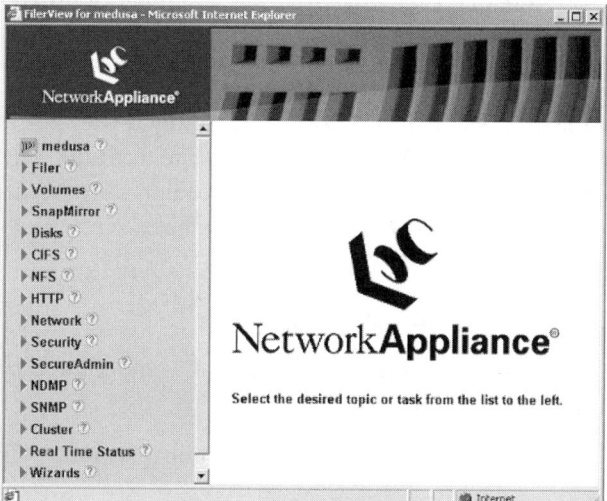

Figure 7.13: The NDMP services portion

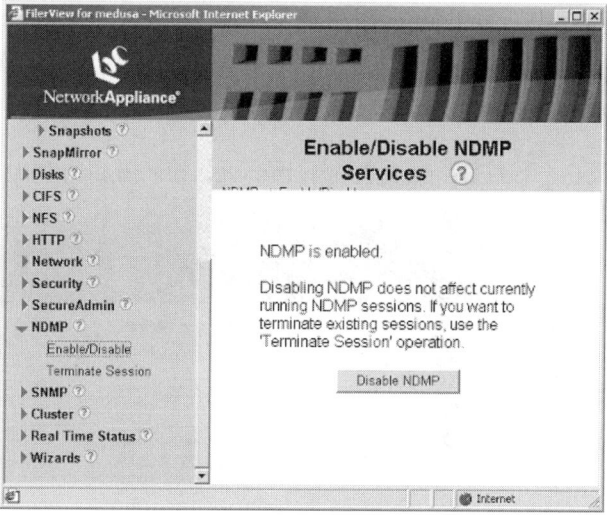

Further, there may be a few other options in which you are interested. For example, if you plan on using LAN-free or three-way backups, then you may want to verify that the tape drive is visible to the filer. You accomplish this by connecting in through the HyperTerminal or through Telnet and running the sysconfig -t command, which will provide you with the various tape device names available that the filer relates with your drive or library. Note that each tape drive has a number of different aliases; choosing an alias, in effect, determines the behavior of the tape device.

Device names with the n prefix are "no-rewind" devices; this means that when an application closes the tape device, it will not automatically rewind the tape. The suffixes—l, m, h, or a—determine the density mode used to write to a tape. The letters stand for low, medium, high, and high density with hardware compression, respectively. (We know, the a doesn't quite fit.) The number is an instance number; zero usually corresponds to the first tape drive.

Use Additional Commands and Options

Use the vol and qtree commands to determine the amount of disk storage available on the filer and note how it is organized.

Of course, you could be asking the very reasonable question, "What is a QTree?"

These are special subdirectories under the root directory of a volume. These are great for quick and easy backups because you can structure your data down into smaller chunks and point your backup software to center in, not on the whole volume but on an individual QTree. They might seem like subfolders of your volume, but they are a bit different in that you can configure them to use different file systems, too.

You can use the qtree command or access the information through the web-based interface, as shown in Figures 7.14 and 7.15.

Figure 7.14: Viewing the QTrees through the web-based administrative tool

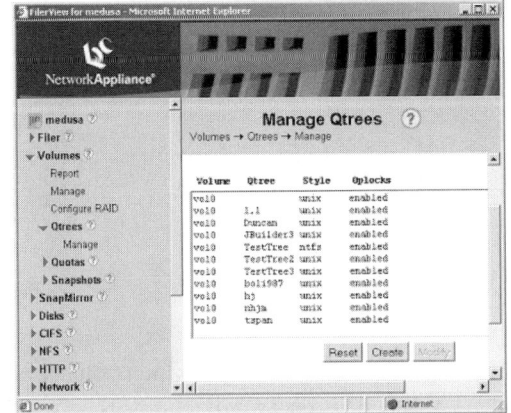

Figure 7.15: Viewing the QTrees through the command-line interface

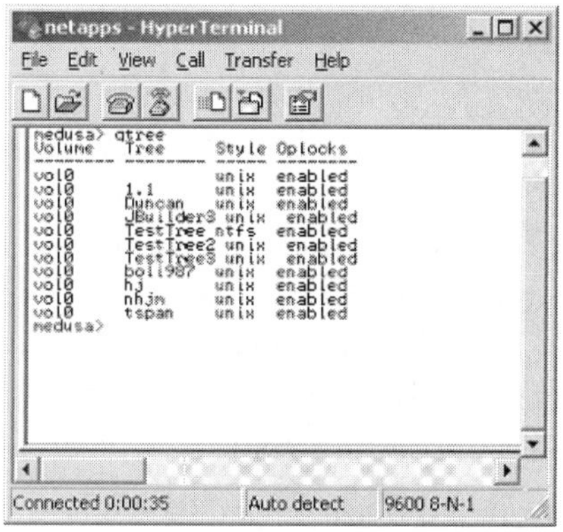

> **NOTE** If you want to learn more about your Network Appliance filer, you can take a class from Network Appliance or visit their website at www.netapp.com.

To round out your knowledge of NAS appliances, we want to also mention the EMC solution.

EMC NAS

Two great products on the market by EMC (www.emc.com) for file services are the Celerra and the IP/FC 4700 Series.

EMC solutions for NAS are not for small-business owners. They include some incredible features that come with a high price. They use all of the aforementioned NAS features, including being NDMP enabled. They come with great failover support, utilizing up to four data movers with a failover data mover. And the EMC product line includes TimeFinder, which is the EMC version of snapshot backup software. The Celerra and the IP/FC 4700 Series are easy to work with, too, as NAS should be.

NAS and the Future

You can honestly say that you are at the forefront of this industry. But the storage field changes daily at times. What do you need to be aware of to keep up with the future of storage? Well, even we aren't mind readers. But we know you should watch out for these three topics:

- iSCSI
- Virtualization
- Millipede technology

iSCSI provides a new approach to storage. It allows you to put native SCSI over IP. Rather than needing Fibre Channel to attach a library to multiple servers for a SAN configuration, you can use iSCSI, which is a cheaper solution and will allow for smaller, localized SANs to be created using a more common Ethernet implementation. However, as good as this sounds, it's still under development. Cisco and IBM are working on solutions, but they are going through hard times with this. See Chapter 14, "The Future of Storage," to read more on IBM's progress on iSCSI.

Virtualization is entering the NAS market and should be watched. Tricord Systems (www.tricord.com), for example, released its Lunar Flare NAS, which gathers the appliances into one mass to create a cluster controlled as a single resource or virtual storage pool. See Chapter 6, "Storage Area Networks (SANs)," for more on virtualization concepts.

Millipede technology is being worked on by several different companies, IBM being at the forefront. In millipede technology, chemical reactions can cause small magnetic particles to formulate mechanically by design. The belief is that this will allow more than 100 times the amount of data storage on disk. Who knows what this technology will cost? See Chapter 14, "The Future of Storage," for more information.

Want to know more? There are tons of places to start. EMC and Network Appliance offers hands-on courses that teach you about their products. Odds are good that if you know how to work with one form of NAS, understand what NDMP is all about, and know how NFS/CIFS comes into play, then you'll quickly be able to port that knowledge to other forms of NAS.

8

RAID Technology

Many professionals in the storage industry are beginning to think differently about storage. For quite some time, we thought of backup as our means of data protection, and magnetic media was used mainly as the primary storage medium for network servers. It was not practical to use tapes as a primary storage device because of their speed (or lack thereof). However, tapes were—and still are—an effective and inexpensive means to archive data. Now think for a moment about the growth of storage over the past 10 years. When upgrading a 120MB hard drive to an 840MB drive several years ago, it seemed like the space could never be filled up. Boy, were we wrong!

Storage requirements have skyrocketed, but the cost of magnetic storage has traveled steadily in the opposite direction. Magnetic media will always be faster than tape, but one of magnetic media's major drawbacks has been cost. So, with the cost of magnetic hard disks falling, this is not a major concern anymore.

Why else is magnetic storage the wave of the future? Consider your organization's mail server. We have spoken with some people at NASA who swear that space shuttles would not launch if NASA employees lost access to their e-mail. This might be an overstatement, but our point is that having a database or mail server down for even an hour is usually too long.

If a hard disk, or even a server fails, data must remain available. Building fault-tolerant disks is the first step to achieving constant availability. In this chapter, you will learn how you can maximize data availability through the use of properly planned and configured magnetic storage. We will look at the alternatives to magnetic storage, such as hardware and software Redundant Array of Inexpensive—or Independent—Disks (RAID), and how to implement these solutions in your environment.

Just a Bunch of Disks (JBOD)

As the need for zero downtime for data continues to grow, so does industry acceptance of RAID technology. Before RAID, and even in some instances today, there was Just a Bunch of Disks (JBOD). Some define *JBOD* as simply having more than one disk in a server. Some simply say, "If you have multiple disks, and they are not configured as RAID, then they are JBOD." After all, you have a bunch of disks together in some type of device. In this sense, you could say that the term fits.

The more recognized and defined use for JBOD is *disk spanning*. Disk spanning is a storage technique not defined by RAID standards. With disk spanning, you can configure several disks to act as one large disk. For example, suppose you have three 10GB IDE hard disks. You can configure all three disks to act as one large disk. Do not confuse disk spanning with *disk striping*, though. With disk striping, if you were to configure three disks, all three disks would be written to simultaneously. With disk spanning, disks are written to sequentially. Thus, the operating system will write to the first physical disk until it is full and then will begin writing to the second disk, and so on. With this configuration, multiple physical disks will act as one large disk but are written to sequentially as opposed to being written to simultaneously (see Figure 8.1).

NOTE If you are still not fully clear on JBOD, consider it to be the opposite of *partitioning*. When you partition a disk, you divide one physical drive into multiple logical drives. With JBOD, or disk spanning, you link multiple physical drives together as one logical drive.

Figure 8.1: As each physical disk reaches capacity, the next physical disk is written to.

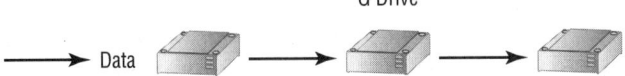

When to Use JBOD

You should use JBOD in these circumstances:

- You have a bunch of mismatched disks (different sizes) that you want to act as a single volume.

- You are not concerned with disk fault tolerance.
- You are not dual booting the server with the spanned volumes configured.

When JBOD Is Not the Answer

You should not use JBOD in these circumstances:

- You need fault tolerance, but spanned volumes in Windows 2000 cannot recover from the loss of even one disk, so all data will be lost.
- You are dual booting and another operating system will need to access the disk, but spanned volumes are not compatible with other operating systems.
- You want to increase input/output (I/O) by combining the disks into a single logical volume, but spanning volumes provides no performance advantage and may even decrease disk I/O.

Some information technology (IT) folks love the JBOD acronym, and perhaps that is why it is still around. But using RAID configurations to support multiple disks is probably the direction you will go in because, as you will see, RAID offers several advantages over JBOD.

Redundant Array of Inexpensive Disks (RAID)

Pick up any book on network servers or certification, and you are bound to see a couple of pages on RAID. To be different, we will concentrate on what you need to know, without boring you with a RAID history lesson.

> **NOTE** Although many use the word *Inexpensive* in the RAID acronym, you may also see RAID defined as a *Redundant Array of Independent Disks*. Both versions of the RAID acronym are accepted throughout the industry.

RAID 0

RAID level 0 is considered to be the first RAID level; however, many do not even recognize RAID 0 as being applicable. Consider the first word in the RAID acronym: *redundant*. RAID 0 does not provide any redundancy. Although RAID 0 allows you to logically create a single volume that uses several physical disks, it does not provide for any fault tolerance. If a single disk crashes, you will lose all the data saved on all disks in the array (see Figure 8.2).

Figure 8.2: One logical drive and three physical drives being written to simultaneously

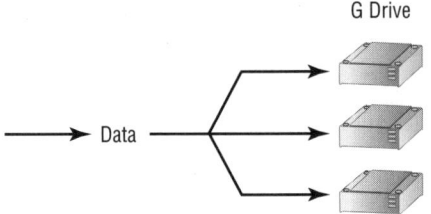

RAID 0 disk arrays are known as *striped volumes* in Windows 2000. A striped volume is the set of disks participating in disk striping. With RAID 0, data is evenly striped across multiple physical disks. To keep the operation simple, let's consider a word analogy. Imagine if you were trying to store the three-letter world *dog*. You have three cups to store the letters, so you place all three letters in the three cups in one motion. Taking the letters out of the cups in the reverse order allows you to retrieve the stored word. However, if you lost any of the cups, the word (data) would be lost. If the cup was lost, you have no way of knowing what data was ever in it. This is the problem with RAID 0. Although it is exceptionally fast, it has no built-in fault tolerance.

When to Use RAID 0
You should use RAID 0 in these circumstances:

- You want optimal disk I/O performance. Nothing is better.
- You do not need redundancy.
- It's great for when you need to temporarily and quickly store files.

When RAID 0 Is Not the Answer
You should not use RAID 0 in these circumstances:

- You need fault tolerance, but striped volumes cannot recover from the failure of a single disk.
- You can afford to sacrifice a slight degradation in performance in exchange for fault tolerance

RAID 1
RAID 1 comes in two forms:

- Disk mirroring
- Disk duplexing

You use RAID 1 to create fault tolerance for a portion of a physical disk. With RAID 1, a second volume will "shadow" another volume. Whatever data is written to or deleted from one volume will be repeated on the second volume. Mirroring volumes is an ideal way to maximize server availability. As with RAID 0, multiple physical disks will act as a single logical volume. For example, suppose users access the mirrored E volume on a file server. If one of the physical disks that make up the mirror fails, users can still read and write data to the second physical disk (see Figure 8.3).

Figure 8.3: Two physical disks acting as one logical drive. Each bit written to the logical drive goes to every physical drive in the mirror set.

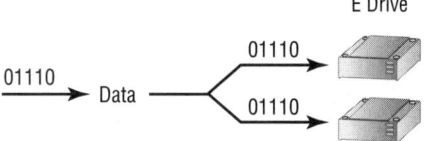

When you implement a RAID 1 array, you can configure it using disk mirroring or disk duplexing. The difference between the two is slight but important:

- Disk mirroring is when you use two physical disks controlled by the same controller to configure the RAID 1 array.
- Disk duplexing is when you use two physical disks controlled by different controllers to configure the RAID 1 array.

> **TIP** You use RAID 1 to eliminate a single point of failure: the failure of a physical disk. By using disk duplexing, each disk in the mirror set is on a separate controller. This eliminates another single point of failure.

When to Use RAID 1

You should use RAID 1 in these circumstances:

- You want to implement a simple (two-disk) form of data redundancy.
- You want to mirror the complete operating system over multiple volumes, providing for redundancy and quick recovery in the event that the operating system's primary volume fails.
- You want to create protection for server databases, which may include mirroring drives that contain system data such as:
    - WINS, DHCP, DNS data
    - Active Directory Database

When RAID 1 Is Not the Answer

You should not use RAID 1 in this circumstance:

- You want to save money. (With RAID 1, you double the amount of storage space you need per megabyte.)

> **NOTE** We are concentrating on the most popular RAID levels. If you want information on other implementations of RAID, search TechNet at www.Microsoft.com/Technet using the keyword "RAID."

RAID 5

RAID 5 is similar to RAID 0 in that data is striped across multiple disks, except for two differences:

- RAID 5 requires three or more disks to implement.
- RAID 5 incorporates the use of parity for data protection, allowing a RAID 5 array to recover from the loss of a single disk.

In Windows terminology, you will typically hear a RAID 5 volume called a *stripe set with parity*. We are going to spare you the details of how the parity bit is distributed across the disk array in a round-robin fashion and how the Exclusive OR (X-OR) process works to fully recover a RAID 5 volume when one of its physical disks crashes. Other books spend several pages on this process, but although knowing it may help you answer a Jeopardy question one day, all you need to know is that it allows you to recover from the failure of one disk. What happens if more disks in the array fail? You're out of luck. Buy better hardware and then restore from a backup.

RAID 5, in offering performance just slightly below that of RAID 0 and in providing for fault tolerance, has emerged as the most popular RAID implementation today.

Sizing Your RAID 5 Array

Parity, while providing data protection, does come at a cost. The basic cost to you will be one physical drive. For example, if your RAID 5 array consists of four 10GB hard disks, you will have 30GB of available storage—meaning you are losing 25 percent of your total storage for parity. As you add more disks, the cost lowers. Say you had five 20GB disks in your array. Although you will have 80GB of available disk space, the cost is decreased to 20 percent.

When to Use RAID 5

You should use RAID 5 in these circumstances:

- You want to optimize file access for a server, while also providing for protection against the loss of a single disk.
- Availability is a primary concern. You cannot afford to have the loss of a single disk down your server.

When RAID 5 Is Not the Answer

You should not use RAID 5 in these circumstances:

- You need more fault tolerance than protection against the failure of a single disk.
- You cannot afford to give up storage space for parity protection (as cheap as magnetic storage is becoming, this is not a good argument).
- You want the I/O performance of RAID 0. If disk write speed is important, you may be better off with RAID 10.

RAID 10

You have already learned the main players in RAID configurations. Now we are going to pair some of them up. RAID 0 is good for pure speed but provides no fault tolerance. There is no cost associated with implementing RAID 0 in terms of disk space. RAID 1 provides fault tolerance but at a high cost. If you are storing 10GB of data to a mirror set, you need 20GB of storage space—10GB on each physical volume.

RAID 10 works by combining RAID 1 and RAID 0. When you build a RAID 10 array, you are creating a stripe set that writes to mirrored disks. The mirrored disks provide the fault tolerance, while striping data to the disks increases disk I/O performance. What you wind up with is a fast RAID 1 array (see Figure 8.4).

When to Use RAID 10

You should use RAID 10 in these circumstances:

- You want better performance than RAID 5 but want to add a level of fault tolerance as well.
- You have money.

When RAID 10 Is Not the Answer

You should not use RAID 10 in these circumstances:

- You do not have the money to buy the additional hardware. RAID 10 inherits the cost of RAID 1. This means that 50 percent of the storage you bought is used for the shadow disks.
- You do not need the I/O boost of a RAID 0 implementation. Instead, RAID 5 is probably ideal for you.

Figure 8.4: Data written to what the operating system believes is one drive. Data is striped across multiple mirror sets.

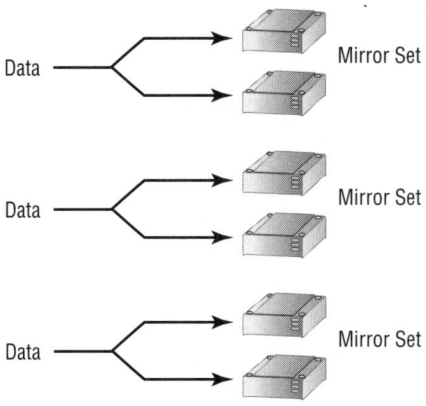

RAID 50

Although RAID 10 adds an element of fault tolerance to RAID 0, it does so at a high cost. You need double the amount of storage (disk) space than the total amount of data you plan on storing on the RAID array. In other words, if you plan to store 500GB of data, you will need a 1000GB (1TB) RAID 10 volume. Another alternative to RAID 10, providing fast I/O and fault tolerance as well, is RAID 50. Instead of combining RAID 1 and RAID 0, RAID 5 combines RAID 5 and RAID 0. Instead of striping data across RAID 1 volumes, with RAID 50, data is striped across RAID 5 stripe sets with parity (see Figure 8.5).

Figure 8.5: Data is written to what the operating system believes is one drive. The data is striped across multiple RAID 5 stripe sets with parity.

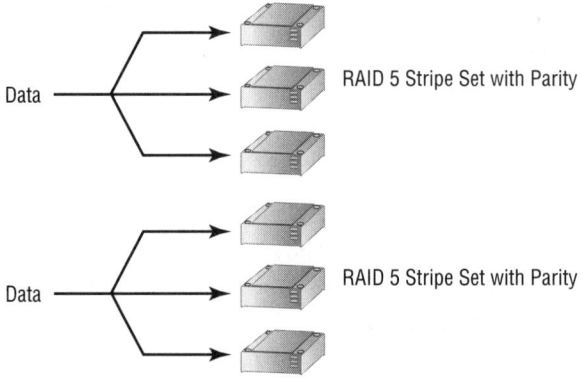

Compared to RAID 5, you will see an increased write performance with RAID 50. However, it has been observed that once a physical drive fails and a RAID 5 array has to be regenerated, overall performance of the RAID 50 array will be slower. RAID 50 does, however, provide you will better fault tolerance than a standard RAID 5 array. Because RAID 50 consists of multiple RAID 5 arrays, the RAID 50 array can withstand the loss of a hard disk in each of its RAID 5 subarrays and still run. For the array shown in Figure 8.5, a disk on each side of the array can fail without taking the logical volume configured to write to the array offline.

When to Use RAID 50

You should use RAID 50 in these circumstances:

- You are looking for improved reliability over RAID 5.
- You have the budget to purchase the additional disk array(s).
- You want to implement a higher level of fault tolerance than what RAID 10 offers.

When RAID 50 Is Not the Answer

You should not use RAID 50 in these circumstances:

- You cannot afford to mirror RAID 5 arrays to provide a high level of availability. RAID 50 is an expensive solution!
- Data stored on the RAID array doesn't require the availability that you get with RAID 50.

Hardware RAID

If you are trying to implement RAID the best way (and some would argue the only right way), then hardware RAID is your answer. Hardware RAID operates transparently to the operating system and presents all physical disks configured in the RAID array as a single disk to the operating system. On the operating system, you can do whatever you want to what is believed to be a single disk.

Hardware RAID is preferred mainly because of its ability to recover from failures. There are no software settings, such as Advanced RISC Computing (ARC) path changes, that you will have to make when a disk fails as you would with software RAID. Once you decide on the RAID configuration you want to implement, most of the RAID setup will be done on the RAID controller's Basic Input Output System (BIOS). This is not much different than any other BIOS. You will simply have to navigate a small series of basic menus. The documentation that comes with your RAID controller should be all you need to configure a hardware RAID array successfully.

Another major advantage of hardware RAID is that a dedicated controller manages the array. With software RAID, a high degree of Central Processing Unit (CPU) cycles is needed to maintain the array. If the CPU on your server is already being heavily taxed, software RAID is probably not even an option for you.

Also, if you want to implement some of the more advanced forms of RAID, such as RAID 10 and RAID 50, you will again need to turn to hardware-based RAID. The RAID configuration itself is set in the BIOS of the RAID controller card. You will do this during bootup. Controller cards usually give you the flexibility to configure your array from the simple BIOS menus. Some of these menus can be a little tricky, so you should consult the controller card's documentation before beginning the configuration.

In most controller card BIOS menus, you will see an option to perform a low-level format of a drive. Remember that formatting is formatting, meaning you will lose everything on a drive. Usually, you use the BIOS to troubleshoot a SCSI bus, such as to see that the bus is recognizing all the drives you have installed. If the controller BIOS does not see the drives, then Windows won't see them either.

One of the detractors to hardware RAID has been its cost. With prices of magnetic storage and SCSI falling drastically, you will find that hardware RAID solutions are pretty cost effective now.

Here are some of the major players in the hardware RAID arena. Go to their websites for information on what they currently offer:

- Adaptec: www.adaptec.com
- QLogic: www.qlogic.com
- Mylex: www.mylex.com
- Advansys: www.advansyscorp.com
- LSI Logic: www.lsilogic.com
- American Megatrends: www.ami.com/raid

Because this is a Windows 2000 book, we will concentrate on Windows 2000 RAID implementations. If you can afford it, hardware RAID is your best bet. If not, Microsoft does allow you to create RAID 0, 1, and 5 volumes using Windows 2000. You can also create JBOD-spanned volumes.

Windows 2000 Software RAID Solutions

You want redundancy, or even better performance, but do not have current plans to upgrade any hardware. If you are in this situation, Windows 2000 RAID might be for you. Before we can even get into how to configure software RAID with Windows, though, you must first understand some terminology new to Windows 2000 storage.

Basic versus Dynamic Disks

Without trying to sound like your grandfather, is it safe to say, "Remember the good ol' days?" Not too long ago, there were just hard disks. Very little distinguished one disk from another, except for how a disk was formatted (FAT16, FAT32, NTFS). With Windows 2000, disk configuration goes far beyond the mere format of a disk. Now a disk can be either basic or dynamic, with significant differences in capability and diversity between the two configurations.

Basic Disks

With Windows 2000, hard disks are characterized as *basic* or *dynamic*. Basic disks are the disks that you have come to know and love. They consist of primary and extended partitions with logical drives. Basic disks, in addition to Windows 2000, can also be accessed by:

- Windows NT
- Windows Me/98/95
- MS-DOS

To create software RAID solutions with Windows 2000, disks must be configured as dynamic; however, if you have software RAID with Windows NT, and the NT Server is upgraded to Windows 2000, the disks will remain as basic. The software RAID will function normally after the upgrade, and you will not have to upgrade those disks to dynamic.

Dynamic Disks

Dynamic disks are new to Windows 2000 and can only be accessed by computers running Windows 2000. To implement a new software RAID solution with Windows 2000, each participating disk must first be converted to dynamic. The process to do this will be covered in the next section.

Physical disks are either basic or dynamic. In other words, you cannot have part of a physical disk be basic and the other part be dynamic. When you partition a disk, it is divided logically.

> **NOTE** Basic disks are divided into partitions; dynamic disks are divided into volumes.

Converting Basic Disks to Dynamic

This is a point of no return. Once a disk is converted to dynamic, it cannot be converted back to basic. To change a dynamic disk back to basic, you will first need to delete its logical volumes. You can then revert the disk bask to basic.

Before implementing a Windows 2000 software RAID solution, you first need to convert any disks in the array to dynamic. When the Windows 2000 Disk Manager detects new disks, it will first ask if you want to write a signature on the disk. Placing a signature on the disk allows Windows 2000 to access and manage the disk. For new disks, you will also be asked if you want to upgrade the disk. If you elect to "upgrade" the disk, Windows will automatically convert it to dynamic.

> **TIP** If you want to use any disks with Windows 2000 Cluster Service, the disks must be basic. Cluster service does not work with dynamic disks.

> **TIP** Make sure any disks you want to upgrade to dynamic are only accessed by Windows 2000. If you are dual booting a disk with another operating system, the down-level (Windows NT, 98/95, or any operating system that pre-dates Windows 2000) operating system will not boot on the dynamic disk.

Follow these steps to convert a basic disk to a dynamic disk:

1. Right-click the My Computer icon and select Manage.
2. From Computer Management, click the Disk Management folder.
3. You will now see all discovered disks listed. Right-click the disk you want to convert and select Upgrade to Dynamic Disk (see Figure 8.6).
4. Select the check box for each disk you want to upgrade and click OK.
5. You will then see a list of disks that will be upgraded. Click the Upgrade button.
6. You will then see a prompt that warns you that you cannot boot another operating system on the disk once it is upgraded. Click Yes.
7. When warned that file systems on the disks to be upgraded will be force dismounted, click Yes.

Figure 8.6: Upgrading a basic disk to dynamic

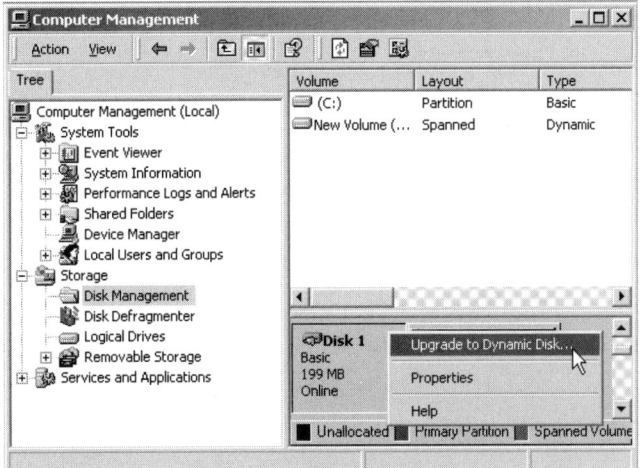

Creating a RAID 0 Striped Volume

If you are looking for better disk performance, creating a striped volume may suit your needs. Remember that with RAID 0, if one physical disk fails, the entire logical volume will be lost.

Follow these steps to create a RAID 0 striped volume:

1. Right-click any physical disk in the Disk Management folder and select Create Volume.
2. At the Create Volume Wizard window, click Next.
3. Select Striped Volume and click Next (see Figure 8.7).
4. Select the two or more volumes to make up the striped volume. Set the size for the volume and click Next (see Figure 8.8).
5. Assign a drive letter or mount path for the volume and click Next.
6. Set the format options for the disk and click Next.
7. Verify that all configuration information is correct for the RAID 0 volume and click Finish.

Figure 8.7: Creating a RAID 0 volume

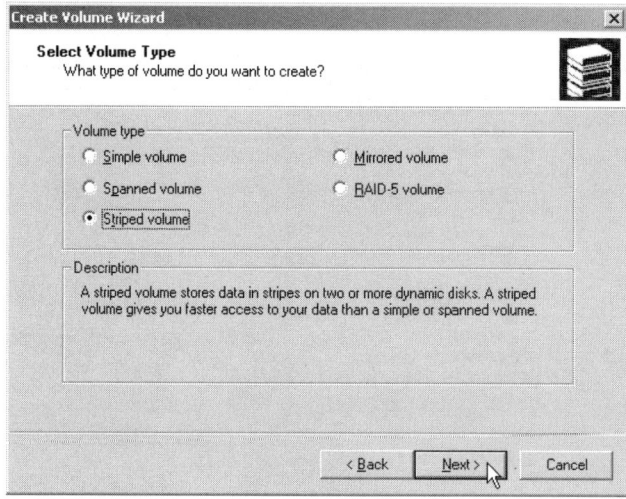

Figure 8.8: Selecting the physical disks and size for RAID 0 volume

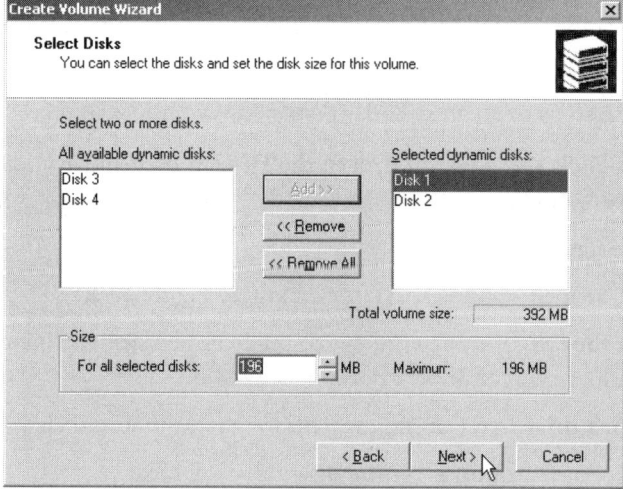

Creating a RAID 1 Mirrored Volume

Disk mirroring gives you an automatic level of fault tolerance. This provides a simple and somewhat transparent means to protect data. If you are looking for better disk performance, creating a striped volume may suit your needs. Remember that with RAID 0, if one physical disk fails, the entire logical volume will be lost.

Follow these steps to create a RAID 1 mirrored volume:

1. Right-click the logical volume that you want to mirror and select Add Mirror (see Figure 8.9).

Figure 8.9: Mirroring a logical volume

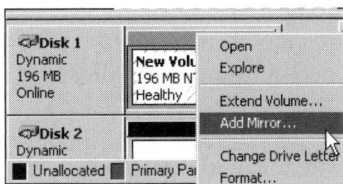

2. Select the disk that you want to form the mirror with and click Add Mirror.

Breaking and Removing Mirrors

Once you have created a mirrored volume, if you no longer need the mirror, you have two choices: break the mirror or remove the mirror. When you break the mirror, you are left with two usable volumes. In other words, you have two separate drives with the same data on them. If you choose to remove a mirror, all data on the disk you choose will be lost and the disk's space will return to being listed as unallocated. The other mirror disk will continue to maintain its data and original drive letter. To either break or remove a mirror, you simply right-click the mirrored volume and select either option.

Creating a RAID 5 Volume

RAID 5 provides you with the performance advantage of striping data across multiple disks while having a safety net with the use of parity. The failure of one physical disk will not cause the logical RAID 5 volume to fail. To configure a RAID 5 volume, you need three separate physical disks that have available space.

Follow these steps to create a RAID 5 volume:

1. Right-click unallocated disk space in Disk Manager and select Create Volume.
2. At the Create Volume Wizard welcome window, click Next.
3. Select RAID-5 Volume and click Next.
4. Select three or more disks for the array and click Next.
5. Assign a drive letter or mount path for the volume and click Next.
6. Set the format options for the disk and click Next.
7. Verify that all configuration information is correct for the RAID 5 volume and click Finish.

Creating a Spanned Volume

Have a volume running out of space and only wish it were bigger? You probably don't want to replace the disk. One solution is to create a spanned volume. Spanning allows a logical drive to span multiple disks. When one drive fills up, the logical volume begins writing to the second disk. The disadvantage to this approach is that you have a single point of failure. If one physical disk fails, the entire spanned volume is lost. When creating spanned volumes, you can take two paths: creating a new spanned volume from scratch or extending an active volume that already has data on it.

Creating a New Spanned Volume

Follow these steps to create a new spanned volume:

1. Right-click unallocated disk space in Disk Manager and select Create Volume.
2. At the Create Volume Wizard welcome window, click Next.
3. Select Spanned Volume and click Next.
4. Select the disks for the spanned volume and click Next.
5. Assign a drive letter or mount path for the volume and click Next.
6. Set the format options for the disk and click Next.
7. Verify that all configuration information is correct for the spanned volume and click Finish.

Extending an Active Volume

Follow these steps to extend an active volume:

1. Right-click the active volume and select Extend Volume.
2. At the Extend Volume Wizard welcome window, click Next.
3. Select an available dynamic disk from the list and adjust the size on the disk that you want to use. Click Next when finished.
4. Verify that all configuration information is correct and click Finish.

Moving Disks

One nice thing about basic and dynamic disks is that they do not have to be married to a single host forever. If the need arises, both basic and dynamic disks can be moved to another server with no loss of data.

> **NOTE** When moving disks to a new computer, all fault-tolerant volumes should be moved at the same time. For example, if you have a RAID 5 volume configured, you should move all of its disks at the same time so as not to cause configuration problems on the new host.

Follow these steps for the safest way to move a hard disk:

1. Before moving any disk, make sure to back up all data on the disk. Once you have a good backup, proceed to step 2.
2. Power down the server that contains the disks you want to move.
3. Remove the disk(s).
4. Power back up the host server (if it will still be used).
5. Power down the destination server.
6. Add the new disks.

> **WARNING** If you are adding SCSI disks, you should consider changing their SCSI IDs to numbers higher than any existing disks on the SCSI bus. This will prevent the added disk(s) from interfering with the current server's ARC Path settings, which could cause the server to fail to boot.

6. Power back up the destination server.
7. The new disks should be discovered. If not, from Computer Management, right-click the Disk Management folder and select Rescan Disks.

Now that the new host can see the disks, it is still possible that you will not be able to use them. That is because the disks could be in either a Foreign or Offline state:

- If the disk is listed as Offline, right-click the disk and select Reactivate Disk.
- If the disk is listed as Foreign, right-click the disk and choose Import Foreign Disks.

Normally, the added disk will be listed as Foreign, meaning that Windows recognizes the dynamic disk but realizes that it is one that it had not originally managed. An Offline status typically points to a missing disk or bad cable. You should check the cable or controller to ensure that a hardware failure is not causing the Offline disk state.

When Good Volumes Go Bad

If RAID was entertaining, this section could qualify to be a special on the Fox network. Unfortunately it's not, and for you, failed RAID can be enough to make you want to lock yourself in your office. Rest assured, if you know the correct steps, recovering data from a failed RAID volume is not that bad.

> **WARNING** RAID 0 is irrecoverable. If your RAID 0 volume fails, your only choice is to rebuild the volume from scratch and then restore from a backup.

Recovering a Failed RAID 1 Mirror

A failed RAID 1 volume can be easy or challenging to recover. If the failed disk contains the operating system, recovering the mirror will most likely be more difficult because you will probably have to boot into the Windows 2000 Recovery Console. Because this is the most challenging recovery, let's get this out of the way first.

When You Can't Even Boot

This usually happens because the ARC path settings in your `boot.ini` file are pointing to a failed physical disk. To get the system to boot, you will have to replace or edit the file. The other option to avoid this would be to move the good disk to where the bad disk is, either physically or logically. For example, if the bad disk was the master on the primary IDE controller, remove the bad disk and change the jumper on the good shadow disk so that it is now the master. You should then be able to boot.

If the two disks were on the same SCSI bus, you could swap their SCSI IDs so that the good disk has the ID of the bad disk and vice versa. By changing the physical layout of your system, you are essentially making it conform to what the `boot.ini` is seeking.

If you cannot change the hardware settings, then you will have to access the Recovery Console. You can get to the Recovery Console in three different ways:

- Boot the system off the Windows 2000 installation CD. From Windows Setup, press R to repair and then C to access the Recovery Console.

- Boot from the Windows 2000 Setup floppy disks. From Windows Setup, press R to repair and then C to access the Recovery Console.

- If the Recovery Console is pre-installed, you can access it by selecting it from the operating system startup menu.

> **TIP** To install the Recovery Console, insert the Windows 2000 installation CD-ROM, and run **<CD-ROM drive letter>\i386\winnt32.exe /cmdcons**.

Edit the ARC path settings in the existing `boot.ini` file. You can also copy a new file in place of the existing one. For example, suppose you had mirrored two IDE drives, both masters on separate controllers. The drive on the primary controller fails. To fix this, you could change the ARC path in the `boot.ini` file from `multi(0)disk(0)rdisk(0)partition(1)` to `multi(1)disk(0)rdisk(0)partition(1)`. With a new `boot.ini` file, you should now be able to boot the system. From that point, you can replace the failed disk and repair the mirror.

Repairing a Failed Mirror

To repair a failed mirror, follow these steps:

1. Right-click the My Computer icon and select Manage to return to Computer Management.
2. Click the Disk Manager folder. The failed disk should be listed as missing.
3. Right-click the failed disk and select Remove Mirror (see Figure 8.10).
4. Click on the missing disk and then click Remove Mirror (see Figure 8.11).

Figure 8.10: Removing a failed disk from a mirrored volume

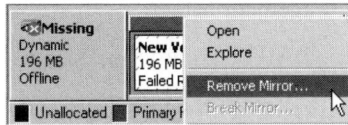

Figure 8.11: Choosing the right disk to remove

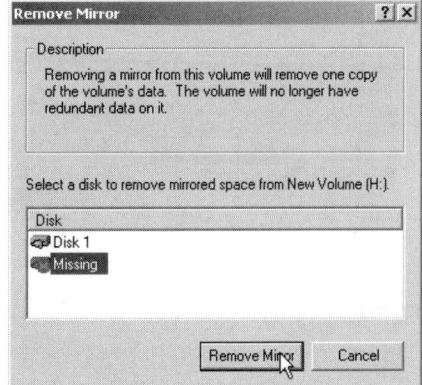

5. When prompted, click Yes to remove the mirror.
6. Now right-click the failed drive and select Remove Disk.
7. You can now "re-mirror" the remaining disk. To do this, right-click the volume you want to mirror and select Add Mirror.
8. Select the dynamic volume you want to use for the new mirror and click Add Mirror.

You have recovered your failed mirror. When the new mirror is created, it will take some time for all the existing data to be copied from the master disk to the shadow disk.

Recovering a Failed RAID 5 Array

When a RAID 5 drive fails, the logical volume will be displayed as having Failed Redundancy. Before attempting to recover the array, make sure that either you have a new disk on the system or an existing dynamic disk has at least as much free disk space as the other disks in the stripe set with parity.

Once you have a replacement lined up, the steps to recovering the failed array are quite simple:

1. Right-click the My Computer icon on the Desktop and select Manage to access Computer Management.
2. Click the Drive Management folder.
3. Right-click the failed RAID 5 volume and select Repair Volume (see Figure 8.12).
4. Select the new disk to replace the failed disk and click OK (see Figure 8.13).

Figure 8.12: Repairing a failed RAID 5 volume

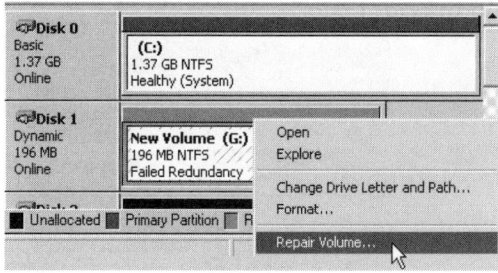

Figure 8.13: Selecting a new disk for the stripe set with parity

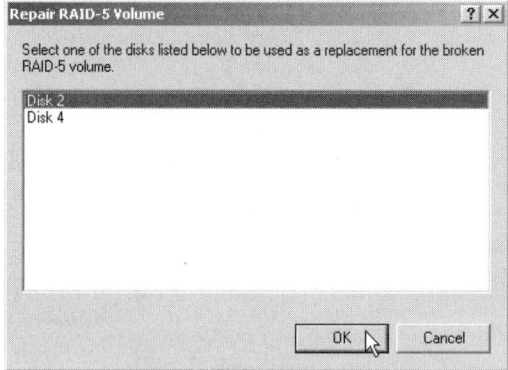

9

Cluster Technology

Clustering is a storage technology that has been on the fast track in the past decade. Although you most likely have a pretty good idea of where and when clustering is needed, it is often best not to assume anything, so we will take a minute to describe the need for clustering. For many organizations today, data must be available practically every second of every day. Unfortunately, computers, networks, and storage all fail, no matter how much we pay for them!

Simply put, a *cluster* is two or more computer systems acting and managed as one. Clients access the cluster using a single hostname or Internet Protocol (IP) address, having requests answered by one of the systems in the cluster.

The purpose of cluster technology is to eliminate several single points of failure. When data availability is essential, clustering is ideal. Using a failover cluster can eliminate these single points of failure:

- Network card failure
- Processor failure
- Motherboard failure
- Power failure
- Cable failure
- Network failure

With a cluster, you can basically eliminate nearly any hardware failure that can be associated with a single computer. If hardware associated with one system fails, another system will automatically take over. If this concept still is not perfectly clear, don't worry. You will soon see the different cluster types available with Windows 2000 Advanced and DataCenter Servers.

Clustering Essentials

Before getting deeper into Microsoft cluster planning and implementation, you should understand some of the lingo. Here are some key terms in the Microsoft cluster vocabulary:

Cluster Communications   Means by which two or more cluster nodes communicate. Communications can occur through a private (cluster node–only) network segment, or mixed (cluster nodes and clients) network segment.

Cluster Disk   Physical hard drive shared by two or more cluster nodes using a shared data bus, which can be a Small Computer Systems Interface (SCSI) or a Fibre Channel bus.

Cluster Node   Physical system participating in the cluster.

Heartbeat   Periodic communication between cluster nodes using User Datagram Protocol (UDP) datagrams to determine if a node is running. Each cluster node will listen for the heartbeat of all other nodes.

Quorum Resource   Disk or disk partition that contains the cluster's management and configuration data and recovery log.

Virtual Server   Typically a collection of cluster nodes that appear as a single server to clients. Like all network servers, a virtual server will have a *network name* and *IP address*.

Configuring Clusters

There are three basic types of Microsoft clusters:

- Server
- Network Load Balanced (NLB)
- Component Load Balanced (CLB)

With Windows 2000 you can implement failover and network load balanced clusters. We will provide an overview of all three cluster types.

NOTE Clustering is too vast a topic to cover everything in a single chapter, so this chapter focuses on implementing and administering server clusters. For information on everything you ever wanted to do or could hope to do with Microsoft clusters, pick up a copy of *Windows 2000/.NET Server Clustering Little Black Book* by Chris Wolf (Coriolis, 2002).

Server Clusters

Server clusters, also known as *failover clusters*, operate under the premise of having two or more nodes share physical storage. Physical disks on the shared storage are managed by individual cluster nodes. One node can manage all the disks, or each node can manage one or more disks. The storage, which is typically a magnetic disk or disk array, is connected to the cluster nodes through either a Fibre Channel or SCSI bus. If one node fails, another node will take control of the disk resources, providing for only a momentary lapse in operation. Failure of a cluster node is discovered by other nodes listening for its "heartbeat." When a cluster node no longer detects that one of its sister nodes is online, it assumes control of the node's shared disk resources. Figure 9.1 shows a simple two-node failover cluster.

Figure 9.1: Two-node failover cluster

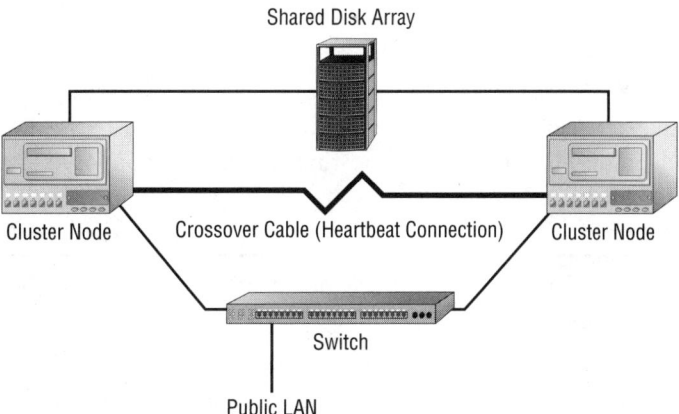

Notice in Figure 9.1 that two network connections exist between the cluster nodes. One connection is used exclusively by the cluster for monitoring its heartbeat, and the other is a public network connection for clients to access the cluster. The crossover cable, although not required, is used to eliminate another single point of failure: a hub. If you used a hub or switch to connect the internal cluster network, failure of that device would cause the cluster to fail.

With the Windows 2000 Server products, there are limitations to the number of nodes in a server cluster:

- Windows 2000 Advanced Server—Two
- Windows 2000 Datacenter Server—Four

With Windows 2000 Server, clustering in any form is not supported. You can only cluster Advanced or Datacenter Servers. Server clusters are described as either *active-passive* or *active-active*. These configurations are explained in the next two sections.

Active-Passive Server Clusters

With active-passive clusters, one node has complete control of the shared resources, and the other nodes monitor the active node for failure. If the active node fails, then a passive node will assume control of the shared resources, which typically is a disk storage array, possibly incorporating hardware Redundant Array of Independent/Inexpensive Disks (RAID). Figure 9.2 shows the basic configuration of an active-passive cluster.

Figure 9.2: Active-passive failover cluster

Active-Active Server Clusters

With active-active clusters, two or more nodes control cluster resources simultaneously. Each node in the cluster is actively hosting resources, as opposed to standing by and waiting for the failure of a node.

> **TIP** Think of an active-active cluster is as two or more active-passive clusters combined.

For example, suppose you want to have failover capability for both your Exchange and SQL Servers. You could cluster both SQL and Exchange, configuring them to store their data on separate physical disks on the shared storage array. Then you could configure one node to actively host the Exchange services and the other to actively host the SQL services. After this configuration, you are left with a node that is active for Exchange and passive for SQL and another node that is passive for Exchange and active for SQL. When the node hosting Exchange or SQL fails, the other node will assume control of the resources. Figure 9.3 shows this configuration.

Figure 9.3: Exchange and SQL active-active cluster

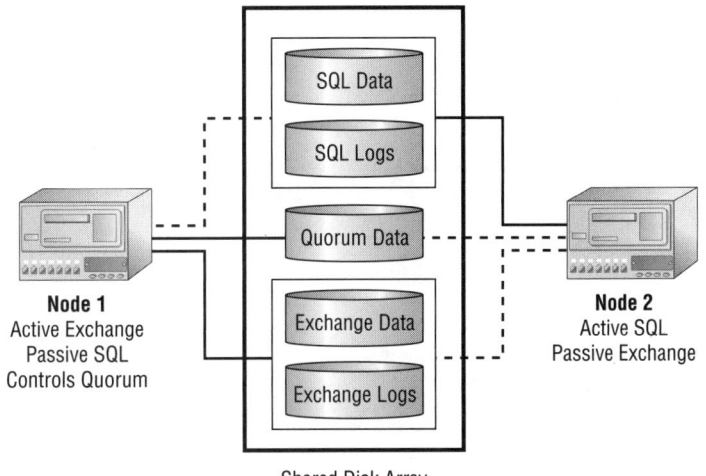

Network Load Balanced Clusters

Network load balanced (NLB) clusters differ from server clusters in that they do not share resources. With NLB clusters, each node stores and maintains its own data, meaning that if you are using an NLB cluster as the frontend for your web presence, you are responsible for ensuring that data remains consistent between all cluster nodes. Unlike failover clusters, NLB clusters do not share resources. Each node in an NLB cluster maintains its own data. A better way to explain data management for NLB clusters would be to say that you are responsible for maintaining data integrity between the nodes. This task can be automated by using tools such as Application Center 2000.

When deciding on whether to choose server or NLB clusters, understand that they are generally used for different purposes. Server clusters are ideal for eliminating single points of failure for data that requires read/write access from users or applications. NLB clusters, on the other hand, are usually used to provide high availability and load balancing for read-only data. Figure 9.4 illustrates an NLB cluster.

As with server clusters, each node in the NLB cluster maintains its own IP address; the NLB cluster will assume its own unique IP address, as well. Clients accessing the NLB cluster by its IP address are directed to one of the nodes in the cluster by the NLB cluster service.

Figure 9.4: Six-node NLB cluster

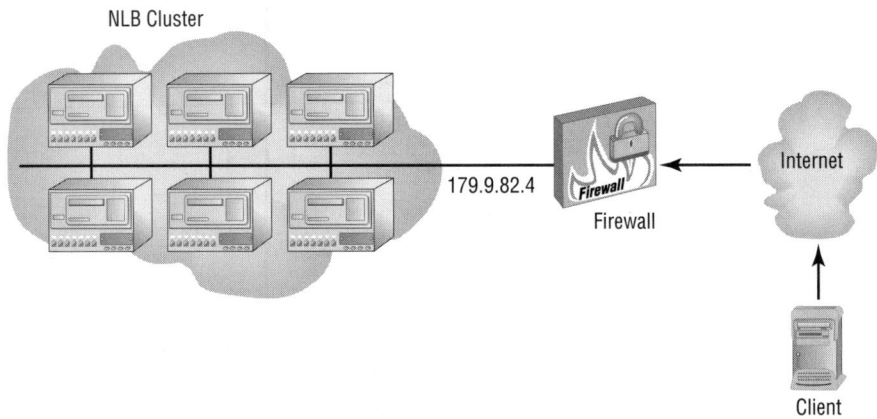

Before Microsoft had NLB clusters, a technique known as *round-robin DNS* was used as a means to distribute client requests to multiple servers. When using round robin, a DNS server would cycle through several IP addresses that referenced a single hostname. Although this in essence works just like NLB, it is not fault tolerant. If a server fails, the DNS server will still periodically direct client requests to the failed server, causing clients to fail to connect. This problem could be corrected by manually removing the failed server's IP address record from the DNS server and also manually clearing any cached records on all other DNS servers involved in the name resolution process. Consider round robin as a solution for load balancing between multiple failover clusters but not as a substitute for NLB clusters. In fact, some even use round robin to distribute client requests among several NLB clusters, adding another level of load balancing.

> **WARNING** You cannot configure a single node to participate in both an NLB and a server cluster. Microsoft does not support this configuration.

Component Load Balanced Clusters

Component load balanced (CLB) clusters can only be implemented on servers running Microsoft Application Center 2000. To understand CLB, you must first understand Component Object Model (COM). To visualize COM, imagine you're going to a department store to purchase a light bulb for a lamp. Although there are some varieties of bulbs from which to choose, the stock is still quite limited. In other words, lamp manufacturers don't invent a new light bulb to go along with each new lamp; instead, they use a standard component in their lamps so that all bulbs work with them. Having standard components available allows all lamp manufacturers to design lamps and not have to worry about some of the pieces for the lamp; they can use what's already there.

COM works under the same premise. COM components can be looked at as pre-labeled building blocks. From looking at the COM component, you can determine its use. Using COM components allows developers to build applications by reusing known components without needing to compile the application.

With an understanding of COM, we can now get to COM+. COM+ is an extension of COM. COM+ is better than COM in that COM+ components can have additional services incorporated into them to do tasks such as alerting and authorization.

> **TIP** For more information on COM+, search for "COM+" at www.whatis.com.

With an overview of COM and COM+ under your belt, let's get to CLB clusters. CLB clusters allow applications built using COM+ components to operate across multiple servers, similarly to NLB clusters. CLB clusters operate differently than NLB clusters in that with CLB, applications and not servers are load balanced. The CLB cluster service maintains an internal list of available COM+ servers participating in the cluster. The service then uses a round-robin technique to distribute application requests between COM+ servers in the cluster. Because the CLB round-robin service is a true cluster service, and not a part of DNS, it is natively fault-tolerant.

If you are wondering where you would use a CLB cluster, consider this scenario: You are tasked with managing an e-commerce site with a 20-node NLB cluster frontend. To ensure tighter security, you decide to segregate the site's electronic shopping cart (a COM+ application) behind a second firewall. The COM+ CLB service could then run on the frontend to distribute application requests to the COM+ components on the backend.

Configuring Resources and Groups

Failover between servers in a server cluster is determined by how resources and groups are configured. Resources are used to define objects and applications controlled by the cluster service. Here are a few examples of resources:

- IP address (IP address of virtual server)
- Network name (virtual server NetBIOS name)
- Physical disk (defines access to shared cluster disk)

Notice that with the IP address and network name resources we used the term *virtual server*. When you place an IP address resource and network name resource in the same group, you have a virtual server. The virtual server, as long as its resources are running, acts just like any other server on your network. For example, you could ping the virtual server while it is online, and it will respond to the ping appropriately.

Resources that work in conjunction with one another are generally placed into groups. For example, when clustering an Exchange Server, you would place all Exchange-related resources, including a physical disk, IP address, and network name, in a single group. This will give you an Exchange virtual server. Like resources are placed into a group because groups define failover. If a resource in a group fails, then the entire group, by default, is moved to another node where the cluster service will attempt to restart all resources.

Addressing Single Points of Failure

Microsoft defines a *single point of failure (SPF)* as anything in your environment that would prevent access to data or to an application if it failed. The single point could be anything including a network card, a hard disk, or an application. We will get to all possible single points of failure shortly. Planning for hardware or software failure is of little value if you do not also consider the possibility of a power failure. Ask yourself these questions before patting yourself on the back for your high-availability infrastructure design:

- Do I have/need redundant Wide Area Network (WAN) or Local Area Network (LAN) links?
- In addition to my servers, are Uninterruptible Power Supplies (UPSs) protecting my other critical network hardware? Protecting your servers from power loss is great, but it means little if clients cannot access the servers because of down network hardware.
- What services, applications, files, and databases require near 100-percent uptime? Wherever possible, anything requiring 100-percent availability should be installed on a cluster.

Table 9.1 organizes SPFs, along with ways to eliminate them.

Table 9.1: SPF Checklist

SPF	Solution
Dial-up connection	Add additional modems to remote-access servers (RAS).
Hard disks/storage	Use hardware RAID to protect data against the loss of a single disk.
Network cabling	Implement redundant paths.
Network cards	Each cluster node should have a minimum of two network interface cards (NICs).

Continued on next page

Table 9.1 (Continued): SPF Checklist

SPF	Solution
Power	Configure a backup generator to power all critical hardware in the event of a complete power failure. Use a UPS to gracefully power down less critical servers.
Routers/switches/hubs	Configure redundant routes, keep spares available.
Software	For critical applications, use cluster-aware software whenever it is feasible and install software on a failover cluster.
WAN links	Purchase multiple WAN links for critical sites to provide redundancy.

Planning Cluster Deployment

Although we would love to just jump right in to explain how to install the cluster service, it is pointless without first understanding the steps to properly plan cluster deployment. You will need to understand what you should cluster and how you should do it, prior to even thinking about the installation itself. So, let's start with some general considerations.

Checking Compatibility and System Requirements

Before purchasing any hardware, or prior to installing the cluster service using your existing hardware, you should first check its compatibility with Windows products. See the Microsoft Hardware Compatibility List (HCL) at www.microsoft.com/hcl.

Also, don't forget about the Central Processing Unit (CPU) and Random Access Memory (RAM). The ideal cluster will have each of its nodes use identical hardware, including the CPU, RAM, hard disks, and network adapters. Using standard hardware for all nodes will make your capacity planning more accurate. Further, when sizing storage for the operating system, do not forget about the swap file (also known as the *pagefile* and saved as `pagefile.sys`). The pagefile is typically set to double the amount of RAM installed in the system. For example, for servers with 512MB of physical RAM, you should allow for 1GB of hard disk space for the pagefile.

Server cluster planning begins with choosing the right model to implement the cluster service. After choosing the appropriate model, you can then plan how you will implement resources and groups. Before deciding on which model you should implement, let's briefly look at the hardware requirements for installing the cluster service:

- A hard disk on a controller separate from the shared storage to store the boot partition

- One external shared disk connected to each cluster node through a SCSI or Fibre Channel bus
- At least one NIC in each node (two recommended)

TIP Although not required, you should consider storing the cluster quorum data on its own physical disk. Otherwise, if an application using the same disk as the cluster quorum fails over, the entire cluster will failover and thus be unavailable for a brief period of time.

When configuring the shared cluster storage, remember the following points:

- Each disk must be configured as a basic disk and formatted as NTFS.
- Each SCSI drive and SCSI adapter on every shared SCSI bus must have a unique SCSI ID.
- Before installing the cluster service, power up each node one at a time and verify that the node can access the shared storage.
- Clustered shared storage does not support the following:
    - Encrypted File System (EFS)
    - Remote storage
    - Reparse points
    - Volume mount points

NOTE The SCSI ID on most host adapters is set to 7 by default, so remember to change the ID of the adapter on all but one cluster node.

Remember the following points when planning the cluster network:

- Each virtual server you plan to configure for the cluster must have a unique NetBIOS name (no more than 15 characters).
- Acquire static IP addresses for each NIC on each cluster node and for each planned virtual server.
- Remember to join all nodes in the cluster to the domain.
- Create a domain user account for use by the cluster service.

Choosing the Right Model

Server clusters are built using the format from any of five different models:

- Single-node model

- Dedicated secondary node (active-passive) model
- Dedicated secondary node (active-passive) split model
- High availability with static load balancing (active-active) model
- Hybrid model

The model you choose will depend on the current and future needs of your organization. This section outlines each model, its pros and cons, and how it is best used.

> **NOTE**   Microsoft loves to classify cluster models as either A, B, and C or 1, 2, 3, and so on. Unfortunately, this approach is not consistent throughout all Microsoft articles; however, the naming conventions used for the models are. Your best bet is to simply remember and plan models by their actual names.

Single-Node Model

A single-node cluster? You may be thinking, "What's the point?" As you will soon see, single-node clusters do have their value (see Figure 9.5).

Figure 9.5: Single-node model

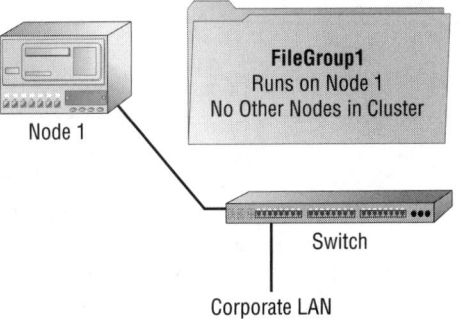

There are several reasons for choosing a single-node model:

- Can provide initial framework for the eventual rollout of a multi-node cluster
- Lets services and applications take advantage of cluster service's automatic-restart ability

And there are several reasons to avoid incorporating the single-node model:

- No other nodes are available for failover.
- The one node is a single point of failure.
- Using server clusters requires an investment in SCSI or Fibre Channel storage, regardless if there are one or more nodes in the cluster.

Taking advantage of the automatic-restart ability of clustering will keep your applications and services up more consistently. Maybe you're also working within a tight budget, and it's not economically possible to roll out a multinode cluster. In this circumstance, you could build one cluster node one year and add additional nodes the following year.

> **WARNING** Not all applications can run in a virtual server on a single-node cluster. Make sure you check the application's documentation for compatibility. For example, you cannot run SQL 7 or 6.5 on a single-node cluster.

Dedicated Secondary Node (Active-Passive) Model

The standard active-passive model offers all the advantages of the single-node model while also allowing for failover (see Figure 9.6).

Figure 9.6: Dedicated secondary node (active-passive) cluster model

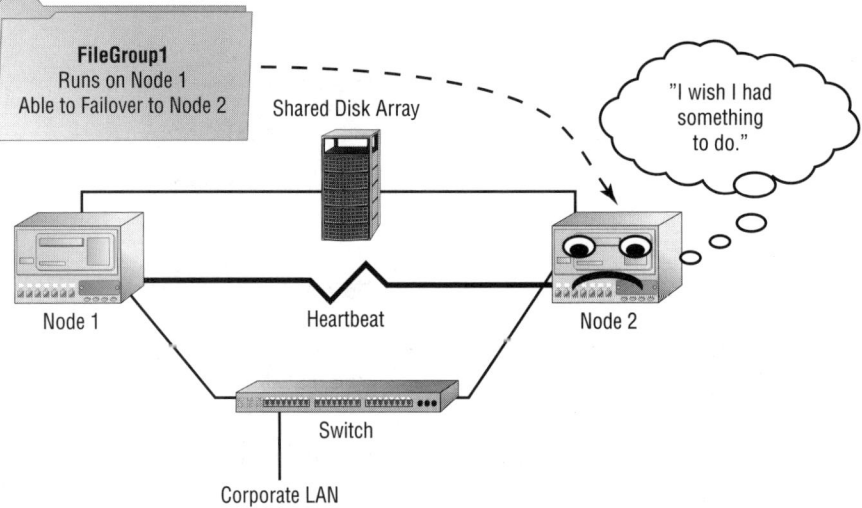

With this model, the active node controls all cluster groups, and the passive node stands by waiting for the active node to fail. If the active node fails, the passive node becomes active and assumes control of all shared cluster groups.

Reasons for using this model include:

- It provides the ability for groups to fail over.
- A cluster node is no longer considered a single point of failure.

Reasons to stay away from implementing this model include:

- Passive node does nothing but waste energy until primary node fails.
- A hardware investment is required for a server that basically sits around waiting for another server to fail.

Some have trouble justifying the cost of a passive server and resort to employing an active-active cluster instead, which will be covered momentarily.

Dedicated Secondary Node (Active-Passive) Split Model

The active-passive split model is similar in configuration to the standard active-passive model. However, in the active-passive split model, the active node runs both clustered and nonclustered applications in the cluster (see Figure 9.7).

Figure 9.7: Dedicated secondary node (active-passive) split cluster

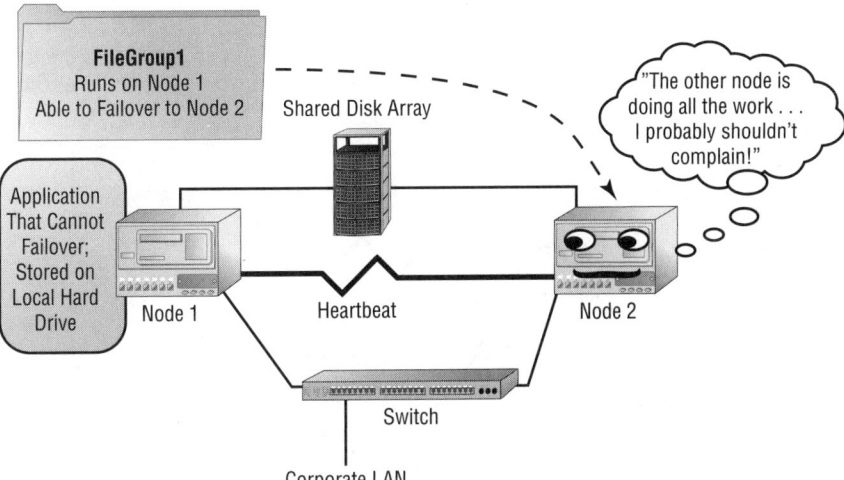

In this model, the applications that do not support failover store their data on a cluster node's local disks. The primary problem with this approach is that if the active node fails, the nonclustered applications do not failover to the passive node and thus are not available.

Reasons for using this model include the following:

- It allows you to get more use out of the servers acting as cluster nodes.
- You have an abundance of processing power and local storage on each node to support running nonclustered applications.

Reasons to stay away from implementing this model include the following:

- When a node fails, its cluster-unaware applications will not be available.
- Clients must access nonclustered applications using the node name and not the virtual server name.
- It provides no fault tolerance for cluster-unaware applications.

High Availability with Static Load Balancing (Active-Active) Model

The static load balanced active-active model is widely popular because it entails running clustered applications on each cluster node, making it easier for you to justify the dollars spent on the cluster implementation (see Figure 9.8).

Figure 9.8: Static load balanced active-active cluster model

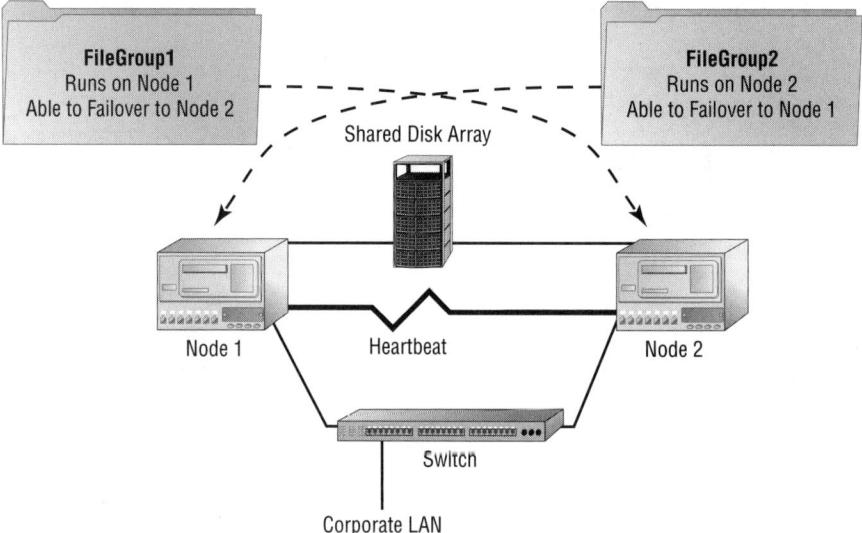

When a cluster is said to be *static load balanced*, it is because each cluster group has a *preferred owner* set. When a preferred owner is specified, it is designated by the cluster service as the first choice for a cluster group. If the node is available, it will host the group. When the node fails, the group can then failover to another node.

There are several reasons why many choose to incorporate this model:

- No nodes are "wasted" as standby servers.
- Multiple applications can be statically load balanced over several nodes, as opposed to running them on a single node.

- Multiple instances of the same application can be statically load balanced over several nodes. This is essential when one node, no matter how powerful, cannot handle the load from network clients.
- Using multiple nodes to run applications generally provides better performance than trying to run several applications on a single node.

This model does have one disadvantage, which is in hardware. Just because you have one clustered application running on each node, for example, that doesn't mean that each cluster node can get away without having the resources to run cluster applications it is not hosting. All nodes must be powerful enough to run all cluster groups at a given time.

Hybrid Model

The hybrid cluster model is one of the more popular cluster implementations. As with other information technology (IT) concepts, *hybrid* refers to a mix, or combination, of other models (see Figure 9.9).

Figure 9.9: Hybrid cluster model

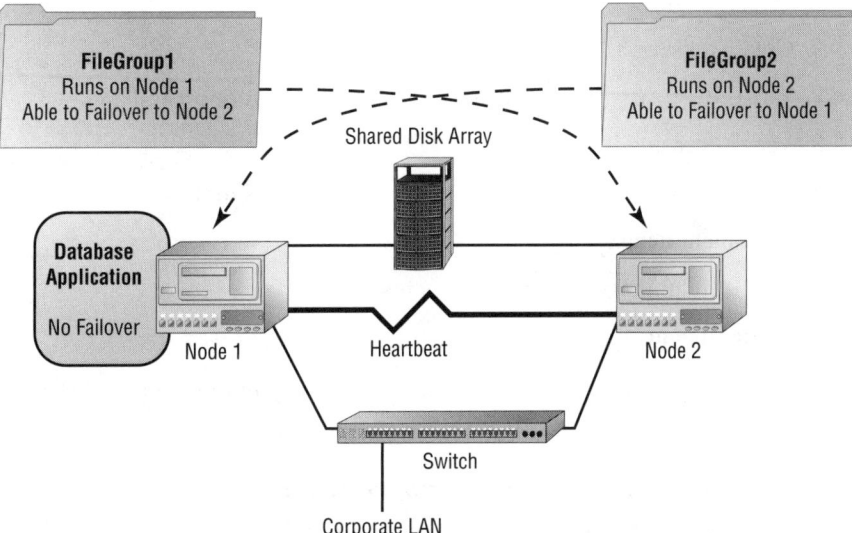

The typical hybrid model involves active-active clusters that also run nonclustered applications. This model allows you to use cluster nodes as stand-alone servers running nonclustered applications, in addition to providing failover for clustered applications.

Reasons for using this model include:

- It provides the ability for groups to failover.
- A cluster node is no longer considered a single point of failure.

Reasons to stay away from implementing this model include:

- Passive node does nothing but waste energy until the primary node fails.

With a decision on how to implement your cluster, you can now work on configuring the cluster's resources and groups.

Planning for Resource and Group Configuration

Creating resources and groups, as you will soon see, is a simple process. This does not mean, however, that you should take shortcuts. For example, we recently worked on installing cluster-aware applications at a large Fortune 500 organization. The organization had one group configured on the cluster: the Cluster Group. This caused a problem because placing everything in one group means that a failure of a single resource will cause everything (by default) on the cluster node to fail over. If the organization had planned their cluster rollout properly, it would never have been in that situation.

With properly planned groups in place, your cluster will run much more efficiently and be less prone to complete failover. Group configuration can be broken down into seven phases:

1. Create a list of all server-based applications.
2. Sort the list by which applications do and don't support failover.
3. Verify licensing.
4. List all nonapplication resources where failover is desired.
5. Document dependencies for each resource.
6. Make preliminary group assignments.
7. Make final group assignments.

The next seven sections outline the considerations you must make during each planning phase.

Creating a List of All Server-Based Applications

When planning resources and groups, you must first document all applications running on each server that will participate in the server cluster. Initially, you may think to document only the applications that you plan on configuring for failover. The problem with this approach is that an undocumented application running on a cluster node can consume memory that you did not consider during planning. Each cluster node must have substantial physical resources to accommodate all applications that might failover onto it. Having an application that is not clustered running on a node consuming 60MB of physical RAM could cause problems if other applications try to fail over onto the node. When planning the physical hardware requirements of each cluster node, if you have each application documented alongside its approximate resource consumption, then it makes it easy to arrive at accurate requirement estimates. For most applications you plan to cluster, you should be able to obtain information on physical memory and storage requirements. On the other hand, you will not see data on CPU loading and bandwidth consumption. This should be estimated through the use of load testing.

Sorting the List

Once you have compiled the list of all applications, you then need to determine which applications will be configured for failover. For any application to support failover, the following are required:

- The application must communicate using TCP/IP.
- Clients must be able to automatically reconnect after a momentary interruption in service.
- The application must allow you to configure where its data is stored.

Remember that even if an application supports failover, that doesn't mean you need to cluster it. Remember to note which applications will be configured for failover.

Verifying Licensing

Before configuring any application for clustering, you must make sure your planned configuration does not overextend the licensing agreement with the applications you plan to cluster. You may find out that when moving an application from a stand-alone server to a cluster, you need an additional license for each node and an additional license for each virtual server. Be careful to validate license requirements before installation.

Listing All Nonapplication Resources Where Failover Is Desired

List the nonapplication-related services that you want to have failover capability, such as file shares and print spoolers. Don't forget that file shares and print spooler services still consume physical resources on the cluster nodes, and their memory and CPU requirements must be considered during planning.

Documenting Dependencies for Each Resource

Be careful to outline the required relationships for each resource. For example, a print spooler resource requires a network name and physical disk resource. The network name resource requires an IP address resource, which means the print spooler's planned group must have at least a network name, IP address, and physical disk resource for the print spooler resource to be created. For all applications that can be clustered, their required dependencies are almost always documented in their installation instructions. When in doubt, it is always safe to assume you will need a network name, IP address, and physical disk for the application.

When grouping resources, remember the following guidelines:

- Resources must be located in the same group as their dependent resources.
- Any single resource can only be located in one group.

Making Preliminary Group Assignments

With dependencies documented, you should at this point have a pretty good idea on how you plan to group resources. Before you plan group assignments, though, remember that managing a few large groups is always easier than managing several small groups. Although you should avoid having too much in a single group, don't get too granular with your grouping either.

A common example of a means to conserve grouping would be to group resources by department, such as marketing, sales, and finance.

Making Final Group Assignments

With the preliminary group assignments document, work to name each group based on its intended purpose. For example, you would want to name a print spooler group as "PrintSpooler," and you would want to name the group of resources for the Exchange Server as "Exchange1." Although this may sound like common sense to you now, we can't tell you how many groups we've seen with the default naming values of "Disk Group 1," "Disk Group 2," and "Disk Group 3." Keeping the default naming convention makes it harder for you to remember the purpose or contents of each cluster group.

Planning for Failover

With related resources grouped together, you should also decide how to configure failover and failback for each group before installing the service. Each group in the cluster will have its own failover policy, which is divided into three settings:

- Failover timing
- Preferred node
- Failback timing

When you set failover timing, you can establish rules for when all resources in a group failover to another node. For example, you could have a resource try and restart itself several times before initiating a failover, instead of initiating a failover automatically upon failure.

During a failover, a group will move to its preferred node, by order of precedence, if it's available. Setting a node as a preferred node for a group does not cause the group to automatically jump to the node. The preferred node configuration is only looked at during a failover. If you want a group to reside on a particular node, you should manually move the group.

One final consideration that should be made regarding groups is failback. By default, when a group fails over from one node to another, it remains there until you manually move it back. With failback enabled, if a group fails over from one node to another, as soon as the failed node comes back online, the group will again move back to its original node. One thing to remember about this configuration, however, is that during a failover, an application will be unavailable for as long as several minutes. If you enable failback, the application would again be unavailable as its group is moved back to its original node. Microsoft recognized this deficiency and added options to allow you to configure failback to run only during a specified timeframe. The method to configure this is discussed later in the chapter in the "Configuring Group Properties" section.

Planning for Active Directory Issues

Active Directory plays an important part in just about everything in a Windows 2000 forest, so why should the cluster service be any different? You read earlier that the cluster service requires a domain user account. If cluster nodes are configured as member servers in the domain, then the cluster service will need to contact a domain controller to validate its logon credentials in order to start. This problem can be eliminated by making each cluster node a domain controller. The problem with this approach, however, is that the cluster will be subject to the replication traffic of the Active Directory forest, thus consuming cluster node hardware resources. Deciding on whether to make cluster nodes domain controllers should be primarily determined by the size of your Active Directory forest. For domains consisting of only a few hundred users, you should consider making each node a domain controller, as replication traffic will be minimal. On the other hand, for large domains, you may want to live with the logon validation as a point of failure. In enterprise environments, you most likely will have more than one domain controller on the network, meaning that fault tolerance will already exist for the logon validation process.

Installing the Cluster Service

If installing the cluster service only meant "installing the service," you would probably be pretty happy right now. Unfortunately, you still have some work to do. For starters, you have to perform some final checks on the cluster hardware. You then need to configure the network for the cluster, as well as the domain user account for the cluster service. This section takes you through the final preparations and then the installation of the cluster service.

Making Final Hardware Preparations

You are almost to the Promised Land—cluster service installation—but first you should run through a couple of additional checks to make sure your cluster is configured properly. After all hardware is configured and ready to go, you should perform the following tasks before installing the cluster service:

- Acquire and configure static IP addresses for each NIC on each cluster node.
- Acquire an IP address for each planned virtual server.
- Verify that all cluster nodes can ping each other using fully qualified domain names.
- Consider promoting one or all nodes to be domain controllers.
- Disable NetBIOS over IP for cluster heartbeat network interfaces.
- Verify that the proper drivers are installed for the cluster shared storage (RAID controllers, Fibre Channel, and SCSI Host Bus Adapters (HBAs).

With server clusters, TCP/IP can be installed on each NIC used by the cluster. A static IP address is only needed for each virtual server, but it is strongly recommended that you use static IPs for all physical NICs used by the cluster.

You should also ensure that each cluster node can resolve fully qualified domain names. If you are still using WINS, then you must edit the `%system root%\system 32\drivers\etc\hosts` file to map all node hostnames, and any other servers the cluster will communicate with, to their proper IP addresses. If you are not sure of how entries in the file are written, just open it. The first entry lists the local loopback IP address, followed by the name `localhost`. To add additional entries, just type the IP address of each needed system, press the Tab key, and then enter the fully qualified domain name associated with the IP address.

NetBIOS broadcast traffic is unnecessary on the cluster heartbeat network, so it should be disabled on the interfaces connected to the heartbeat network.

> **TIP** The steps to disabling NetBIOS over TCP/IP are covered later in this chapter in the "Disabling NetBIOS over IP" section.

One last hardware check you should perform is to verify that all hardware is recognized in Device Manager. If any of the cluster-shared storage devices are listed under a yellow question mark, that is a sign that Windows does not have the proper driver for that device. Make sure all drivers are installed before continuing with the cluster service implementation.

Configuring the Final Network Settings

Prior to installing the cluster service, you must first decide how each network interface in each cluster node will be used. With Microsoft cluster service, network connections can be defined as:

- Public (client access only)
- Private (internal cluster communications only)
- Mixed (communicates with both clients and cluster nodes)

When installing the cluster service, you will have the opportunity to determine the role of each network interface. When considering NIC usage, remember these points:

- If each node only has one NIC, configure the NIC as mixed.
- If each node has two NICs, set the NIC that offers the lowest bandwidth as private and the NIC with the higher bandwidth as mixed.
- If each node has three NICs, configure two NICs for private communications and the third NIC for public communications. If the cluster sees a heavy load of network traffic from clients, you could then also consider configuring a private, public, and mixed network to load balance client traffic over multiple network interfaces.

With the final touches of your plan in place, you can now move to install and configure the cluster service. If each cluster node has more than one NIC, your first course of action should be to disable NetBIOS on the cluster heartbeat network.

NetBIOS broadcasts do nothing more than waste bandwidth and resources on a private heartbeat network, so you should disable NetBIOS on the NIC for the private network on each node before installing the cluster service. To do this, perform these steps:

1. Log on to the node as a user with administrative privileges.
2. Click Start ➢ Settings ➢ Network and Dialup Connections.
3. Right-click the network that will be used for the cluster heartbeat and select Properties.
4. In the LAN Connection Properties dialog box, click the Internet Protocol (TCP/IP) object and then click the Properties button.
5. Click the Advanced button.
6. Click the WINS tab and then select the Disable NetBIOS over TCP/IP radio button, as shown in Figure 9.10.

Figure 9.10: Disabling NetBIOS over TCP/IP

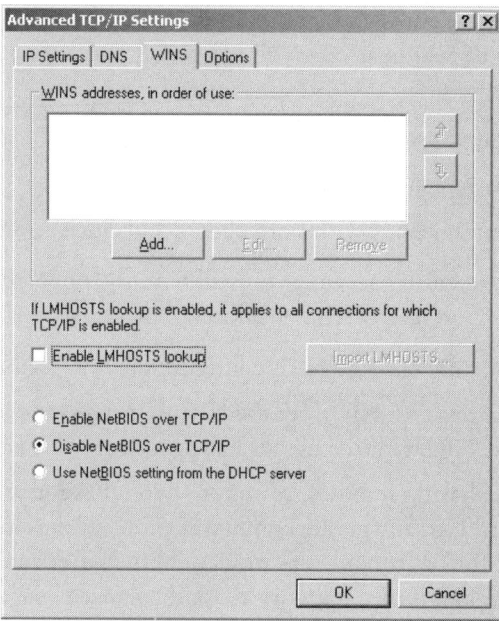

7. Click OK. If you are prompted that the connection has an empty WINS address, click Yes to continue.

8. Click OK to close the TCP/IP Properties dialog box.

9. Click OK to close the LAN Connection Properties dialog box.

10. Repeat steps 3 through 9 for all other heartbeat network connections.

Creating a Domain Account for the Cluster Service

During installation, you will be prompted to provide a domain user account for the cluster service. This account must have local administrative privileges on all cluster nodes. The easiest way to achieve this is to simply create an account for the cluster service and place the account in the Domain Administrators group. It is also required that the account have the following advanced user rights:

- Act as part of the operating system
- Log on as a service
- Lock pages in memory

You don't have to worry about adding these rights because this is done automatically during the cluster service installation. One final consideration with the cluster service domain account is password management. If the password for the cluster service account expires, it will not be able to start. To prevent this problem, you should select these two options when creating the account:

- User cannot change password
- Password never expires

This is the procedure for creating the domain user account for the cluster service:

1. Log on to a domain controller as a user who has administrative privileges.
2. Click Start ➢ Programs ➢ Administrative Tools ➢ Active Directory Users and Computers.
3. Right-click the Users folder, select New, and then select User.
4. In the New Object–User dialog box, enter a username and logon name, and click Next.
5. Enter and confirm a password for the cluster user account. It is recommended that you also check the User Cannot Change Password and "Password Never Expires boxes and click Next.
6. Verify that the user information is correct and click Finish.
7. Right-click the newly created user account and select Properties.
8. Click the Member Of tab and then click the Add button. Select the Administrators group and click OK. Then click OK to close the User Properties dialog box.

> **Infinite Password? Do You Want Me to Get Hacked?**
>
> Having the password for the cluster domain account never expire prevents the cluster service from failing because of a logon failure at intervals when the password must be changed. Although this is good from an availability perspective, many network security gurus would frown on this.
>
> Follow these steps to change the domain cluster account password:
>
> 1. Log on to a domain controller using a user account that has domain administrative privileges.
> 2. From the desktop, select Start ➢ Programs ➢ Administrative Tools ➢ Active Directory Users and Computers.
> 3. Click the Users folder, or whichever folder contains the cluster service user account.
> 4. Right-click the cluster user account and select Reset Password.
>
> *Continued on next page*

> **5.** In the Reset Password dialog box, enter and confirm a new password and click OK.
>
> Once the password is reset, you will need to update the cluster service properties on each cluster node to reflect the new password. To do this, follow these steps:
>
> **1.** Log on using an account that has local administrative privileges.
>
> **2.** From the desktop, select Start ➢ Programs ➢ Administrative Tools ➢ Services.
>
> **3.** Right-click the Cluster service and select Properties.
>
> **4.** Click the Log On tab.
>
> **5.** In the This Account field, enter and confirm the new password and click OK.
>
> Remember to repeat steps 1 through 5 on every cluster node.

Assigning Drive Letters to Shared Storage

It's hard to believe we have been talking about clustering this much, as we haven't even installed the service yet, isn't it? Well, this is the final pre-installation step you need to take, and then we'll get to the service installation. When new disks are discovered, the operating system will assign drive letters sequentially after the letters that have already been assigned. The problem with this is that if one node has more local drives than another, the letters assigned to the shared storage by each node will by out of sync. To prevent this problem, you need to manually assign drive letters to each shared storage disk partition. Typically, we start with the letter Q for the quorum drive and continue upward through the alphabet for all additional drives (R, S, T, U, and so on). Your first disk partition should be a minimum of 500MB for the quorum disk, and all other partitions can be solely based on the needs of your clustered applications. To assign drive letters to shared storage, power down all cluster nodes, then power up the first node, and follow these steps:

1. Log on using an account with local administrative privileges on the node.

2. Click Start ➢ Programs ➢ Administrative Tools ➢ Computer Management.

3. Right-click the shared partition and select Change Drive Letter and Paths.

4. If more than one drive letter is listed, click each additional drive letter and then click Remove.

5. With one drive letter listed, click the letter and then click the Change button.

6. Click the Assign the Following Drive Letter radio button, select a new drive letter from the pull-down menu, and click OK (see Figure 9.11).

7. Once drive letters have been assigned to all shared drives, power down the node.

8. Repeat steps 1 through 6 for all remaining cluster nodes.

Figure 9.11: Using Disk Manager to change drive letters

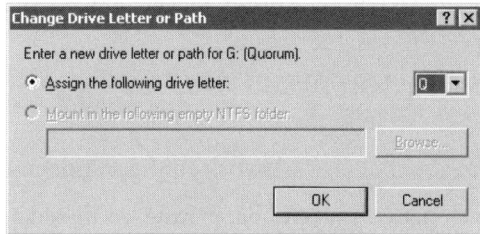

Installing the Cluster Service

Before beginning the installation, power down all nodes in the cluster. Then power up only one node to install the cluster service. Once the installation is complete on the first cluster node, you can then move to power up the remaining cluster nodes and install the service on each of them.

Installing the Cluster Service on the First Node

Perform these steps to set up the cluster service on the first node:

1. Open the Control Panel and double-click the Add/Remove Programs icon.
2. Click the Add/Remove Windows Components button.
3. Select Cluster Service from the list of Windows components and click Next.
4. If prompted, insert the Windows 2000 Advanced or Datacenter Server CD-ROM, or provide the path to the location of the i386 installation folder and click OK.
5. Click Next.
6. The Cluster Service Configuration Wizard appears. Click Next.
7. Click I Understand to verify your acceptance that hardware not on the Microsoft HCL is not supported by the cluster service.
8. Click the radio button to indicate that the server is the first node in the cluster and click Next.
9. Enter the NetBIOS name that clients or cluster administrators will use to access the cluster and click Next.
10. Provide the username, password, and domain for the cluster service account and click Next.

11. Use the Add and Remove buttons to select the disks in the shared storage array that will be managed by the cluster. Once you have selected the desired disks, click Next.

12. Select a partition at least 500MB in size as the location for the Quorum Resource and click Next.

13. Read the note about cluster network configuration and click Next.

14. Configure each network as public, private, or mixed and click Next (see Figure 9.12).

Figure 9.12: Configuring a network connection as a mixed network

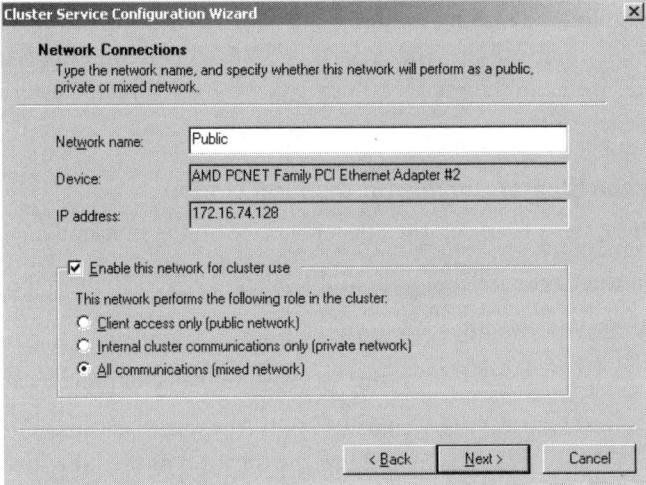

15. Input the TCP/IP settings that the cluster will use to communicate with the rest of the network. Then select the interface the cluster will use to communicate with the public network and click Next.

16. Click Finish to complete the installation of the cluster service.

17. Close the Windows Components Wizard.

Joining Additional Nodes to the Cluster

With installation completed on the first node, you can now install the cluster service on the remaining nodes. First, power up all remaining nodes and then perform these steps on each node:

1. Open the Control Panel and double-click the Add/Remove Programs icon.

2. Click the Add/Remove Windows Components button.
3. Select the Cluster Service checkbox from the list of Windows components and click Next.
4. If prompted, insert the Windows 2000 Advanced or Datacenter Server CD-ROM, or provide the path to the location of the i386 installation folder and click OK.
5. Click Next.
6. When the Cluster Service Configuration Wizard appears, click Next.
7. Click I Understand to verify your acceptance that hardware not on the Microsoft HCL is not supported by the cluster service.
8. Click the radio button to signify that the server is the second or next node in the cluster and click Next.
9. Now type the NetBIOS name of the cluster you want to join the node to, make sure the Connect to Cluster As box is cleared, and click Next.
10. Enter the password for the cluster account listed and click Next.
11. Click Finish to complete the installation of the cluster service.
12. When prompted that the cluster service started successfully, click OK.
13. Close the Windows Components Wizard.

Verifying Failover

Now that the cluster service is installed, it's not a bad idea to make sure the cluster is working properly. Testing failover is actually an easy process. To verify that the cluster group can fail over from one node to another, perform these steps:

1. Click Start ➢ Programs ➢ Administrative Tools ➢ Cluster Administrator to open the Cluster Administrator utility.
2. Expand the Groups folder so that you see a list of preconfigured groups. You should see the cluster group and Disk Group x, where x is a number beginning with 1 for each additional physical disk configured on the cluster's shared storage array.
3. Right-click each group and select Move Group.
4. The group will go offline, then move to another node, and come back online.

After successfully verifying failover, the cluster service is ready to go. At this point, you can install and configure other applications and services on the cluster.

Administering the Cluster Service

When administering the cluster service, you basically have two options:

- Use the Cluster Administrator
- Use the `Cluster.exe` command

Using a graphical interface–driven or command-line tool to administer the cluster is your choice. Both are equally as powerful. Because most administrators choose the graphical tool, which is shown in Figure 9.13, that is where this section will primarily focus. We have included an explanation on the `cluster.exe` command in the "Using the Cluster Command" section.

Figure 9.13: Cluster Administrator Microsoft Management Console (MMC)

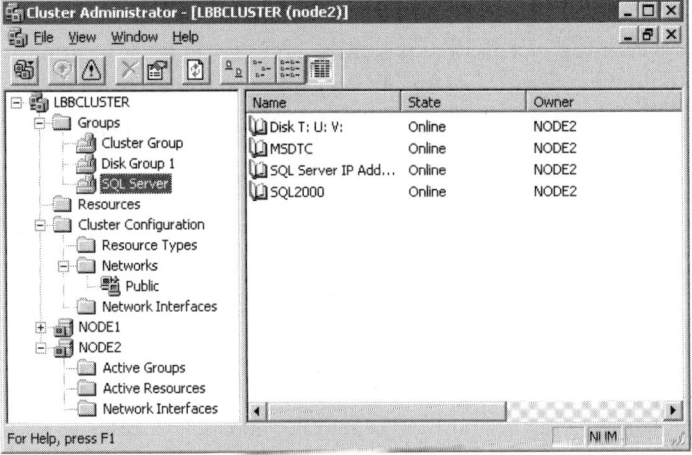

Using the Cluster Administrator

Cluster Administrator is located in the `Program Files\Administrative Tools` folder from the Start menu. Once you open the tool, you should be immediately connected to the cluster you just installed and configured. If not, select Open from the Cluster Administrator's File menu and then enter the name of the cluster. There are countless administrative tasks that can be performed with the Cluster Administrator, so we will concentrate on covering the most frequently used tasks.

Granting User Groups the Right to Manage the Cluster

By default, only members of the Administrators group have permission to manage the cluster. For any cluster, you can grant other users and user groups permission to manage the cluster. A best practice is to create a domain local Cluster Administrator group and then add users to the group that you would like to manage the cluster. Granting individual users permission to manage the cluster could quickly become an administrative nightmare in any enterprise-level network.

Once you have created and added members to the user group, perform these steps to grant the group permission to manage the cluster:

1. In the Cluster Administrator, right-click the cluster icon and select Properties.
2. Select the Security tab.
3. You should now see a list of groups allowed to access cluster resources. To add a new group, click the Add button.
4. Select the user group (or user) you want to add and click OK.
5. You should now see your user group added to the access list. Click OK to close the Cluster Properties dialog box.

Pausing or Resuming a Cluster Node

At this point, you may be wondering if *paused* is the same as *stopped*. The difference between pausing and stopping the service lies in a paused node's ability to still service cluster groups. When a node is stopped, all groups on the node fail over to another node. On the other hand, when a node is paused, any groups running on the node will remain on the node, but no other groups can fail over to the paused node. When a node is nearing its peak processing capacity and you don't want any more groups to run on the node, it is a good idea to pause the node. Also, pausing nodes is often done during a software upgrade.

A node can be paused by right-clicking the node in the Cluster Administrator and selecting Pause Node. If you want to resume the node, simply right-click the node again and select Resume Node.

Evicting Nodes from the Cluster

If you want to permanently remove a node from participating in the cluster, then you will need to *evict* the node.

> **NOTE** When you evict a node from a cluster, the cluster service is not uninstalled on that node. This allows you to quickly rejoin the node to a cluster at a later time.

Follow these steps to evict a node from the cluster:

1. In Cluster Administrator, right-click the node you want to evict and select Stop Cluster Service.

2. Wait a moment for the cluster service to stop, then right-click the node again, and select Evict Node.

3. When warned that evicting the node will permanently remove it from the cluster, click Yes to evict the node.

Creating Groups

Groups are commonly used as containers for related resources and as a definition for a virtual server. Usually, you should have a group for nearly each virtual server you plan to run on the cluster. Many of the latest cluster applications automatically create a group during their installation, but for older applications and to cluster Windows services, you will need to manually create groups.

Some examples of where you would create a group for clustering a Windows service would include:

- Creating virtual file servers
- Creating virtual Internet Information Server (IIS) servers
- Creating virtual print servers

One consideration before creating a group is to decide on which nodes will act as preferred owners for the group. When a group fails over, the node that the group moves to is determined by its configured preferred owners. The highest available node listed as a preferred owner will assume control of the group.

To create a group, follow these steps:

1. Right-click the Groups folder, select New and then Group.

2. Name the group and enter a description for the group and click Next. We generally will name a group after its planned virtual server name, making it easy to identify.

3. Set a preferred owner for the group, as shown in Figure 9.14, if desired and click Finish.

Bringing a Group Online or Offline

When a group is created, it is initially placed in an offline state. If you would like to make the group available to be accessed by clients, you will need to bring the group online. Like many other tasks, taking groups online and offline with Cluster Administrator is easy:

- To bring a group online, right-click the group and select Bring Online.
- To take a group offline, right-click the group and select Take Offline.

Figure 9.14: Configuring preferred owners for a group

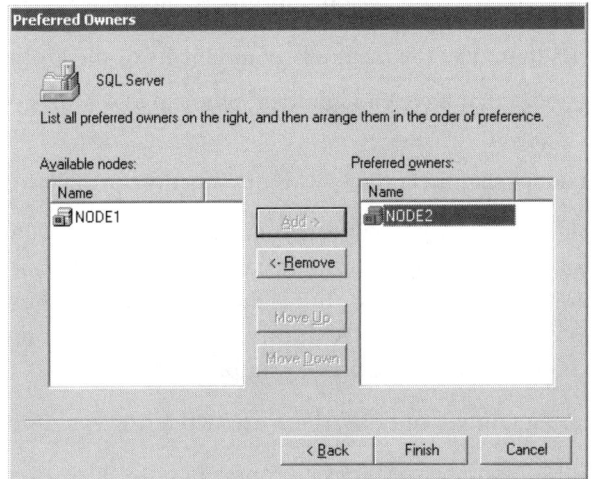

> **NOTE**   Taking a group offline does not cause it to fail over to another node. If you want the group to move to another node, you should right-click the group and select Move Group.

Configuring Group Properties

When a group is initially created, rarely are any advanced group settings configured. To optimize the performance of your cluster, you may find it necessary to apply more granular control to each cluster group. Settings that you can alter on each group include:

- Group name
- Preferred owners
- Failover settings
- Failback settings

You may decide you need to rename a group if its planned purpose changes. Otherwise, if you use the default groups created by the cluster installation (Disk Group 1, Disk Group 2, and so on), you may want to name the group after its intended use to make it easier to identify.

Setting preferred owners for a group allows you to provide a list of nodes that the group will attempt to move to during a failover. The order of nodes listed as preferred nodes will determine to which node a group will first attempt to move. Before just making every node a preferred owner for a group, though, consider the following points:

- List nodes that meet the memory requirements of the group's applications.
- List the nodes that have enough local physical disk storage required to run the group's applications.
- List the nodes that meet the CPU requirements for the group's applications.

When you configure the list, don't forget about nodes that are already hosting groups and applications. For example, if a node has 512MB of RAM, it will meet the minimum requirement for most applications. But if the node is already hosting two groups that collectively consume 350MB of RAM, then the node may not meet the requirements to be a preferred owner for an additional group.

When configuring failover options, there are two terms you need to know:

Threshold   Number of times a group can failover to another node within the specified period

Period   Number of hours allowed for failovers within threshold

To understand the meaning of threshold and period, let's look at an example. Suppose that the threshold is set to the default value of 10, and the period is set to 6. What these numbers mean is that a group can only failover to another node 10 times within a six-hour period. If the group tried to failover an 11th time during the six-hour period, the cluster service would not allow the group to failover to another. Configuring failover boundaries allows you to restrict how many times a group can bounce between cluster nodes. Normally when a group repeatedly fails over, a single resource in the group is malfunctioning. When a resource continually fails, it is better to leave the group on a single node by not allowing it to attempt to failover anymore.

During any failover, a group may be offline for a long as several minutes, depending on how long it takes all of the group's services to stop on one node and then start on another. Now close your eyes and imagine your Exchange Server being unavailable. (You have probably already had this nightmare with your eyes closed, but do it again for this example anyway!) We know that normally a down Exchange Server can cause an organization's help desk to be flooded with calls. If you enable failback, as soon as the Exchange group's original host node comes back online, it will again stop to move back to the node. This means that during production hours, your Exchange Server could go down twice, which is not something most administrators would want to have happen.

By default, failback is disabled so that group downtime is reduced. If you enable failback, you have two options:

- Allow Failback Immediately, which means failback occurs as soon as a group's previous owner is back online.
- Allow Failback Between..., which allows failback to occur only during specified hours.

For critical groups, most administrators will configure failback to occur only between specific hours. For example, if you want a group to be able to automatically move back to its original node during off-peak hours, you could set failback to occur between 19 and 7. This configuration would allow failback to happen only between 7:00 P.M. and 7:00 A.M.

With a solid grasp of the configuration options available for cluster groups, let's now take a look at the steps to configure group properties:

1. Right-click the group and select Properties.
2. From the General tab, you can rename the group or change the preferred nodes for the group. To modify preferred nodes, click the Modify button. The general configuration options for a cluster group are shown in Figure 9.15.

Figure 9.15: Setting preferred owners for a group

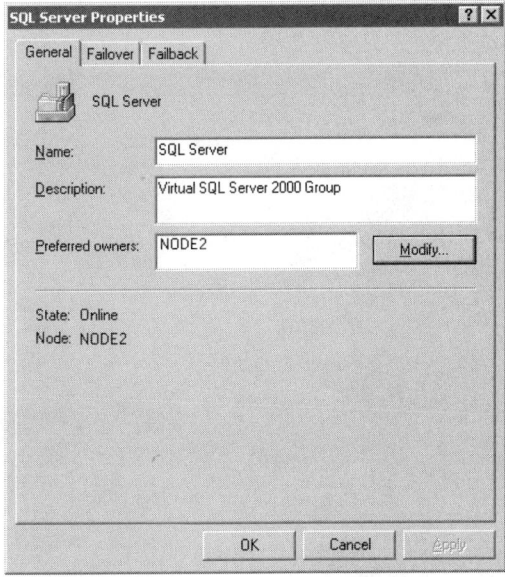

3. To modify failover properties, click the Failover tab.
4. Enter values for failover threshold and a period as required (see Figure 9.16).

Figure 9.16: Setting group failover properties

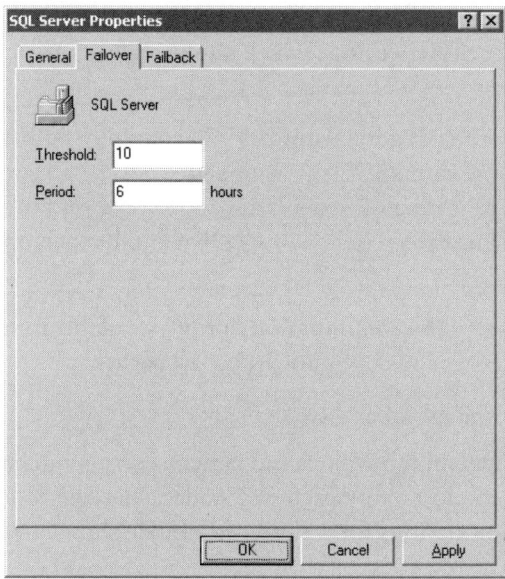

Figure 9.17: Setting failback parameters

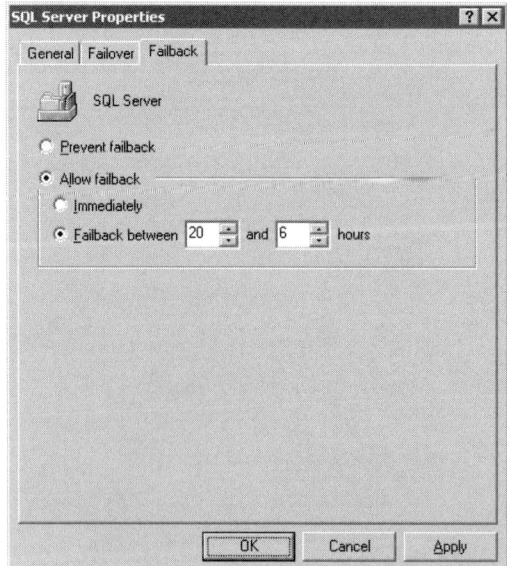

5. To modify failback parameters, click the Failback tab.
6. To allow and configure failback, click the Allow Failback radio button.
7. Click the button to either allow failback immediately or allow failback between specific hours.
8. If you decide to allow failback between specific hours, set the hours and click OK to close the Group Properties dialog box (see Figure 9.17).

Configuring Resource Properties

As when groups are initially created, resources are often created with their default options. Depending on your availability requirements, you may find it necessary to modify resource properties after installing an application on the cluster. Modifying resource properties allows you to change the following parameters:

- Modify general properties to:
    - Change the name or description of resource
    - Set possible owners for resource
    - Configure resource to run in a separate resource monitor
- Set resource dependencies
- Configure advanced resource properties to:
    - Set restart parameters
    - Set Looks Alive poll interval
    - Set Is Alive poll interval
    - Set pending timeout value
- Modify resource parameters

When configuring the general properties of a resource, aside from naming the resource, you have two more configuration options:

Possible Owners This allows you to list the nodes that have the ability to run the resource, thus preventing the resource from failing over to a node that does not have the hardware or software requirements to host the resource.

Run in a Separate Resource Monitor. This allows you to have the resource run in a separate resource monitor process separate from other resources. This option is cleared by default, which is usually fine. If the resource is a DLL file that may conflict with other DLLs running in the same process, then you should run it in a separate resource monitor.

> **TIP** If the resource continually fails, an easy troubleshooting step is to check the option to run the resource in a separate resource monitor before attempting to troubleshoot further.

Many resources cannot run if others aren't already running. For example, a Network Name resource needs to be associated with an IP Address resource to run. These associations are known to the cluster service as *dependencies*. Dependencies also define how resources fail. In the previous example with a network name resource being dependent on an IP Address resource, if the IP Address resource goes offline, the Network Name resource will go offline as well.

Under the advanced resource properties, there are several options. Here is a brief description of each advanced property:

Do Not Restart When selected, the cluster service will not try and automatically restart a failed resource.

Affect the Group If selected and the resource fails, the entire group will fail over to another node.

Restart Threshold Value for the number of times the cluster service will attempt to restart a resource within the specified period.

Restart Period Value for the number of seconds that restarts within the restart threshold are allowed. For example, with the Restart Threshold value set to 6 and the Period set to 300, the cluster service will attempt to restart the resource after failure six times within 300 seconds (5 minutes). If a resource cannot restart within the restart threshold/period, it is left as failed, and the cluster service does not attempt to restart it again.

"Looks Alive" Poll Interval This value specifies an increment of time when the cluster service will check the resource to see if it is running. Usually, the default value is fine for this option.

"Is Alive" Poll Interval This value specifies an increment of time where checks that are more extensive than Looks Alive checks are run. This test is run less frequently than Looks Alive checks because it consumes more resources. Usually, the default value for this option is fine.

Pending Timeout This value is used to set the maximum time that a resource can be in a pending state (Offline Pending or Online Pending). If a resource represents a service, this value is the time the cluster service will wait for the service to start or stop. When a resource does not start within its pending timeout period, it is marked as "Failed."

Resource parameters are settings that are specific to a particular resource. For example, for a Network Name resource, you would see its NetBIOS name values under its Parameters tab.

With a sound understanding of resource properties, let's now look at the steps to modify the properties:

1. In Cluster Administrator, expand the Groups folder.

2. Click the group whose resources you want to modify, and you will see its resources listed in the right pane of the Cluster Administrator.

3. Right-click the resource you want to modify and select Properties.

4. Under the General tab, you can change the name, description, or possible owners for a resource, as shown in Figure 9.18. When finished setting these values, click the Dependencies tab.

Figure 9.18: Setting general resource properties

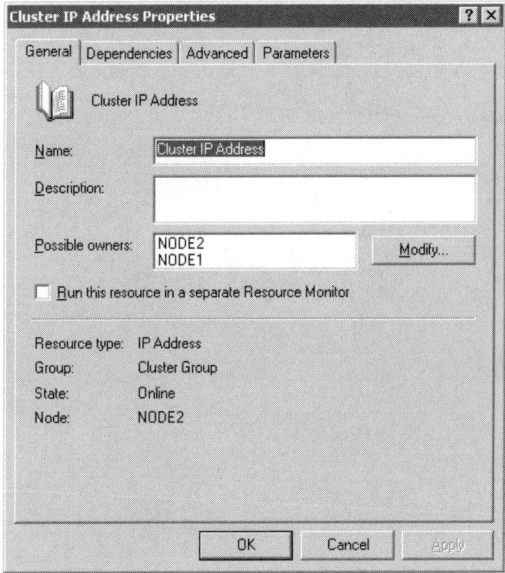

5. The Dependencies tab enables you to see the resources on which the selected resource is dependent. To change resource dependencies, click the Modify button.

6. Select the resources that the selected resource will be dependent on and click OK, as shown in Figure 9.19. You will only see resources listed that are in the selected resource's group.

Figure 9.19: Modifying resource dependencies

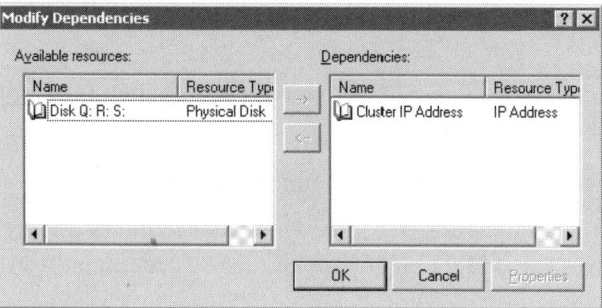

7. Now click the Advanced tab.
8. As shown in Figure 9.20, set the advanced properties for the resource.

Figure 9.20: Setting advanced resource properties

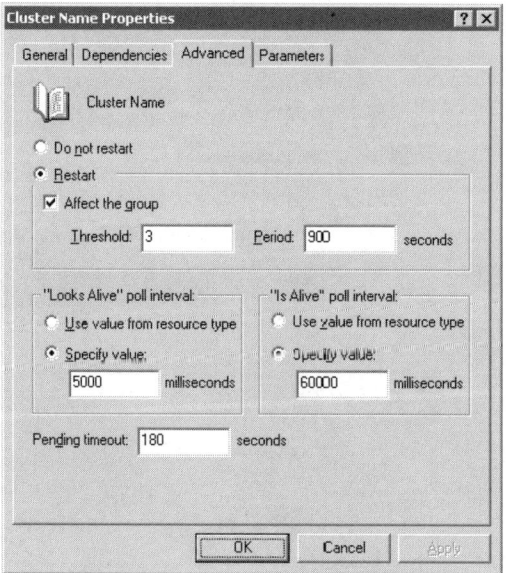

9. Now click the Parameters tab.
10. Modify the parameters for the resource and click OK to close the Resource Properties dialog box (see Figure 9.21).

Figure 9.21: Modifying parameters of an IP address resource

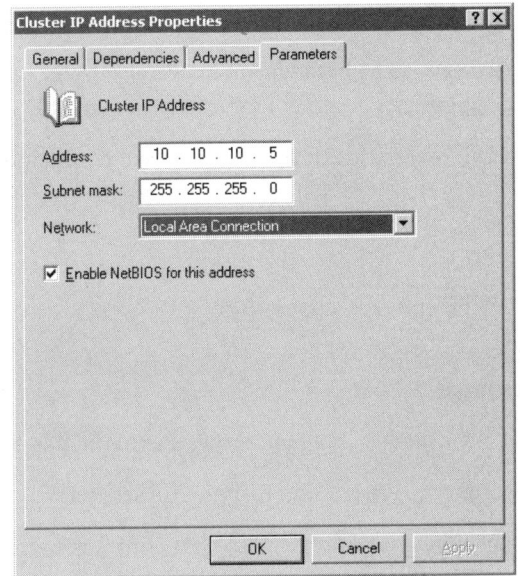

Initiating Resource Failures

Before waiting for a real failure to test failover, you should manually initiate a failover to test your group's failover to other nodes.

To initiate the failure of a resource:

1. In Cluster Administrator, expand the Groups folder.
2. Click the group whose resource you want to fail. You should now see its resources listed in the right pane of the Cluster Administrator.
3. Right-click the resource and select Initiate Failure.

Using the Cluster Command

Practically anything that can be done from Cluster Administrator can also be performed from the command line or even scripted. The cluster.exe command-line utility is installed by default into the %systemroot%/system32 directory when Cluster Service installed. The command-line utility is installed once the Cluster Administrator is installed and can be run from any of the following platforms:

- Windows 2000

- Windows NT Workstation 4.0 (with Service Pack 3 or later)
- Windows NT Server 4.0 (with Service Pack 3 or later)

When identical tasks have to be performed on several clusters, it is often easier to use `cluster.exe` and script the tasks rather than run each manually using Cluster Administrator.

The five most common versions of the `cluster.exe` command are:

- Cluster
- Cluster Group
- Cluster Network
- Cluster Node
- Cluster Resource

Each variation of the `cluster.exe` command is explained in the next five sections.

Before using the `cluster.exe` command-line utilities, remember these points:

- Whenever specifying a name or path that contains spaces, place quotes (") around the name or path.
- If setting properties to true or false, use a 1 for true and a 0 for false.
- `<data>` signifies required syntax.
- `[data]` signifies optional syntax.

Using the Cluster Command

The Cluster command can be used to administer the cluster as a whole. The basic syntax for using the `Cluster.exe` command is as follows:

```
Cluster [cluster name] /options
```

Several options can be run in conjunction with the Cluster command (see Table 9.2).

Table 9.2: Cluster Command Options

Option	Description
/Add: <node1, node2, etc.>	Adds one or more specified nodes to an existing cluster
/Create: <path to answer file>	Creates a cluster using information in the specified answer file
/List: <domain name>	Displays a list of all clusters within the specified domain

Continued on next page

Table 9.2 (Continued): Cluster Command Options

Option	Description
`<new cluster name> /create /ipaddr: <static IP address>[, subnet mask, network connection name] /password:<password> /domain:<domain name> /node:<node name> /user:<domain\cluster user account name> /verbose`	Creates new cluster with information specified
`/Properties`	Displays cluster properties
`/Privproperties`	Displays cluster private properties
`/Quorum: <resource name>`	Renames quorum resource to the name specified
`/Quorum /path:<path>`	Changes the path to where the quorum resource is stored to the path specified
`/Quorum /maxlogsize: <maximum value of quorum log in KB>`	Sets a new maximum value for the size of the quorum log
`/Rename: <new cluster name>`	Renames the cluster and changes value for network name resource in the Cluster Group
`/Version`	Displays the version number of the cluster service software

Here are a few examples of using cluster.exe on a cluster named ESSCluster.

- To rename the cluster to W2KESSCluster:

    `cluster ESSCluster /rename: W2KESSCluster`
- To view all clusters in the Sybex.com domain:

    `cluster /list: Sybex.com`
- To view the properties of the cluster:

    `cluster /properties`

Using the Cluster Group Command

The Cluster Group command is used to administer a single cluster group. The basic syntax for using the command is as follows:

`Cluster [[/cluster:]cluster name] group <group name> /options`

Table 9.3 describes the options that can be run with this command.

Table 9.3: Cluster Group Command Options

Option	Description
/create	Creates a group with the name specified in the *group name* portion of the syntax.
/delete	Deletes the group specified in the *group name* portion of the syntax.
/move [:node name] [/wait: <*timeout value in seconds*>]	Moves a group to another node. When used in conjunction with the wait switch, the cluster service will wait the specified period before timing out and canceling the command if it has yet to complete.
/online [:node name] [/wait: <*timeout value in seconds*>]	Brings a group online. If a node is specified, the group will be brought online on that node. If a wait value is specified, the cluster service will wait the specified period before timing out and canceling the command if it has yet to complete.
/offline [:node name] [/wait: <*timeout value in seconds*>]	Takes a group offline. If a node is specified, the group will be taken offline on that node. If a wait value is specified, the cluster service will wait the specified period before timing out and canceling the command if it has yet to complete.
/Properties	Displays group's properties.
/Privproperties	Displays group's private properties.
/Rename: <*new group name*>	Renames the group to the name specified.
/Setowners:<*node name*>[,node name...]	Sets preferred owner(s) for group.

Here are a couple of examples of using the Cluster Group command on a cluster named ESSCluster.

- To create a new group named Exchange:

    `cluster ESSCluster group Exchange /create`
- To move the Exchange group to a node named Node1:

    `cluster ESSCluster group Exchange /move:node1`

Using the Cluster Network Command

The Cluster Network command is used to administer a cluster's network configuration. The basic syntax for using the command is as follows:

`Cluster [[/cluster:]cluster name] network <network name> /options`

Table 9.4 describes the options that can be run with this command.

Table 9.4: Cluster Network Command Options

Option	Description
/listinterfaces	Lists network interfaces associated with the cluster network
/Properties	Displays or can be used to set cluster network's properties
/Privproperties	Displays or can be used to set cluster network's private properties
/Rename: <new network name>	Renames the network to the name specified
/Status	Displays the status of the network

Here are a couple of examples on using the Cluster Network command on a cluster named ESSCluster:

- To display the status of the Public network:

    `cluster ESSCluster network Public /status`
- To display the interfaces used on the Public network:

    `cluster ESSCluster network Public /listinterfaces`

Using the Cluster Node Command

The Cluster Node command is used to administer a cluster's network configuration. The basic syntax for using the command is as follows:

`Cluster [[/cluster:]cluster name] node <node name> /options`

Table 9.5 describes the options that can be run with this command.

Table 9.5: Cluster Node Command Options

Option	Description
/evict	Evicts the node from the cluster.
/force[cleanup] [/wait:<timeout value in seconds>]	Cleans up all cluster-related metadata and restores the cluster configuration on the specified node to its original state prior to ever participating in a cluster. When used in conjunction with the wait switch, the cluster service will wait the specified period before timing out and canceling the command if it has yet to complete.
/Listinterfaces	Lists the node's network interfaces.
/Pause	Pauses the node.
/Properties	Displays or can be used to set the node's properties.
/Privproperties	Displays or can be used to set cluster node's private properties.
/Resume	Resumes a paused cluster node.
/Start [/wait:<timeout value in seconds>]	Starts the cluster service on the cluster node. When used in conjunction with the wait switch, the cluster service will wait the specified period before timing out and canceling the command if it has yet to complete.
/Status	Displays the status of the cluster node as either up or down.
/Stop [/wait:<timeout value in seconds>]	Stops the cluster service on the cluster node. When used in conjunction with the wait switch, the cluster service will wait the specified period before timing out and canceling the command if it has yet to complete.

Here are a couple of examples on using the Cluster Node command on a cluster named ESSCluster and a node named Node2:

- To pause the node:

    cluster ESSCluster node node2 /pause

- To start the cluster service on the node, allowing the service to try and start for 10 minutes before timing out:

    cluster ESSCluster node node2 /start /wait:600

Using the Cluster Resource Command

The Cluster Resource command is used to administer resources on a cluster. The basic syntax for using the command is as follows:

```
Cluster [[/cluster:]cluster name] resource <resource name> /options
```

Table 9.6 describes the options that can be run with this command.

Table 9.6: Cluster Resource Command Options

Option	Description
/Create /group: <group name> /type:<resource type> [/separate]	Creates a new resource in the group specified. The resource type must be input as well. The separate switch is used if you want the new resource to run in a separate resource monitor. You can use a separate cluster resource command with the properties switch to configure the properties for the resource.
/Adddependency: <resource>	Adds a dependency for the resource.
/Addowner: <node name>	Adds the specified node to the list of possible owners.
/Delete	Deletes the resource.
/Fail	Initiates failure of the resource.
/Listdependencies	Displays the dependencies for the resource.
/Listowners	Lists the possible owners for the resource.
/Moveto:<Group name>	Moves the resource to the specified group.
/Offline	Takes a resource offline.
/Online	Brings a resource online.
/Properties	Displays and modifies the properties of a resource.
/Removedependency: <resource>	Removes a dependency for a resource.
/Removeowner: <node name>	Removes the specified node from the list of possible owners.
/Rename: <resource name>	Renames a resource.

Here are a couple of examples of using the Cluster Resource command on a cluster named ESSCluster and a node named ExchangeIP:

- To initiate the failure of the resource:
    ```
    cluster ESSCluster resource ExchangeIP /fail
    ```
- To take the resource offline:
    ```
    cluster ESSCluster resource ExchangeIP /offline
    ```

The Cluster command is a powerful tool, allowing you to do practically any task from the command line that you could perform using the Cluster Administrator.

10

File System Backup and Recovery

You might have been surprised that for a book about storage, you have had to wait nine chapters before reading about backing up and restoring files. That's because, with proper planning, this is the easy part.

Although earlier we told you to stay away from using Windows Backup, we will be using it in this chapter's examples. The main reason for doing this is because it is the one standard everyone has. Besides, backup and restore is what it does. Some of the high-end backup and restore products will automate some of your work for you, but they basically all do the same thing.

In this chapter, we dive into the basics of backing up and recovering Windows 2000 servers. For the most part, we concentrate on the simple parts of file system backup and recovery. We talk about how to back up and restore files and the Active Directory. In Chapter 11, "Operating System Rebuilds: The Gotchas," you will learn all the issues that exist between the lines.

Creating an Emergency Repair Disk

Although Emergency Repair Disks (ERDs) were mentioned earlier, we have waited until now to give you the full story. If you already have an enterprise backup solution that you trust, you may think that maintaining ERDs are not necessary. Restoring from a backup is always a viable option, but you also have to consider restore time.

> **NOTE** You can say *goodbye* to ERDs with the Windows XP and .NET Server platforms. For more information, turn to Chapter 14, "The Future of Storage."

> **TIP** You should create an ERD for each server you have. In some situations, you can repair a server much faster from an ERD than from a backup.

With Windows NT, you could run the Rdisk utility to create an ERD. With Windows 2000, ERDs are created using Windows Backup. From within Backup, the ERD is created using a wizard.

> **NOTE** With Windows NT, a backup of the Registry was stored on the ERD. Because of the rules regarding Windows 2000 System State components, this in no longer the case. When the System State is backed up, backup Registry files are stored in the %systemroot%\Repair\Regback folder. You can use these files to repair a corrupted Registry.

Creating an ERD

You should create an ERD:

- After you first install Windows 2000
- After a hardware upgrade
- After changing the existing disk configuration
- After any service pack, hot fix, or driver update

Follow these steps to create an ERD:

1. Click Start ➢ Programs ➢ Accessories ➢ System Tools ➢ Backup.
2. From Backup, click Tools and then click Create an Emergency Repair Disk.
3. Insert a blank, formatted disk into the A drive and click OK (see Figure 10.1). Notice that you can also select to have the Registry backed up to the Repair folder.

Figure 10.1: Creating an Emergency Repair Disk

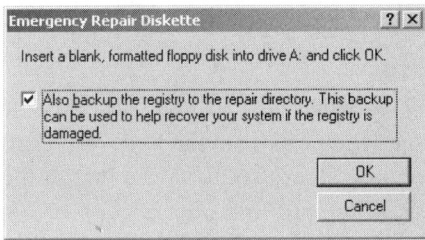

4. Once finished, you will receive a message telling you to label the disk as an ERD, along with the date you created it, and store it in a safe location.

Using Windows 2000 Repair

The Windows 2000 Repair option lets you use an ERD to repair the Windows Server, or you can get to the command line through the Recovery Console option. To repair a Windows Server, you can boot the server from the installation CD-ROM or you can boot from the setup boot disks. You can create setup disks by running `makeboot.exe`, which is in the Bootdisk folder of the Windows installation CD-ROM. To use `makeboot.exe`, you need four blank floppy disks.

Once you boot from the installation CD-ROM or setup disks, press R to repair the server. When you do this, you will see the following options:

```
To repair a Windows 2000 installation by using
the recovery console, press C.
To repair a Windows 2000 installation by using
the Emergency Repair Process, press R.
```

The following sections explain each of these options.

Windows 2000 Recovery Console

Although similar, the Recovery Console is not the Windows 2000 command prompt. Microsoft defines the Recovery Console as "a text-mode command interpreter." When you select to enter the Recovery Console, you will first be asked to choose the Windows installation to which you would like to log on. If there is only one operating system on your system, just type **1** and press Enter. After you provide the Administrator password, you will be logged on to the console. The Recovery Console gives you limited command-line functionality to repair the operating system.

You can use the Recovery Console to perform the following tasks:

- Fix the master boot record.
- Start, stop, enable, and disable services.

- Check and repair disk sectors for errors.
- Copy files.

Console Commands

The following are the most useful Recovery Console commands. Do not assume that each console command when run from the Recovery Console is the same as if it were executed from the command line. You will find that in the Recovery Console, these commands execute slightly differently and offer fewer switches and options in their syntax.

Chksdk

Chksk runs a simple diagnostic routine on a hard disk and reports any errors it finds. It does have the ability to recover information from any bad disk sectors that it finds.

This is the syntax:

chkdsk [drive:] [/p] [/r]

[drive:] is used to specify the drive you want chksk to scan. By default, chksk will scan the drive on which it is being run.

[/p] causes chksk to scan a drive, even if it has not been marked as "dirty."

[/r] causes chksk to locate and recover and usable data found on bad disk sectors.

Figure 10.2 shows an example of executing chksk.

Figure 10.2: Chksk execution

NOTE Chksk requires the autochk.exe file to run. If this file is not present in the boot folder, chksk will retrieve the file from the Windows 2000 setup CD-ROM.

Copy

Copy allows you to copy a replacement file from a source, such as the Windows 2000 installation or service pack CD, to a specified destination. This lets you replace a bad file with a known good equivalent. When run in the Recovery Console, copy has the following limitations:

- Wildcards cannot be used.
- Copying between folders is not permitted.

Another nice feature with copy is that when copying compressed files from the installation or service pack CD-ROM, they are automatically decompressed.

This is the syntax:

    copy source [destination]

source is the full path to the source file.

[destination] is the path to the destination folder of the copied file. With no destination specified, the copied file will be written to the folder where the copy command is run.

Disable
This command allows you to disable services. This is useful if some services are hanging during the bootup of the operating system.

This is the syntax:

    disable <service name>

<service name> is the name of service or driver you want to disable.

Enable
This command is used to enable a service or driver.

This is the syntax:

    enable <service name> [start type]

<service name> is the name of service or driver you want to enable.

Fixboot
The command will write a new boot sector on the system partition. You also have the option of specifying the drive that you would like the boot sector written to.

This is the syntax:

    fixboot [drive:]

[drive:] is the drive where the boot sector will be written. When not specified, a new boot sector is written to the system boot partition.

Fixmbr
Fixmbr is used to check and correct a bad master boot record on the boot partition. Before running fixmbr, run antivirus software against the boot partition. You can actually damage the master boot record when running fixmbr when a virus is present.

This is the syntax:

fixmbr [device name]

[device name] is the name of device that has the faulty master boot record. When a device name is not specified, the master boot record on the boot device is checked and fixed.

Listsvc

This is used to display a list of all services and drivers installed on the computer.

This is the syntax:

listsvc

Map

Used by itself, map allows you to see the drive letter to physical drive associations for the computer. When used with the arc parameter, you will see the drive letter to ARC path associations displayed.

This is the syntax:

map [arc]

[arc] displays the drive letter to arc path associations for each physical drive.

Figure 10.3 shows the execution of the command map arc.

Figure 10.3: Map arc output

Reasons to Use the Recovery Console

Although there are several good reasons for using the Recovery Console (primarily when a system cannot boot to the GUI), we will stick with situations particularly relevant to backup and recovery. After restoring a system, you may find it necessary to use the Recovery Console to:

- Fix the boot.ini file
- Restore the Registry

These two instances are explained next.

Fixing the boot.ini File

From the Repair Console, you can copy a good `boot.ini` file over the existing version. If you copy the existing `boot.ini` file to a floppy disk, you can use a text editor on another computer to edit the `boot.ini` file and then copy it back to the root folder on the down system.

Restoring the Registry

There is quite a bit of talk that because the Registry is a part of the System State, the only way to recover it is to restore the System State data. Although restoring the System State is one way to recover the Registry, it is not the only way. If you created an ERD, the Registry will be backed up to the `%system root%\Repair\Regback` folder. You can use this backup to repair the Registry from the Recovery Console.

If you do not see a Regback folder, you will see Registry files also located in the `%systemroot%\repair` folder. These files are a backup of the Registry that was created when you first installed Windows 2000. To restore a corrupted Registry, you can copy the backup Registry files from the Repair directory to the `%systemroot%\config` folder.

Repairing a Windows 2000 Server with the ERD

You can use repair to fix your server using your ERD. When you run the emergency repair process, you have two choices:

- Manual Repair
- Fast Repair

Fast Repair

Fast Repair is the quick and easy method that requires no user input. All you will have to do is insert the ERD. Windows will take care of the rest. With Fast Repair, Windows will try and fix everything it has the ability to fix. This includes:

- Boot sector on system disk
- Registry
- System files

Although this option is useful, you may want to have a little more control over the repair process. You can do this by choosing the Manual Repair option.

Manual Repair

With Manual Repair, you are presented with the choice to perform one of three different repairs or checks.

Inspect Boot Sector

Choosing this option will cause Windows to make sure the boot sector on the system partition still points to NTLDR. As long as the system partition is on the first hard disk (referenced by `boot.ini`), Windows will be able to fix the boot sector if necessary.

Inspect Startup Environment

Windows checks the boot files. If the `boot.ini` file cannot be found, Windows will replace it with a new one. Windows will also check for NTLDR and `ntdetect.com`. If either of these is missing they are copied from the Windows 2000 CD-ROM.

Verify Windows 2000 System Files

If you choose this option, Windows will verify the system files against the installation CD-ROM for validity. Any files that Windows believes may be corrupted will be displayed, and you will be asked if you want to replace the file with its generic equivalent found on the Windows 2000 installation CD-ROM.

Using ERD Didn't Work! Now What?

Full system restores are time-consuming and may place a load on your network, depending on whether you backed up the Windows 2000 system over the local area network (LAN). Using the ERD or Recovery Console to fix your system may not solve your problem, but it is a fast way to try and bring a Windows system back to operation. Because trying to repair a system with an ERD only takes a couple of minutes, you have nothing to lose by at least trying the repair. When a basic repair using an ERD fails, you have two choices:

- Reinstall Windows, choosing to repair the existing Windows installation.
- Restore the system from a backup.

> **TIP** Never forget about the obvious. Pressing F8 at bootup and selecting to boot using the Last Known Good Configuration might be all you need to do.

Performing Backups

You were introduced to backup basics in Chapter 2, "Storage Terminology," so we won't dwell on them in this chapter. The most important issue regarding backups is restores. If your backups do not meet your restore requirements, then they are worthless. Keep this in mind when performing or scheduling backups.

Depending on the backup software you use, creating a backup schedule is most likely relatively automated by a wizard. For those looking for small, office-level backup and recovery solutions, you might be able to use Windows Backup. Because everyone who has Windows 2000 has Windows Backup, the examples in this chapter refer to Windows Backup. Keep in mind that the process for nearly all backup solutions is pretty much the same. After all, clicking a couple of buttons with a mouse is the easy part. Understanding the underlying issues behind backups and restores is a little tougher.

Full Backups: The Foundation

Any backup scheme should begin with a full backup. The regularity with which you perform full backups depends on how frequently data is changed or added and on the restore efficiency for which you are looking. Frequent fulls will result in faster restores, so plan to do them regularly. You might consider a scheme that uses weekly fulls and daily incrementals. Or your needs may be better suited by monthly fulls, weekly differentials, and daily incrementals.

Backup Options

Backups are generally broken down into two parts:

- File system backup
- System State backup

With Backup, the System State can be explicitly chosen or can be backed up when you back up My Computer. Chapter 3, "Windows 2000 Storage Enhancements," provided you with details on the contents of the System State. Remember that the Active Directory is included in backups of the System State.

> **NOTE** Only members of the Backup Operators or Administrators groups can back up the System State.

Active Directory Backup Considerations

The following Active Directory files are backed up as a part of the System State:

- `ntds.dit`   Active Directory database
- `edb.chk`   Checkpoint file
- `edb*.log`   10MB transaction log files
- `Res1.log` and `Res2.log`   Reserved transaction logs

When dealing with replicated data, some ask, "Why should I bother? If I have multiple domain controllers, I can always rebuild a server and run `dcpromo.exe` to re-promote it back to a domain controller." Although this approach might be good for some, it certainly is not good for all. When planning your backup scheme for Active Directory, consider the following:

- Do you back up and restore data over the same network that your domain controllers replicate over?
- Does your environment consist of multiple sites distributed over several wide area network (WAN) links?
- Do you compress data during backup?

If you are doing full backups on your domain controllers, you should be backing up the System State and thus the Active Directory at that time as well. If you are restoring system data uncompressed over the LAN, you may find little difference between using your backup software to restore a domain controller or just reinstalling Windows and re-promoting the domain controller.

> **NOTE** Windows Backup only supports the backup and restore of System State data to a local computer. This means that a restore of Active Directory data across your network is not possible using Backup. Any of the major enterprise backup solutions (CommVault, Veritas, Legato) will give you this ability.

If your Active Directory forest traverses multiple sites, then regular backups should be your course of action. Microsoft provides the following performance benchmark for replicating a 2GB Active Directory database over a WAN:

- 128Kbps link   12 hours
- 1.544Mbps   5 hours

Benchmarks are only considered a general reference, and your particular performance will directly depend on the hardware you have. In Microsoft's test, they used Compaq Proliant 1600s with dual 266MHz CPUs, 256MB RAM, and a single hard drive.

If your network resides in more than one physical location, then recovery via replication also is probably not the answer for you. You will need to back up to some form of removable media, such as tape, and locate the media at an offsite location so that you can recover your domain in the event of a natural disaster such as a fire or a flood.

Active Directory Tombstone Lifetime

Active Directory objects, when deleted, are not completely removed for 60 days, by default.

> **WARNING** You can modify the 60-day tombstone lifetime value by editing the Active Directory schema. Microsoft does not recommend any user-performed schema modifications. Do so at your own risk!

The 60-day lifetime value means that deleted objects are not fully removed from the directory until 60 days after their date of deletion. Windows will protect the consistency of the Active Directory by not allowing you to restore deleted Active Directory objects older than their tombstone lifetime.

> **TIP** For domain controllers, make sure your System State backup interval falls within the Active Directory tombstone lifetime, meaning that when leaving the default settings, you should back up the System State on domain controllers at least once every 60 days.

Effect of Open Files on Backups

Files that are locked by either an application or a user will be skipped during a backup. For example, if you are performing a file system backup on a SQL server, the data and log files will be locked by SQL, and you will not be able to back them up using a default file system backup. You will also see that files such as NTUSER.dat are missed as well if the system is backed up while a user is logged on. We will cover backup and recovery of SQL in Chapter 13, "SQL 7/2000 Backup/Recovery."

Open Files: Issue or Non-issue?

First, you need to determine if the files skipped by the backup are even needed. Nearly all backup solutions have a means of logging unsuccessfully backed up files. If these files are backed up by another agent, or are simply missed once and backed up during the next backup, then don't worry. If you notice a trend in needed files that are continually missed, then you have two choices:

- Script a shutdown of the application, copy the locked file to a temporary directory, and restart the application; the copied file will be backed up.
- Purchase an open file management solution.

> **NOTE** You will find sample shutdown/startup scripts in Chapter 12, "Exchange 5.5/2000 Backup/Recovery," and in Chapter 13, "SQL 7/2000 Backup/Recovery."

Some of the higher-end backup solutions bundle Open File Manager (OFM) with their software. If your backup solution has an integrated OFM, odds are that the backup solution is currently managing the backup of open files on your servers. If your backup solution already integrates with an open file manager, then you have the ability to back up open files the day you install the backup software. If your backup solution does not have a built-in OFM, and you find it necessary to back up all open files during a backup, then you can purchase open file management software separately from your backup solution. OFM software vendors usually publish the backup solutions with which they integrate. Basically, all you have to do is install the OFM application, and it will run behind the scenes. The standard for open file management has been St. Bernard's Open File Manager. You can find information about their products at www.stbernard.com.

Another up-and-coming method to manage open files is through snapshot technology. You have already read about some of this technology in the NAS chapter and will see more in Chapter 14, "The Future of Storage." With snapshots, you can achieve guaranteed backup of data, regardless of time and independent of which files are open or locked. Because snapshots work at the block level and not at the file level, open files are not a concern.

Setting Up a Backup Schedule

For most situations, your backup schedule will coincide with times of low utilization of your server. Often, this will be at night. For database servers, discussed later, this may not be an option. For typical division or departmental level file servers, this is usually the case, and this is the scenario that we will concentrate on in this section.

Scheduling Weekly Full Backups

To schedule a weekly full backup, follow these steps:

1. Click Start ➢ Programs ➢ Accessories ➢ System Tools ➢ Backup.
2. From the Welcome tab in the Backup dialog box, click the Backup Wizard icon.
3. When the wizard opens, click Next.
4. You are now presented with three choices on what to back up:
   - Back up everything on my computer
   - Back up selected files, drives, or network data
   - Only back up the System State data

   Now select how you want to back up the system and click Next. Choosing to back up everything is the easiest means to ensure that the system is protected, but it requires the most backup media. In this example, we elected to back up selected files, drives, or network data.

5. If you chose to back up selected files, drives, or network data, you will now need to specify what you want to back up. Select the data to back up as shown in Figure 10.4 and click Next.

Figure 10.4: Selecting drives and the System State to back up

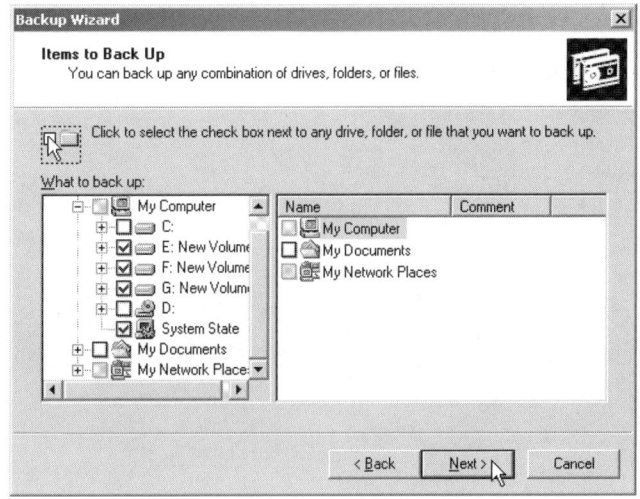

6. Select the media to back up to and click Next.
7. Now click Advanced to set additional options.
8. Select Normal for the backup type. Notice that you can also elect to back up migrated Remote Storage Service (RSS) data here as well. RSS administration was covered extensively in Chapter 4, so you can turn back to that chapter for a refresher on that service.

> **TIP** RSS is a service designed for random access. Randomly accessing files on a tape will significantly slow down your backup. We have seen backup times increase over six hours when backing up RSS-archived files. Another option would be to use RSS's own copy feature to make a disaster recovery (DR) copy of archived files.

9. If you would like the backup data verified for integrity, check its associated box and click Next. Otherwise, just click Next.
10. Select to append the backup to the existing backup set on the media. Otherwise, it will be overwritten.
11. Enter a label for the backup job and media and click Next.
12. Enter a job name, such as **Weekly Full**. For When to Backup, choose Later and click the Set Schedule button.

13. For a backup that runs each week, set the schedule options as shown in Figure 10.5.

Figure 10.5: Configuring the backup to run every Sunday

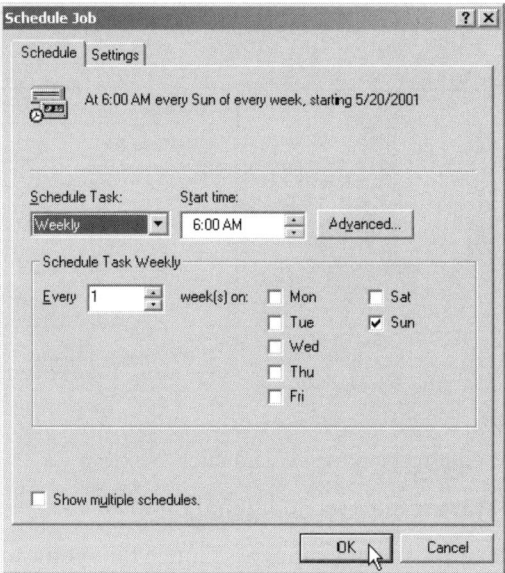

14. Make sure all settings are correct and click Finish to complete the scheduling of the job.

Scheduling Daily Incremental Backups

Now that you have seen how easy setting up a weekly full is, configuring incrementals to run each day of the week is simple as well. To schedule daily incrementals, you would follow steps 1 through 7 of the full backup scheduling procedures, and then do this:

1. Select Incremental as the backup type and click Next.

2. Choose whether to verify the backup data and click Next.

3. Choose to Append the backup to the current backup files on the backup media and click Next.

4. Enter a label for the backup job and media and click Next.

5. Select to run the backup Later and give the job a name, such as **Daily Incremental**. Then click the Set Schedule button.

6. For a backup that runs each business day, set the schedule options as shown in Figure 10.6.

Figure 10.6: Configuring daily incremental backups

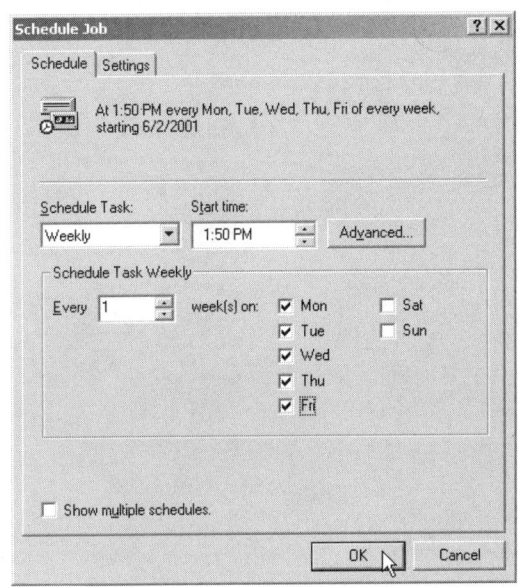

7. Make sure all settings are correct and click Finish to complete the scheduling of the job.

Modifying Scheduled Jobs

Scheduled jobs can be modified from Windows Backup or by using the Task Scheduler. Both options provide the same functionality. Backup will show jobs in a Calendar format, but the Task Scheduler does not. Viewing jobs using the Backup calendar lets you see if you have too many jobs stacked up on a certain day, compared to just using the Task Scheduler.

To see your scheduled backup jobs, click the Schedule Jobs tab in the Backup window. You will then see a window similar to what is shown in Figure 10.7.

You can change the scheduled job's parameters by clicking the icon that represents a specific job in the window. From there you can edit the same parameters that you configured when first creating the scheduled backup, including the days on which the job runs.

Figure 10.7: The Scheduled Backup Calendar

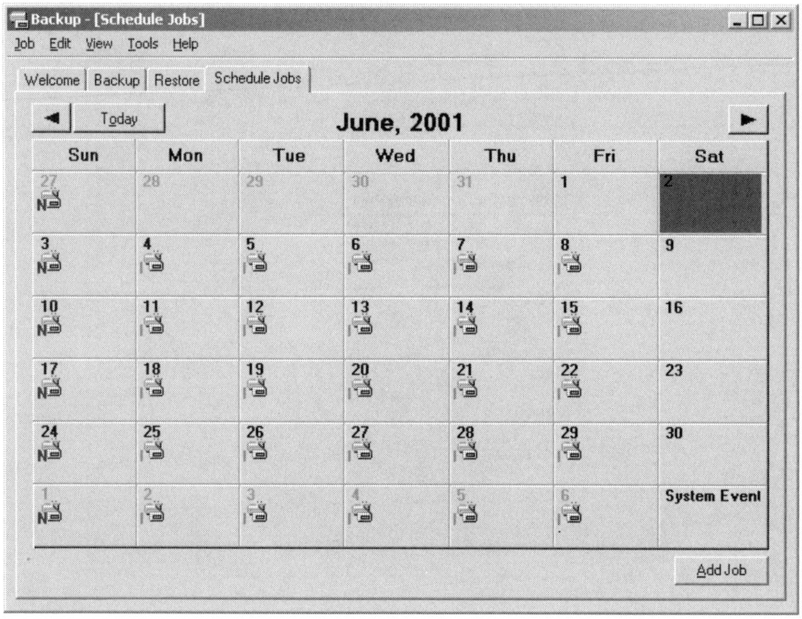

Automatically Filtered Data

By default, there are certain files that Windows will not back up because from a restore perspective, these files are useless. You do not need to back up everything, considering that many files are re-created each time the operating system starts, and others are temporary files that are deleted.

Default Filtered Data

Windows 2000 maintains a Registry key that lists the default filtered data. Windows Backup uses this key when backing up your system. If you are not using Backup, your enterprise backup solution most likely has its own graphical user interface (GUI)–driven filter tool. If you are using Backup, additional filtering of files for backup can be achieved through editing the Registry or by using the Backup GUI. As shown in Figure 10.8, you will see a list of filtered files and folders in the HKEY_LOCAL_MACHINE\SYSTEM\CurrentControlSet\Control\BackupRestore\FilesNotToBackup key.

You can also use Backup to filter files from being backed up. Because Microsoft recommends that you only run Regedit as a last resort, you should use the GUI tool.

Figure 10.8: Default backup filtered data

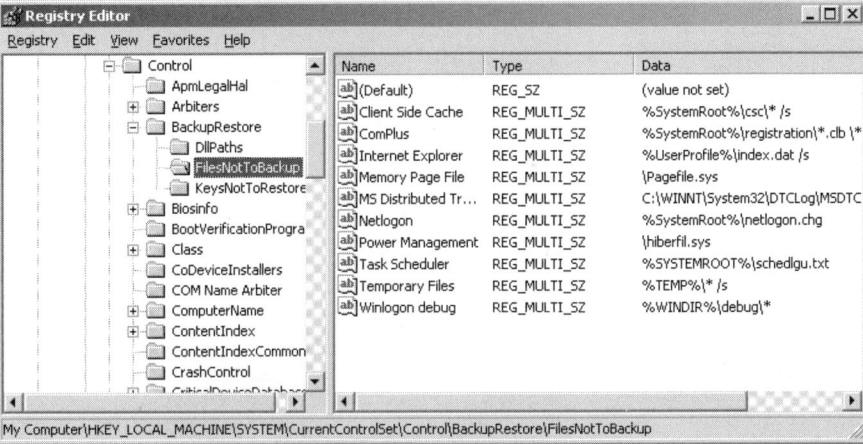

To filter data using Backup, from the Backup window, click Tools and then Options. Then click the Exclude Files tab (see Figure 10.9). From here you can add additional files or directories to filter. You can do this on a user basis, or you can have backup filters applied to all users.

Figure 10.9: Using the Backup GUI to filter backup data

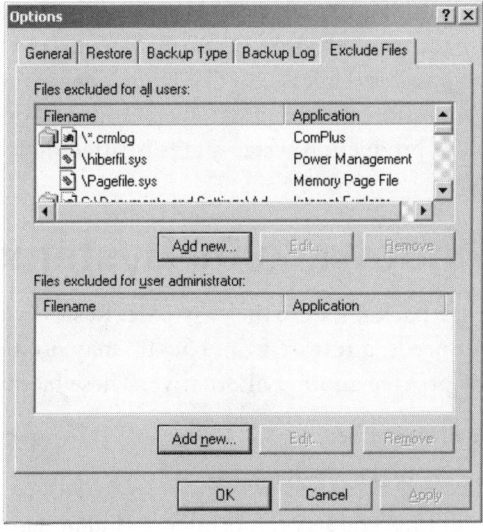

New filters are added by clicking the Add New button. From there you can enter the criteria for a new filter. Figure 10.10 shows a filter added so that all files with the TMP extension will not be backed up.

Figure 10.10: Filtering temp files

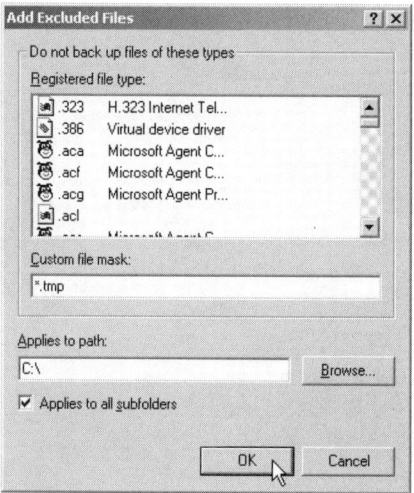

Verifying Your Backups

Many backup programs have built-in data verification. You read earlier how Backup has verification as a check box option when you run or schedule a backup. All verification does is check the validity of the data. Having good backup data is great, but if it does not meet your restore needs, it is meaningless. If you have the resources available, you should try and perform a backup and restore on a test system. Try and simulate your production scenario as close as possible. Unless you like living dangerously, we would never suggest that you try a system restore in a production environment unless it is needed. Do not wait until one of your production systems fails to attempt your first restore.

Restoring Windows 2000 Systems

As mentioned earlier, backups were the easy part. Restores can be a little more tricky. Depending on your needs, a restore from backup may not be necessary. Simply rebuilding the system may provide another alternative. These factors will mainly depend on:

- The purpose of the server
- The backup data you have available
- The amount of time you have to bring the system back online

Restoring Files, Folders, and Volumes

We have all seen that over time, all systems become a little "dirty." As our servers are tinkered with by several administrators, they will inevitably acquire some degree of user-added instability. With this in mind, if time permits, you may find it easier to rebuild a file server by first reinstalling Windows. Then you can use a backup to restore only the files that users access.

Taking this approach will guarantee you a clean system, but it will also take additional time. If you have time to manually configure the pre-existing services, the approach will leave you with the most stable system. Once you restore the necessary files and folders, you may have to reconfigure some shares and network settings. For most backup solutions, restoring a file, folder, or volume is a matter of selecting a check box and clicking OK. As long as you have the backup media available, the restore operation will run relatively seamlessly.

As you will see in this example, volume-level restores are a relatively painless process. To use Windows Backup for file-, folder-, or volume-level restores, follow these steps:

1. From Backup, click the Restore Wizard icon.
2. At the Wizard Welcome window, click Next.
3. Select the data you want to restore and click Next (see Figure 10.11).

Figure 10.11: Selecting data for restore

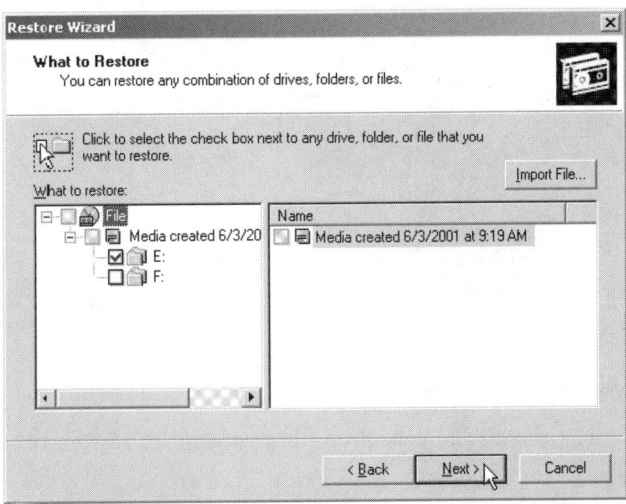

4. Click Advanced to set additional restore options.

5. Select the destination where you would like the data restored. The default is the original location.

> **TIP** For file servers, some administrators like to restore everything to a new folder. This way you can bring everything back at once and then simply move the files and folders you need.

6. Select how you want like files restored. You can select from three options:
   - Do not replace the file on the disk (the recommended option).
   - Replace the file on disk only if it is older than the backup copy.
   - Always replace the file on disk.
7. Select any advanced restore options, if desired, and click Next (see Figure 10.12).

Figure 10.12: Advanced restore options

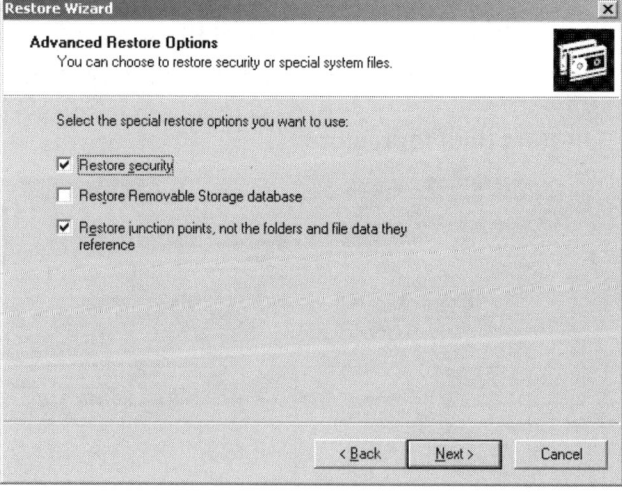

8. Verify that the restore information is correct and click Finish.
9. Now select the media or backup file you want to restore the data from.
10. Once you click OK, the restore will begin. After the restore completes, you can click the option to view a report and see details on the restored data.

Restoring the System State

You may need to perform a System State restore for several reasons. If you want to fully recover a system from a backup, you will inevitably need the System State as well. Unfortunately for you, if any System State component becomes corrupted, you will need to restore the entire System State. For example, say you just wanted to restore the Active Directory database, or just the boot files. For either of these, you would still have to restore everything in the System State. Remember that this is for your protection. Although you will be restoring more data, all core operating system data will be synchronized, thus causing fewer headaches for you.

Follow these steps to use Backup to restore the System State:

1. Open Backup by clicking Start ➢ Programs ➢ Accessories ➢ System Tools ➢ Backup.
2. Click the Restore Wizard button.
3. At the Wizard Welcome window, click Next.
4. Check the System State box associated with the backup you want to use for the restore and click Next, as shown in Figure 10.13.

Figure 10.13: Selecting to restore the System State

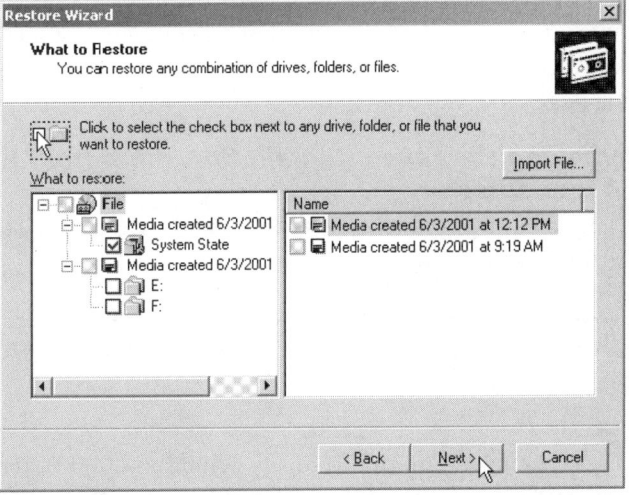

5. If you would like to control the actual System State data that is restored, click the Advanced button and select to restore the files to an alternate folder. Otherwise, click Finish to begin the restore job. This will give you flexibility in choosing what current System State data you want replaced.

6. Select whether you would like existing files replaced and click Next.

7. If you would like the RSM database also restored, check its associated box and click Next. Otherwise, just click Next.

8. Verify that the restore settings are correct and click Finish.

9. Verify the backup file you want to use for the restore and click OK.

10. Once the restore completes, click Close in the Restore Progress window.

11. You will then receive a prompt that the system needs to be rebooted. Click Yes to reboot the system.

Recovering Domain Controllers

As you read earlier, you have two choices when recovering domain controllers. You can either reinstall Windows 2000 and then re-promote the domain controller, or you can restore the domain controller from a backup.

Recovery through Replication

If you have the available bandwidth to support the Active Directory replication, this is probably the most foolproof method of recovering a domain controller. Remember that the only way this method can work is if you have another domain controller in your domain and, preferably, another domain controller is located at your site. Otherwise, you might wind up causing major congestion on your WAN while the DC promotion is running. Recovery through replication is a three-part process, each part is outlined on the following pages.

Part 1: Removing the Failed Domain Controller from the Existing Active Directory

To do this, you must run `metadata cleanup` using the `ntdsutil`. The steps to remove the domain controller from the forest are listed next.

> **NOTE** To perform this process, you must be a member of the Enterprise Administrator's group.

1. Access the command prompt from any Windows 2000 system in your domain. The system does not have to be a domain controller.

2. Now type **ntdsutil** and press Enter.

3. From ntdsutil, type **metadata cleanup** and press Enter.

4. From the `metadata cleanup` prompt, type **connections** and press Enter.

5. Now type **connect to server** *<name of any active domain controller in your forest>* and press Enter. For example, type **connect to server dc1.domain.com**.

6. Now type **quit** and press Enter. You will be brought back to the metadata cleanup menu.

7. Type **select operation target** and press Enter.

8. Type **list domains** and press Enter.

9. Locate the domain that contains the failed domain controller. It will have a number next to it.

10. Type **select domain** *<domain number>* and press Enter.

11. Type **list sites** and press Enter.

12. Type **select site** *<failed domain controllers site number>* and press Enter.

13. Type **list servers in site** and press Enter.

14. Locate the failed domain controller by number. Now type **select server** *<failed DC server number>* and press Enter.

15. Type **quit** and press Enter.

16. To remove the failed domain controller from Active Directory, at the `metadata cleanup` menu, type **remove selected server** and press Enter.

At this point, you are finished. You can close the command-prompt window. If the replacement domain controller will not retain the same host name as the failed domain controller, you will need to perform these additional steps:

1. Remove the failed domain controller object from the Active Directory Sites and Services snap-in.

2. Click Start ➢ Programs ➢ Administrative Tools ➢ Active Directory Sites and Services.

3. Expand the Sites folder until the failed domain controller's site is showing.

4. Now expand the site's Servers folder until you see the domain controller listed.

5. Right-click the failed domain controller and select Delete.

6. Remove the failed domain controller computer account from the Active Directory Users and Computers snap-in.

7. Click Start ➢ Programs ➢ Administrative Tools ➢ Active Directory Users and Computers.

8. Click on the container that contains the failed domain controller.

9. Right-click the domain controller and select Delete.

Part 2: Reinstalling Windows

We are not going to waste your time giving you step-by-step instructions on how to install Windows 2000 Server. At this point, you need to reinstall the operating system, selecting the installation options that the server requires.

Part 3: Re-promoting the Server

Once the server is installed, click Start ➤ Run ➤ and type **dcpromo** and press Enter. This will launch the Active Directory Installation wizard. Choose the options you need to rejoin the domain controller's old forest and domain.

Recovery Using a Backup

Simply reinstalling Windows and then re-promoting a failed domain controller is not the answer for all situations. There will be times when you inevitably will have to restore from a backup. For example, if the failed domain controller were the sole owner of a Single Master Operations (SMO) role in its domain or forest, restoring from backup would be the easiest solution. Not to mention, any kind of rebuild that requires manual input will be time consuming. Letting your backup software do the work for you is much easier. This section will give you the steps to perform "perfect world" restores of domain controllers from backups. In the next chapter, you will be exposed to the main recovery issues that exist between the lines when recovering domain controllers.

Sysvol Restore Types

When you are restoring a domain controller, you will have to decide how you want its replicated data in the Sysvol brought back. You will have to choose between performing a nonauthoritative, authoritative, or primary restore. Your decision will mainly depend on the state of the existing domain.

A nonauthoritative restore will bring the domain controller back to its state at the time of the last backup. Any changes made to the domain after that point will be updated with the restored domain controller via replication. Replication will occur as soon as the restored domain controller reboots following the completed restore.

Choose nonauthoritative when

- You are unsure of which option to choose.
- You want to recover a domain controller under normal circumstances.
- You need to rebuild the entire system.

An authoritative restore will cause the restored Sysvol data to replicate out to the other domain controllers in your domain. A full authoritative restore will roll your domain back to the point of its last backup. Any updates to the domain after that point will be overwritten. When an authoritative restore is performed, the attribute version number for each restored Active Directory object will be incremented by 100,000. This will cause each restored object to overwrite like objects in the directory during replication (unless the object on the other domain controller has been modified more than 100,000 times!). During replication, the object with the highest version number will overwrite like objects with lower version numbers.

Choose authoritative when

- You need to undo changes that were previously made to the Active Directory.
- You need to restore single Active Directory objects, such as a user, group, or organization unit.

Primary restores are the least often used. You would only perform a primary restore if no other domain controllers existed in your domain. A primary restore will cause a new NT File Replication Service (NTFRS) database to be built. The new NTFRS database will be built by loading the restored Sysvol data from the restored domain controller.

In the following sections, you will see the steps for restoring domain controllers. These steps are based on restores using Windows Backup. Again, the steps are not much different using any other enterprise-level backup application.

Performing a Nonauthoritative Restore

Follow these steps to perform a nonauthoritative restore:

1. Reinstall Windows.
2. After a successful installation, reboot the server. During the reboot press F8 as soon as you see "Starting Windows" to access the Windows 2000 Advanced Options menu.
3. Move the down arrow to select Directory Services Restore Mode and press Enter.
4. Log on as the Administrator.
5. Open Windows Backup and click the Restore Wizard icon.
6. At the Wizard Welcome Window, click Next.
7. At a minimum, select to restore the System State and the system disk. The easiest bet would be to check the My Computer box, which will restore everything on the system. Click Next.
8. Click the Advanced button.
9. Select to restore the files back to their original location and click Next.
10. Make sure the advanced restore options shown in Figure 10.14 are selected. For nonauthoritative restores, the ...Mark the Restored Data as the Primary Data for All Replicas check box should not be selected. Click OK.

Figure 10.14: Advanced Restore Options

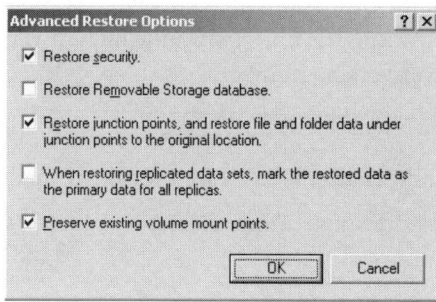

11. Verify that the restore settings are correct and click Finish.
12. Verify the backup file you want to use for the restore and click OK.
13. Once the restore completes, click Close in the Restore Progress window.
14. You will then receive a prompt that the system needs to be rebooted. Click Yes to reboot the system.

Performing an Authoritative Restore

With Windows Backup, you will actually have to restore the System State twice for a full authoritative restore. Most likely, you will not have to go through as much work with your backup software:

1. Create a temporary folder for the restored system state data. For example, you could create an AD_Restore folder in the Winnt\temp folder.
2. Perform steps 1 through 13 of the nonauthoritative restore process. Do not reboot the computer.
3. Reinitiate a second restore using the Windows Backup Restore Wizard.
4. At the Wizard Welcome window, click Next.
5. Select to just restore the System State and click Next.
6. Click the Advanced button.
7. Select to restore the files back to an Alternate Location, as shown in Figure 10.15. Browse to and select the folder that you created.
8. Make sure the advanced restore options are consistent with what is shown in Figure 10.14. Click OK.
9. Verify that the restore settings are correct and click Finish.

Figure 10.15: Restoring to an alternate folder

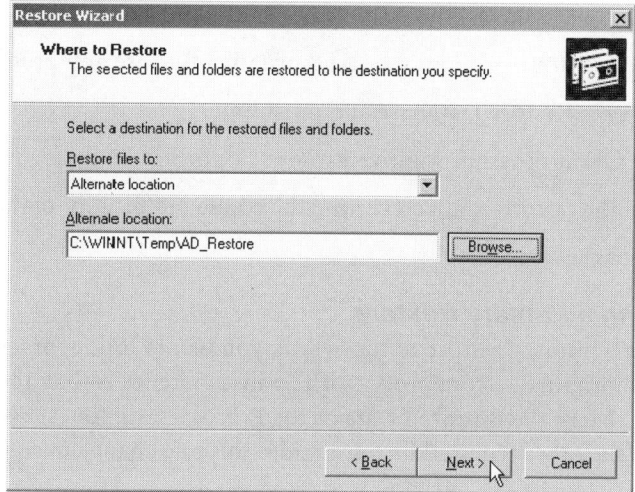

10. Verify the backup file you want to use for the restore and click OK.

11. Once the restore completes, click Close in the Restore Progress window.

12. You will then receive a prompt that the system needs to be rebooted. Do not reboot the system!

WARNING Do not reboot once the restore completes. If you do, no restored objects would be marked authoritative for replication, and you would have to restart the restore process from the beginning.

13. Open Windows Explorer and locate the Sysvol folder in the `<restore folder>`\Sys Vol\c_\winnt folder. Copy the folder and paste it into the `%System Root\winnt` folder. Click Yes to All to overwrite the existing files. The result should be `%System Root%\winnt\sysvol\(dirs)`.

NOTE Step 13 may not be required, depending on the backup software you use. Some backup programs do not restore the Sysvol directly to its original folder on an authoritative restore, and thus you will need to manually copy it yourself. Others copy the Sysvol back to its original location. If you are in doubt, you should always manually copy the restored data before proceeding to step 14.

14. Access the command prompt.

15. At the command prompt, type **NTDSUTIL** and press Enter.

16. At the NTDSUTIL prompt, type **Authoritative Restore** and press Enter.

17. Now type **Restore Database** and press Enter.

18. Click OK at the Authoritative Restore Confirmation dialog box.

19. When the restore completes, close the command prompt dialog box.

20. Reboot the system.

Performing a Primary Restore

To perform a primary restore of the Sysvol, you would follow practically all the steps in the nonauthoritative restore process. The only difference is that at step 10 you would select the ...Mark the Restored Data as the Primary Data for All Replicas check box, along with the other required boxes. Besides this one change in step 10, the process is the same.

Restoring Active Directory Objects

Sometimes, you may mistakenly modify the wrong organizational unit or delete a user group or user account. In these instances, restoring the Active Directory object might be quicker than re-creating it manually. This might be especially true for user groups and organizational units. Some documentation says this cannot be done, but you won't hear this from Microsoft. The unfortunate part of object-level restores, as it stands now, is that to bring an object back, you have to bring back the entire System State. In the future, you will be able to circumvent this step with some third-party backup applications.

Despite this step, under most circumstances using the procedures you will see momentarily, Active Directory objects can be restored in under an hour. If this is quicker than manually creating the objects and their associations, then do the restore. If not, choose then to re-create the object. Remember that Active Directory objects that have been deleted for more than 60 days (by default) cannot be restored.

Bringing Back the Database

As with other procedures, we will use Windows Backup to show the general procedure for restoring Active Directory objects.

> **WARNING** You will need more than one domain controller in your domain for these procedures to work.

First you will follow the standard System State restore procedures. The only difference, however, is that you will restore the System State to an alternate folder:

1. Create a temporary folder for the restored System State data. For example, you could create an AD_Restore folder in the `Winnt\temp` folder.
2. Open Backup by clicking Start ➢ Programs ➢ Accessories ➢ System Tools ➢ Backup.
3. Click the Restore Wizard button.
4. At the Wizard Welcome window, click Next.
5. Check the System State box associated with the backup you want to use for the restore and click Next.
6. Click the Advanced button and select to restore the files to an alternate folder. Browse to and select the folder that you created in step 1.
7. Because the folder is empty, select to not replace existing files (although any option will work) and click Next.
8. Select the options to restore Security and Junction Points and click Next.
9. Verify that the restore settings are correct and click Finish.
10. Verify the backup file you want to use for the restore and click OK.
11. Once the restore completes, click Close in the Restore Progress window.
12. You will then receive a prompt that the system needs to be rebooted. Do not reboot the computer!
13. Open Windows Explorer and locate the Sysvol folder in the `<restore folder>\Sys Vol\c_\winnt` folder. Copy the folder and paste it into the `%System Root\winnt` folder. Click Yes to All to overwrite the existing files. The result should be `%System Root%\winnt\sysvol\(dirs)`.
14. Access the command prompt.
15. At the command prompt, type **NTDSUTIL** and press Enter.
16. At the `NTDSUTIL` prompt, type **Authoritative Restore** and press Enter.

From here, the path you take will depend on the object you need to restore. The next section shows some examples for restoring different Active Directory objects and containers.

Marking Objects Authoritative

The objects that you make authoritative for replication will replicate out to the other domain controllers as soon as the system is rebooted. They will, in essence, cause only the restored objects to replicate out to the other domain controllers in your domain. The system you performed the restore on will receive updates from the other domain controllers for any new object information.

This is the syntax for restoring an organizational unit:

```
restore subtree ou=<OU name>,dc=<domain name>,dc=<extension>
```

For example, this is a sales organization unit at sybex.com:

```
restore subtree ou=sales,dc=sybex,dc=com
```

and this is an organizational unit in a child west.sybex.com domain:

```
restore subtree ou=sales,dc=west,dc=sybex,dc=com
```

This is the syntax for restoring a user group:

```
restore subtree cn=<group name>,cn=<users>,dc=<domain name>,dc=com
```

For example, this is a writer's user group at sybex.com:

```
restore subtree cn=writers,cn=users,dc=sybex,dc=com
```

and this is a writer's user group contained in a sales organizational unit:

```
restore subtree cn=writers,ou=sales,dc=west,dc=sybex,dc=com
```

Figure 10.16 shows the execution of using ntdsutil to restore the Training OU.

Figure 10.16: `ntdsutil` execution

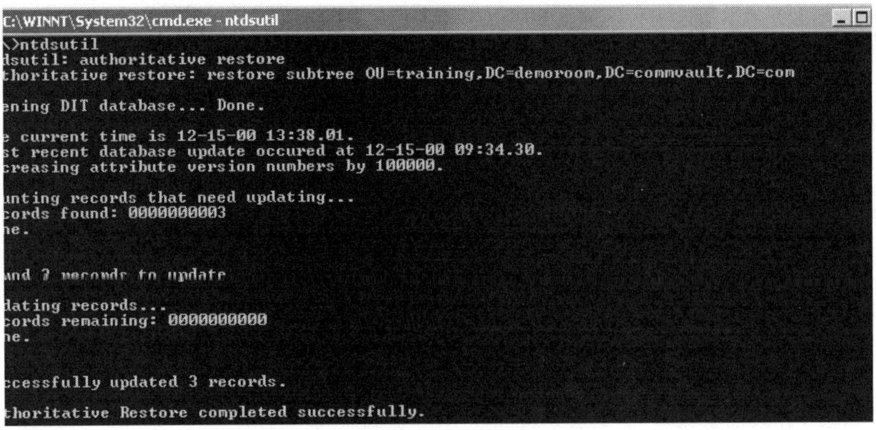

Finishing the Job

To finish the job, follow these steps:

1. Once you enter the command syntax you need and press Enter, click OK at the Authoritative Restore Confirmation dialog box.

2. When the restore completes, close the command prompt dialog box.

3. Reboot the system.

11

Operating System Rebuilds: The Gotchas

In the last chapter, you experienced the beginnings of Windows 2000 Recovery. Unfortunately, recovery is never that easy. We cannot just say, "Restore this backup, and you're finished," although we'd like to say that.

If you already have an enterprise-level backup solution, odds are that many of the issues we discuss in this chapter are handled "behind the scenes" by the software. In the event that they are not, we tell you how to properly back up and restore Windows 2000 services, databases, and files that would otherwise give you headaches. If you are deciding on which enterprise-level backup software suite to purchase, this chapter gives you plenty of pointed questions to ask.

As with any recovery plan, when in doubt, practice! Perform test restores to standby systems, if available. With the day-to-day file-level recovery situations presented in the previous chapter, you can most likely get away without testing backup data for restore, although this too is not recommended.

Windows 2000 servers have several services, databases, and files that require special attention. In this chapter we show you how to take on these challenges and succeed. Along the way, you will probably find some issues with services you may have normally taken for granted, so hold on tight. You are about to learn some things about Windows 2000 that may scare you. We are not here to dissuade you from using Windows 2000; rather, we want to help you get through the inevitable failure that will occur when you least expect it.

Overlooking the Obvious

Don't assume that if a system experiences hardware failure, or even worse, if a natural disaster occurs, that you will be able to bring everything back "lickity split." If recovery were that easy, your company would not need you.

The easy path to backup and recovery is to build up a server, back it up regularly, and use software to restore the server in the event of a crash. What if you never did the initial install of a server but are expected to rebuild it in the event of a natural disaster? Consider these questions:

- Do you know the fully qualified domain name and Internet Protocol (IP) address of the system?
- Do you have the disk configuration and install directories documented?
- Do you know what services or applications were run on the server?

If you do not have the answers to these questions, you are not ready for disaster recovery. When you perform a full system restore, your backup software will most likely default to placing everything where it was originally stored. If you do not rebuild a new system with the same logical configuration as the old, the restore will most likely fail. For example, if the old system had three physical disks, each with four partitions, then the new system should have this setup, as well.

How are the disks configured? To which controller is each physical disk attached? If these settings are configured wrong on the new system, consider how the new boot.ini file will look. This can cause several headaches for the restored applications. For physical disks and all Small Computer Systems Interface (SCSI)–attached devices, you should have the following documented and stored somewhere offsite:

- SCSI controller model number and firmware revision number
- Configuration information from the SCSI Basic Input Output System (BIOS) setup
- A detailed map of each SCSI bus, including the location of each termination, as well as location and SCSI ID of each device on each SCSI chain
- For IDE drives, the jumper settings (Slave, Master, CS) and the IDE controller to which the device is connected (primary, secondary)

Although collecting partition information for each system you back up can be a headache, Diskmap will make your life a little easier.

Using Diskmap

The Windows 2000 Server Resource Kit contains a utility (diskmap.exe) for collecting and storing disk configuration information. When wanting to document disk configuration information for a particular server, Diskmap can be invaluable. When run, the utility will display the number and size of each partition on a specified disk. Sure, you could use the Logical Disk Manager Graphical User Interface (GUI) tool to collect this information, but with Diskmap being a command-line tool, you can run the executable and redirect its output to a file, allowing you to easily maintain disk configuration information for your servers on a floppy disk or other storage medium.

This is the Diskmap syntax:

    diskmap /d<drive number> [/h]

For example:

    diskmap /d0
    diskmap /d0 > C:\disk_info\disk0.txt

When the first example is executed, the disk 0s (the first hard disk's) information would be displayed on the screen. In the second example, the disk's information would be saved to the disk0.txt file. Figure 11.1 shows a sample execution of Diskmap. The Diskmap output shows drive configuration information for a single drive with three partitions.

Figure 11.1: Executing Diskmap

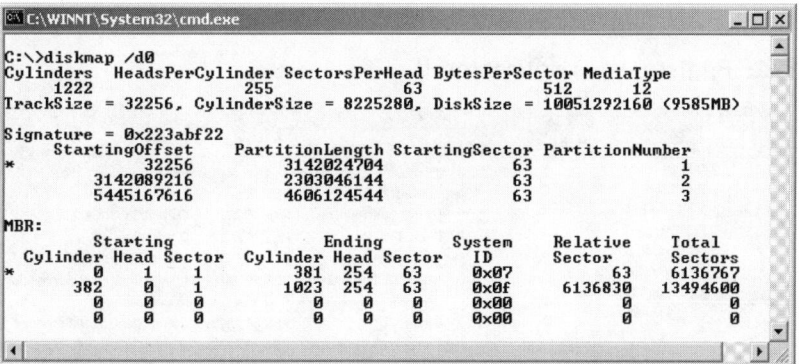

OK, so we got disk issues out of the way, but we are not done yet. There are a lot more hardware issues on your servers you should consider. You should also document this information for each system you back up:

- CMOS or NVRAM information
- BIOS information and firmware revision level
- Computer make, model, and serial number

Restoring to Different Hardware

Now that you have all the hardware information you need to rebuild a system documented and stored offsite, you may find yourself with one other problem. If you have to rebuild a site, or even a system, you may not be able to match the exact hardware configuration of the system that was lost. In the NT days, this situation was not as painful because Microsoft did not have the System State or any of the issues associated with it. Having the System State does ensure that recovery is more predictable because all system databases that have inter-dependencies are brought back in sync.

When you need to perform a full system restore to new hardware, you will need to exclude certain Registry keys from the restore. Otherwise, keys will reference hardware that no longer exists. A simple rule of thumb is to bring back what you need. A Registry key actually exists that contains restore filters for the Registry. In other words, Backup (or your backup solution), can check this key to see what Registry keys not to restore. If you would like to check these default settings, or want to add additional keys to the "not to restore" list, run Regedit and navigate to the following key: HKEY_LOCAL_MACHINE\SYSTEM\CurrentControlSet\Control\BackupRestore\KeysNotToRestore. Figure 11.2 shows the default settings for this key on a Windows 2000 member server.

> **NOTE** If the system is a domain controller, you will also see the Ntfrs key listed as a key not to restore.

Figure 11.2: Registry keys not restored

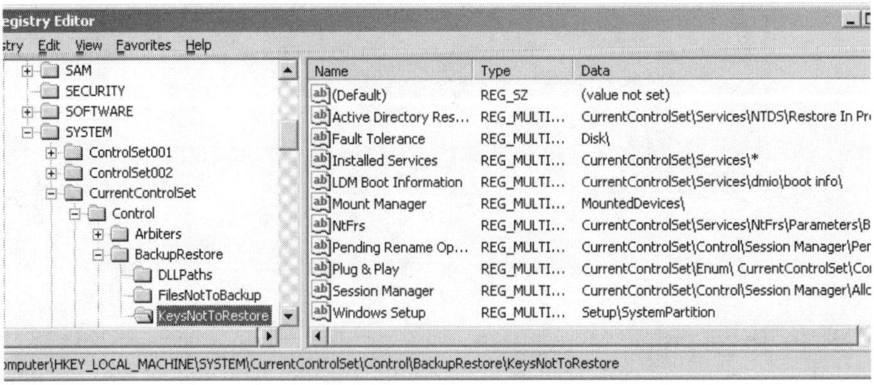

The Longer but Safer Road to Recovery

Now, you may be one who prefers to leave the Registry alone, whenever possible. If you would like to avoid having to locate and filter Registry keys from a restore operation, there is another alternative. The steps in this section show a process that, although lengthy, will enable you to safely restore a full system backup from one computer to another with dissimilar hardware. This process assumes you have a good full backup of the source computer, including boot and system volume(s), System State, SYSVOL volumes (for domain controllers), and any other pertinent volumes configured on the system.

> **TIP** Windows Backup only allows you to restore System State data to a local system. So, you cannot perform a cross-server restore over the network. When using Windows Backup, you will have to perform the restore using a locally attached storage device (tape drive, library, and so on).

Follow these steps:

1. Reinstall the Windows operating system on the destination computer to its original configuration.
2. Configure the hard disk partitions on the new system to match the configuration of the old system. By default, Backup will restore files to their original location. Having the new system's directory structure configured the same as the old system's will help to ensure the success of the restore operation.
3. On the new (destination) system, load the medium that contains the backup data into its drive or library.
4. Open the Computer Management MMC (Start ➤ Programs ➤ Administrative Tools ➤ Computer Management).
5. From Computer Management, navigate to the RSM Import media pool. From the Import pool, locate the medium that contains the backup of the original system. Drag and drop the medium into its associated Backup media pool. This will allow Backup to see and use the medium for the restore.
6. Close Computer Management.

> **NOTE** As mentioned in Chapter 10, "File System Backup/Recovery," remember that to restore the System State on a domain controller, you must boot the system into Directory Services Restore Mode.

7. Start Windows Backup (Start ➢ Programs ➢ Accessories ➢ System Tools ➢ Backup).

8. Click the Tools menu and select Options.

9. In the Options dialog box, click the Restore tab. Select the Always Replace the File on My Computer option and click OK (see Figure 11.3).

Figure 11.3: Configuring like files to always be overwritten

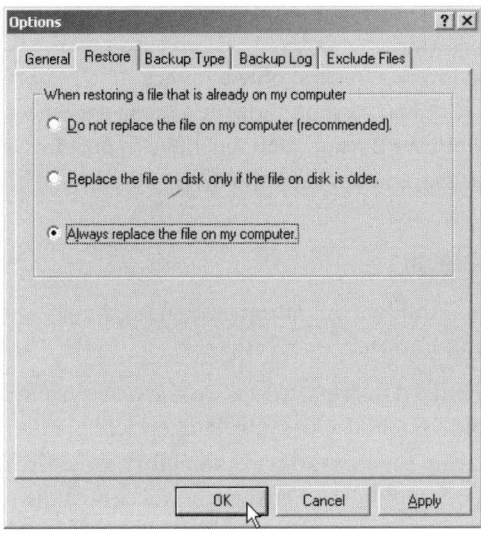

10. Now in the Backup window, click the Restore tab.

11. Select to restore all necessary volumes, and the System State from the backup medium, make sure that the Original Location is selected as the destination, and click the Start Restore button.

12. Once the restore completes, power down the original (source) system or remove it from the network. This will prevent IP conflicts with the restored system.

13. Reboot the new system.

After rebooting, if everything starts up fine, consider yourself lucky. Odds are that the system might try and locate hardware installed on the original system, or you might find that a mismatch exists with the Hardware Abstraction Layer (HAL) of the original system and the new system. If the restored system encounters errors during startup, you will have to perform a repair of the operating system. You do this by booting from the Windows 2000 setup disks or CD-ROM. Once booted, select the option to repair the

Windows installation. The repair process will re-enumerate all hardware, including the HAL settings, and perform an in-place upgrade of the operating system. Once complete, the operating system will be fully functional. Performing a repair will not affect any of the restored program or user settings.

> **TIP** Following a repair, you should reinstall the latest service pack to replace any updated files that were overwritten during the repair process.

> **NOTE** It is possible that after the completed restore, depending on the date of the backup that was used, the domain controller may not accept the restored system's Security ID (SID). In this circumstance, you will have to rejoin the computer back to the domain.

Now that we got the big picture out of the way, it's time to examine all the between-the-lines issues you might normally forget. Let's start with Encrypting File System.

Encrypting File System

Encrypting File System (EFS) is relatively simple, from a backup or restore perspective. Backup products can back up and restore encrypted files in their encrypted state. If you are worried about sensitive data contained on backup media stored offsite, you can use EFS to provide some protection for the data. Even if someone stole an offsite tape, the data on the tape is worthless without a decryption key. For these reasons, you may choose to assign certain sensitive folders the encrypted attribute. When this is done, all files saved to the encrypted folder will become encrypted.

Encrypting Data

Encrypting folders can be done using Windows Explorer. To do this, follow these steps:

1. With Explorer open, right-click the folder you want to encrypt and select Properties.
2. Under the General tab, click the Advanced button to access the advanced folder attributes.
3. Click the Encrypt Contents to Secure Data box and click OK (see Figure 11.4).

Figure 11.4: Assigning a folder the encrypted attribute

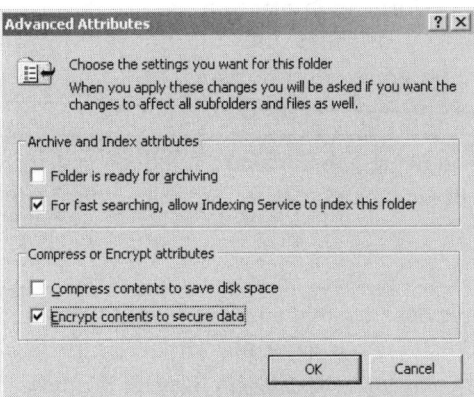

4. At the folder properties window, click OK. You will then be prompted to either apply the encrypted attribute to the current folder or add the attribute to the folder, as well as all of its files and subfolders (see Figure 11.5). If you elect to just encrypt the folder, any file that is saved to it will gain the encrypted attribute.

Figure 11.5: Selecting where to apply the encrypted attribute

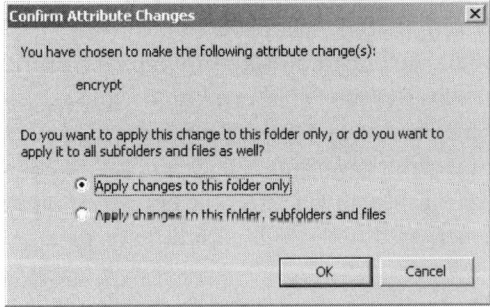

The Gotchas of EFS Management

When managing and designing your enterprise storage topology, you should consider these points:

- When a user encrypts a file, only that user or an Encrypted Data Recovery Agent can decrypt it.
- Users could theoretically encrypt a file, delete their encryption key, and leave the organization with encrypted data. How do you recover it?

- Plan a recovery strategy for domain users.
- Plan a recovery strategy for users on stand-alone servers or workstations.

If you cannot guarantee you are already prepared to restore and recover encrypted files, then this section is important. Remember that with Windows 2000, nothing prevents users from encrypting their own files, unless you take the steps to do so.

If you choose to allow users to encrypt their files (default EFS configuration), then you must take the necessary steps to ensure you can get any encrypted file back. This is why Recovery Agents are so important.

Recovery Agents

Plenty of books and resources on the intricacies of EFS architecture and operation are available. For the sake of looking at EFS from a backup and recovery perspective, we will keep the explanation short and sweet. When a file is encrypted, two decryption keys are created. One key is for the user who encrypted the file to decrypt it. The other key is so that any designated Recovery Agent can decrypt the file. Think of Recovery Agents as locksmiths. They possess all the needed master keys to open any encrypted files. Just like losing your car keys, if your encryption key is lost, a Recovery Agent can log on and retrieve any data you need. The agent could then decrypt all files for you. If you want, later you can encrypt them again, with a new key that will be generated. A user's encryption key is automatically created if one is not present when the user first encrypts a file.

By default, the domain administrator account is the Recovery Agent for files encrypted by domain users, and the local administrator account is the Recovery Agent for files encrypted by local users. You can view a list of Recovery Agents using the Domain Security Policy (or Local Security Policy) administration tool. Figure 11.6 shows the default settings.

Figure 11.6: Viewing domain Recovery Agents

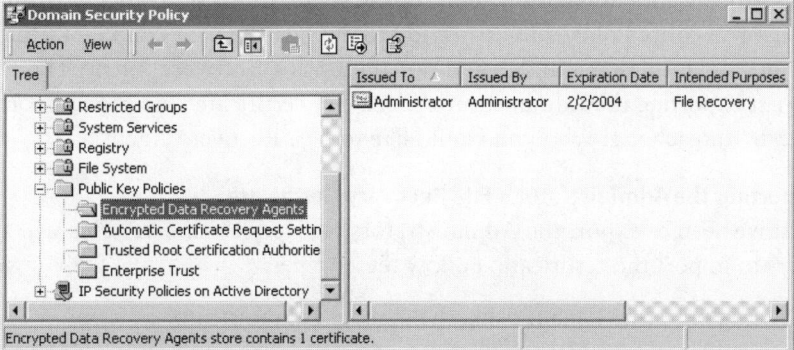

Unfortunately, this default configuration does complicate things a little bit. Odds are that you have several users in the Domain Administrators group that you would like to act as Recovery Agents. Unfortunately, only user accounts, and not user groups, can be configured as Recovery Agents. For you, this means additional work is required to delegate authority for specific users to be able to decrypt all encrypted files.

When you want to designate additional user accounts as Recovery Agents, you have two choices:

- You can configure a Windows 2000 Server in your Enterprise as a Certificate Server.
- You can manually export the Encrypted Data Recovery Certificate from the Administrator account and import the certificate for each user you want to act as a Recovery Agent.

If your only need for using a Certificate Server is for EFS protection, then you probably should not configure a Certificate Server. For starters, Microsoft recommends that when you use a Certificate Server, you should take the root server and store it in a safe place, off the network. If you are administering a large network and can afford the extra system, you might consider taking this approach. Otherwise, for small- to mid-sized organizations, where only a handful of administrators exist, having a Certificate Server just for EFS can be looked at as an unnecessary expense. If you already have or plan to use a Certificate Server in your Windows 2000 Forest, then your choice is easy.

Let's start with the small office, or easy, solution.

Designating Additional Recovery Agents: The Shortcut

When you only have a few administrators in your domain, the easiest solution is to export the Administrator account's Recovery Certificate and then import the certificate for each user account you want to act as a Recovery Agent. When you export a certificate, it is saved to a disk and password protected, so you should not consider exported certificates to be a security risk. Keep in mind that this process is a "back-door" approach that requires you to manually track users who have the recovery certificate. This process does not allow you to see the standard list of Recovery Agents using the Domain Security Policy administration tool. Over the next couple of pages, you will see the process for designating an additional user as a Recovery Agent. The process consists of first exporting the Administrator's recovery certificate, and then importing the certificate for each user who you would like to be a Recovery Agent.

Exporting the Administrator's File Recovery Certificate
First we need to export the Administrators recovery certificate. This will allow other users to import the certificate. Follow these steps:

1. Log onto the domain using the domain Administrator account.

2. Click Start ➤ Run, type **MMC**, and press Enter to open the Microsoft Management Console.

3. Click the Console menu and select Add/Remove Snap-in.

4. Click the Add button. .

5. In the Add Standalone Snap-in window, select Certificates and click the Add button.

6. Select to manage My User Account and click Finish.

7. Close the Add Standalone Snap-in window.

8. Click OK to close the Add/Remove Snap-in window.

9. You should now see the Certificates snap-in displayed in the console. Expand the Certificates snap-in so that you see the `Personal\Certificates` folder.

10. Click the Certificates folder, right-click the Administrator File Recovery certificate, choose All Tasks, and then click Export (see Figure 11.7).

Figure 11.7: Exporting the Administrator File Recovery certificate

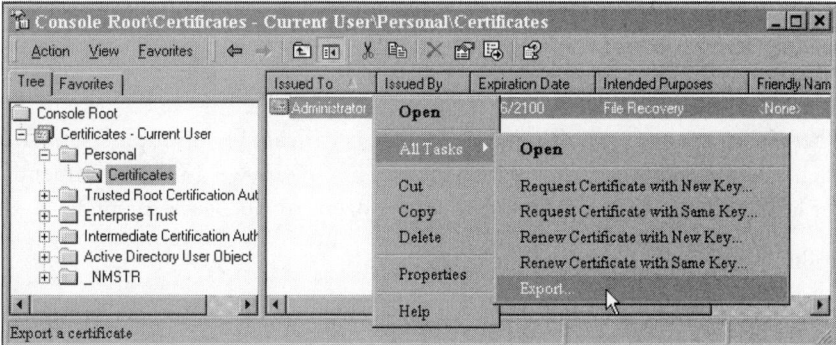

11. At the Certificate Export Wizard welcome window, click Next.

12. Choose the default setting to export the private key and click Next.

13. Choose the default export file format and click Next, as shown in Figure 11.8.

14. Enter and confirm the password that will be used to import the certificate and click Next.

15. Provide the path and filename for the exported file. The file will automatically be given the `.pfx` extension. Click Next when finished.

16. Confirm the settings you have selected and click Finish to complete the export operation.

17. When prompted that the export was successful, click OK.

Figure 11.8: Selecting the certificate export file format

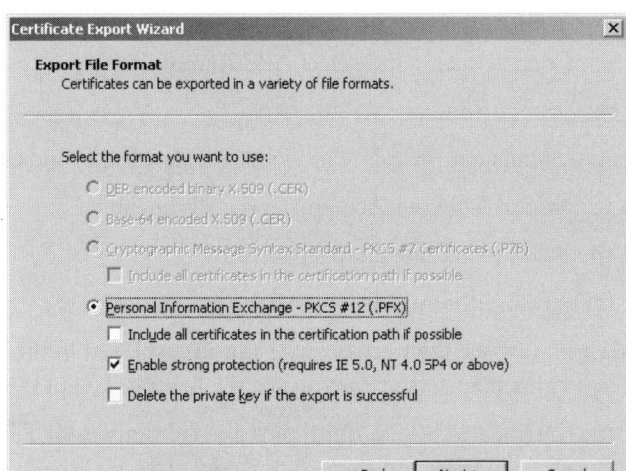

Now with the certificate exported and saved on a disk, other users can log on and import the certificate.

Importing the File Recovery Certificate
There is no method to bulk-import a single certificate for multiple users. You must have each user log on to import the certificate. This is why we don't recommend this process for large organizations that want to have dozens of Recovery Agents!

Follow these steps to import the certificate:

1. Log on using the user account that you would like to import the certificate to.

2. Repeat steps 2 through 9 of the previous procedure to reach the user's certificates configuration.

3. Right-click the Certificates folder, select All Tasks, and then choose Import.

4. At the Certificate Import Wizard welcome window, click Next.

5. Enter the path for or browse to the certificate file you want to import and click Next (see Figure 11.9).

6. Enter the password for the private key and click Next.

7. Click Next to place the certificate in your personal store.

8. Click Finish to complete the import operation.

9. When prompted that the import was successful, click OK.

Figure 11.9: Selecting the certificate file

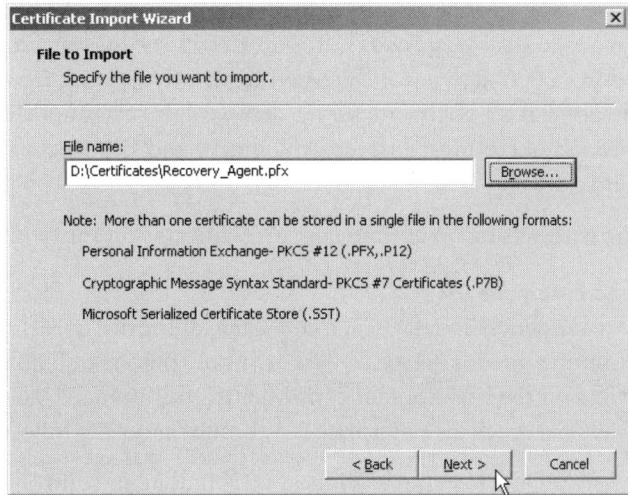

10. The user's Certificates folder should now appear similar to the one in Figure 11.10. You should see the Administrator's File Recovery certificate displayed.

Figure 11.10: Configuration complete for giving a user account the Administrator's File Recovery certificate

Now the user will be able to decrypt any file encrypted with any domain user account. If this solution is not feasible for you, then your only other choice is to install, configure, and use a Certificate Server to manage File Recovery certificates. This is what we will look at next.

Designating Additional Recovery Agents: The Enterprise Solution

The enterprise level, and the only Microsoft-documented and Microsoft-supported method to manage Recovery Agents, is with Certificate Server. Chances are that with a sound Windows 2000 network infrastructure already in place for your organization, you may already have a certificate server deployed. If this is not the case, we will cover the entire process of certificate server deployment and EFS Recovery Agent delegation, just to be safe.

We will start with setting up an Enterprise Certificate Authority (CA).

Setting Up an Enterprise CA

Before users can request certificates, a certificate authority must first be present. This begins with setting up an Enterprise CA, or simply put, installing and configuring Certificate Services on the first domain controller in your domain. To configure a Windows 2000 Server as an Enterprise CA, it must meet the following prerequisites:

- Host Active Directory (be a Windows 2000 domain controller)
- Have DNS installed
- Installing user must have Enterprise Administrative privileges

> **NOTE** Microsoft recommends configuring subordinate CAs in conjunction with the Enterprise CA for increased security. You can find more information on Certificate Authority configuration by searching TechNet (www.microsoft.com/technet) for "Step-by-Step Guide to Setting Up a Certificate Authority."

Follow these steps to configure an Enterprise CA:

1. Log on to the domain controller you want to act as the Enterprise CA using an account that has Enterprise Administrative privileges.
2. From the Control Panel, double-click the Add/Remove Programs applet.
3. Click the Add/Remove Windows Components icon.
4. Click the Certificate Services check box.
5. When warned that you will not be able to rename the system or remove it from the domain, click Yes to acknowledge the warning.
6. Ensure that the Certificate Services box is checked and click Next to continue.
7. If the Terminal Services box is checked (regardless of whether it is already installed), you will be prompted to select the mode in which Terminal Services will run. Select the appropriate mode and click Next. Otherwise just go to step 8.

8. Make sure that Enterprise Root CA is selected and click Next.

9. Now enter your organization's information for the Root CA and click Next (see Figure 11.11).

Figure 11.11: CA identifying information

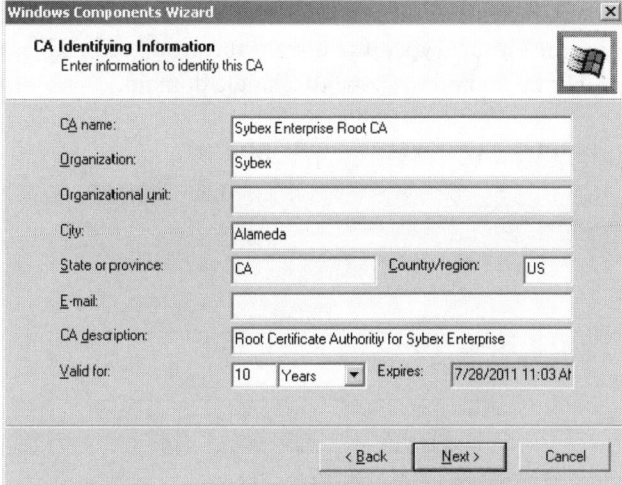

10. Select the installation location for the Certificate Server database and log files and click Next. You can, if desired, choose to store this information on a network share.

11. If IIS is running, you will be prompted that it must be stopped. Click OK.

12. If prompted, insert the Windows 2000 Server CD-ROM and click OK.

13. Once the file copy process complete, click Finish.

Now that the Enterprise CA is set up, you can work to configure additional domain users as Recovery Agents. To do this, it is recommended you follow conventional Microsoft user-management techniques. To do this, we will begin by creating a Recovery Agents user group. Once the user group is created, you can add any users to the group that you would like to act as Recovery Agents.

Creating a Recovery Agents User Group

After getting Certificate Services up and running, the remainder of the process will be relatively simple. To create a Recovery Agents user group, follow these steps:

1. Log on to a domain controller in your domain as a user with Domain Administrative privileges.

2. Click Start ➢ Programs ➢ Administrative Tools ➢ Active Directory Users and Computers.

3. Right-click the Users folder (or an Organization Unit folder if one is created) and select New and then Group.

4. Now enter a Group Name, select Global under Group Scope, and choose Security under Group Type, as shown in Figure 11.12. (You could choose Domain Local for the Group Type, if you want the group to be able to contain other groups, but be limited in scope to a single domain.)

Figure 11.12: Creating a Recovery Agents group

5. Click OK to create the group.

Members can now be added to the group by right-clicking the group and selecting Properties. From the Members tab you can then add members to the group.

Granting Members of the Recovery Agents Group the Right to Request Certificates
Before users can request the EFS Recovery certificate, they must first be granted proper rights. You do this by performing the following steps:

1. Log on to a domain controller as an enterprise administrator.

2. Click Start ➢ Programs ➢ Administrative Tools ➢ Active Directory Sites and Services.

3. Click the View menu and select Show Services Node.

4. Expand the Services folder until the Certificate Templates folder is shown. Click the Certificate Templates folder, and then right-click the EFS Recovery certificate and select Properties (see Figure 11.13).

Figure 11.13: Accessing the EFS Recovery certificate properties

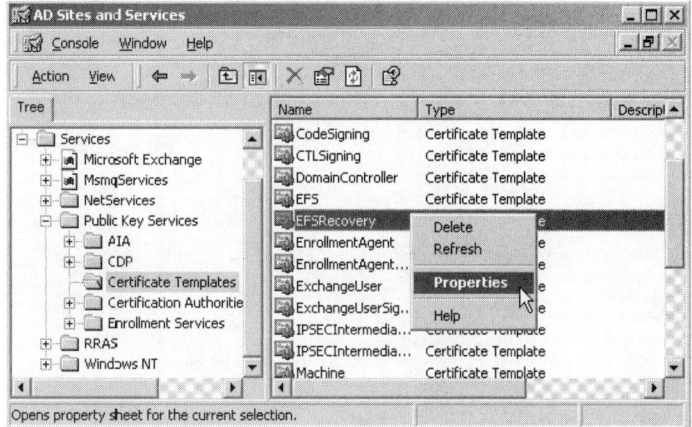

5. Click the Security tab.
6. Now click the Add button.
7. Select the domain Recovery Agents user group that you created and click Add.
8. Click OK to close the Select Users dialog box.
9. Make sure the Recovery Agents group is highlight in the top pane of the EFS-Recovery Properties window, and then check the Enroll box in the lower portion of the window (see Figure 11.14).
10. Now click OK to close the EFS Recovery Properties dialog box.
11. Close the Active Directory Sites and Services snap-in.

Members of the Recovery Agents group are now able to request the EFS Recovery certificate. To act as a Recovery Agent, members of the Recovery Agents user group will not have to log on and request the EFS Recovery certificate.

Figure 11.14: Granting the Recovery Agents group enroll permission

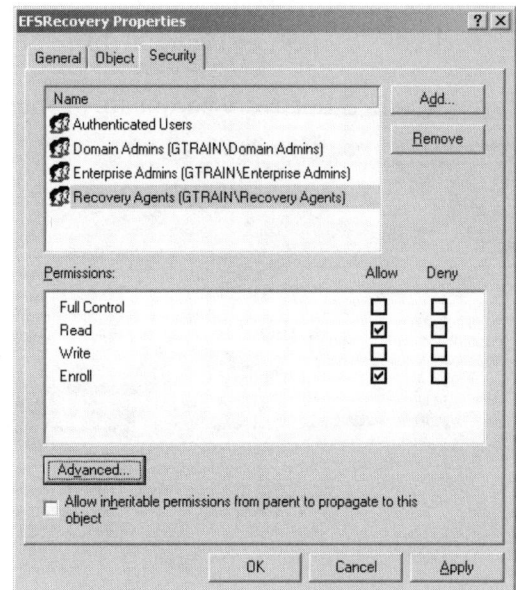

Requesting the EFS Recovery Certificate

The steps that each user must perform to obtain the certificate are listed below. Once they have the certificate, they will be able to decrypt files that were encrypted by any domain user.

1. Log on as a user who is a member of the Recovery Agents group.
2. Click Start ➢ Run, type **MMC,** and press Enter to open the Microsoft Management Console.
3. Click the Console menu and select Add/Remove Snap-in.
4. Click the Add button.
5. In the Add Standalone Snap-in window, select Certificates and click the Add button.
6. Select to manage My User Account and click Finish.
7. Close the Add Standalone Snap-in window.
8. Click OK to close the Add/Remove Snap-in window.
9. You should see the Personal folder listed right under the Certificates snap-in. Right-click the Personal folder, select All Tasks, and then choose Request New Certificate.

10. You will then see the Certificate Request Wizard welcome window. Click Next.
11. From the displayed list of certificate templates, click EFS Recovery Agent and then click Next.
12. Enter a friendly name for the certificate, so that you can distinguish it from others, and then click Next.
13. Ensure the settings in the Completing the Certificate Request Wizard window are correct and click Finish.
14. When prompted that the certificate request was successful, select the option to install the certificate.
15. When prompted that the request was successful, click OK.

Once each user has the certificate, your work is almost finished. All that is left is to export the certificates as .cer files and then add the exported certificates to the domain recovery policy. To export certificates, you have two options:

- You can have each user export their own file recovery certificate to a disk or share.
- As an Enterprise Administrator, you can use the Certification Authority MMC snap-in to export the file recovery certificate for each user.

Waiting on each user to export their certificates may be a task you do not want to undertake. Most network administrators, being busy individuals, may take some time performing a task for you. The easiest way, and the way we will show you, is to do it yourself. With that in mind, we will show you the method of using the Certification Authority tool. This enables you to export all File Recovery certificates yourself (one for each user) and then add each certificate to the domain recovery policy once they are exported.

Exporting the EFS Recovery Certificate

Individual users can use the Certificates MMC snap-in to export their issued certificates, but it is faster as an administrator to export all needed certificates yourself. With this in mind, we will show you how to use the Certification Authority tool to get the job done quickly.

Once each user requests their recovery certificate, as was outline in the previous section, you can locate and export their certificates. Follow these steps:

1. Log on to a Certificate Server as an Enterprise Administrator.
2. Click Start ➢ Programs ➢ Administrative Tools ➢ Certification Authority.
3. Click the Issued Certificates folder.
4. You can associate certificates granted for each user account by checking the username field. When the EFS Recovery Certificate was issued, the requesting

user received an encryption and file recovery certificate. You are interested in the File Recovery certificate. To locate it, double-click the first certificate listed for the user after the date the certificate was requested. Under the General tab, you will see the certificate listed as File Recovery, as shown in Figure 11.15.

Figure 11.15: Verifying the file recovery certificate

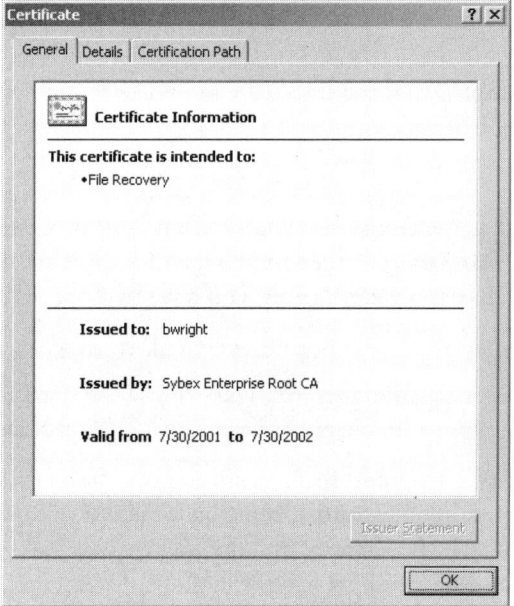

5. If you did not see File Recovery, then select another certificate for the user. Once you have found the File Recovery certificate for the user, click the Details tab.

6. Click the Copy to File button to export the certificate.

7. The Certificate Export Wizard should open. Click Next.

8. Select the file format to use for the export operation and click Next. If unsure, choose the default value (DER encoded binary).

9. Provide a path and filename for the exported certificate, as shown in Figure 11.16. The file will receive the .cer extension.

10. Click Finish to close the Export Wizard.

11. Click OK when notified that the certificate was exported successfully.

12. Click OK to close the Certificate Information dialog box.

13. Repeat steps 4 through 12 for each user that has the File Recovery certificate.

Figure 11.16: Designating a path and filename for the exported certificate

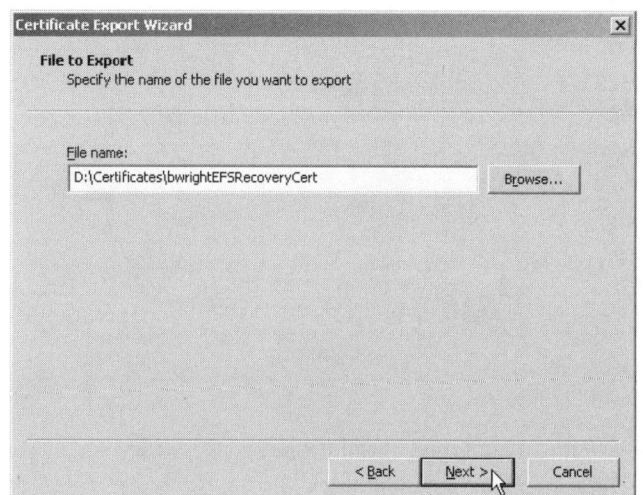

Adding Certificates to the Recovery Policy

Now that you have exported the certificates to files, you can finally designate each user as a Recovery Agent. Follow these steps for this final action:

1. Log on to a domain controller and click Start ➢ Programs ➢ Administrative Tools ➢ Domain Security Policy.

2. Expand the Public Key Policies folder and then click the Encrypted Data Recovery Agents folder. You will see a list of all configured Recovery Agents.

3. To add a new user to the list, right-click the Encrypted Data Recovery Agents folder and select Add.

4. At the Add Recovery Agent Wizard welcome window, click Next.

5. When prompted to Select Recovery Agents, click the Browse Folders button.

6. For each user that you have exported an EFS Recovery certificate for, browse to the location of their .cer file, click the file, and then click Open (see Figure 11.17). You can repeat steps 5 and 6 for each user account.

7. Once all user certificates are selected, click Next.

8. Verify the selected certificates and click Finish to close the wizard.

Figure 11.17: Selecting exported certificates

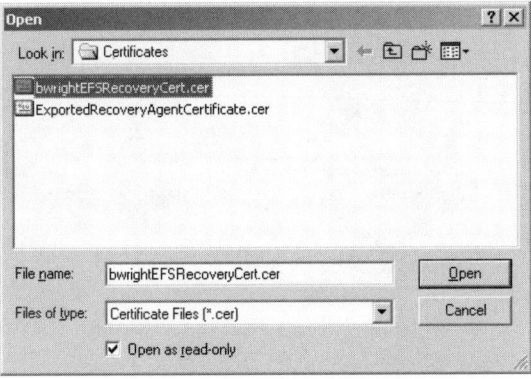

As shown in Figure 11.18, you should now the Recovery Agent certificates listed in the Encrypted Data Recovery Agents folder.

Figure 11.18: The Recovery Agent certificates

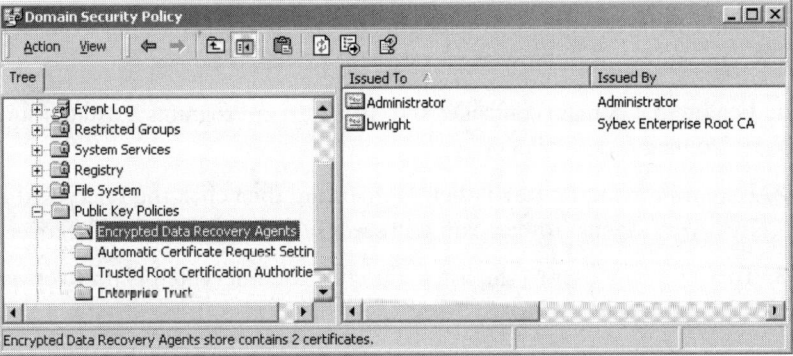

Sure, this has been a long journey, but it has been at the expense of greater management in the long run. If you have a large organization and intend on using EFS, then configuring and using a Certificate Server is your answer. Otherwise, you can take the small-scale approach outlined earlier.

Disabling EFS

After reading the amount of work involved to ensure you can recover an encrypted file when a user's private key is deleted or lost, you may have decided that EFS is not that important. Remember, there always is the chance that a "rogue employee" will encrypt all of his files and then delete his encryption key! Even if you have configured domain

Recovery Agents, you still have to concern yourself with stand-alone workstations or servers. Domain controllers maintain users' domain certificates, making management relatively simple. Users who have a local account on a system can also use their local privileges to encrypt files. Files encrypted this way cannot be decrypted by domain Recovery Agents.

As an alternative to having to worry about individual Recovery Agents for each system, you could disable EFS for local accounts on each system, allowing only users logged onto the domain to encrypt files. This way you will only have to configure select domain administrator accounts as Recovery Agents.

If you do not even want domain users to be able to encrypt files, you can disable EFS for your domain, as well. No matter what you choose, if anything at all, the process is the same. The easiest way to disable EFS is to simply remove all Recovery Agents. Windows will not allow users to encrypt files when there are no Recovery Agents to decrypt them, in the event a user's key is lost.

To disable EFS for the domain, follow these steps:

1. Log on to the domain controller as a domain administrator.
2. Click Start ➢ Programs ➢ Administrative Tools ➢ Domain Security Policy.
3. Click the `Public Key Policies\Encrypted Data Recovery Agents` folder.
4. Now right-click each certificate listed in the Encrypted Data Recovery Agents folder and select Delete.
5. When prompted to permanently delete the selected certificate, click Yes.

To disable EFS for a stand-alone system, follow these steps:

1. Log on to the stand-alone system as the local administrator.
2. Click Start ➢ Programs ➢ Administrative Tools ➢ Local Security Policy.
3. Click the `Public Key Policies\Encrypted Data Recovery Agents` folder.
4. Now right-click each certificate listed in the Encrypted Data Recovery Agents folder and select Delete.
5. When prompted to permanently delete the selected certificate, click Yes.

> **TIP** With the use of Group Policy Objects, it is possible to enable EFS for specific groups, or Organizational Units, and deny EFS usage to other users.

Backing Up and Restoring Encrypted Files

As mentioned earlier, any Windows 2000 backup product should be able to back up or restore encrypted files. So why are we mentioning it then, as a "gotcha," you ask? The trouble occurs when a user's private key is lost. Suppose a user left the company, deleted all his files, and was smart (or foolish) enough to delete his private key. You attempt to restore his files back to their original file server but cannot open them. They are encrypted! All files were encrypted using the user's domain account. However, you are not worried because you are a Recovery Agent for the domain.

Here's the trick you must remember: To decrypt the file as the Recovery Agent, you must decrypt the file on the system where the decryption key physically resides. In other words, if the file was backed up from a member file server of your domain, the file must be restored to a domain controller (the system that holds decryption key) to decrypt it. Once the file has been decrypted, you can move it back to its original location.

> **NOTE** We just touched on the most important issues surrounding EFS file backup and recovery. For more information, search TechNet (www.microsoft.com/technet) using the phrase "Step-by-Step Guide to Encrypting File System."

DHCP Database Recovery

Odds are that your enterprise-level backup and recovery solution handles Dynamic Host Configuration Protocol (DHCP) properly. With that being the case, you only have one consideration following your restore: You must take action to prevent your DHCP server from handing out duplicate IP addresses. How can this happen? When you restore a server, it is being "rolled back" to the time of the last backup. For example, if the DHCP server was backed up six hours before the restore, it could have handed out several IP addresses since that time. After the restore operation, the DHCP server would have no record of the IP addresses it handed out after its last backup and, as a result, could distribute them again. How do we prevent this? Use Server Conflict Detection.

Using DHCP Server Conflict Detection

With Windows 2000, Microsoft realized the potential problem of DHCP servers handing out an already assigned IP address. To prevent this problem from occurring, Conflict Detection was devised. The idea behind conflict detection is simple. When enabled (set to a value higher than 0), the DHCP server will ping an IP address and check for a response before it assigns the IP address to a system. When the server receives a reply from an IP address, it will assign that address a BAD_ADDRESS value in the DHCP scope and will no longer try to use the address.

By using the DHCP administrative tool, you can edit the server's properties to set a number of conflict detection attempts. Each attempt represents a one-second ping attempt for an IP address before it is assigned. The default value is 0 (no conflict detection). Microsoft recommends that after a restore of a DHCP server you set the conflict detection attempts value to 1 and leave that setting for at least half the longest lease duration. For example, if all systems were assigned eight-day leases, you would leave the conflict detection attempts value for the server to 1 for a minimum of four days.

Each attempt you set results in a one-second delay (or waiting period for conflict detection) for an IP address to be assigned. Conflict detection will slow down your DHCP server, which is why you should use it only when needed. To configure conflict detection after a restore of the DHCP database, follow these steps:

1. Click Start ➢ Programs ➢ Administrative Tools ➢ DHCP to open the DHCP administrative tool.
2. Right-click the DHCP server and select Properties.
3. Click the Advanced tab in the DHCP Server Properties dialog box.
4. Change the Conflict Detection Attempts value to 1 (see Figure 11.19).

Figure 11.19: Setting conflict detection attempts

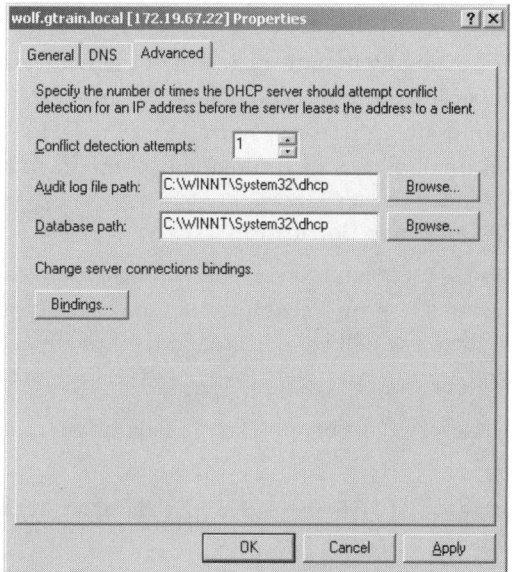

When Trouble Arises

With a solid backup solution, being aware of DHCP conflicts after a restore is most likely all you will need to know. However, not all backup solutions are perfect. Although their backups might run perfectly, the restore may not. With this in mind, it is always better to be careful, so we will show you methods to getting a guaranteed good backup of the DHCP database. Windows 2000 provides you with several options in backing up the DHCP database. By default, the database is stored in the `%systemroot%\system32\dhcp\dhcp.mdb` file.

Here are some valid ways to back up the DHCP database, if your backup application is having trouble backing it up while it is running:

- Stop the DHCP Server Service before the backup and then restart it after the backup. You can use this command-line syntax:

    ```
    net stop DHCP Server
    net start DHCP Server
    ```
- Manually initiate a backup "dump" of the DHCP database using the `Netsh` command. You can use Task Scheduler, for example, to run a regular dump of the database before a backup is run. To create a backup of the DHCP database to its default backup folder, you could use the following command:

    ```
    netsh dump dhcp server >
    %systemroot%\system32\dhcp\backup\dhcpserv.dmp
    ```

Even if you do not manually initiate a backup of the DHCP server, the service will automatically run backups periodically and place them in the `%systemroot%\system32\dhcp\backup` folder. If after a restore you find that the DHCP database is corrupted, you can use a previous dump file or an automatic backup file to recover the database.

Detecting DHCP Database Corruption

After a restore, and subsequent reboot, you will be alerted to a problem with the DHCP database by receiving a pop-up alert on the system that says a service failed to start. A corrupted DHCP database will be indicated in the System event log by any of these three errors:

- Event ID 1014 – DHCP Server – The JET database returned the following Error: -510
- Event ID 1014 – DHCP Server – The JET database returned the following Error: -1022
- Event ID 1014 – DHCP Server – The JET database returned the following Error: -1850

Once you see one of these events, you will need to recover the DHCP database from one of its backups in the dhcp\backup folder. Before attempting manual recovery of the database, you can attempt to run a Jetpack compaction of the database first. This may not fix the problem, but if the database is already corrupted, you have nothing to lose.

First Action for a Corrupted DHCP Database: Use Jetpack

To attempt to fix the DHCP database with Jetpack, use the following syntax from the command line:

`jetpack <path to dhcp database> <name of temp database file>`

For example, you could use this line:

`jetpack %systemroot%\system32\dhcp\dhcp.mdb dhcptmp.mdb`

After running Jetpack, try and start the DHCP Server service. If it starts, you're fixed!

When Jetpack does not work, you can restore the database from another backup, or you can restore from one of its automatic backups or manually created dump files.

Second Action for a Corrupted DHCP Database: Use Automatic Restore

So, Jetpack did not work, and your DHCP Server service still won't start. Your next action should be to let it automatically repair itself. You do this by setting the Database Restore Flag to 1. The restore flag tells the DHCP Server service to automatically load the database from the automatic backup the next time it starts. To do this, follow these steps:

1. Click Start ➢ Run, type **cmd,** and press Enter.
2. From the command prompt, type **netsh - c dhcp** to access the DHCP console.
3. Now type **server \\<name of DHCP server>** to reach the dhcp server prompt.
4. Type **set databaserestoreflag 1**.
5. Type **exit**.
6. Close the command prompt window.
7. Start (or restart) the DHCP Server service.

Figure 11.20 shows the result of running this syntax.

Figure 11.20: Setting the DHCP database restore flag

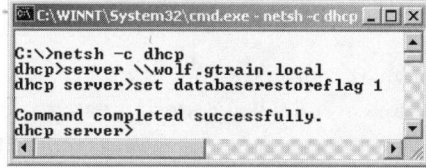

Once the service restarts, the automatic backup file will replace the existing DHCP database file. If you are wondering how to set the automatic backup interval, you can also achieve that from the *Netshell dhcp server* prompt. The backup interval is measured in seconds, so to set the backup interval to 24 hours, you would use the `set databasebackupinterval 1440` command, as shown in Figure 11.21.

Figure 11.21: Setting the DHCP database backup interval

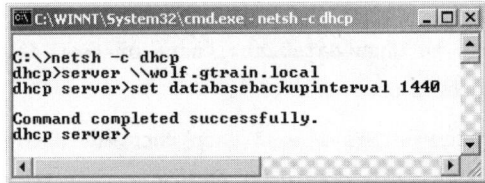

If you had used the `netsh dump` command to create a backup of the DHCP database, you could then use `netsh exec <path to backup dump file>` to restore the database. For example, for the dump command used earlier, you would enter from the command prompt: `netsh exec %systemroot%\system32\dhcp\backup\dhcpsrv.dmp`.

> **NOTE** Even Windows Backup does not have any backup or restore issues with the DHCP database, so if your backup program is designed for Windows 2000, you should not have to take any of these precautions.

SIS Volume Recovery

You were introduced to Single Instance Storage (SIS) in Chapter 3, "Windows 2000 Storage Enhancements." When you install and configure Remote Installation Services (RIS) on a Windows 2000 Server, SIS is automatically set up on the volume that contains the RIS images. With multiple images containing duplicate files stored on the same partition, SIS saves space by placing a single instance of all duplicate files in a common hidden directory (SIS Common Store). Files that have duplicates on the partition will contain pointers to the SIS Common Store folder, which is the only true location where the actual file data is stored. You can again relate this concept to the idea of Windows shortcuts. Shortcuts are not the actual executable that runs a program, but rather they act as a virtual pointer that transparently directs a user to an executable.

Unfortunately, although SIS may save you disk space, it will also cause you some headaches if you are not careful when restoring data to volumes managed by SIS. SIS is a volume-management service, meaning it manages more than the RIS directory. Because it manages an entire volume, you must be careful when restoring anything to a volume managed by SIS.

Rebuilding a SIS Volume

Though you have been warned about SIS, you should not be discouraged from using the service. Problems with SIS mainly arise when rebuilding a partition managed by the service. Suppose a server crashes and you must rebuild it from scratch. Another time to be careful would be if the SIS volume crashed and had to be replaced, or if you were upgrading the volume to a larger disk. Following the steps in the next section will make the restore of data backed up from a SIS managed volume a seamless process.

Restoring SIS Data When RIS Is Already Installed

Take these steps when you need to rebuild a volume on a server already running Remote Installation Service:

1. Install and format the hard drive for the SIS data using NTFS. Assign the same drive letter as the drive that failed.
2. Click Start ➤ Run, type **risetup -check**, and press Enter.
3. Now follow the screen prompts to reconfigure the volume. When asked for the volume name, use the volume that you re-created in step 1.
4. Restore data to the volume.

Restoring Data When RIS Is Not Installed (Rebuilding a System)

Take these steps when you have to completely rebuild a server that uses RIS:

1. Reinstall the Windows operating system.
2. From the Control Panel, double-click Add/Remove Programs.
3. Click the Add/Remove Windows Components button.
4. Check the Remote Installation Services check box and click Next.
5. Select the Terminal Services mode, if asked, and click Next.
6. Once the installation completes, you will need to reboot the server.
7. After the reboot, use Disk Management to create a new partition for the RIS images.
8. Click Start ➤ Run, type **Risetup**, and press Enter.
9. Follow the prompts on the screen to setup RIS. When prompted, select the volume created in step 7.
10. Restore data to the volume.

Now that RIS is out of the way, let's take a look at Dfs.

Dfs Recovery Considerations

For the most part, file and folder backup of Dfs trees is no big deal. You have to know that files restored as part of a Dfs replica set are restored authoritatively, and it is also important to understand how to back up and recover the Dfs Structure Table. Aside from these two issues, backing up and restoring Dfs files are no different than backing up and restoring files from any other network share.

Dfs Structure Table

An easy way to recover the Dfs root structure of a Dfs server is by backing up its Structure Table. With a good backup of the Dfs root configuration, you can regenerate a Dfs root and all its associated pointers on another server in a matter of seconds. This is extremely useful if a Dfs server crashes and you need to recover immediately. If hardware failure is preventing the system from recovering immediately, you can use a backup of the Dfs Structure Table to implement the Dfs configuration on another server.

Follow these steps for backing up the Dfs Structure Table:

1. Click Start ➢ Run, type **cmd,** and press Enter to access the command prompt.

2. Now type **dfscmd /view \\<Dfs Server Name>\<Dfs Root Share Name> /Batch >> <path\filename.bat>**. Figure 11.22 shows the execution of this command, followed by use of the dir command to verify the new file.

Figure 11.22: Backing up the Dfs Structure Table

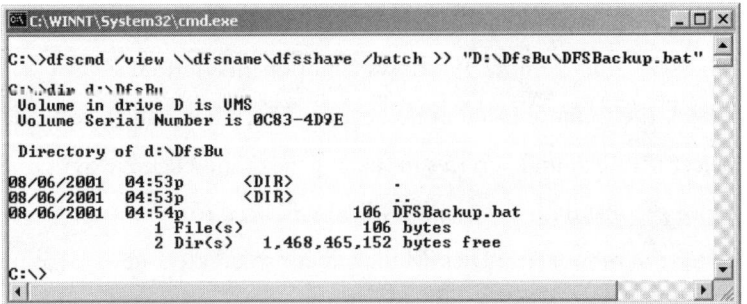

With a good backup of the Dfs Structure Table, follow these steps to restore the Dfs structure to the same or another system:

1. First, you must manually re-create the Dfs root. Open the Dfs administrative tool by clicking Start ➢ Programs ➢ Administrative Tools ➢ Distributed File System.

2. Click the Action menu and select New Dfs Root.
3. When the New Dfs Root Wizard opens, click Next.
4. Select the Dfs root type (domain or stand-alone) for the server and click Next.
5. For domain Dfs, select the domain and click Next.
6. Enter the server that will host the Dfs root and click Next.
7. Choose the share the will become the Dfs root share, or enter the name and path for a new share, and click Next.
8. Enter the name for the Dfs root, and comments, if desired, and click Next.
9. Verify that the configuration settings are correct and click Finish.
10. From the command line, run the batch file you created when you backed up the Dfs Structure Table.

When the batch file executes, it will run several instances of the `dfscmd /map` command to re-create the Dfs structure.

Recovering Dfs Replicas

Under most circumstances, it should not be necessary to restore data to a replicated Dfs share. One of the reasons for using replication in the first place is to maintain a high degree of data availability. However, if the need arises to restore a file that resides on a Dfs replicated share, you must know that the restore will be authoritative. Once the file is restored, it will replicate out to other shares in the Dfs replica set, overwriting any like files. If someone errantly modified a file and you want to revert back to an earlier version of the file, then you should restore the file from a backup.

In the event that you want to nonauthoritatively restore a file to a share in a Dfs replica set, you would need to perform these steps:

1. Remove the share from the Dfs replica set.
2. Restore the file.
3. Re-add the share to the replica set.

Losing WINS

Some backup products seem to have difficulties backing up the WINS database when it is in an online state. This does not mean you will have to shut down the WINS service to get a valid backup of the WINS database. Instead, you can let WINS do its own backups.

When running its own backups, WINS will store a good backup of its data files on any local directory you specify. Once you specify a backup directory and manually run one backup using the WINS administration tool, the WINS service will automatically run a backup of the WINS database every three hours. This automatic backup will ensure your backup software gets a backup of your WINS database; however, the backup might not be current.

Configuring Automatic Backup

Automatic backup will allow you to have peace of mind regarding how your backup software backs up the online WINS database. Once automatic backups are configured, your backup software will always be able to, at a minimum, back up the offline backup copy of the WINS database.

To configure an automatic backup, follow these steps:

1. On the WINS server, click Start ➢ Programs ➢ Administrative Tools ➢ WINS to open the WINS administrative tool.

2. Right-click the WINS server icon and select Properties.

3. Specify the database backup directory (see Figure 11.23). Microsoft recommends you use `%systemroot%\system32\wins`.

Figure 11.23: Setting WINS database backup parameters

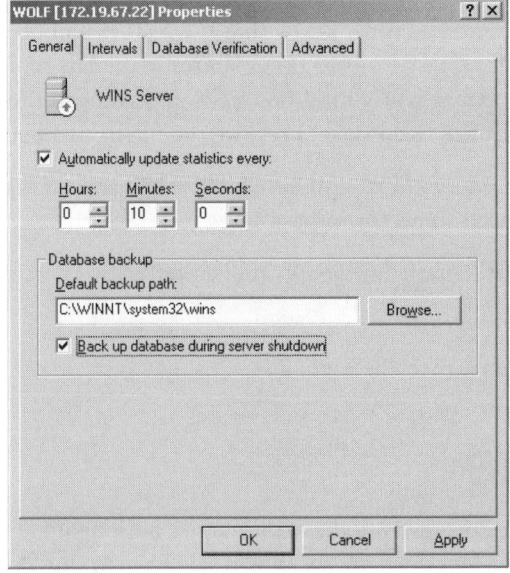

4. If you would like to have an automatic backup run each time the WINS service shuts down or restarts, then select the Backup Database during Server Shutdown check box.

5. Click OK to save the configuration.

6. Now right-click the WINS server and select Back Up Database. This is necessary because automatic backups will not run until after you have manually backed up the database.

7. Click OK to select the backup destination directory you set in step 3.

8. When prompted that the backup completed successfully, click OK.

9. Repeat steps 2 through 8 for each WINS server in your forest.

Restoring the WINS Database from a Backup File

If your backup application could not restore the WINS database from its live backup version, then you can recover the database from the automatic backup file. Before doing this, you must first stop the WINS service. After stopping the service, follow these steps to recover the database:

1. On the WINS server, click Start ➢ Programs ➢ Administrative Tools ➢ WINS to open the WINS administrative tool.

2. Right-click the WINS server for which you need to restore the database and select Restore Database.

3. Select the folder that contains the wins_bak directory, and click OK.

4. Once the restore completes, the WINS service will be automatically started on the server.

NOTE Another alternative to restoring the database from a backup is to recover the database through replication with other WINS servers.

12

Exchange 5.5/2000 Backup and Recovery

Time is money. In modern business, e-mail is money, too. So how much time can you afford to waste while your Exchange Server is down? There is zero time for what we term as being *e-mail inhibited*. As an administrator, it's your job to ensure that your Exchange 5.5/2000 is up and stays up or, at least, is recoverable in a short period of time.

Accomplishing this task requires three things:

- Knowing your Exchange cold. In this chapter, we provide you with a strong overview of where your Exchange databases live and what you need to do to preserve your structure.

- Choosing a reliable data management software. Reliability and functionality are key features of your backup application. This chapter helps you make your decision.

- Practice. So, you want to wait until a problem to test those recovery skills of yours? Nice going, you're fired! A little practice and some detailed documentation on recovery are in order. This chapter gets you ready.

> **NOTE** We cover both Exchange 5.5 and Exchange 2000 because their architectures are quite different from each other. Exchange 5.5 is more widely deployed, but Exchange 2000 is the newest form of Microsoft's mail application, so we should be seeing more of it as Active Directory becomes more widely implemented.

The best place to start is with Exchange 5.5; let's discuss the Exchange architecture involved.

Understanding Exchange 5.5 Architecture

There are several items that combine to create the architecture of Exchange 5.5. There are various log files, which hold all of the immediate changes to the database, and there are the data files (or database files), which are the most important files to back up. Further, you can perform different types of backups under the Exchange structure. Let's start with the logs.

Exchange 5.5 Log Files

The following types of logs are used within Exchange 5.5: transaction logs, previous logs, checkpoint files, patch files, and circular logging.

Transaction Logs

Data for the directory or information store is written at high speed to a sequential transaction log file and to a memory cache simultaneously. The data in the cache is later written to the directory database or the information store database files as necessary. When a log file has 5MB of transactions, a new log file is generated. Log files are named with hexadecimal serial numbers.

The size of log files is always 5MB, so you cannot determine whether a log file is filled to capacity by checking the file size.

The transaction logs are used to bring a database up-to-date during a restore operation. The public and private information stores share a transaction log located in the Mdbdata folder, and the directory database has its own transaction log located in the Dsadata folder. Both transaction logs are named edb.log.

Previous Logs

When a transaction log becomes full, it is renamed in the format edb*nnnnn*.log (*nnnnn* is a incrementing hexadecimal value), and a new edb.log is started.

One distinction between the two types of backups is that a full or incremental backup will delete log files that have all transactions committed to the database. Differential backups will back up the transaction log files but will leave the log files on the hard disk. Copy backups will back up the system like a full backup but leave the transaction logs intact.

Checkpoint Files

The checkpoint file indicates exactly which transactions have been committed to the .edb database. It serves as more of a speed index of transactions committed than anything else. If it is missing, the database service will simply start from the beginning of the log files and match it with the database to confirm that each operation has been entered.

Patch Files

During an online backup, transactions made to the part of the database that has already been backed up are recorded in a patch file. The private information store uses a file called priv.pat, the public information store uses pub.pat, and the directory database uses dir.pat.

Circular Logging

Circular logging recycles transaction log files by overwriting logs that have been committed to the database with new transactions. This prevents the continuous buildup of transaction log files and reduces the disk space required to store them. You turn the option off from within the Exchange administrator program from within the Server properties on the Advanced tab.

> **WARNING** The Circular Logging option is turned on by default in Exchange 5.5. Keep in mind that circular logging is great for keeping transaction logs from growing out of control, but this prevents you from getting proper backups of the logs, which are essential for restore issues. Only use circular logging on Exchange Servers that hold less-sensitive data such as newsgroup servers.

When the Circular Logging option is enabled, you cannot perform incremental or differential backups. In fact, Windows Backup will have these options disabled. So, remember to turn this off.

Additional Terms

A few terms are used in relation to backing up Exchange, but they generally refer to your individual Outlook clients. They still become necessary in the case of restore issues:

Personal Message Store (.PST) Located on the client and hold the data that would be stored on the Exchange Server in a personal message store on the local system. These can work with the Exchange data as an additional part of the profile. If a .pst file is corrupt, you can restore it if it is backed up off the client (not the Exchange Server). If the .pst is not backed up and becomes corrupt, then that data is lost. (To fix a damaged .pst you can use the Scanpst program).

Offline Message Store (.OST)   Allows users to work offline and then synchronize with the Exchange Server.

Personal Address Book (.PAB)   Can be placed on the server or the client. It is safer if it is on the server because if it is lost you'll spend a long time putting it back together.

Exchange Database Structure and File Locations

Microsoft Exchange Server 5.5 includes three specific databases: an information store (which is split into a public information store and a private information store) and a directory store. These databases must reside locally on the Exchange Server. In addition to the database files, the transaction logs, checkpoint files, and patch files are part of the process for Exchange functionality. All related files are backed up together in what is referred to as a *database set*:

Private Information Store   This database is stored in a `priv.edb` file. It holds individual users' mailboxes and folders.

Public Information Store   This database is stored in a `pub.edb` file. It holds folders containing information that is publicly accessible to the entire Exchange organization. A wide range of access configurations can be implemented for public folders.

Directory Store   This database is stored in a `dir.edb` file. It holds information about resources and users within the Exchange organization. The directory service manages information with the database and provides an interface through which users and other services can access the data.

Table 12.1 describes the databases and their locations.

Table 12.1: The Database Filenames and Locations

Database	Database Filename	Patch Filename	Transaction Log Filename
Private information store	`Priv.edb`	`Priv.pat`	`Mdbdata\Edbnnnn.log`
Public information store	`Pub.edb`	`Pub.pat`	`Mdbdata\Edbnnnn.log`
Directory database	`Dir.edb`	`Dir.pat`	`Dsadata\Edbnnnn.log`

Exchange uses write-ahead transaction log files in addition to the database (.edb) files to improve server data write performance and to provide fault tolerance for the directory and information stores. In addition to log files, we describe checkpoint files, patch files, and reserved files to give you a better understanding of how Exchange can recover from various types of failures.

> **NOTE** It is important to note that recovery is the key to an Exchange failure, not necessarily restore. Restoring your Exchange Server is the final solution to recovery. By understanding the underlying structure of Exchange database activity, you will have a better possibility of recovering your server without the need to fully restore the system.

Putting It Together

You might be wondering about how all of these different files work together to provide a functioning mail server. Well, consider how an Exchange Server works. For example, an e-mail is sent to a user's mailbox with a large attachment file. The Exchange Server receives the message and, according to Microsoft, places the message into the database (or, in the case of a private message, into the priv.edb) while simultaneously entering the full record of the message, including the attachment, into the current transaction log file. In reality, the transaction log gets the data first, and the database follows shortly after. The checkpoint file keeps track of what changes have gone from the transaction logs to the database itself. If the transaction log exceeds its 5MB limit, it is renamed and considered a previous log file. A new "current" log is created. This process continues and logs fill until you run out of room on your server and all services stop or until you back up the server in a way that purges these transaction logs. In the case of a message that contains enough data to exceed the 5MB limit of the transaction log, the patch file will keep track of where logs are connected by their data.

> **NOTE** Purging logs occurs during the online backup. All transaction logs that have been written to the .edb file are purged (deleted and not backed up, because the .edb files are backed up). Any new transaction logs created during the backup process are copied to tape so that the .edb files and new transactions are saved.

There is only one way to avoid the crash that will eventually come from data overflow: either use circular logging and forget about fault tolerance or prepare yourself for backup/recovery solutions. Before considering backups, Microsoft has a best-practice solution for Exchange configuration of hard disks, as shown in Figure 12.1.

Figure 12.1: Fault-tolerant Exchange disks

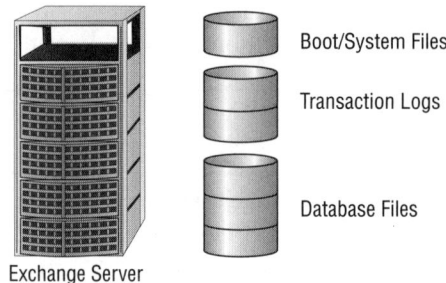

You might notice the following configuration for fault tolerance:

- A disk for the operating system and the page file
- A disk for the transaction logs that is mirrored
- A stripe set with parity for the database itself for fast access and fault tolerance

> **NOTE** In the case of a disk failure where the database is lost, the transaction logs would still be valid for restore. To restore the server, you would simply restore your database information and allow the transaction logs to replay themselves until the server is up-to-date. Do not restart your services until all transaction logs have been restored from backup.

One of the reasons for this configuration is that transaction logs are written to simultaneously, and by dedicating them their own disks, the read/write heads of the drive do not have to fight for time.

Backing Up Exchange 5.5

You have a hundred different ways to back up and recover your Exchange Server's data, but where to start depends on where the data resides. The data for your mail clients could reside on the Exchange Server (as in the case of a corporate mail server) or on the client (as in the case of an ISP-provided mail server).

- Server-based backups include backing up all of the directory information and information stores directly off the Exchange Server.
- Local includes the Personal Message Store (.pst files), the personal address books, and the offline folders.

> **NOTE** Server-based data is the primary concern in this chapter. If you need more information on backing up .pst files, visit Microsoft's Exchange site at www.Microsoft.com/exchange.

With an Exchange Server, there are two types of backup directions:

- Online is when the services are up, and the system is still able to accept information. During an online backup the information store, directory, Message Transfer Agent (MTA), and system attendant remain in service during the backup.
- Offline is when the services have stopped.

Understanding Offline Backups

An offline backup is a normal file-level backup made with services stopped. To get an offline backup you simply stop the services and then do a direct copy to an alternate location of your database and transaction files. Or you can use backup software to do a file-level backup of these files. Any backup software can perform an offline backup; you just have to manually or, through the use of a script, turn off the Exchange services. However, when you restore an offline backup, it does not automatically play through the log files as does its online counterpart. For this reason, Microsoft does not recommend offline backup for daily backups. Nonetheless, an offline backup can really save you when online backups fail.

Restoring Offline Backups

Restoring an offline backup would involve the following:

- Restore the directory store to the location of the DSADATA folder and start the service for the directory store.
- Restore the information store to the MDBDATA folder and start the service for the information store.
- Run the Isinteg program. (You must use the -patch option with the isinteg command.)
- Stop the service for the information store, and it will start up again on its own.
- You may need to run the Data Consistency Adjuster to fix some issues between your databases, which will be covered shortly.

Running Isinteg

Isinteg finds and eliminates common errors from the Exchange Server's public and private information store databases. These errors can prevent the information store from starting or prevent users from logging on and receiving, opening, or deleting mail.

Isinteg has three modes that can run independently of each other: Check mode, Check and Fix mode, and Patch mode. In Check mode, Isinteg will search the information store databases for table errors, incorrect reference counts, and unreferenced objects. The results will be displayed and written to a log file. Check and Fix mode goes to the next level by attempting to correct the errors that are found. Patch mode is specifically used when you've attempted a restore from an offline backup.

Isinteg (-fix) or (-patch) modes should not be used without the advice of Microsoft technical support. In reality, there are Exchange administrators who have never used Isinteg because they have never needed to utilize an offline backup. Although this is the normal and hoped-for scenario, this information may just get you out of a problem.

Isinteg, however, can perform 33 tests. Although Microsoft requests involvement for this tool, the likelihood of losing data is minimal because Isinteg doesn't throw out any information, even if it doesn't find a place for it. (Eseutil, described in "Using Eseutil," has that destructive capability and should be used if Isinteg doesn't do the trick.)

NOTE For more information go to Microsoft's Exchange site at www.microsoft.com/Exchange and search for "Isinteg." Or you can read the isinteg.rtf file located on the Exchange 5.5 CD-ROM under the \Server\Support\Utils folder.

Using the Data Consistency Adjuster

Every public folder and mailbox is represented in two places on your server: in the directory database and in the information store. The information store contains mailboxes, public folders, and their contents. The directory database contains the mailbox and public folder properties.

The Directory Service/Information Store (DS/IS) Consistency Adjuster—or Data Consistency Adjuster for short—resolves inconsistencies between the directory and the information store on a server. These typically occur after you restore the directory of the information store from a backup. It is used to ensure that the directory and information store objects are synchronized. Inconsistencies between the information store and the directory occur when there is an entry for a public folder or mailbox in the information store without a corresponding entry in the directory database, or vice versa.

To start the Data Consistency Adjuster you must navigate your way from within the Exchange administrator tool down to the server level and select the server you are looking to adjust. Go into the properties of the server and select the Advanced tab, as shown in Figure 12.2.

Figure 12.2: Advanced tab of a server's Properties dialog box

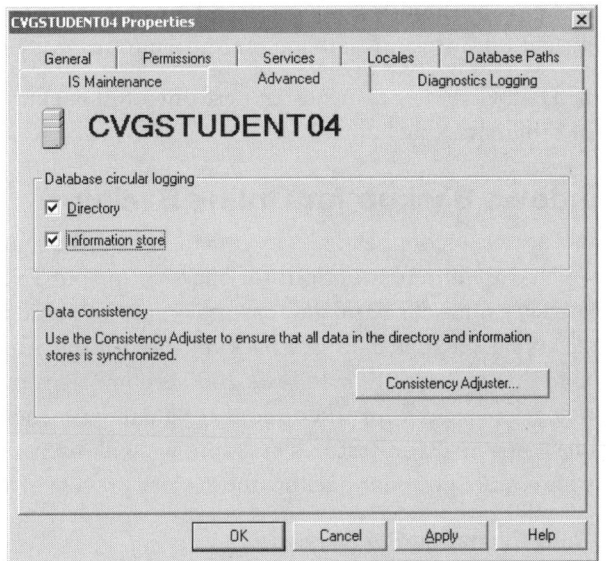

The Data Consistency Adjuster creates an entry in the directory if a public folder or mailbox exists in the information store. It deletes from the directory any public folder entries that don't exist in the information store, but it won't delete any mailbox entries from the directory. It also removes users who are no longer valid from public folder permissions and reports on public folders with no owners. Once you select the Data Consistency Adjuster option, you can then specify a latency period, as shown in Figure 12.3.

Figure 12.3: Some of the options available with the Data Consistency Adjuster

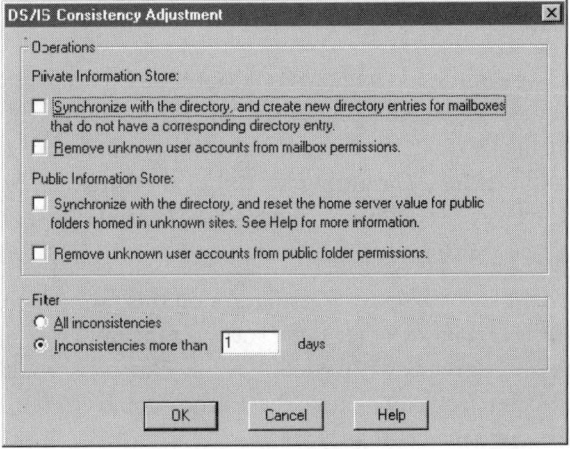

The latency period allows you to specify a time wherein only inconsistencies older than a given number of days are adjusted. This is useful for preserving entries in the directory or the public information store and enabling replication to resolve inconsistencies.

After using the Data Consistency Adjuster, perform a full backup before doing the next incremental or differential backup.

Using Windows Backup for Online Backups

Online backups are the recommended way to handle your Exchange Server according to Microsoft. There are different options for backing up your Exchange Server, but the process is relatively simple for basic database backups. You could use third-party software to handle your Exchange database backups, but for the most part the Windows Backup software that comes with Windows 2000 is competent in this area. We will now take a look at the procedure and options for a database backup. Later in the "Brick-Level Backups for Item Restores" section, we will discuss additional software backup types for a more granular backup and restore process of your Exchange Server.

Backing Up Your Exchange 5.5 Server

If your Exchange Server is located on a Windows 2000 system, then you have the built-in option of using the Windows Backup application. Follow these steps:

1. Select Start ➢ Programs ➢ Accessories ➢ System Tools ➢ Backup. Windows Backup opens.

2. Go to the Backup tab.

> **TIP** You are not able to select the Microsoft Exchange check box. You must double click Microsoft Exchange or click the plus sign (+) to expand the Exchange Server tree. You can expand the tree down to the directory or information store for any server.

3. You can expand the Exchange Server option by double-clicking on it. If you don't see your server, you can search for it from within the Backup tool. Expand your server until you get to the option to choose the Information Store (Public and Private Information Stores) or the Directory Store or both. In Figure 12.4, we've selected both for a CVGSTUDENT04 server in the EDSERVICES Organization.

4. You can choose the Backup Destination on this tab, which allows you to choose a file format or other type, such as tape (and the tape type). In our case, we chose File; in the Backup Media or File Name group, it gives a file with a .bkf extension. You can change these (and should) to retain multiple copies within the same magnetic location.

Figure 12.4: Backup procedure for Exchange

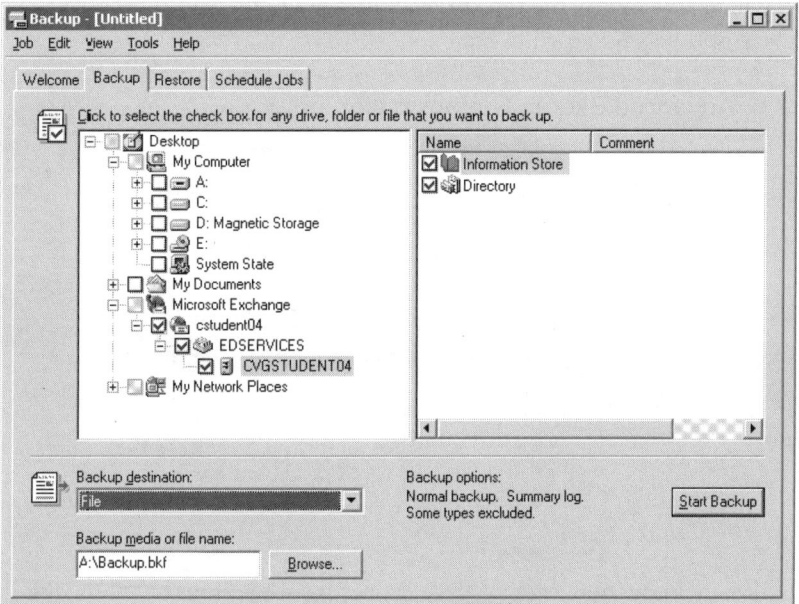

When you hit Start Backup, another set of options appears, as shown in Figure 12.5.

Figure 12.5: Backup Job Information dialog box

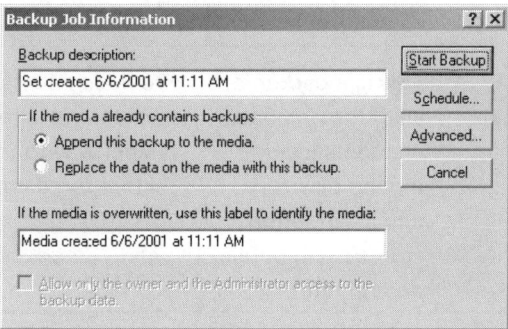

From within these settings you can choose how the media will be written to. You can create your own easily identifiable descriptions or use the ones already provided for you. You can choose to append this backup to media that has already been written to. You can choose to overwrite the existing data.

By selecting the Advanced button, you go into the Advanced Backup Options dialog box, where you choose the type of backup you would like to perform. There are five primary options, as shown in Figure 12.6.

Figure 12.6: Advanced Backup Options dialog box

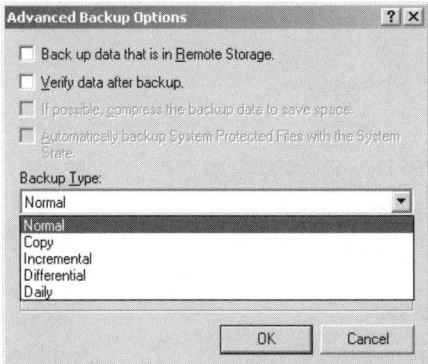

You already know how each of these works from previous chapters, but it is important to consider how these are handled in Exchange backup in relation to the logs. Table 12.2 describes the five backup types.

Table 12.2: Backup Types

Backup Type	Description	Advantages	Disadvantages
Full (purges the transaction logs).	This is a backup of all of the database elements including the directory and information stores (both public and private).	Provides a full backup and is the fastest way to restore the data.	Time consuming. Requires more free media than a differential or incremental backup.

Continued on next page

Table 12.2 (Continued): Backup Types

Backup Type	Description	Advantages	Disadvantages
Incremental (purges the transaction logs).	Backup of only those portions of the database that have changed since the last backup. Essentially it back ups the database transaction logs.	Much faster than a full or differential backup. Consumes a relatively small amount of media. Also places fewer burdens on resources than full backups.	Many incremental backups will result in lengthier restores as compared to full and differential backups.
Differential (does not purge the transaction logs).	Contains only those databases that have changed since the last full backup.	Like incrementals, these consume less media and place less of a burden on resources than full backups.	More time consuming and consumes more media than incremental backups.
Copy (does not purge the transaction logs).	Makes a backup of whatever is currently residing in your Exchange database; however, it will not delete the transaction logs.	Gives you a full backup without hindering your backup cycles in any way. Allows you to retain the logs for your incremental backups.	Doesn't fit within your backup cycle structure. More of a secondary precaution. Very handy for testing.
Daily (does not purge the transaction logs).	In this regard, the daily backup performs the same as a copy backup.	Gives you a full backup without hindering your backup cycles in any way. Allows you to retain the logs for your incremental backups.	Doesn't fit within your backup cycle structure. More of a secondary precaution. Very handy for testing.

Once you hit OK, you are taken back to the Backup Job Information dialog box where you can then start the backup or determine when you want to schedule your backup structure. In starting the backup, you will get the Backup Progress dialog box, shown in Figure 12.7.

Figure 12.7: Backup Progress dialog box

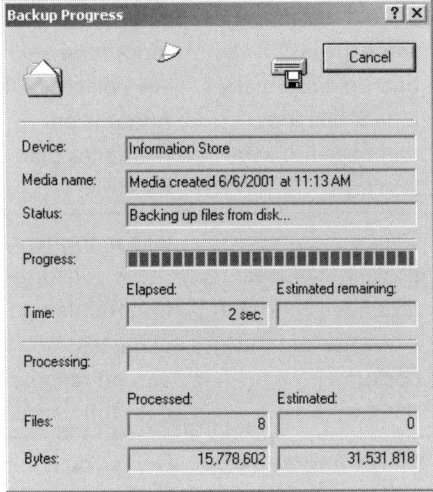

When the job is complete, you will (if the backup was successful) see the dialog box in Figure 12.8.

Figure 12.8: The backup is complete.

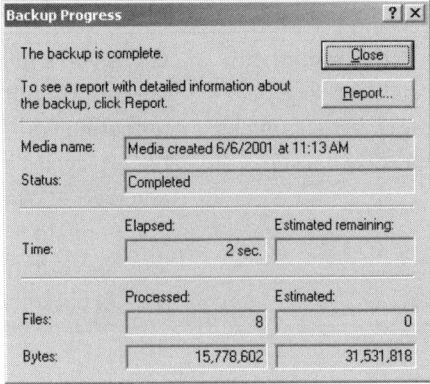

Restoring Your Exchange 5.5 Server Databases

Using Windows Backup to restore your databases is as easy as the backup; however, there are several issues that need to be addressed in handling your Exchange Server restoration. First, we'll take a look at the restore options; second, we'll look at the various methods involved in the restore process.

To restore your Exchange Server, do the following:

1. Select Start ➢ Programs ➢ Accessories ➢ System Tools ➢ Backup. Windows Backup opens.
2. Go to the Restore tab.
3. Select the backup you want to restore, as shown in Figure 12.9.

Figure 12.9: The restore process

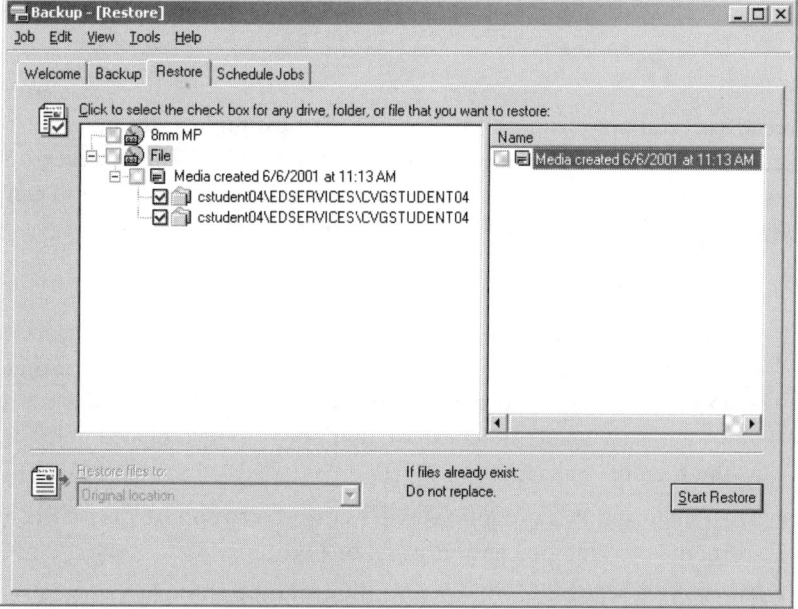

You may wonder about different restore options that you would like to perform; for example, what if you only want to restore the information store? When you hit the Start Restore option, the Restoring Microsoft Exchange dialog box appears, as shown in Figure 12.10.

Figure 12.10: Restoring Microsoft Exchange dialog box

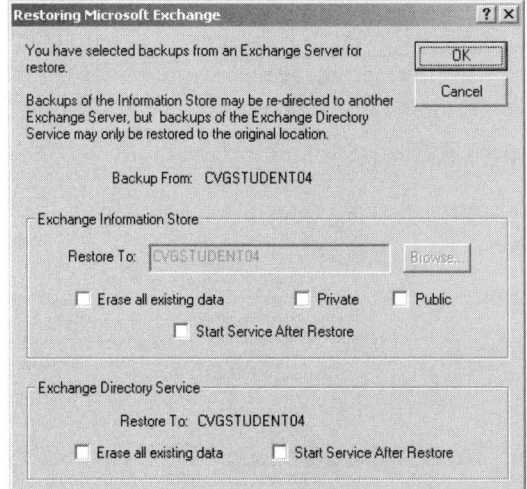

There are several options in this dialog box. For example, right up at the top you are directed that the information store can be restored to a different server, but the directory store cannot. If you restore the information store alone, then you can choose to browse for another Exchange Server to restore to.

Some of the options for the information store include the following:

- The Erase All Existing Data option will overwrite existing transaction logs. If this option is not selected, then the logs that currently reside for that database will be replayed and those messages will not be lost. This is a great feature when you have a corrupt database that needs to be replaced but you want "up-to-the-minute" messages.
- The Public and Private options will allow you to choose the public information store, the private information store, or both.
- The Start Services After Restore option is important when your server is back up and running after your restore process.

With the directory store, the options include Erase All Existing Data or Start Services After Restore, which hold the same meaning as above.

When the restore is complete, you'll see the Restore Progress dialog box, as shown in Figure 12.11.

Figure 12.11: The restore is complete.

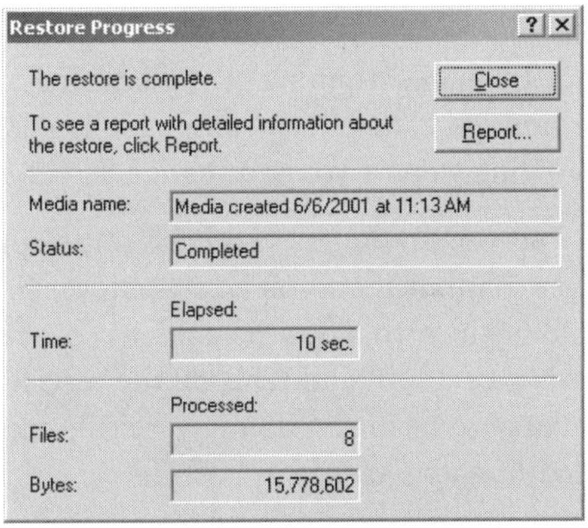

The backup process is great for restoring corrupt databases. It can also be used for larger issues such as full server restores or mailbox restores. So, no more worries with the Exchange process, right? Wrong. There are additional factors involved in Exchange restoration, such as the following:

- Performing a full Exchange restore
- Restoring a mailbox
- Restoring individual messages

The theory behind these restores may save you hours worth of unnecessary work.

Backup/Restore Strategy for Exchange 5.5

Considering the many different problems you can have with an Exchange Server (from database corruption to an angry employee throwing the box out of a 30-story window), we could go through hundreds of scenarios. Let's just start off with the worst case: the full server restore.

Performing a Full Server Restore with 5.5

This is no easy discussion. We are talking about reinstalling Windows NT/2000 and service packs, working up a new Registry and a new security ID (SID). Depending on your current arrangement, this could be easy. For example, if you had your Exchange 5.5 Server located on a member server within your domain (not a problem), most of your underlying structure should be fine. If you had your Exchange 5.5 server located on the Primary Domain Controller (PDC) of your NT domain (or a Windows 2000 domain controller), then you have to go through the process of reinstalling the Security

Accounts Management database (SAM) (or the Active Directory). So, a great deal depends upon your arrangement.

Assuming you have your Exchange running on a member server (running Windows 2000), with your domain controllers (running NT or 2000) still intact, you should perform the following steps if your Exchange Server goes down:

1. Create a Recovery Server. To do this you have some options to consider. You could use the server that failed and replace whatever hardware caused the crash, or you could begin with a new machine. You need to reinstall the operating system (either NT or 2000) and reinstall the service packs you originally had running. Don't try to be fancy; if you were running SP 4 on your NT Server, don't try loading up 6a.

   a. Also, you may need to delete the NT/2000 account from the domain and then re-create it using Server Manager in NT or Active Directory Users and Computers for 2000.

   b. This newly created system needs to have the same name as the crashed box. It needs to have the same role (in the easiest case, a member server). It should have plenty of disk space for the restoration.

2. You then need to install Microsoft Exchange Server on the new or repaired server. You cannot just do a simple install, but rather you must use the `Setup /r` procedure to install the Exchange Server.

   a. Setup /r will not create the `dir.edb`, `pub.edb`, or `priv.edg`. These are normally created during the installation and are taken from the organization and site name given. The /r will copy these files directly from the CD-ROM, and the services will not be able to start.

> **WARNING** If you are going to restore the information store and not the directory store, then you do not want to run `Setup /r` because this switch requires you to restore all database files, including the directory store.

   b. During the installation you want to give the server its original organization and site name. You do not want to use Join an Existing Site even if there are other servers in your organization. Remember, you are restoring your information, not creating a new machine in an existing environment.

   c. Use the same Service Account for the installation when requested.

   d. Install the same connectors that were used in the original server. (By the way, can you see the need for some good documentation to survive this type of crash?)

3. Run Exchange Optimizer. This tool will help you to put your configuration back to its original configuration with the location of transaction logs and such going back in the correct locations.

4. Make sure you are using the same Exchange service packs. Again, don't be fancy here by installing SP4 when SP3 was on your original production server. If you want to upgrade, do it after your server is restored. Use the `Update /r` to restore the service pack, which will, again, not start the services and is pretty much telling your Exchange Server that you are going to restore from a backup.

5. Restore the directory store from your latest backups from your original production server.

6. Restore the public/private information store from your latest backups from the original production server.

NOTE During the restore process, you should select the Erase All Existing Data option, unless a server has transaction logs that are recoverable. For example, if your production server goes down and you can recover the disk that held the transaction logs, then you can restore from your latest backup and choose to not erase all existing data. Then these transaction logs will be replayed. This would depend upon how well you followed the instructions to let Exchange know where those logs are located by using the Performance Optimizer and configuring your server like the original production system. Another option would be to copy the logs from their current location to the location that you have newly established for your DSADATA folder or MSADATA folder.

7. You can now restart your services, if you hadn't selected that as a restore option during the restoration process.

8. As a final step you might do well to run the Data Consistency Adjustment tool.

Testing the Restore

Testing the restore is not a difficult process. You know when your Exchange Server isn't working. If the services don't start, that is a good indication something went wrong in the process, and you'll need to start fishing for solutions. But for some quick verification of restore, you might try the following:

- Go into the Recipients container on the Exchange Server and check to see if you have mailboxes restored and if they have Windows NT/2000 account associations. Do this by selecting the mailboxes and checking out their properties to see the association.

- Have some users log on and check their mail. Can they get into their Outlook with their current password (which shows that the accounts are linked properly between the domain controller and the mailbox)? Can they send and receive mail? Can they get into their calendar and such?
- If the services haven't started, try manually starting them. Sometimes they get a little confused, and you need to push them along.

Troubleshooting the Process

Ah, troubleshooting is where the fun begins. What could go wrong, you ask? Ha, ha. You don't want to know. If you do, then the most conclusive database of knowledge on the matter is Microsoft itself (http://support.Microsoft.com/support/).

We'll cover some of the common problems.

What if your services fail to start, for example, your information store? Look within your Event Viewer for error messages that contain Exchange entries, such as MS-ExchangeIS, MSExchangePriv, or MSExchangePub. The Event Viewer will usually give a clear reason for the problem and sometimes even a solution.

What if a log is corrupted and the restore process fails at this log? By checking through Event Viewer in the application log, you would be able to see a message for each log file played back during the restore. If a log is corrupt, you need to remove that log and all logs higher than that one and test to see if the services will start then. In that case, the server will be restored, but not with the most recent data; all logs after the corrupt one will be lost.

What if you suspect there are database errors, and you want to defragment your newly restored databases? Now, this is a dangerous prospect, but, hey, what have you got to lose at this point? You can use the `edbutil.exe` or `eseutil.exe` to defragment the database you suspect and then run the `isinteg -fix` to clean up inconsistencies. You should have Microsoft technical support talking you through this.

Now, why two tools? Eseutil replaces Edbutil in Exchange 5.5. So for those who are using older versions of Exchange, go for Edbutil (or maybe you should go for an upgrade). For those running 5.5, Eseutil offers more strength.

Using Eseutil

Remember the Isinteg tool mentioned earlier? Eseutil is its irate older brother. This utility will scan through the physical structure of the databases looking for (and fixing) errors. It can repair the database in one of two ways, either by recovery mode, which will fix problems without discarding pages that it finds to be bad, or by repair mode, which will throw away all pages considered bad.

The following are some of the more important features:

`eseutil /g` checks database integrity at speeds of about 10GB per hour.

`eseutil /p` can perform an integrity check and repair corrupt tables.

`eseutil /d` can defragment the Exchange database (offline). Online defragmentation takes place automatically but doesn't compact the database. Eseutil will allow the database to shrink in size.

Defragmenting the databases in Exchange is done automatically in the background. You have messages slated for deletion and tombstoned; during periodic maintenance, these are removed. The online process will defragment the files. That doesn't compact the database, however, so it will not reduce in size.

Compaction is performed offline (with services stopped) and through the Eseutil tool. The tool will reclaim space and reduce the database size.

Doing Authoritative Restores

For those of you who are familiar with Active Directory and some of the problems involved in restoring the directory to a domain controller, the process for Exchange will be easy.

When you restore an Exchange Server within an Organization, the database that is restored is considered "old," so the other Exchange Servers within the organization will check in with the server, see that it is out-of-date, and force the directory to change. What if you didn't want this to occur? What if you accidentally deleted some important configuration information or mailboxes with their directory information? Every time you restored the server, the others would overwrite the old information, thinking it was out-of-date, when in reality you want that information brought back.

The solution is `authrest.exe`. This tool can allow you to perform authoritative restores so that the system you restore will propagate its information to the other Exchange Servers, rather than the other way around. The tool does this by advancing object versions and Update Sequence Numbers (USNs) on the objects within the directory so that it tricks the other servers into thinking it has the most recent data. The program `authrest.exe` is located on the Exchange CD-ROM under \support\utils*your platform*. Additional support information can be found on the Exchange CD-ROM.

Restoring a Mailbox

In the case of an entire information store going bad, you can (and should) restore the entire database for the information store (public or private). But what about a scenario where you need to restore a single mailbox? Some third-party software (such as CommVault Galaxy and Veritas Backup Exec) make this a simple matter of finding the mailbox in an index and clicking a simple restore button. Without the purchasing of third-party software, you would need to perform the following with Windows Backup.

> **NOTE** You can also use an Exchange Resource Kit utility, Exmerge, for restoring mailboxes. See the "Using Exmerge" section.

You need to create a recovery server that is not considered part of the production environment. The server should have access to a domain controller for account validation.

1. To create the recovery server you need to install the server as a Backup Domain Controller (BDC) or member server. You can call the server whatever you choose because you are only restoring the mailbox, not the directory store. Also install the correct service packs for the server.

2. Install Exchange Server as a new Organization and Site using the same names and being careful not to join the existing server's site. Install the service packs that are on the production server.

3. Install an Exchange client such as Outlook on your new recovery server. (Installing an Outlook client is not always recommended on your Exchange Server, but this is just your recovery server, so you don't have to worry about it.)

4. Ensure that you have a backup of the information store database. Remember, you cannot restore a directory store to an alternate location, but the information store is capable of that feature.

5. Perform a restore of your backup and make sure you indicate the name of the recovery server as the server to restore to. Select the Erase All Existing Data and Start Service After Restore options.

Now you have a recovery server, but it happens to be worthless to you for your production environment. However, its original purpose was to pull out one mailbox. Let's grab that one:

1. On the recovery server you should open up the Exchange Administrator program. It would be good to run the Data Consistency Adjuster to handle inconsistencies. This will take the information store details and match them up to mailboxes.

2. From within the Exchange administrator program, select the Recipients container and find the mailbox you need to restore.

3. Now go into the properties of the mailbox. On the General tab, select the Primary Windows NT Account button and match the mailbox up with your account (the Administrator).

4. Configure an Outlook profile for the user and add a personal folder file to the profile.

5. Then run the Exchange client. Once you have the client open, you will see the mail that was backed up. Of course, it does you no good like this. You have to get it to the user who needs it.

6. From the Outlook mailbox, choose to Export the mailbox to a .pst file.

7. Finally, take that .pst file (either through a network share or a backup) and bring it to the production client and Import it.

Restoring Individual Messages

If you wanted to restore a single message or multiple messages, you would need to create the recovery server in all the same ways as in the previous section:

1. Through the Mail applet in Control Panel, go through the process of creating an additional Personal Folder file. Then open up your Outlook client, and you should see the two Personal Folder files.

2. Your functioning folders should include your message. Select the individual messages you would like to retain and copy them off to your extra Personal Folder file, which is an extra .pst file.

3. Once those messages are in the .pst file, you can copy that .pst file to your client system.

4. Configure the profile for that user to include the moved .pst file. Open Outlook, and you should see both the normal Inbox and the moved .pst messages.

5. Copy the moved messages into the standard Inbox.

6. At that point, you could remove the .pst file and the indication toward that file from within the user's profile.

This may seem like an awful lot of work just to restore a single message or mailbox. There are two ways to handle these types of single item recoveries. The first is included within Exchange and is easy to use for short-term recovery of deleted items. The second involves a price as you search through backup/recovery data-management software to find what you are looking for.

Deleted Item Retention

When you delete a message in Outlook and your Exchange Server holds that message, where do you think it goes? Well, in some cases it disappears forever, unless you restore from backup either through third-party software or through the process outlined previously. Within Exchange 5.5, however, there is a Deleted Item Retention setting that you can configure for your stores.

When you go into the private information store properties, for example, you can choose the number of days that the messages will be retained before being permanently purged from the server (see Figure 12.12). You can choose not to permanently delete items until the store has been backed up, as well.

Figure 12.12: Deleted Item Retention time

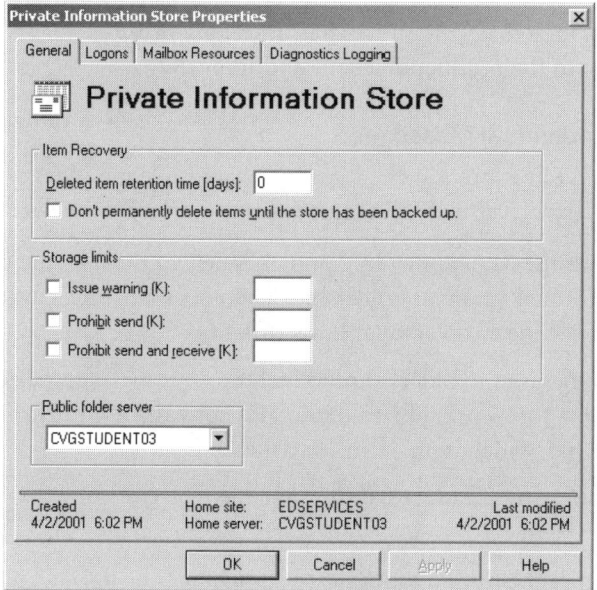

Another way to configure Deleted Item Retention time is on a specific mailbox basis. From within the properties of a mailbox within the Exchange Server, go to the Limits tab and choose Use Information Store Default or override the information store and create your own setting. This may be handy when you want to configure the more important mailboxes to retain items for a longer period of time.

So, how does this work? Most users are already aware that they have a Deleted Items folder from which they can retrieve mail. That isn't the concern here. What about mail that has been permanently deleted? With Deleted Item Retention parameters, you can instruct users who want deleted mail back to go into their Deleted Items folder from within Outlook. Specifically, follow these steps:

1. Choose Tools ≻ Recover Deleted Items.

2. Select the item or folder that you want to retrieve and choose Recover Selected Items.

That's it! It's a neat trick if you have it enabled on the Exchange Server and if the deleted item doesn't exceed the time parameter. If it does, then you have to go toward the long recovery process. Sorry!

There are two things to keep in mind. First, if you work with Offline folders a great deal, then you may run into problems finding these options. You have to be logged on to your mailbox on the server to see these options because they are carried out through the mail server. Also, we keep indicating Outlook as the client. That is because most of these features are Outlook oriented (Imagine that!) But even Outlook Express will not carry this functionality (because it is designed to retain messages on the client through .pst files, as opposed to retaining the data on the server).

Brick-Level Backups for Item Restores

Cool name, huh? *Brick-level backups* is a term given to the backup/restore process of items such as messages, mailboxes, folders, public folders, and so on. Windows Backup doesn't support this type of backup/recovery method. Imagine if it did? Keep in mind that Windows Backup is a light version of Backup Exec (currently owned by Veritas Software). How would Veritas sell its product if all the best stuff was wrapped directly into the operating system?

So, how does this work? Well, for one thing, it works slower on the backup process. That is because these types of backups do not just grab the .edb file and run; it has to scan through and grab each item as a separate piece. But what these backups cost on the backup time side, they make up for with the ability to restore an item quickly.

Let's say the Vice President of Marketing calls up and says, "Hey, I deleted a message that was a million-dollar deal. I want it back now." Now, you say, "No problem," because you're thinking of your seven-day deleted retention time. But then you find out that the VP deleted the message a month ago. You have a problem. You can either get out the recovery process detailed previously, or you can use your third-party software to find the message-level backup and restore the individual message, which is much quicker.

Figure 12.13 shows an example of an information store index, made by a CommVault Systems product called Galaxy.

By selecting the message, right-clicking, and choosing Restore, the workload has reduced dramatically from all the aforementioned recovery steps.

It is up to you and your company to research and choose a third-party solution. The key considerations are cost, functionality, support, and reliability. Do your research.

Figure 12.13: Galaxy Index of an Exchange mailbox backup

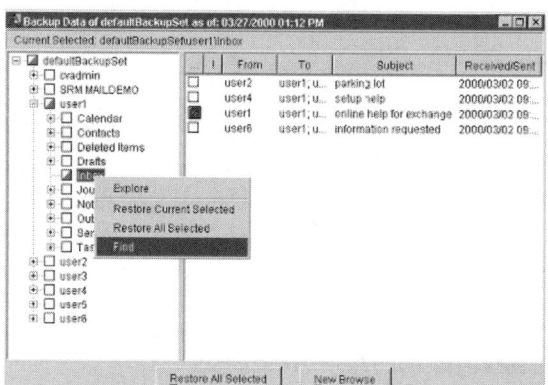

The Full Recovery Server Issue

Some have made it a practice to retain a server that is ready to perform at all times as a spare. In other words, the production Exchange Server goes down, you disconnect it from the network, connect the new server, and you're up and running and fully functional.

You can do this, but the requirements are strange, though. The recovery servers we mentioned earlier could not function in a production environment because we couldn't restore the Directory store to these systems because they didn't have the same computer names as the systems that were backed up.

So, why not just create a server that has the same computer names? Well, because of the conflicts that arise from two systems with the same name on the same network. You could take it off the network, but it needs access to the domain controllers for account validations. This is quite a situation.

There are a couple of fixes to this problem: one is a workaround, and the other is administratively intense.

The first solution is to keep an NT Server with service packs ready to go. Ensure that it is the same role (domain controller or member server) as the existing production server (if it is Windows 2000, then it won't matter because you can promote member servers). You might want to copy the Exchange installation files and service packs to the recovery server, but don't install Exchange. You can use this server in some light role, but in the event of a failure you can change the name of the server and install Exchange as the same Organization and Site. Then restore from backup, as described previously. Granted, this only shortens the process; it doesn't exactly give you up-to-the-minute solutions.

> **TIP** For 24/7 reliability you should maintain the mirrored/striped set with parity configuration of your disks, mentioned earlier in "Putting It Together."

The second solution is to configure your production environment Exchange Server to back up to a tape. Create a recovery server on a separate subnet with no ability for one to "see" the other. Ensure that the recovery server is using the same computer name, Organization, and Site name. Perform a backup and recovery of the production Exchange Server's directory and information stores. Because the names are the same, the recovery server should think it's simply getting a restored copy of the data. Some dilemmas come into play with this type of configuration; for example, the recovery server still needs to be able to validate accounts, which may be done by making it a Backup Domain Controller (BDC) in the domain initially.

One idea to speed up setup for this type of configuration is to use a third-party imaging solution. Image your Exchange and then you have an exact duplicate (SIDs and all) of the original. From that point, all you have to do is maintain the changes that occur from the time of your image date.

Disaster Recovery Spare

Gaylord Friend, a systems engineer for CommVault Systems, has worked on these "hot spare" configurations. This is what he has to say about them: "To maintain competitiveness in the marketplace, businesses must be able to quickly recover in case of a failure of those critical messaging systems."

To accomplish this, make sure you have the following configurations:

- A mirrored server is maintained on an unconnected disaster recovery and testing network segment. An exact replica of an Exchange Server cannot exist on the same network in the same Exchange site.
- The hostname and IP address of the mirror Exchange Server are not the same as the production server; all other configuration items are identical.
- The hardware of the recovery server does not need to be exact but must meet or exceed the storage requirements and configuration of the production server.
- The connection between the production and recovery site is of sufficient bandwidth to support the backup and recovery requirements.

> **NOTE** This solution is only one kind and is specific to CommVault Galaxy. Other software vendors would provide similar solutions, but the terms might change a bit.

The CommServe Server (which controls the entire backup CommCell, a logical data management structure) and MediaAgent (which intermediates between the Comm-Server and the Library) do not have to be on the same server, but both must have connectivity to the production and recovery segments. The appropriate Exchange database backup agents must be installed on both the production and recovery Exchange Servers.

The CommServe Server is configured in a workgroup and not in the domain. The production Exchange Server is installed with a valid production IP address and hostname. All backups of production data will happen via this interface on the CommServe Server (see Figure 12.14).

Figure 12.14: The "hot-spare" solution played out

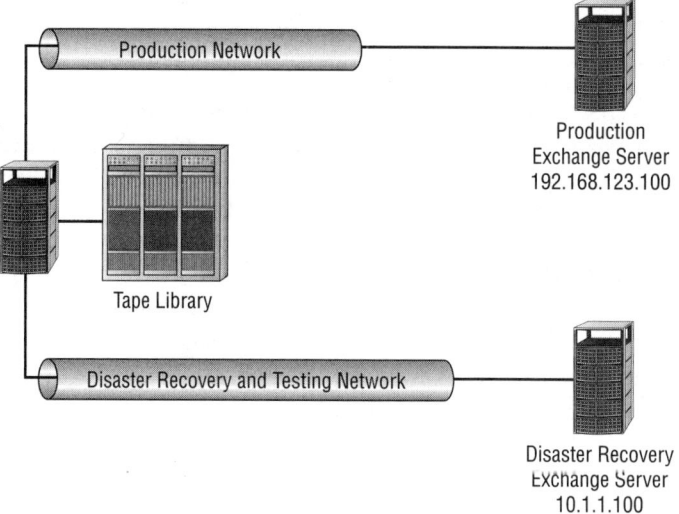

The recovery Exchange Server will be restored over the non-production interface. It will be an exact replica other than the hostname and IP address. In a total failure of the production server, the disaster recovery (D/R) server can be quickly re-cabled to the production network after changing the hostname and IP address to match the production server, allowing a minimum downtime for the messaging users.

The backups of the production server and the restores to the recovery server can be scheduled to minimize user intervention. By performing full restores to the D/R server, backup data can be verified to be valid and media tested to be functional.

Any requirement to recover old data can be made to the recovery server to minimize impact to the production network.

> **NOTE** This is one way to configure this solution. Other vendors may have additional solutions or may suggest other methods. Check with your vendor for more information.

Best Practices for Exchange 5.5 Recovery

We've already been through the recovery process, but how would you as an administrator put yourself in the best possible position to protect your data? Do the following:

- Make sure you back up all essential information. This includes your Registry, which is crucial to Exchange Server. The Registry contains most of the configuration information for certain connectors (such as Microsoft Mail) and service-related information. You need to make sure you have backups of your domain controller's SAM (or System State for Windows 2000 systems) because those accounts are essential.
- Turn off circular logging. It doesn't help you in terms of data protection. If you perform full backups each day, then you could leave it on.
- Monitor your event and application logs to see that your backups are successful.
- Set limits on mailbox sizes and perform regular cleanup operations on mailboxes to ensure a faster backup and recovery process.
- Remember the information presented earlier about mirroring and RAID 5 configuration of your transaction logs and database information. This is a fault-tolerant option and a performance booster for your Exchange environment.
- Periodically remember to run your database tests and defragmentation tools such as Isinteg and Eseutil.

So, that's it, huh? You wish! These are some great starting points, but you may run into problems, or you may have additional questions. And, of course, your configuration is going to be unique. Microsoft's support pages are always a great place to track down your errors or problems. You might start with `http://www.microsoft.com/exchange/techinfo/`.

Now let's look into the changes in Exchange 2000.

Understanding Exchange 2000 Architecture

Although you may be familiar with procedures for backup and restore of earlier Exchange versions, which is a great foundation, you will need to learn the new processes for Exchange 2000. You are well on your way if you have Exchange 5.5 experience; there are just a few changes in the structure of Exchange 2000 to be concerned about. For example, the database for any given store in Exchange 5.5 is contained in one file (.edb), but the Exchange 2000 database is contained in two linked files (database.edb and database.stm). For backup and restore processes, these two files must always be treated as one. They both need to be backed up, in addition to the transaction logs and checkpoint files.

An important enhancement in Exchange 2000 is the concept of multiple storage groups, multiple mailbox stores, and public folder stores in each storage group. A database contains data in a mailbox store or a public folder store. You can back up and restore databases in a storage group individually or together. A single set of log files contains entries for all databases in the storage group. These concepts will be explored further in this portion of the chapter.

Active Directory and Exchange 2000

In previous versions of Exchange, the directory database was held within the Exchange structure and was part of the backup of the Exchange databases. In Exchange 2000, the servers use Active Directory as their directory structure. Active Directory replicates Exchange mailbox and configuration information throughout an entire Windows 2000 forest.

From a backup and restore perspective, this complicates the procedural precedence from former versions. You can no longer back up the directory within an Exchange backup; rather, you need to perform this type of backup with a file system backup including your System State.

Because your Active Directory can have similar problems with restores that are nonauthoritative, Microsoft teaches you how to restore the directory in an authoritative way using the ntdsutil.exe tool. This has been described in Chapter 11, "Operating System Rebuilds: The Gotchas."

System State

The term *System State* refers to system-specific data that can be backed up and restored. The Windows 2000 System State includes the following:

- Boot and system files
- System File Protection catalog
- System File Protection files

- Performance monitor configuration files
- Active Directory (if client is a domain controller)
- SYSVOL (if client is a domain controller)
- Certificate Server database (if client is a certificate server)
- Cluster database (if client is part of a cluster)
- Registry
- COM+ database

Microsoft dictates that the System State be backed up and restored as an entire unit, using only full backups. You cannot selectively back up and restore individual System State components.

What does this new twist mean in terms of recovery of the Exchange Server? Well, for one thing, there's no more `dir.edb` file, so that is out of the equation for backups. That may seem like a good thing, but now your directory is in Active Directory and so your backups involve two separate processes. Both need to be solid in order for you to restore.

Understanding the New Storage Structure

To fully understand the new concept of storage groups and multiple stores, we need to first look at some of the different file types that assist in holding a store. We'll also look at an entire storage group and see how Exchange 2000 handles these efficiently and in a fault-tolerant manner.

Exchange uses write-ahead transaction log files, in addition to the database (`.edb`) files, to improve server data write performance and to provide fault tolerance for the storage groups and stores. In addition to log files, checkpoint files, patch files, and reserved files are all described within this section to give you a better understanding of how Exchange can recover from various types of failings.

You already received a good background on how these various logs work in Exchange 5.5; they continue to work the same way in Exchange 2000. However, the directory side has been removed, and the storage group has been developed. So, it's more important to get an understanding of these newer pieces, particular stores and storage groups.

There are two things you need to clearly understand for Exchange 2000 architecture to make sense: what a store is and what a storage group is. You'll also want to know where these storage groups keep their database and transaction log files.

Stores

A *store* is a database that houses data. That data can comprise private information, such as in the case of a mailbox, or public information, such as in the case of public folder structures. Each store contains two files that are inseparable from a working perspective, the .edb file and the .stm file. The .stm extension stands for Streaming Database File (contains common Internet-formatted content, which protocols other than MAPI place in the store). The .edb file is a rich-text database file that contains data placed in the store through MAPI.

Exchange 2000 can support multiple stores on each server. They have no programmed size limit, but you will want to keep an eye on their size, so you can use multiple stores to enhance the flexibility of backup and restore tasks.

Storage Groups

With Exchange 2000 you can configure up to four storage groups on each Exchange Server. You can configure up to five databases in each storage group, for a maximum number of 20 configurable databases on a single server.

Each storage group uses its own set of transaction log files, as shown in Figure 12.15. Five stores are all recorded in a single series of transaction log files. You can determine where to locate the transaction logs for each storage group. Where are they located by default? The First Storage Group files are located in the C:\Program Files\Exchsrvr\Mdbdata folder.

As you begin to create additional storage logs, they take on the name of the group; for example, the second storage group files are located in the C:\Program Files\Exchsrvr\Second_Storage_Group name folder.

Figure 12.15: Storage group with multiple stores and transaction logs visible

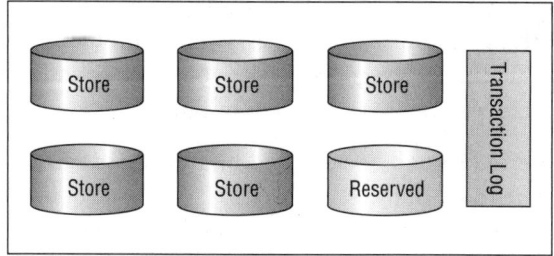

Exchange 2000 Reminders

Microsoft still recommends that you keep the transaction logs on separate physical disks from the database files. This will enhance performance because the database and logs do not have to struggle for equal time with the hard disk controller. It may also increase recovery speeds in case your store is corrupt or a hard disk crashes.

Circular logging is disabled by default in Exchange 2000. Unless you plan on doing full server backups each night, leave this feature disabled. It prevents you from doing incremental and differential backups. For a full explanation of circular logging, see the "Circular Logging" section earlier in this chapter.

Transaction logs are not purged unless you back up the entire storage group. If you only back up individual stores, the backup takes place, but the logs remain. This is because you have one set of logs for all the stores in the storage group.

> **TIP** You can back up and restore all databases (stores) individually, but it's most efficient to perform these operations on the storage group level because of the transaction logs and speed comparisons. Another point is that Exchange 2000, because of the multiple storage group arrangement, allows you to back up storage groups in unison to different tapes. That should decrease your backup time and may fit better within your backup window.

Keeping in mind that this chapter is about backup and recovery, we will move forward into the nitty-gritty details; however, you may want to work with storage groups and stores, if you haven't done so already, to ensure that you understand their features.

Backing Up Your Exchange 2000 Server

If your Exchange Server is located on a Windows 2000 system, then you have the built-in option of using Windows Backup. Windows 2000 Backup is not, by default, capable of backing up Exchange, but the installation of Exchange will enhance the backup program to allow for Exchange 2000 backups.

Follow these steps to back up your Exchange Server:

1. Select Start ➤ Programs ➤ Accessories ➤ System Tools ➤ Backup.
2. Select the Backup tab.
3. You can expand out the Microsoft Exchange Server option by double-clicking on it. If you don't see your server, you can search for it from within the backup tool. Expand the server until you get to the option to choose the Microsoft Information Store, where you can then find the Storage Groups and corresponding stores.
4. Select your server. For instance, we've selected the First Storage Group, the mailbox, and the public folder store for the MAVERICK server (see Figure 12.16).

Figure 12.16: Backup procedure for Exchange 2000

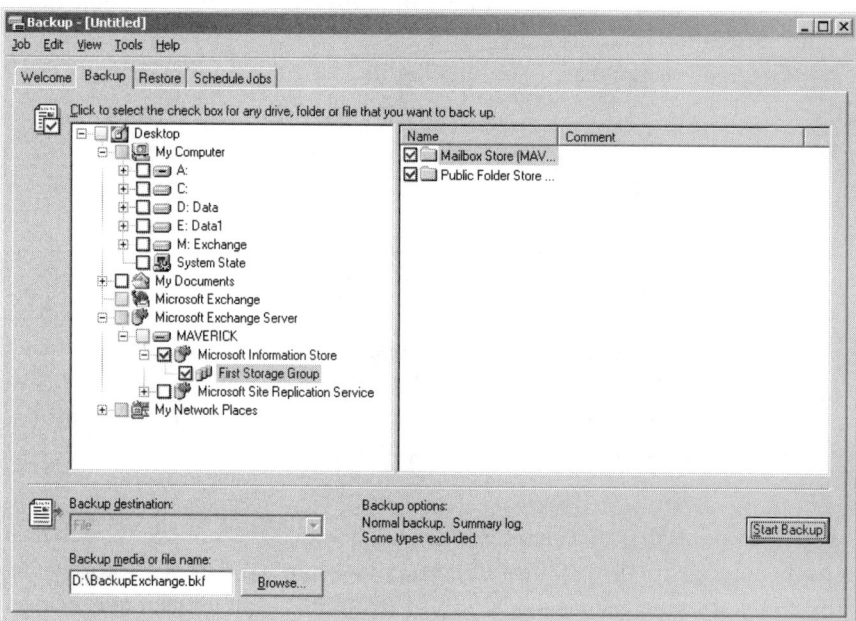

It's important to note that you can back up the entire server or portions of it. This is the nice feature about storage groups. You can break your mailboxes up into smaller, more manageable chunks.

5. Select Backup Destination (in the bottom left of the Backup tab) if you want to choose a file format or other type, such as tape (and the tape type). For example, choose File. In the Backup Media or File Name group, you'll notice it gives a file with a .bkf extension. You can change these (and should) to retain multiple copies within the same magnetic location.

6. Once you are satisfied with your selections, click Start Backup. The Backup Job Information window will appear, as shown in Figure 12.17.

7. From within these settings you can choose how the media will be written to. You can create your own easily identifiable descriptions or use the ones already provided for you. You can choose Append This Backup to the Media that has already been written to, or you can choose to overwrite the existing data by selecting Replace the Data on the Media with This Backup.

Figure 12.17: Backup Job Information window

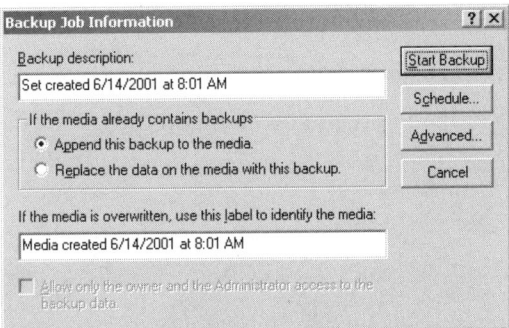

8. Select the Advanced button to get into Advanced Backup Options. There are five primary backup options from which to choose, as shown in Figure 12.18.

Figure 12.18: Advanced Backup Options dialog box

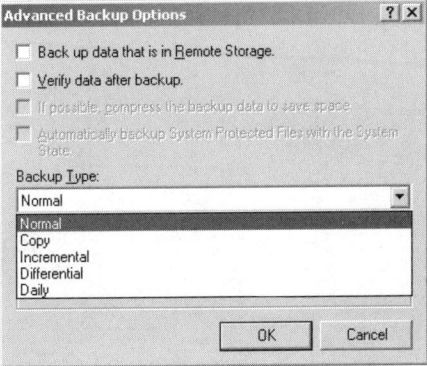

The earlier part of this chapter described these options for Exchange 5.5; those explanations hold true for Exchange 2000.

Choose your backup type, hit OK, and you are taken back to the Backup Job Information dialog box, where you can then determine you want to schedule your backup structure or choose Start Backup. When the job is complete, then you will be notified.

Restoring Your Exchange 2000 Server Databases

Using Windows Backup to restore your databases is not a difficult process; however, there are several issues that need to be addressed in handling your Exchange 2000 Server restoration. First we'll take a look at the restore options, and then we'll look at the various methods involved in the restore process.

To restore your Exchange Server, do the following:

1. Select Start ➢ Programs ➢ Accessories ➢ System Tools ➢ Backup.
2. Go to the Restore tab.
3. Expand the backup options you have and then select the backup you want to restore, as shown in Figure 12.19.

Figure 12.19: The restore process

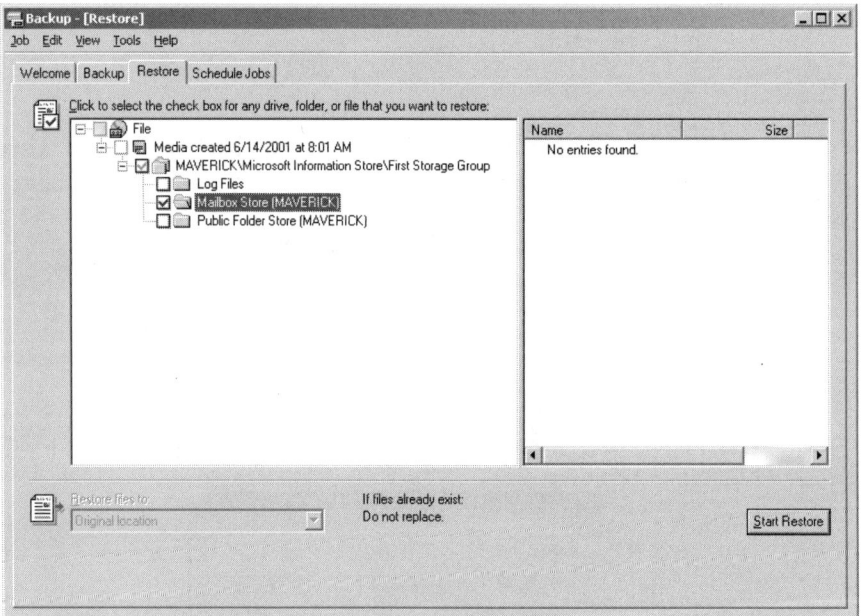

TIP At this point you can choose to restore all or part of your backed-up data. (Whatever you do restore, although the services remain online, you need to take the store or storage group offline if you want your restore to work.) Microsoft, again, recommends that you back up and restore storage groups as complete units.

5. Once you choose what you want to back up, you are then presented with the options shown in Figure 12.20. You need to select which server you are restoring to, and you need to indicate the location of the transaction logs and patch files that Exchange will use. (This is a temporary location for these files, only for the purpose of restoring the database to completion.)

Figure 12.20: Restoring Database Store dialog box

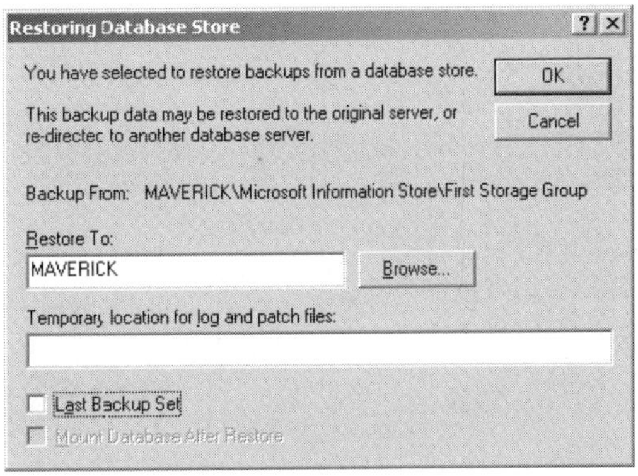

Additional options involve the Last Backup Set (which you should choose if this is the last online backup set) and the Mount Database After Restore, which work in conjunction to determine if the database should replay all restored logs or if there will be additional restores.

When you're done, choose OK.

And that is how it's done. At the end of the restore you are shown a "Complete" message that includes a Report tab. This can be helpful in conjunction with your Event Viewer.

Consider the following scenario: You perform a restore of your data and the message indicates that the restore completed. You take a closer look, though, and it indicates that certain files didn't complete, as shown in Figure 12.21. You also notice that 0 bytes have been restored.

Figure 12.21: Restore complete but files not restored

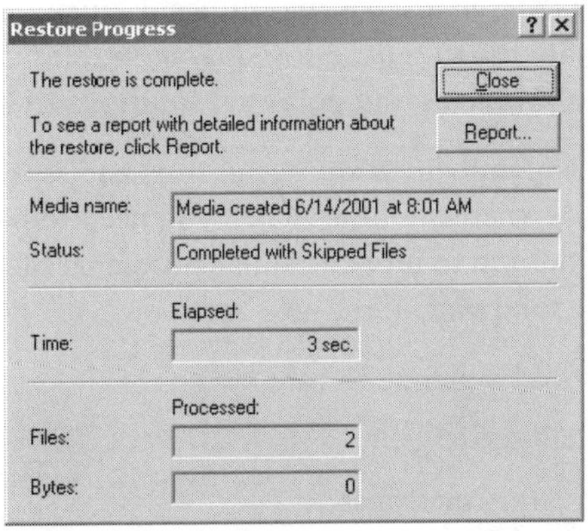

You decide to hit the Report button just to make sure, and you see the messages in Figure 12.22.

Figure 12.22: The report

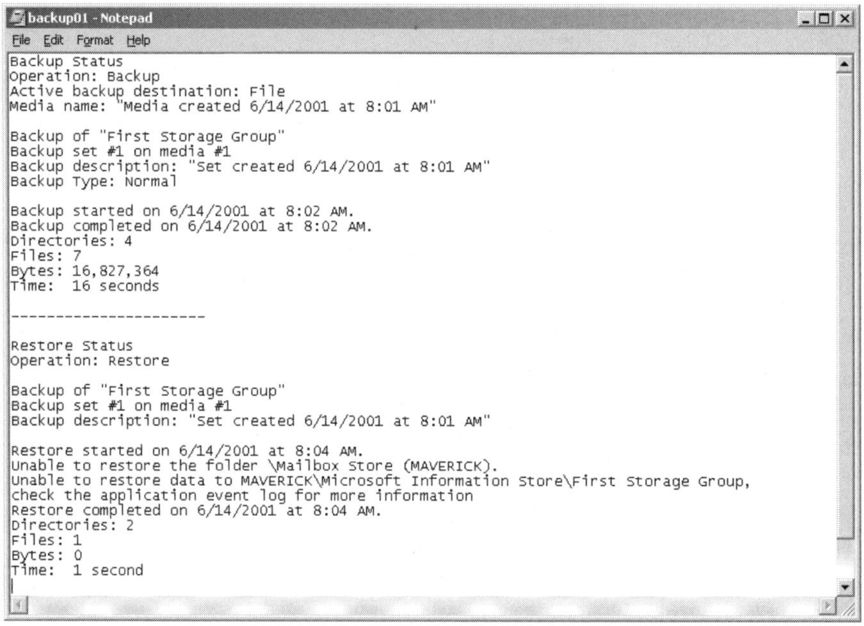

```
Backup Status
Operation: Backup
Active backup destination: File
Media name: "Media created 6/14/2001 at 8:01 AM"

Backup of "First Storage Group"
Backup set #1 on media #1
Backup description: "Set created 6/14/2001 at 8:01 AM"
Backup Type: Normal

Backup started on 6/14/2001 at 8:02 AM.
Backup completed on 6/14/2001 at 8:02 AM.
Directories: 4
Files: 7
Bytes: 16,827,364
Time: 16 seconds

----------------------
Restore Status
Operation: Restore

Backup of "First Storage Group"
Backup set #1 on media #1
Backup description: "Set created 6/14/2001 at 8:01 AM"

Restore started on 6/14/2001 at 8:04 AM.
Unable to restore the folder \Mailbox Store (MAVERICK).
Unable to restore data to MAVERICK\Microsoft Information Store\First Storage Group,
check the application event log for more information
Restore completed on 6/14/2001 at 8:04 AM.
Directories: 2
Files: 1
Bytes: 0
Time: 1 second
```

The report confirms that files weren't restored and indicates that you should check the application log within your Event Viewer to see the problem. You go into Event Viewer and notice several different error messages, including the one shown in Figure 12.23.

From this message you realize that you have attempted to restore to a database that is still mounted. This example teaches two things: Remember to dismount the stores or storage groups you are looking to restore manually, and use your reports and Event Viewer to determine problems and potential solutions to backups.

In addition to restoring individual storage groups and stores during an online backup and restore procedure, there are times when you need to handle complete server disaster/recovery issues, in addition to more granular problems such as individual mailbox issues. We will consider the following in the next section:

- Performing a full Exchange restore
- Restoring a mailbox
- Restoring individual messages

Figure 12.23: Error in Event Viewer

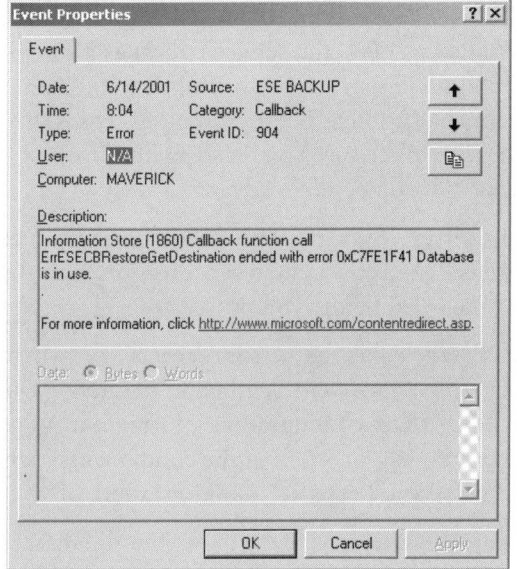

Similar in format to their Exchange 5.5 predecessor, these steps will come in handy.

Backup/Restore Strategy for Exchange 2000

There is no quick answer to Exchange 2000 recovery. It's not a simple program. There are multiple points of failure and multiple points for backup/recovery failure. This is probably not what you want to hear, but if you want to administer an Enterprise Exchange 2000 environment, then you should be prepared for the worst. Let's start with the full server restore.

Full Server Restores of Exchange 2000

The restore of Exchange will depend upon your Active Directory placement. In other words, if your Exchange 2000 and Active Directory servers are on separate machines, your restore process will be much easier. In either case, though, you will need to restore your System State data.

To fully restore, proceed with the following:

1. If the system is new, then the hardware should be configured to match what you've lost. If the system is the original production server that crashed, then ensure that you are using new hardware. (Some of the drivers may be incompatible with

your System State when using new hardware. You may need to go into Safe Mode after the restore of the System State and reconfigure drivers.)

2. Reinstall Windows 2000 (and service packs) as a stand-alone server with the same computer name as your production server. Install the operating system files to the same location as before. (In other words, if you originally installed as C:\WINNT, then make sure you do so again. The best way to remember all of this is to have it documented in advance.)

3. Restore your server's System State (whether a domain controller or member server) and ensure that the system synchronizes with the Active Directory and is network functional before you proceed.

4. Reinstall Exchange using the /disasterrecovery switch. This will tell setup to look for a domain controller to gather all the Active Directory information it can get including setup configuration information. When using this switch, you need to make sure you select all of the components manually that existed on the production server. Leave no room for failure of your restore.

5. Finally, restore the Exchange backup of your databases (storage groups and stores) to their original paths.

WARNING The key to your recovery lies in your preparation for disaster. You need to ensure that you have proper backups of your system, your System State, and your Exchange. You need to have a documented plan of your restore process, including a layout of your current server, including service packs, hotfixes, location of specific files, disk configuration, and so on. And if you have a large environment with multiple Exchange Servers, or if you are using Cluster Services or Key Management Server services (KMS), then be prepared to handle these issues, as well.

These are the highlights to restoring an Exchange 2000 server from the ground up; however, you may want to be aware of certain issues that arise.

For example, there is a file called restore.env that is used to control the hard recovery process, which makes sure that the log files are replayed in the correct order after a restore. This file is restored during the restore process to a temporary folder. If you restore a backup of a store from a storage group and the restore.env file goes in the temporary folder, and at the same time you restore another store from the same storage group to the same temporary folder, the restore.env file will be overwritten. Therefore, it is recommended that you perform separate store recovery individually, rather than at the same time. You can restore multiple storage groups at the same time without worrying about the restore.env file because separate temporary folders are created.

If you want to perform parallel restorations of your stores from the same storage group, without restoring the entire storage group, then you can do this, but you have to use the eseutil.exe utility with a /cc switch command, rather than using the standard restore option of Last Restore Set. For more information on these types of restores, visit the Knowledge Base at http://support.microsoft.com or read this article: http://support.microsoft.com/support/kb/articles/Q232/9/38.ASP.

Restoring a Mailbox

Once again this chapter visits the implications of a deleted or corrupt mailbox that needs to be revived. What do you do? Again, much like Exchange 5.5, Windows Backup doesn't have the ability to handle brick-level backups, so if you need that functionality, then you should start looking for third-party software. Restoring a mailbox involves restoring an entire database.

One of the nice conveniences to Exchange 2000 is that now—rather than in the old days of Exchange 5.5 when you had a server with an information store of 500 mailboxes that you needed to restore to bring back a single mailbox—you might want those mailboxes broken up into five 100-mailbox stores. That will save you time and energy. Or perhaps you want to give the most important personnel in your organization (the CEO, partners, and so on) their own storage group with individual stores per person. This provides a greater degree of flexibility with quicker backup/restore times as a fringe benefit.

The process of restoring a mailbox, however, can be a bit more complex if you need to restore one mailbox without restoring the entire mailbox store of your production server. Think about it: You have a mailbox that is deleted and you need to restore it from backup, but if you restore the store over the existing one, this affects all other users in the store. You need simply to recover the one mailbox. Unfortunately, without third-party software, the recovery process involves creating a recovery server.

Creating a Recovery Server

The principals are the same as the Exchange 5.5 recovery server, but there are a few twists involved because Active Directory is used rather than an individual directory store. Because of this, you cannot create your recovery server on the same production network, as you were able to before with Exchange 5.5. Without being on the production network, your recovery server will need to be a domain controller running Active Directory for your Exchange 2000 to work.

The recovery server needs to be reconfigured with the following information being identical: the Organization, the Administrative Group name, the Storage Group name, the Logical database name, and the LegacyExchangeDN name on certain important system objects. What does this involve? Well, check out your production server and record what you are dealing with. What is the correct Organization and Administrative

Group names? Map out the names of your storage groups and the database logical store names. You will need to restructure these in your recovery server (and it doesn't take long to do) if you are going to restore the mailbox to that server.

Now, if your production Exchange Server is new, then the LegacyExchangeDN doesn't have an effect, and you can proceed with your recovery server without gathering this information. If, however, you did an upgrade on your Exchange 5.5 server to 2000, then the LegacyExchangeDN is necessary to locate and correct on the recovery server.

The LegacyExchangeDN is an attribute carried by most Exchange 2000 objects. It is not a Registry key; it is an Active Directory object attribute for objects in your Exchange environment. The standard LegacyExchangeDN for objects would be the /O=organization/OU=administrative group on newly installed systems. On upgraded systems these settings might not be correct. Another possible problem may exist on systems where the administrative group name has changed, if the LegacyExchangeDN doesn't reflect the changes. If this match is not made between the production and recovery servers, then you will have difficulty restoring your mailbox to the recovery server.

To find your LegacyExchangeDN, you can use the following tools:

- ADSIEDIT
- LDP
- LDIFDE command

You can drill down into the Configuration container to locate the LegacyExchangeDN. If you find that the production and recovery servers are using different LegacyExchangDNs, then you need to change this.

To change the LegacyExchangeDN, you need to first change the name of the First Administrative Group on your recovery server to match the production Administrative Group. Then perform an LDIFDE export. Use a text editor to change the OU portion of the LegacyExchangeDN and then import the file back in.

> **NOTE** There are other ways to make these changes and other ways to check the LegacyExchangeDN, but this will suffice for now. For more information, search Microsoft's Knowledge Base for "Mailbox Recovery for Exchange 2000."

Once your LegacyExchangeDN is located and you've determined if you need to change it, then you can return to the process of creating your recovery server for mailbox restores.

Mailbox Restores

This is the procedure for a recovery server implementation:

1. Install Windows 2000 and all proper service packs. Upgrade the server to be running Active Directory and use the DNS installation at this time, too, to make life easier.

2. Install Exchange and use the same Organization name as your production server. Make sure the LegacyExchangeDN is correct before moving forward.

3. Create a new Storage Group and give it the same name as the one on the production network (unless the production network is using the First Storage Group, which will automatically be the same on your recovery server). You do not have to match store names; the restore will handle that.

4. Make sure you dismount the database to be restored or the entire storage group. You saw earlier how the restore process fails without doing this. You need to go into the properties of the store and choose the This Database Can Be Overwritten by a Restore option.

5. Restore the database or storage group from your backup and remount the database.

6. Through the Exchange System Manager you want to go to the restored database, right-click Mailboxes and choose Run Cleanup Agent. You'll notice all the red X marks that show you have mailboxes without Active Directory objects to which to connect.

7. Next, create a user account for each mailbox. During the mailbox creation you do not want to choose to create a mailbox because you already have one. You do not have to perform this manually; you can use the Mbconn utility that is located on the Exchange 2000 CD-ROM in the \Support\Utils\i386 folder.

NOTE The Mailbox Reconnect Tool (Mbconn) allows you to connect users in Exchange 2000 to their orphaned mailboxes. You may find the tool especially helpful in either of the following situations: when you install a replacement server and need to restore a database or when you move databases between storage groups.

8. Link those mailboxes to their user accounts. This can be done manually or, again, through the Mbconn utility.

9. Convert the mailbox contents for those users you are attempting to recover by logging on as that user on the recovery server and creating a .pst file (as

described earlier for Exchange 5.5) and then copying the files from your Exchange mailbox over to your .pst folder. Then you can move that .pst file off to your production client and restore it. (Another tool you can use, rather than manually logging on and creating .pst files per user, is the Exmerge utility.)

Using Exmerge

This utility has several great functions. Located on the Exchange 2000 Resource Kit, the utility comes with a 71-page document on how and when to use the tool. One of the features we want to discuss involves the ability of Exmerge to back up your Exchange mailbox to a .pst file. The tool can do this in bulk, and these .pst files can be backed up or they can be used to restore the mailbox to your production clients or to do cross-server restores between Exchange 5.5 and 2000.

The Exmerge utility will work for Exchange 5.5 and 2000.

Now, this might seem a bit overwhelming at first, but don't worry; the documentation provides the command-line options, and there is a wizard, too. Install the Resource Kit, find the tool, and kick it off by double-clicking on it.

You'll come up to a welcome screen that gives you an overview of the program and what you can do with it. It will also explain that you will be able to handle the process of migrating your information in either a one-step or two-step process.

The one-step process will take the data from the source mailbox, place it in an intermediate .pst file, and then merge the data into a mailbox on the destination server. In this case you need to have a production and recovery server set up and structured in the previous descriptions for recovery servers. You can also use this tool to merge that data into a mailbox with a different name, if specified.

With the two-step process you can move the data from the server to a .pst file and in a second step, merge that data.

So, why bother with the command-line approach? Because, you can run the command as part of a batch file that can be scheduled, and this requires you to know the commands to handle this.

This tool goes beyond the functionality not only of Windows Backup but also of third-party software. It can help you out in specialized scenarios.

Message-Level Restores

If you wanted to restore a single message or multiple messages, you would need to create the recovery server described previously for your Exchange mailbox restore. Through the Mail applet in Control Panel, go through the process of creating an additional Personal Folder file. Then open up your Outlook client and you should see the two Personal Folder files, similar to your mailbox restore.

Your functioning folders should include your message. Select the individual messages that you would like to retain and copy them to your extra Personal Folder file, which is an extra .pst file. Once those messages are in the .pst file, you can copy that .pst file to your client system. Configure the profile for that user to include the moved .pst file. Open Outlook and you should see both the normal Inbox and the moved .pst messages. Copy the moved messages into the standard Inbox.

At that point you could remove the .pst file and the indication toward that file from within the user's profile.

As mentioned for Exchange 5.5, this is an awful lot of work. Isn't there an easier way? Well, Exchange 2000 has a Deleted Item Retention that can assist in the process.

Deleted Item Retention

Under the properties for the mailbox store you can define a few settings that will specify when deleted messages and mailboxes are permanently removed from the server, as shown in Figure 12.24.

Figure 12.24: Deleted item settings

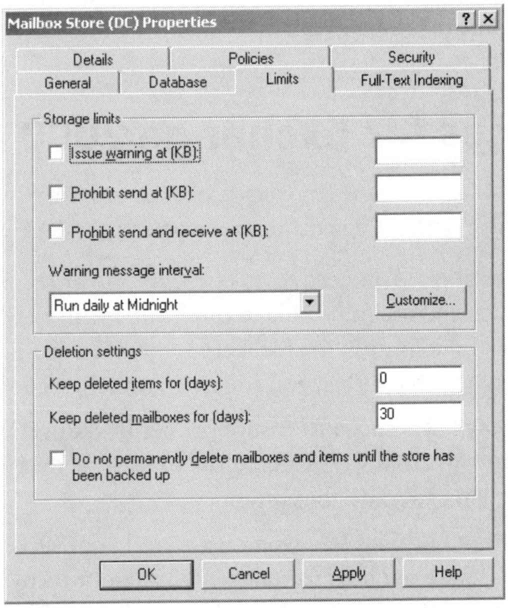

You can specify through the settings that you want to keep deleted items for a certain number of days (with 0 indicating that you want deleted items to be removed immediately) or you can go as high as 24,855 days. The same is true of the deleted mailboxes.

The Do Not Permanently Delete Mailboxes and Items option will keep deleted mailboxes and items until a backup is performed.

With these settings in place, users can recover their own files, and you can restore mailboxes that have been deleted. So, how does it work?

Most users are already aware that they have a Deleted Items folder from which they can retrieve mail. With Deleted Item Retention parameters, you can instruct users who want deleted mail back to go into their Deleted Items folder from within Outlook. Go to the Tools menu and choose Recover Deleted Items. Select the item or folder that you want to retrieve and choose Recover Selected Items.

Brick-Level Backups for Item Restores

Brick-level backups is a term given to the backup/restore process of items such as messages, mailboxes, folders, public folders…the little things. Windows Backup does not support these types of backups, so you need to find third-party software that will allow you to restore backups of your mailboxes, your messages, and even your other items such as Deleted Items, Sent Items, and so on.

To choose an appropriate enterprise solution, you need to research the various vendors and consider ability, flexibility, scalability, support, and cost.

Best Practices for Exchange 2000 Recovery

We've already been through the recovery process, but how would you as an administrator put yourself in the best possible position to protect your data? Consider the following:

Documentation You need to ensure that proper records have been kept of your current structure to be able to duplicate it. Another thing you might try in the process of duplication for recovery servers is third-party disk imaging software. Whether you use this, you should definitely record your current structure.

Backup Daily You need to ensure proper backups. Don't use circular logging (which is already disabled by default). Set up a recovery server for "hot spare" recovery if you can spare the equipment.

Record a Plan and Test It Don't wait until your server has gone down before you start to figure out how to restore it. Test your recovery process. Record your plan. Keep the record of your plan handy and with your offline copies. You never know when a complete disaster will ruin your existing structure.

Going Forward

We wouldn't dare to claim that this is all you would ever need to know about the backup/recovery of your Exchange environment. These are the strongest topics, but what about the following:

- Active Directory, the directory service that Exchange runs on top of. How do you restore the System State? What if you encounter errors? How do you correct these? How do you defragment the directory database?

- Internet Information Server (IIS) is used by Exchange 2000 for SMTP support and NNTP support. Configuration settings for these protocols are part of the IIS metabase that needs to be restored. How do you do it? What if you don't have a backup of your IIS metabase; how do you recover?

- Site Replication Service (SRS) is used for directory replication in a mixed site, one that uses both Exchange 2000 and Exchange 5.5. How do you recover in the case of an Exchange Server running SRS?

And what about Key Management Service (KMS)? This is one of the most important services to restore if you are using a KMS server. You cannot lose even one component of your KMS infrastructure. You need backups of everything. Where do you start? How do you restore your KMS? Each of these issues is covered in greater detail on Microsoft's site. These white papers are a good place to start:

www.microsoft.com/TechNet/exchange/dbrecovr.asp

www.microsoft.com/TechNet/exchange/exrecovr.asp

13

SQL 7/2000 Backup/Recovery

Although we could write hundreds of pages about SQL backup and recovery topics, we will instead concentrate on what you need to survive as an administrator. For the most part, as with many topics in this book, your enterprise-level backup software should automate the management of backup and recovery for your SQL databases. There are, however, many between-the-lines issues we will point out to you, as well as showing you what you need to know to plan for backup and recovery of your SQL Servers.

The process of initiating a backup or restore is relatively easy. People often run into problems because of improper planning, so that is where we will spend quite a bit of time during this chapter. To fully understand the importance of planning, consider this situation, which happened to one of our clients: Sean installed his new backup software and immediately performed a full backup. After running an initial full backup of one of his SQL databases, he decided to run transaction log backups every hour. He loved how fast transaction log backups completed, compared to the hours of time required to complete a full backup. Sean's idea to run nothing but transaction log backups each day and week, followed by running a monthly full, was embraced by the organization. After all, backups took minutes to complete, thus having the lowest impact on the SQL Server.

Sean's life as a SQL database administrator (DBA) was great, until one of his databases became corrupted and he had to perform a restore. Sean began his restore Friday morning and began waiting for the restore to complete. He figured that with transaction log backups only taking minutes to complete, his restore would be finished by lunch, and he eagerly informed management of this. By dinner, the restore still hadn't finished, and there was no end in sight. Sean had no idea why the restore was taking so long. His library didn't seem very active, so he blamed the performance on the backup software. Sean then called customer support to get to the bottom of the problem and found that the software was performing just as it should. It was restoring the transaction log files as the SQL Server was requesting them. The problem, Sean realized, was his backup plan. Although transaction log backups can often be completed in minutes, on a restore, each transaction in the log must be written to the database. With hundreds of log backups, Sean soon realized that he was in for a long weekend. The restore, in case you're wondering, finally finished late Sunday night. On Monday, Sean was looking for a new job.

The lesson learned by Sean, and the one we hope you will learn in this chapter, is that with SQL recovery, knowing how to run SQL backups and restores is something anyone can do, but planning and implementing a sound SQL backup and recovery strategy is something that will keep you employed.

In Sean's story, we made assumptions that you had some basic knowledge of SQL terminology, but in case you don't, we start this chapter with a brief discussion of SQL terminology.

Understanding SQL Basics

In this section, we keep the SQL basics "basic." With dozens of books already devoting hundreds of pages to SQL architecture, we don't want to take jobs away from other authors, so if you want to learn every detail about SQL architecture, pick up a SQL book. Otherwise, you can simply log on to a SQL Server and click Start ➤ Programs ➤ Microsoft SQL Server ➤ Books Online to get plenty of easy-to-read documentation on SQL Server.

As a backup administrator, you should be aware of several fundamental terms regarding SQL architecture. Before getting to know how to back up SQL databases, it is a good idea to understand what it is you're backing up. To get to that level of understanding, we explain the following terms:

- SQL databases
- Transaction log
- Filegroup
- Data file

- Enterprise Manager
- Transact-SQL (T-SQL)

Defining SQL Databases

SQL uses four databases that are required for operation, which are known as *system databases*. System databases are parallel to core components of the operating system, such as the Active Directory, Registry, and pagefile. Without its system databases, SQL cannot run. When system databases are lost, don't think that it's necessarily the end of your SQL Server, because there are ways of bringing system databases back to life (discussed later in this chapter in the "Restoring SQL Databases" section).

The four SQL system databases are:

- Master
- Model
- Msdb
- Tempdb

If a database is not a system database, it is considered to be a user database. After we cover each essential system database, we will then examine user databases.

> **NOTE** When replication is configured on SQL Servers, you may see up to three additional system databases. These databases are discussed later in this chapter in the "Replicated Databases" section.

Master

Of these four databases, the Master database is the most crucial. You can think of the Master database as the equivalent of a core operating system database, such as the Registry. Much like the Registry, the Master database is responsible for maintaining records on the SQL Server, including:

- User accounts
- System configuration settings
- Information (metadata) on all other SQL databases

> **NOTE** If you are not sure of the term *metadata*, it's basically no more than data about data. Although not referring to the actual data stored in SQL databases, SQL metadata includes information such as data file location settings and database configuration.

Model

Think of the Model database as nothing more than a template. If you were working with a template in Microsoft Word, it would be a document that has some basic configuration settings for you to build a document around. With SQL, the Model database serves the same purpose; it is nothing more than a template on which newly created databases are based.

> **NOTE** You may be thinking that because the Model database is merely a template, you can get rid of it. But you can't. The Model database is needed because it is used to re-create the Tempdb database each time the SQL Server starts.

Msdb

Besides the Master database, Msdb is the other critical SQL database. Losing the Model or Tempdb database (described next) is really not a big deal, but you do need to be concerned with Master and Msdb. Msdb is so important because it is the database that maintains tables used by the SQL Server Agent for job scheduling and alerting. Many backup applications write their backup history of SQL databases to the Msdb.

Tempdb

Think of Tempdb as the SQL equivalent to the Windows swap file (`pagefile.sys`). With operating systems, the swap file is used for temporary storage of data. The Tempdb serves the same purpose with a SQL Server. When the SQL Server needs to temporarily store data for operations such as sorting, the data is stored in the Tempdb database. The Tempdb is created by default each time the SQL service is started, so there is never a need to back it up. Backing up the Tempdb is no different than backing up the swap file. In fact, some backup applications won't even let you back up the Tempdb, even if you wanted to do that.

User Databases

System databases allow a SQL Server to run, and user databases are the databases created by users or applications running on the SQL Server. User databases are created to store your organization's or an application's data and are usually your primary focus for backup and recovery.

Defining Transaction Logs

Data is stored in databases, but databases can grow to be large (terabyte databases are not rare) and can be subject to intense input/output (I/O) traffic. Transaction logs solve several problems with large databases:

- Storing data prior to writing it directly into the database. Database modifications are first written to its transaction log and then are later committed to the database.

- Making backup and recovery much more feasible. In many organizations, it is not possible or practical to back up large databases on a daily or even hourly basis. Remember that your server is only as good as the time of your last backup. With this in mind, it is much easier to perform frequent backups of small log files than to frequently back up a large database.

> **TIP** To see an improvement in database I/O performance, you should configure SQL to store the transaction log on a separate physical disk than its associated database.

Transaction logs are divided into two portions:

- The *active portion* contains transaction log entries that either have not yet completed or have been aborted.
- The *inactive portion* contains transaction log entries that have been completed.

Now the big picture is starting to come together. So far, you know that data is written to the transaction log before it is committed to the database. But when is it actually committed? That is what recovery is for!

A simple definition of *recovery* is the process of updating a SQL database through the use of its transaction log files. Each time the SQL Server is started, a recovery is automatically initiated.

During a database recovery, two processes occur:

- Transactions completed between the last recovery and the current recovery are rolled forward. *Rolling forward* refers to writing or committing completed transactions to the database.
- Incomplete transactions are rolled back. *Rolling back* is the process of undoing partially committed or aborted transactions from the database.

Defining Data Files

SQL Server databases are made up of both data files and log files. Each database will have an associated log file with it. Data files are identified by their .mdf or .ndf extensions, and log files normally have an .ldf extension. Every SQL database has at least one data file and one log file, which is the default configuration.

Data files are characterized as either:

Primary Data File (.mdf) Each SQL database will have one primary data file. The primary data file will always contain:

- Database startup information
- Pointers to secondary data files (if they exist)
- Information on database tables and objects

Secondary Data Files (.ndf) Secondary data files can be created to store data and objects not located in the primary data file. In other words, instead of having one great big primary file, you can divide it into several smaller files, the way you would partition a large hard disk. The advantage to dividing a database into several files is clear when you consider backup and restore performance. It is much easier to plan to back up several relatively small files as opposed to one large file.

Now, with a database divided into data files, you may be wondering how these files can be organized for easy backup and recovery administration. That is the job of filegroups.

Defining Filegroups

In addition to allowing you to group files for administrative purposes, such as performing backups and restores, filegroups also give you the flexibility to store database indexes and tables over several disks.

> **TIP** For high-traffic, I/O-demanding databases, you should strongly consider creating several data files grouped into filegroups to store a single database's contents on two or more physical disks.

> **WARNING** Although the data file and filegroup-level backups are supported by the SQL Server backup engine, not all enterprise-level backup solutions support filegroup-level backups and restores. Before planning to divide your high-traffic databases into filegroups, make sure you will be able to back them up as you expect!

You may encounter three different types of filegroups:

Default Contains all pages for tables and indexes that do not have a selected filegroup

Primary Maintains the system tables for each database on the SQL Server and holds the primary and any secondary data files not placed in a filegroup

User-Defined Filegroups created by SQL administrators, which contain tables or indexes manually selected by the administrator

As you can see, SQL Servers are powerful in how you can configure them to support backup and restore. Before we get to the planning phase of SQL data recovery, let's take a quick look at the available tools for configuring and executing backups and restores.

Enterprise Manager

Enterprise Manager is the graphical user interface (GUI) tool that administers SQL Servers. In addition to providing you with an easy interface with which to manage SQL Servers, Enterprise Manager also provides tools to allow you to easily back up and restore SQL databases.

You can access Enterprise Manager on any SQL Server by clicking Start ➢ Programs ➢ Microsoft SQL Server ➢ Enterprise Manager. Figure 13.1 shows Enterprise Manager.

Figure 13.1: SQL Enterprise Manager

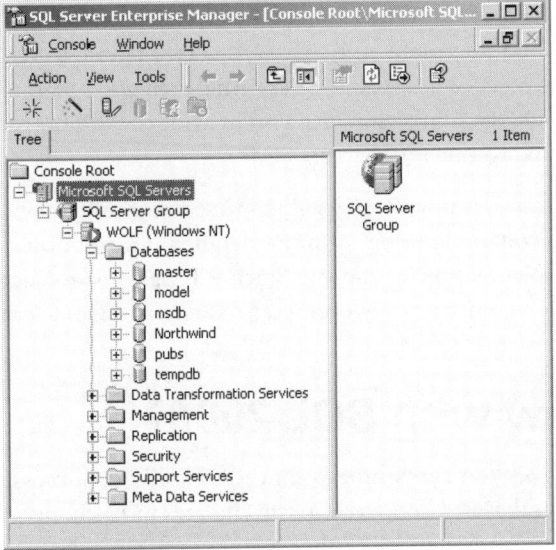

Transact-SQL (T-SQL)

Another popular method for administering SQL Servers is through Transact-SQL (T-SQL) commands. If you are one who likes using command-line scripting for administrations, then T-SQL is the choice for you. As with all aspects of network administration, if you have several databases to create or modify, you can create a simple T-SQL script to make your modifications and then execute the script on each server. This approach, as opposed to manually creating or changing databases using the Enterprise Manager GUI, will undoubtedly save you time (depending, of course, on how much time it takes you to get the script to execute properly).

Although T-SQL commands can be executed right from the command prompt, they do require you to connect to a SQL Server to run. You can do this by entering the following syntax at the command prompt:

```
OSQL -U <user name> -P <password> -S <server name>
```

Figure 13.2 shows an example of using Object Structured Query Language (OSQL) to connect to a SQL Server.

Figure 13.2: Using OSQL to connect to a SQL Server

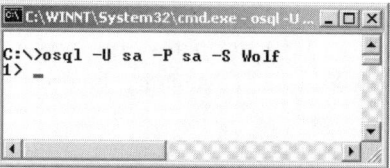

One other method for connecting to a SQL Server to run T-SQL commands is through the Query Analyzer. To access the Query Analyzer, click Start ➤ Programs ➤ Microsoft SQL Server ➤ Query Analyzer. Once you provide a valid username and password, you will be connected to the SQL Server.

SQL administration is a book in itself, so we cannot tell you everything about SQL in this chapter. If you are looking for more detailed information on SQL Server, access the SQL Server Books Online by clicking Start ➤ Programs ➤ Microsoft SQL Server ➤ Books Online or point your web browser to www.microsoft.com/sql.

What's New with SQL 2000?

This chapter gives you everything you need to know to successfully plan, back up, and restore SQL databases. Compared to the changes in Exchange architecture from Exchange 5.5 to Exchange 2000, the changes in SQL architecture are minimal. From a purely backup and recovery perspective, there is little to know about SQL 2000. Regardless of whether you are running SQL 7 or 2000, the steps, theory, and procedures presented in this chapter apply to both SQL platforms.

However, you should be aware of a few improvements with SQL 2000 when studying backup and recovery:

- Multiple instances
- Log shipping
- Fast differential backups

- Copy Database Wizard
- Recovery models

There are several other improvements with SQL 2000, but they are not significant in this discussion on backup and recovery. The next six sections will provide you with an overview of the significant improvements to SQL 2000 that will affect your backup and recovery strategy.

Multiple Instances

With SQL 7 and earlier versions, if you had two SQL Servers, you had two physical systems running the SQL Servers. In other words, you had one occurrence, or *instance*, of SQL running on one box. An instance can simply be looked at as a logical representation of a SQL Server. With multiple instance support you can configure multiple virtual SQL Servers to run on the same physical box. This enables you to have two or more SQL Servers on the same physical system. Many applications have incorporated instance support with the growth of computer horsepower. As systems have become stronger and faster, many organizations have looked to consolidate servers. Oracle has long seen and supported this trend by offering multiple instance support for quite some time. With SQL 2000, Microsoft has jumped on the bandwagon.

If a server is upgraded from SQL 6.5 or SQL 7 to SQL 2000, you will see a SQL 6.5 or 7 instance, as well as a SQL 2000 instance on the system, giving you two virtual SQL Servers. SQL 2000 only supports one SQL 6.5 or 7 instance on one system, but you can have several SQL 2000 instances on that same system.

To summarize, using multiple instances offers the following advantages:

- You can consolidate several SQL Servers onto one box.
- If you back up to a local library or tape drive, consolidating several servers onto one box can lessen backup overhead and network-bandwidth consumption during backups.
- Each SQL instance runs independently in its own process, allowing you to group databases by the application they support, providing for better performance on the SQL Server.

Log Shipping

With *log shipping*, you can easily maintain a warm or standby server in the event that your primary SQL Server fails. If you are not sure of the idea of a warm (standby) server, consider it to be the second node in a "poor man's" cluster. With server clusters, if a node fails, the cluster service automatically switches control to the second node with no need for administrator intervention. When standby servers are used for fault tolerance, the hot (live) server is backed up, and the backup files are used to perform regular restores to the standby server. This way, if the primary server fails, then the standby server can be brought online to maintain data availability. Of course, when this happens, clients and applications will have to be alerted to connect to the new server, unless you rename the standby server to the name of the failed server.

With SQL 7, working with standby servers was a standard practice, so the concept of standby servers is nothing new. In fact, many administrators, maybe yourself included, have been burned too many times when performing restores to instinctively trusted backups. Because of this, they like to have a secondary server to which to restore backup data. This way, the backup administrator can test a backup for its validity before a restore is actually needed.

Now back to log shipping. This feature of SQL 2000 makes it easier to maintain standby servers by providing the ability to continually dump and copy transaction log backups from one SQL Server to another. Log shipping can automatically perform the dump of the log files, copy the dump, and then load the logs onto the destination server. The complete process of configuring log shipping for SQL 2000 Servers is covered later in the "Backing Up SQL Databases" section of this chapter.

Fast Differential Backups

With SQL 7, differential backups (covered later in this chapter) were not run very efficiently. When a differential backup would run, the SQL engine would scan every page in the entire database to determine what data had changed since the last full backup. The scan process would take several minutes to complete, if not longer.

With SQL 2000, database backup architecture has been restructured so that differential backups are not slowed down by database scans. Database changes are now tracked by SQL at the extent level, allowing SQL to quickly record a list of changes to the database for differential backups.

Copy Database Wizard

With the Copy Database Wizard, you may be thinking, "I could always make database copies." By backing up a database on one server and restoring it to another, you are essentially copying the database. The problem with this approach is that the copy process requires two separate operations.

With SQL 2000 you can use the Copy Database Wizard to quickly copy a database to another SQL Server. Why copy databases, you ask? You may be testing a new application and do not want to impact the production database, or even if you want a quick backup for offsite disaster recovery, the Copy Database Wizard gives you a fast way to get a redundant copy of a SQL database.

Recovery Models

With SQL 2000, you can select a *recovery model* for each SQL database. Microsoft devised the recovery model concept for SQL 2000 to simplify backup strategy and configuration for SQL Servers on a database-by-database basis.

When configuring SQL databases to fit into your enterprise backup and recovery strategy, you always had to weigh certain trade-offs:

- Backup performance (time)
- Simplicity
- Data loss exposure
- Transaction log space

Before SQL 2000, you had to manually consider each of these trade-offs when formulating your SQL Server backup plan. With SQL 2000, the data availability–database performance tradeoff is easier managed by configuring a recovery model for each database, based on the usage of the database. The three available recovery models are:

- Full
- Bulk logged
- Simple

Each of these models is explained in the next three sections.

Full

When this recovery model is selected, all operations on the database are recorded in its transaction log, including any bulk copy or bulk loading of data. With SQL 7, for example, bulk copy operations were not logged, meaning that for data protection, any bulk copy had to be followed by a full backup of the database. The full recovery model gives you the best data protection but at a small cost in performance.

If you need nearly up-to-the-minute protection for a database, and need to have the ability to recover it to a point in time, then you should configure the database to use the full recovery model. This model is best suited if you plan to perform frequent transaction log backups, combined with regular full backups. Depending on the size of the database, it may be practical to mix in differential backups as well. If you're not sure about what backup to perform when and where, don't worry, because we will spend time discussing backup and recovery strategy in the next section.

Bulk Logged

With this recovery model, all transactions except for bulk operations are recorded in the transaction log. This model provides more balance between data protection and performance than provided by the full model.

When considering implementing this model in your existing backup and recovery plans, you need to consider how easy it would be to perform the bulk operation on a restore. If having to redo a bulk operation after restoring a database is more management than you are looking for, then you could avoid this step by performing a full backup immediately after any bulk operation is performed. Some enterprise storage software is intelligent enough to check each database as it is backed up to see if any bulk operations have been performed since the last backup. If the software detects that a bulk operation was performed, it can be configured to convert its current backup automatically into a full backup. You should check with your enterprise storage vendor to see if it supports this feature.

Now, the problem with backup software automatically converting a transaction log backup into a full, for instance, is that a transaction log backup scheduled for 9:00 A.M. could be converted into a full and run all day, which is something most administrators and users would want to avoid because of the performance hit that would result on the SQL Server.

To summarize backup strategy for databases configured with the bulk logged recovery model, you can perform full, transaction log, and differential backups on the database, but you must remember to account for any bulk operations performed on the database.

Simple

With the simple recovery model, you cannot perform transaction log backups. That is because the SQL Server will automatically truncate the log at each recovery checkpoint, thus keeping the size of the database's transaction log file to a minimum. With the other two models, transaction logs are truncated as a part of a transaction log backup. Once a log is backed up, its committed transactions are automatically pruned from the log, thus keeping its size within reasonable boundaries.

Because you cannot perform transaction log backups on a database configured to use this recovery model, only full and differential backups are allowed. Without having log backups, you only have the ability to recover a SQL database to the time of the last backup. The simple model, although providing for the best database performance, offers the lowest level of data protection. Nonetheless, this model is ideal for small databases where it is easy to perform regular full backups and for the SQL Server system databases.

Backup and Recovery Planning

The story that introduced this chapter conveyed the importance of a plan. Organizations today often worry about backup plans, wanting to make sure that all backups are completed within a specific backup window, such as 12 hours, for example. With a fixed window in which backups must be completed, administrators sometimes feel forced into a backup scheme that is adequate from a purely backup perspective. To meet a tight window, for instance, sometimes it is necessary to perform daily incremental backups of file systems or to perform transaction log backups of SQL databases as opposed to performing full backups.

Although an operation window might dictate your backup plan, have you considered its effect on restores? With SQL databases especially, just because a backup took 10 minutes doesn't mean that the restore will be equally as quick. If a server can be down for no more than four hours, then that's where your plan should focus—on the restore. With restore requirements documented, then formulate a backup plan that supports the restore requirements.

As you can see, you have quite a bit to think about when planning your backup and recovery strategy. If some of the SQL backup terminology presented thus far in this section is new to you, don't worry, as we will get to that next. We will first document the supported SQL Server backup types and then will take a look at how to build a sound strategy around these backup types.

Backup Types

The different backups you can perform on a SQL database are:

- Full
- Differential
- Transaction Log
- Filegroup
- Data File

When planning backups, odds are that you will not be performing just one backup type. Instead, you are likely to use several of the backup types in conjunction with each other to meet your restore requirements and stay within your backup window. Each of these backups is explained in the next five subsections. After arriving at an understanding of what each backup type accomplishes, we will then move to how to formulate a backup and recovery plan based on the advantages and disadvantages of each backup type.

Full (Complete)

A full backup is a backup of an entire database, including all filegroups and data files contained in the database. From purely a restore perspective, full backups are the best. If you run nothing but full backups, on a restore you will only have to restore the most recent full backup. If you are working with small- to mid-sized databases, you may be able to get away with doing nothing but regular full backups of the database.

For most enterprise-level SQL implementations, though, performing only full backups is not practical, especially when you're talking about terabyte databases. The other issue with full backups is that they're uninterruptible. You'll probably hear the salespeople from your backup software vendor telling you how their SQL backups can automatically restart from the point of failure. We have no doubt that this is true, but what you should notice is that there is no mention of where the job is restarted. All SQL full backups, when paused or interrupted, are restarted from the beginning. The reason for forcing the restart from the beginning is to guarantee data integrity. Although it is a small issue and most backups will normally complete without incident after they are started, the fact that a full must be able to run to completion once it is started, coupled with the fact that they take the longest time to complete, should factor into your backup and recovery planning strategy.

> **NOTE** We use the term *full* for this backup type, instead of *complete*, because full is an industry standard. However, the SQL Server backup and restore interface will reference a full backup as a complete backup. Understand that these backups are the same.

Differential

With a SQL database, differential backups operate by the same means that they would with file systems. With differentials, all changes made to the database since the last full backup are recorded. Because differentials only record changes to the database, they are faster to perform than full backups; however, if you perform too many differentials between full backups, the differential could grow to be as large as the full. Earlier in this chapter, it was mentioned that differential backups perform significantly faster with SQL 2000 than they did with SQL 7. If you are used to not running differentials based on what you learned about SQL 7 and are moving to SQL 2000, you may want to consider implementing differential backups into your backup scheme.

> **WARNING** To ensure data integrity, when a differential backup is used as a part of a SQL database restore, some backup applications will automatically convert the next SQL database backup to a full backup. Keep this in mind if the next planned backup following a restore is an hourly transaction log backup that runs during the middle of production hours.

Transaction Log

Transaction log backups are simply backups of the transaction log files. By default, when this backup is performed, the inactive portion of the transaction log is automatically truncated. This feature allows your backup software to more or less maintain the SQL transaction logs. Transaction log backups are important because they give you the ability to recover a database to a point in time. Also, because transaction log files are relatively small, you can perform frequent backups of the transaction log. Some large organizations perform transaction log backups as frequently as every 10 minutes. When weighing how frequently you should perform transaction log backups, if you desire to do so, consider the value of your data and build your strategy around that value. If you can afford to lose up to two hours of data, then you can run log backups every two hours. If the limiting factor for the frequency with which you run backups is storage space, then buy more storage. Most likely the lost data has a much greater value than the cost of additional storage.

> **NOTE** Not all enterprise storage software supports file- and filegroup-level SQL backups. Before even thinking of including these two backups into your backup plan, check to see if your storage software supports these backups.

Data File and Filegroup

A filegroup backup is a backup of all the data files associated with a single filegroup in a database. Because this backup is a direct backup of data files, consider it to operate similarly to a full backup.

Although a filegroup backup is a backup of associated data files, a data file backup simply secures a single data file. In large-scale enterprise organizations, the ability to perform these two backups is often a paramount concern. For high gigabyte- to terabyte-sized databases, it is often unreasonable to be able to back up the entire database in one backup operation. Instead, you can divide the database into files and filegroups, allowing you to back up portions of the database each night. For example, you may find that you need to divide a database into three data files to back up the database within your window. You can perform transaction log backups during the day and back up one data file each night using a full backup.

Backup Strategy

With an understanding of how each backup operates, we can now get to formulating a well-rounded backup plan.

> **TIP** Always plan your backups from a restore perspective. Although the transaction log backups can often complete in minutes, too many transaction log backups will have the reverse effect on a restore.

The key to any backup plan is to document restore requirements. It does little good to run successful backups for months, if it takes three days to recover a server after a failure. At that point, no one will remember how quickly and efficiently your backups ran.

As a general rule of thumb, you should plan your SQL Server backups to balance point-in-time recoverability with restore performance. To this end, many perform weekly full backups, daily differential backups, and hourly transaction log backups. Of course, all of this is relative to your specific SQL configuration. For example, transaction log backups that run every 10 minutes may be needed for your recoverability requirements. No matter how you plan, always remember to balance periodic full backups with the rest of your backup schedule, as full backups equate to faster restores.

When planning to back up SQL Servers, you can't necessarily use a "one-size-fits-all" approach. Most likely, the requirements for the SQL system databases will not be the same as for the user databases; therefore, you must plan the backup and recovery for each SQL database as its own entity to ensure that its specific requirements are met. We will now look at how to approach backup planning for system and user databases, as well as replicated databases.

SQL System Databases

The most important SQL system database is Master. Like trying to run the operating system with a corrupted Registry, odds are that the SQL Server will not even start if the Master database becomes corrupted. When this happens, you need to manually rebuild the Master database to start the SQL Server. Once this is done, you will be able to restore the Master database from a backup. The entire process of manually rebuilding the Master database is covered later in this chapter in the "Rebuilding the Master Database" section.

Aside from the Master database, you should also perform regular backups of Msdb and Model. Because Tempdb is re-created each time the SQL Server starts, there is no need to back it up. Because of their relatively small size, you should generally just perform full backups of the three major system databases. To support this configuration and allow for optimal performance, you should make sure that SQL 7 and SQL 2000 have the following database properties set:

- SQL 2000: Configure the database recovery mode as Simple (see Figure 13.3).
- SQL 7: Make sure the Truncate Log on Checkpoint database option is selected (see Figure 13.4).

Figure 13.3: Setting Master database recovery mode to Simple

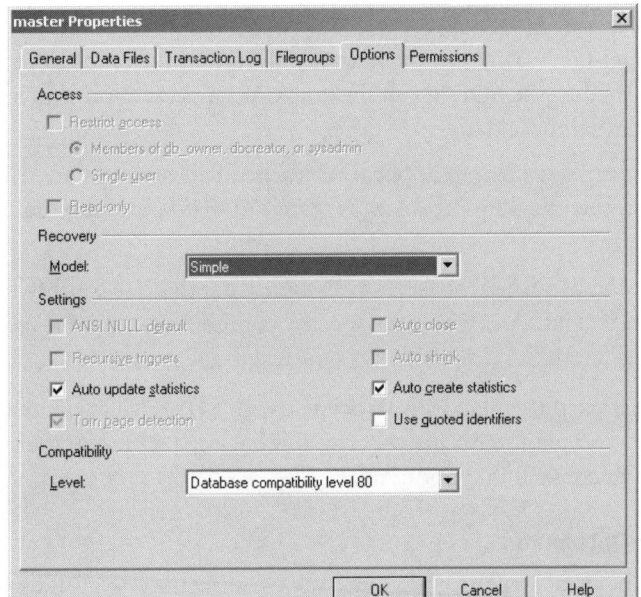

Figure 13.4: Selecting the Truncate Log on Checkpoint option

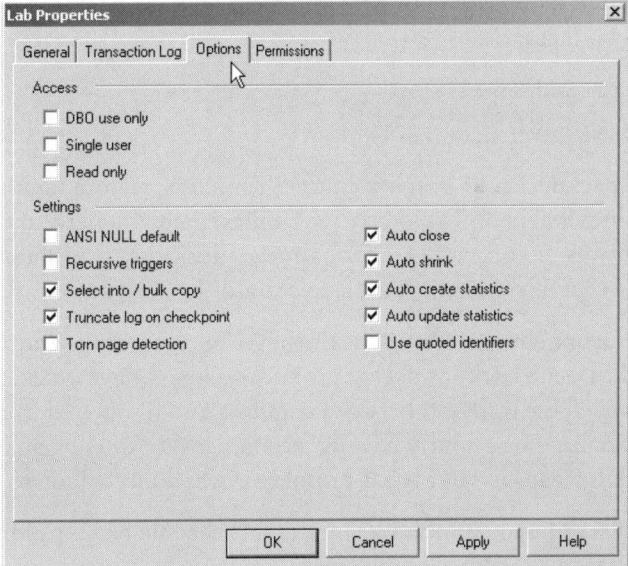

To summarize the frequency of when you should back up SQL system databases, remember these guidelines:

- Back up the Master database after any configuration changes or new databases are added to the SQL Server. For maximum protection, run a full backup of the Master database daily.
- If you or your backup application's scheduled backups are using the SQL Agent, then backup metadata is stored in Msdb, and it should also be backed up daily.
- Treat the Model database as a read-only database. Monthly backups are usually sufficient. Any time user-specific configuration data is used to modify the Model database, it should also be backed up.

For the most part, the planning associated with SQL system databases is relatively easy, especially if you plan to exclusively run full backups. User databases often require more planning, which we'll talk about next.

SQL User Databases

The frequency and structure of your backups surrounding SQL user databases will primarily be determined by the database's purpose. For example, if the database is read-only, monthly full backups should be your course of action. This can also change depending on how often the read-only database is updated.

For production databases with dynamic content, your backup schedule should be driven by two factors:

- Restore requirements
- Database server resources

As with all backups, your primary concern should be restore requirements. If the most data you can possibly do without is 10 minutes, then you need to run backups in 10-minute intervals. If you cannot afford any data loss, then you should look at a clustering solution that incorporates a fault-tolerant disk array, such as RAID 5.

Your other major concern should be the physical resources of the database server. What impact will running backups during production hours have on clients and applications? You must weigh the trade-off between data loss and resource demand. Although running log backups on an hourly basis is certainly less resource demanding, it does, however, leave large gaps in your point-in-time recoverability window.

If you're still confused about how you should schedule backups for your SQL user databases, here are a couple of examples:

Maximum Protection   Schedule weekly full backups, daily differential backups, and run transaction log backups every 10 minutes. For a restore, the daily differential backups will significantly cut down on restore time by limiting the number of transaction log backups that will need to be applied.

Good Protection   Schedule weekly full backups, daily differential backups, and hourly transaction log backups. On a restore, you would still need to restore one full and one differential backup, but you would have far fewer log backups to restore. This approach will give you better restore performance but at the cost of data availability.

Minimal Protection   Schedule transaction log backups to run twice a day (or more frequently depending on the size of the database), weekly differential backups, and monthly full backups. From a backup perspective, this approach is clearly the fastest, but it can be very painful for restores. With only weekly differentials and daily transaction log backups, you could be looking at restoring five days' worth of log backups in addition to the monthly full and weekly differential. If the SQL Server has to replay a week's worth of transactions, you may want to call home and ask someone to bring you a sleeping bag. At the least, grab a Snickers because you won't be going anywhere for a while.

Replicated Databases

Another way to maintain data availability with SQL Server is to replicate a database between several servers. If one server goes down, another version of the same database is still available. Although in theory replication is good for data availability, it does so at the expense of backup and recovery planning.

In a replicated SQL environment, you will have three additional system databases to worry about:

- Distribution
- Publication
- Subscription

The strategy with which you decide to back up these three databases should again be determined by your restore strategy. In a perfect world, you would back up all system databases together, at daily intervals. Although this offers the best level of protection, it does so at the cost of additional storage.

If backing all databases up together is not realistic, you should then, at a minimum, attempt to back up both the Publication and Distribution databases with the Master and Msdb. SQL Server replication has the built-in ability to reinitialize a subscription database on demand, so if you prefer to wait for SQL reinitialization as opposed to restoring the Subscription database (meaning you won't have to back it up), understand that doing so may cause a SQL Server slightly longer to recover from a complete failure.

One final factor determining the frequency for backing up replication databases is the period in which modifications are made to the SQL replication topology. Each time replication objects are added or modified, or when the SQL schema is changed, you should run full backups of both the Distribution and Publication databases.

Parallel Backups

Have several available drives in your library? Why not put them all to work? Unlike other Microsoft products that offer average-at-best backup and restore performance, SQL Servers are built to be "backup beasts." When a SQL database is divided into multiple data files, each data file on its own disk can be backed up in its own thread. Many enterprise backup solutions take advantage of this architecture by allowing you to set the number of streams the solution should use for the backup. For example, for a database divided into three data files stored on three disks, you could configure your backup application to use three streams for all backup and restore operations. SQL has the intelligence to pull a stream off each disk all running as individual threads, and then the backup application will direct each stream to an appropriate backup drive. Unless your backup application supports multiplexing several streams to a single drive (which is usually a mess in a restore), as a general rule you should set the number of backup streams to equal the number of available drives in the library you want to use for the backup.

> **TIP** Always remember that when performing parallel backups, you should make sure the same number of drives you used for the backup are available for the restore.

Backing Up SQL Databases

This section shows you how to use SQL Server's tools for performing backups. If your enterprise storage software is being used to back up SQL databases, then the processes in this section will not be of much relevance to you. However, that does not mean you should skip the restore section of this chapter. Issues can come up when rebuilding a SQL Server that may not be documented by your backup software vendor. In any case, the "Restoring SQL Databases" section has what you need to be aware of before, during, and after a restore.

Configuring Logical Backup Devices

If you're still reading this section at this point, then we can assume you are planning on using the SQL backup tools to back up your SQL databases. If so, your first course of action should be to define a backup device for SQL to use for backups. You can do this using either SQL Enterprise Manager or T-SQL commands. Both methods for configuring logical backup devices are described in the next two sections.

Configuring Backup Devices with Enterprise Manager

Configuring backup devices with Enterprise Manager is a simple process. If you have not already done so, open Enterprise Manger (click Start ➤ Programs ➤ Microsoft SQL Server ➤ Enterprise Manager) and follow these steps:

1. Expand the console root to the SQL Server for which you want to configure the backup device.
2. Expand the SQL Server's Management folder and locate the Backup object.
3. Right-click the Backup object and select New Backup Device.
4. Enter a name for the device in the Name field and select the type of device (tape drive or filename) and click OK (see Figure 13.5).

Figure 13.5: Configuring a backup device with Enterprise Manager

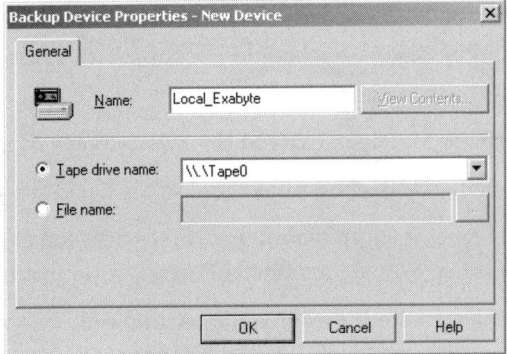

Configuring Backup Devices with T-SQL

With T-SQL, configured backup devices is also easy. To set up a backup device, you need to use the `sp_addumpdevice` stored procedure. The syntax for this command is:

```
sp_addumpdevice '<device type>', '<logical name>', '<physical name or file path>'
```

From OSQL, you would then type **go** to commit the command. Figure 13.6 shows an example of using this command to configure a file as a backup device.

Figure 13.6: Using T-SQL to create a backup device

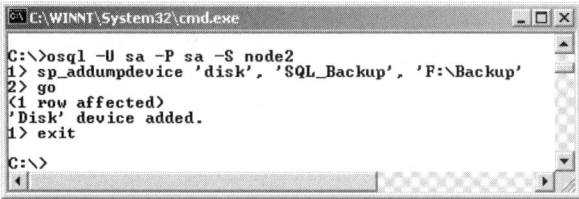

With a backup device configuring, you are now ready to run or schedule backups, so that's what we'll cover next.

Running Backups with Enterprise Manager

If your backup software does not natively support live SQL database backups, then an alternative to stopping the SQL services and then backing up the database offline is to use SQL to back up the database to a file. You can then use your backup software to back up the SQL backup file.

Scheduling Backups

To run on-demand backups or schedule backups with Enterprise Manager, follow these steps:

1. From Enterprise Manager, expand the SQL Server's Management folder.
2. Then right-click the Backup object and select Backup a Database.
3. In the SQL Server Backup dialog box, first select the database you want to back up and then provide a name and description for the backup.
4. Click the proper radio button for the backup type you want to perform. (For full backups, click the Complete radio button.)
5. You must now select a destination for the backup data. To do this, click the Add button.
6. Select a File Name or preconfigured backup device and click OK (see Figure 13.7).
7. With the device set, you can now select the Overwrite option. Your choice is to have the backup append an existing backup, or to overwrite existing media.
8. After selecting the Overwrite option, you can click OK to perform the backup on demand and then skip to step 11. If you would like to schedule your backup, proceed with step 9.

Figure 13.7: Selecting backup destination

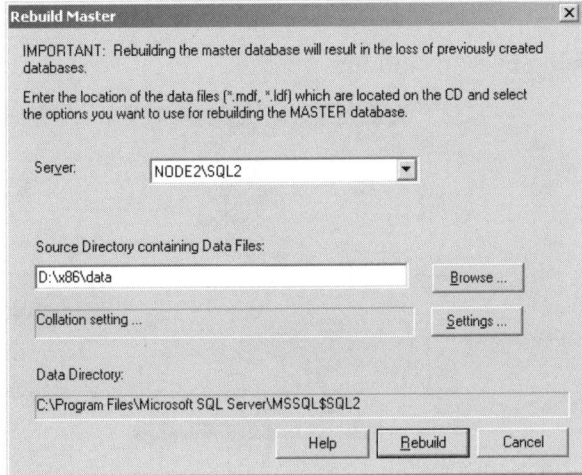

9. To schedule the backup, click the Schedule check box and then click the Browse button to set the schedule frequency.

10. In the Edit Schedule dialog box, name the schedule and click the Change button, if desired, to configure the schedule date, time, and frequency. Once these parameters are set, you should see the Edit Schedule dialog box appear (see Figure 13.8).

Figure 13.8: Editing schedule frequency

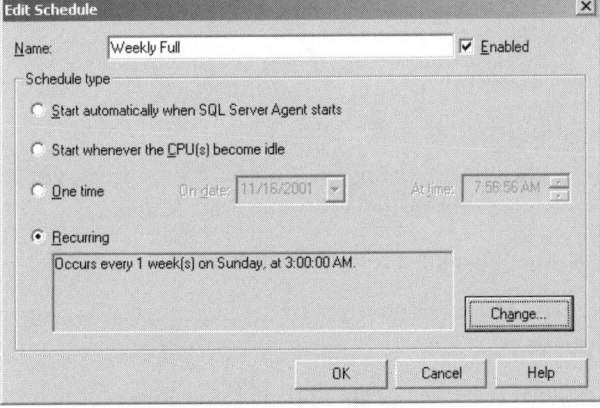

11. Click OK to close the Edit Schedule dialog box.

12. Verify that all backup configuration settings are correct and click OK (see Figure 13.9).

Figure 13.9: Verifying backup settings

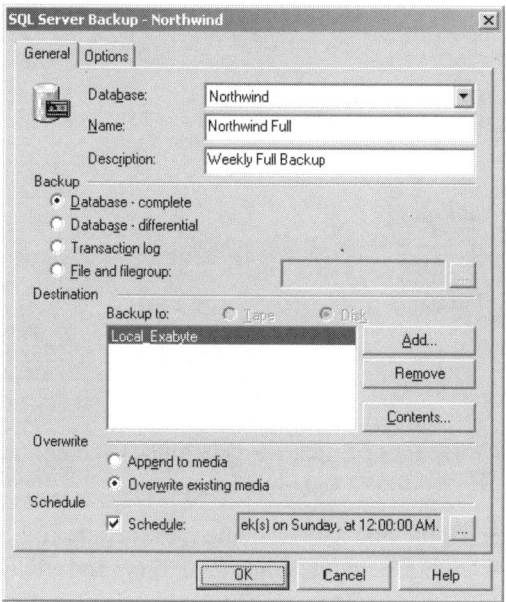

NOTE SQL Server Agent must be running for scheduled jobs to execute. If the agent is not running, right-click the SQL Server Agent object under the Management folder and select Start.

Viewing Backup Schedules

Once you have scheduled backups for your SQL databases, you can view, delete, or modify any scheduled jobs using SQL Enterprise Manager.

To see a list of scheduled jobs, follow these steps:

1. In Enterprise Manager, navigate to the SQL Server/Management/SQL Server Agent object.

2. Expand the SQL Server Agent and click the Jobs object.

3. In the right pane of Enterprise Manager, you will see your scheduled jobs listed (see Figure 13.10).

Figure 13.10: Viewing a list of scheduled jobs

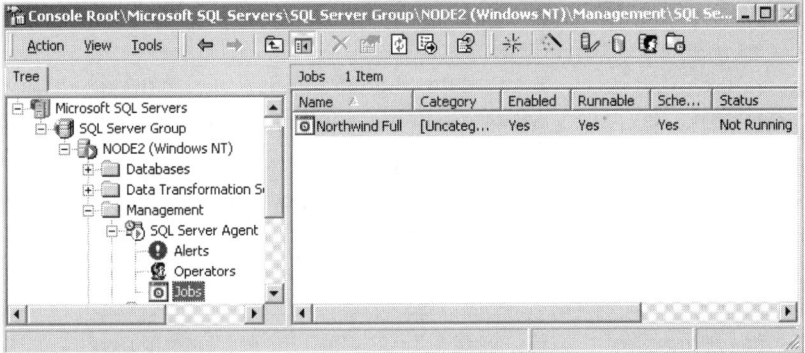

4. To delete a scheduled job, simply right-click the job and select Delete.

5. To modify a job's parameters (scheduled day, frequency, and so on), right-click the Job and select Properties. From the Properties dialog box, modify the desired parameters and then click OK.

Running Backups with T-SQL

Everything you can do with Enterprise Manager in terms of executing backups, you can also do with T-SQL commands. The T-SQL command for executing backups is Backup, and its syntax is:

```
Backup <Database|Log>
To <Backup Device>
[With <options>]
```

The Backup Database or Backup Log parameter, followed by To, are required. With <options> is not required. Table 13.1 lists the options for the T-SQL Backup command. After the table, we will show you details on how to execute the commands.

Table 13.1: T-SQL Backup Command Options

Option	Description
Blocksize	Specifies the size of the data blocks written to the backup media.
Description	Provides a description (up to 255 characters) for the backup.
Differential	Used in conjunction with the Backup Database command. Allows you to designate the backup as a differential backup.

Continued on next page

Table 13.1 (Continued): T-SQL Backup Command Options

Option	Description
Expiredate = <date>	Sets a date when the backup data can be overwritten; otherwise the settings configured for the SQL Server are applied.
Format	Causes the media's tape header to be overwritten during the backup, effectively formatting the media.
INIT	Leaves the media header intact but deletes all other data on the media.
Mediadescription = <description>	Provides a description for the backup media.
Medianame = <media name>	Specifies the name of the media for the backup.
MediaPassword = <password>	If a password is required to access media, this option allows you to enter a password to be used by the backup process.
Noformat	Prevents the backup from overwriting the media header.
Noinit	Backup data is appended to the media, as opposed to overwriting all other backups on the media.
Norewind	Causes tape not to be rewound after backup completes.
Noskip	Causes backup operation to check if media is expired before overwriting its data.
Nounload	Causes tape to remain in drive after backup operation completes.
Password = <password>	Allows you to set a password to access the backup data, protecting it from unlawful access.
Restart	Allows you to restart a backup that abnormally aborted before completion.
Retaindays = <days>	Lets you specify the number of days a backup must be retained before it is overwritten.
Rewind	Causes tape to be rewound after backup completes.
Skip	Causes the backup operation to ignore media expiration information and write to the media regardless of whether its data has surpassed its retention requirements.

Continued on next page

Table 13.1 (Continued): T-SQL Backup Command Options

Option	Description
Stats [= percentage]	Causes percentage of job completion to be displayed while backup is running. If no percentage increment is input with the command, the default increment of 10 is displayed.
Unload	Causes backup to unload the media from its drive once the backup completes.

As you can see, the T-SQL Backup command, with its many options, is powerful. We didn't want to leave you in the dark on how to use this command, so next are some examples of using the command to execute backups.

Performing a Full Backup

These are the T-SQL commands to perform a full backup of a database called Northwind:

```
Backup Database Northwind
To Local_Exabyte
With
       Description = 'Weekly Full Backup - Northwind',
       Retaindays = 180,
       Mediadescription = 'Northwind Offsite Full',
       Medianame   = 'NWT1',
       Unload
Go
```

Performing a Transaction Log Backup

This is an example of a log backup script for the Northwind database:

```
Backup Log Northwind
To Local_Exabyte
With
       Description = 'Daily Log Backup - Northwind',
       Retaindays = 180,
       Mediadescription = 'Northwind Offsite Logs',
       Medianame   = 'NWT2',
       Unload
   Go
```

The benefit of using T-SQL commands to script backup jobs lies in the ability to run the scripts on several SQL Servers. This will save you time configuring backup jobs if you have several SQL Servers in your enterprise.

Configuring Log Shipping on SQL 2000 Servers

Although running scheduled backups and restores is a means to maintain a standby SQL Server, the process of maintaining a standby server with SQL 2000 Enterprise is much easier. With SQL 2000 Enterprise, log shipping automates the process of backing up data on one server and effectively restoring it on another. The benefit of log shipping as opposed to using backup and restores is that it can be done with one operation. Before attempting log shipping, you must have two installed instances of SQL Server, installed on either the same or separate machines. It is recommended that you have separate instances running on separate machines if you're using log shipping as a means to facilitate faster recovery.

To configure log shipping, follow these steps:

1. Create a shared folder on the production SQL Server. The shared folder is used for the standby server to access and copy the production server's log files.

2. In Enterprise Manager, expand the Management folder on the production SQL Server.

3. Right-click the Database Maintenance Plans object and select New Maintenance Plan.

4. At the Database Maintenance Plan Wizard window, click Next.

5. Select the databases you want to maintain on the multiple SQL instances, select the Ship the Transaction Logs to Other SQL Servers check box, and click Next, as shown in Figure 13.11.

Figure 13.11: Selecting databases for log shipping

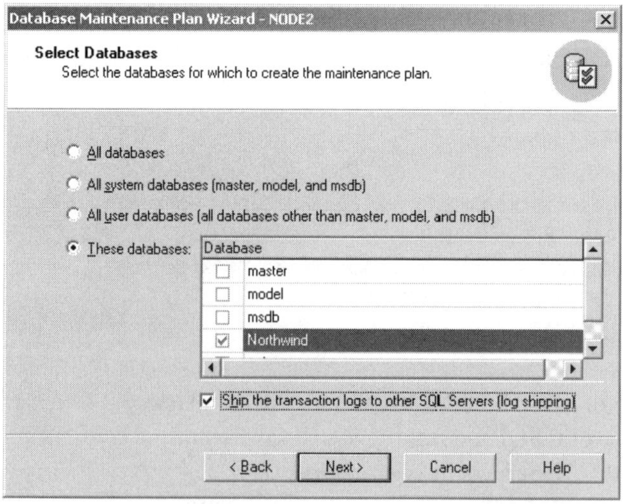

6. At the next window, you do not have to select any database optimization settings. Leave all check boxes cleared and click Next.

7. Leave the Check Database Integrity box cleared and click Next.

8. Select and configure the backup parameters for the database backup and click Next.

9. Enter your shared directory for the location of the backup files. Select the duration that files should be retained, if desired, and click Next (see Figure 13.12).

NOTE   You don't have to store the database backup files in the shared directory. It is only required that you store the log backups there.

10. Specify the shared directory to store the transaction log backups, as you did in the previous step, and click Next.

11. Enter the UNC for the log share folder on the primary SQL Server, as shown in Figure 13.13.

Figure 13.12:   Specifying database backup directory

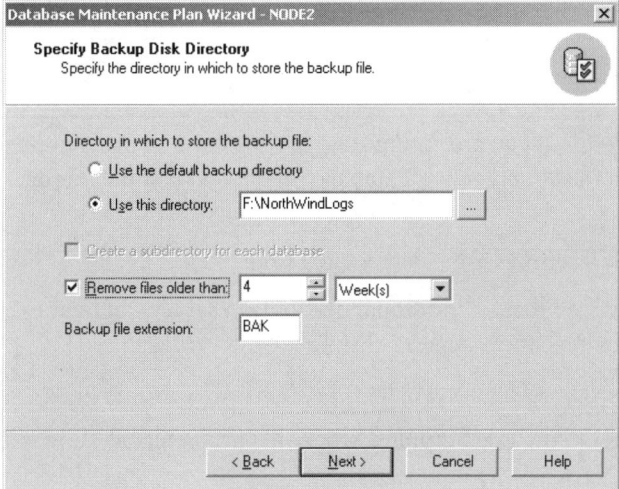

12. Click the Add button to specify a log shipping destination.

13. Configure the settings, as shown in Figure 13.14. You will need to select:
    - Destination standby server name.
    - Transaction log database directory.
    - Destination Database.

- Select Standby for the Database Load State and select the box to Terminate Users in Database.
- Check the box to Allow Database to Assume Primary Role.

Figure 13.13: Specifying shared directory for log file access

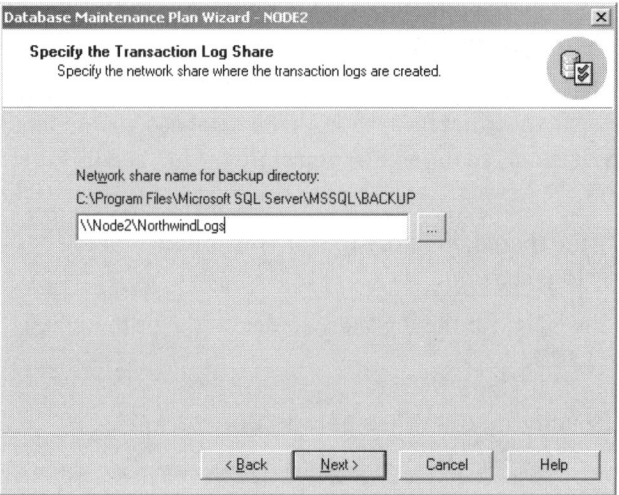

WARNING If you are configuring log shipping to use a pre-existing database on the standby server, the database must be in standby mode.

14. Once all settings are entered, click OK.
15. If you need to add additional destination servers and databases, do so at this time by repeating steps 12 through 14.
16. Click Next.
17. Configure the Log Shipping Schedule parameters as shown in Figure 13.15 and click Next.
18. Configure the log shipping thresholds for Backup Alerts and Out of Sync. If the threshold limit is exceeded, an alert will automatically be generated.
19. Select the central server that will take the role of monitoring log shipping. If another SQL Server is available besides the servers participating in log shipping, you should allow that server to perform the monitoring. Otherwise, you can select either the primary or standby server.

Figure 13.14: Configuring destination database options

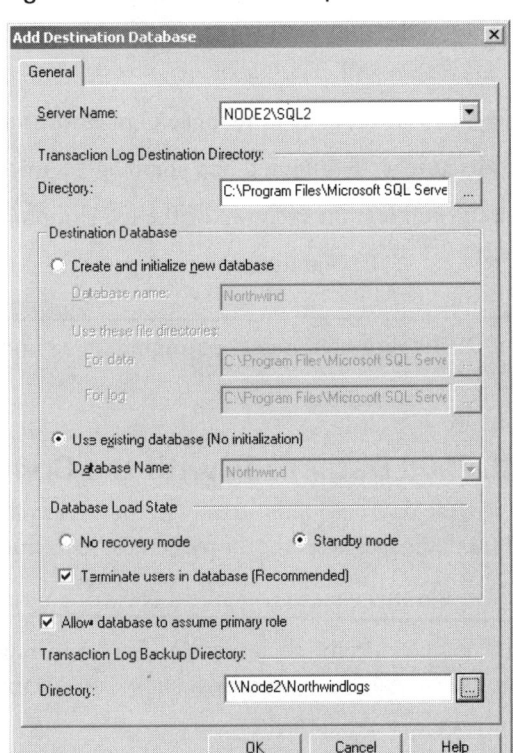

Figure 13.15: Configuring log shipping schedules

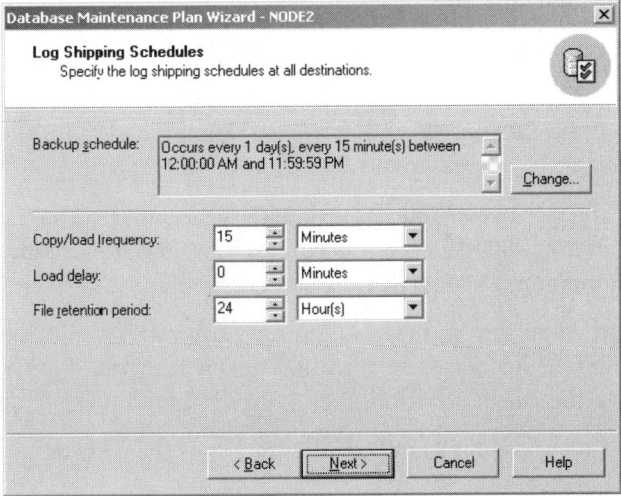

20. Set the authentication to be used for the central server and click Next.
21. If desired, select a directory for reports to be written to that are generated by the maintenance plan and click Next.
22. Select the server to store the maintenance plan records and click Next.
23. Name the plan, such as "Northwind Log Shipping" in this example, and click Next.
24. Click Finish to complete the creation of the log shipping maintenance plan.
25. When prompted that the maintenance plan was created successfully, click OK.

WARNING SQL Server Agent must be running on all nodes participating in log shipping.

Copying SQL 2000 Databases with the Copy Database Wizard

Another way to provide database redundancy in the event of failure is by generating copies of SQL 2000 databases with the Copy Database Wizard.

Follow these steps to use this wizard to make a copy of a database:

1. In Enterprise Manager, right-click the SQL Server instance whose database you want to copy, select All Tasks, and then click Copy Database Wizard.
2. When the wizard opens, click Next.
3. Select the source server for the copy operation, choose the authentication method, and click Next.
4. Select the destination server for the copy operation, choose the authentication method, and click Next.
5. Select to move or copy databases to the destination and click Next (see Figure 13.16).
6. Leave the default, or select a new destination location for the database files and click Next.
7. Select the tasks you want to move with the database. You have the option to move logins, shared stored procedures, jobs, and user-defined error messages. At a minimum, leave the Logins box checked and click Next.
8. Select the time you want the job to run. You can have the job only run once, or you can schedule the copy operation to run at regular intervals. Once you have selected the schedule option, click Next.
9. Click Finish to complete the configuration of the copy database operation.

Figure 13.16: Selecting databases to move or copy

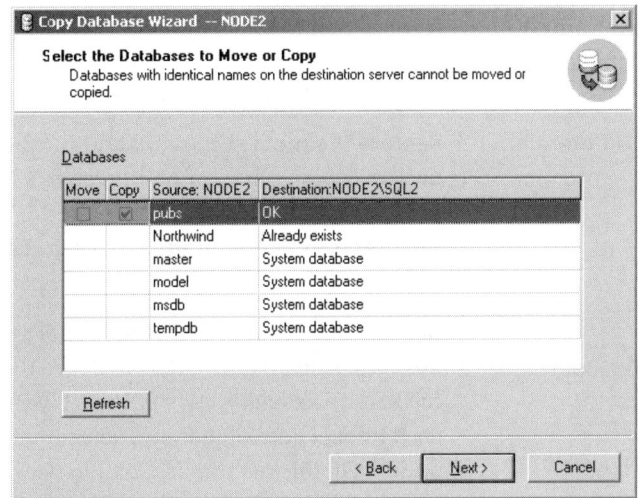

10. If you selected to copy the database immediately, click OK once the operation finishes.

Restoring SQL Databases

You have just read of several ways to back up SQL databases. Backups are relatively simple to configure and execute, and so are restores.

For restore operations, if you are using enterprise storage software such as CommVault, Legato, or Veritas, the restore process should be well documented and automated. If you need to manually restore databases without the help of storage software, then you must remember the order in which you need to restore databases.

Any complete database restore will begin with restoring the last full backup of the database. If you have run differential backups, then you should restore the most recent differential backup after the restore from the full backup completes. After the differential restore completes, your final task is to restore all transaction log backups completed after the last differential backup.

If you still feel a little in the dark on the process for restoring SQL databases, Table 13.2 provides you with the process you should take depending on the backup strategy you used.

Table 13.2: SQL Database Recovery Strategy

Backups Performed	Recovery Strategy
Fulls only	Restore the most recent full backup.
Fulls and differentials	Restore the most recent full and most recent differential backup. When performing the restore from the full backup, select the NoRecovery restore option. When performing the restore from the differential backup, select the Recovery restore option.
Fulls and transaction logs	Back up the current transaction log for the database (if desired), selecting the NO_TRUNCATE option. Restore the full backup selecting the NoRecovery restore option. Restore each transaction log backup, selecting the NoRecovery option. On the last transaction log backup restore, select the Recovery restore option (if you backed up the current log, this would be the log file you restore).
Fulls, differentials, and transaction logs	Back up the current transaction log for the database (if desired), selecting the NO_TRUNCATE option. Restore the full backup, selecting the NoRecovery restore option. Restore the most recent differential backup, selecting the NoRecovery option. Restore each transaction log backup, selecting the NoRecovery option. On the last transaction log backup restore, select the Recovery restore option (if you backed up the current log, this would be the log file you restore).

Sometimes restoring all transaction log backups is not the best solution for your database recovery. If the database became corrupted at a certain point, and you have a good idea of about when corruption occurred, you should restore all log backups up to the point before corruption occurred.

Once you know the order that you need to restore backup files, the restore process using either Enterprise Manager or T-SQL is relative straightforward.

System Database Restore Issues

The process to restore any database is the same, regardless of whether it is a system or user database. (The only problem you may have with system databases is the Master database; see the next section.) However, some services must be stopped before restoring other system databases.

> **WARNING** Microsoft does not support the restore of SQL 7 system databases to SQL 2000 Servers.

These are the services you should stop before attempting a restore for particular system databases:

- Msdb: SQL Server Agent
- Distribution (If SQL Server instance participates in replication):
  - Replication Distribution Agent Utility
  - Replication Log Reader Agent Utility
  - Replication Merge Agent Utility
  - Replication Snapshot Agent Utility

There are no issues when attempting to restore the Model database.

If Master is corrupted, you will not even be able to start the SQL Server. In this case you will have to manually rebuild the master. Once the master database is rebuilt, you can then move to restore it.

Rebuilding the Master Database

If the Master database is corrupted to such a point that SQL cannot even start, or if you don't have a valid backup of Master, you can manually rebuild it. When rebuilding the Master database, SQL Server will also re-create the Model and Msdb databases. After the Master is rebuilt, you should then perform a restore of Model and Msdb so that they are current.

To rebuild the Master database, follow these steps:

1. If the SQL Server service is running, stop the service.
2. Run the `rebuildm.exe` utility. By default, it is located in the `80\Tools\Binn` folder of the SQL installation directory. For SQL 7, you would run the executable from `70\Tools\Binn`.
3. In the Source Directory field, provide the location of the SQL installation files or browse to their location.
4. If needed, click the Settings button to specify the character set, sort order, and Unicode collation settings you manually used when installing SQL Server. If you used the default installation, this is not necessary.
5. Once you have configured these settings, click Rebuild (see Figure 13.17).

Figure 13.17: Rebuilding the Master database

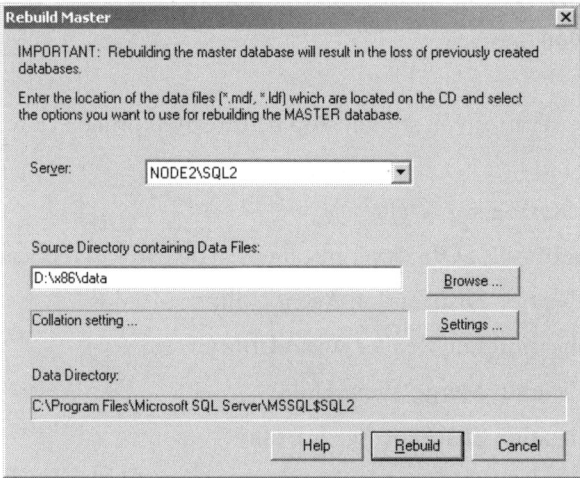

6. When warned that you are about to overwrite system databases, click OK.

7. Once the rebuild completes, start the SQL Server service.

Restoring Databases with Enterprise Manager

Performing restores with Enterprise Manager is just as straightforward and automated as performing backups.

To restore a SQL database using Enterprise Manager, perform these steps:

1. In Enterprise Manager, expand the SQL Server instance that you want to restore.

2. Right-click the Databases folder, select All Tasks, and then Restore Database.

3. In the Restore Database dialog box, select the database you want to restore.

4. Select the backup to base the restore on (see Figure 13.18). If you have a collection of fulls, differentials, and log backups, you can select the backups to restore so that the restore completes as one operation.

5. To restore particular data files or filegroups, click the Filegroups or Files radio button and then choose the files and filegroups to restore.

6. Click the Restore Device radio button to choose the device to use for the restore operation.

7. Now click the Options tab.

Figure 13.18: Selecting database to restore

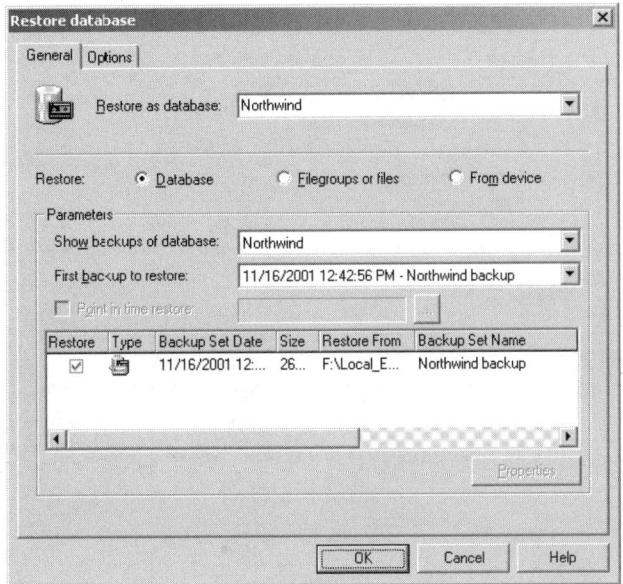

8. Under the Options tab, you can select the state the database should be in following the completed restore. These are the options you should choose, based on the progression of the backup:

   - Recovery: Click the Leave Database Operational... radio button.
   - NoRecovery: Click the Leave Database Nonoperational... radio button.
   - Standby: Click the Leave the Database Read-Only... radio button.

9. Select the recovery option for the restore and click OK to initiate the restore, as shown in Figure 13.19.

10. The restore progress bar will increment as the restore moves closer to completion. Once the restore finishes, click OK.

> **NOTE** The wording in the restore dialog boxes will appear slightly differently in SQL 7 than in SQL 2000, shown in Figures 13.18 and 13.19. The differences, however, are insignificant.

Figure 13.19: Selecting restore options

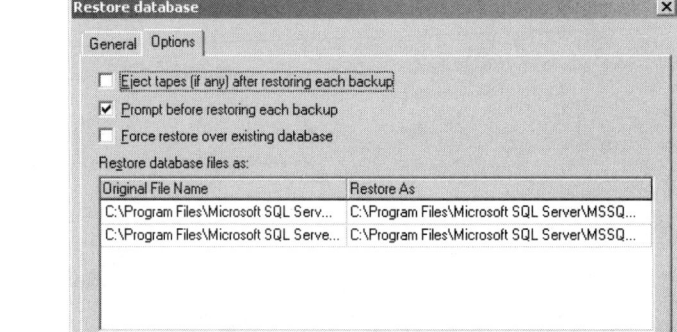

Restoring Databases with T-SQL

The T-SQL restore commands are almost identical to the T-SQL backup commands. Instead of using Backup in the command syntax, instead you will use Restore. Otherwise, the process is nearly completely the same. Here is the command syntax for the T-SQL Restore command:

```
Restore <Database|Log>
From <Backup Device>
[With <options>]
```

The Restore Database or Restore Log parameters, followed by From, are required. With <options> is not required. Table 13.3 lists the options for the T-SQL Restore command. After the table, we will show you details on how to execute the commands.

Table 13.3: T-SQL Restore Command Options

Option	Description
DBO_Only (SQL 7)	Leaves restored database in state, so only the database owner can access it.

Continued on next page

Table 13.3 (Continued): T-SQL Restore Command Options

Option	Description
`File = <file number>`	Specifies the file in a backup set to restore.
`Keep_Replication`	Preserves the database's replication settings following the restore.
`MediaName = <name of media>`	Causes SQL to verify that the media used for the restore operation matches the name specified with this option.
`Mediapassword = <password>`	If media is password protected, this option is needed to provide a password for SQL to use to access the data for restore.
`Move '<logical file name>' to '<physical file>'`	Tells SQL to restore logical files to a different physical location. For file and filegroup restores, a separate Move statement can be entered for each file or filegroup.
`Norecovery`	Used when additional restore operations will be performed. Tells SQL not to roll back uncommitted transactions.
`Norewind`	Causes tape not to be rewound after restore completes.
`Nounload`	Causes tape to remain in drive after restore operation completes.
`Partial`	Tells SQL only specific files or filegroups will be restored and not the entire database.
`Password = <password>`	Allows you to set a password to access the backup data for restore, protecting it from unlawful access. For password-protected data, this option must be used.
`Recovery`	Used when you are restoring the last backup for a database. Causes uncommitted transactions to be rolled back and database to be brought online.
`Replace`	Tells the SQL restore to overwrite a database with the same name.
`Restart`	Restarts a previously uncompleted restore operation.
`Restricted_user`	Configures the restored database so that only db_owner, dbcreator, or sysadmin accounts can access it.
`Rewind`	Causes tape to be rewound after restore completes.

Continued on next page

Table 13.3 (Continued): T-SQL Restore Command Options

Option	Description
Standby = <undo file path>	Creates a file that can be used to allow SQL administrators to undo recovery operations.
Stats [= percentage]	Causes percentage of job completion to be displayed while restore is running. If no percentage increment is input with the command, the default increment of 10 is displayed.
Unload	Causes restore to unload the media from its drive once the restore completes.

As with the T-SQL backup, T-SQL Restore gives you a multitude of options for performing restores from the command line. Use these T-SQL commands to perform a restore of a database called Northwind:

```
Restore Database Northwind
From Local_Exabyte
With
      File = 2,
Medianame = 'NWT1',
Recovery,
      Unload
Go
```

14

The Future of Storage

The phrase *the future of storage* conjures up different things to different people depending on what their job entails or what their storage goals are. However, if we had to sum up what we think the future of storage will be in a single word (as lacking in technical meaning as it may be), we'd say it's going to be *profitable*. In fact, the companies that deliver strong solutions to the current storage capacity problem will lead the information storage market of the future.

Yes, storage is on the rise. As the latter part of the 1990s proved, data has increased and will continue to do so. Two factors are driving the market: 24/7 access to that data (which is expected to grow by 50 and 100 percent each year) and disaster recovery of that data (in the case of catastrophic scenarios).

The future of storage will include both software and hardware advancements as well as corporate battles for the prominent market space. Several companies are making a run for the gold already. For example, EMC is developing high-end solutions for storage and recovery. IBM is making a play for the iSCSI market and holographic technology. Veritas, CommVault Systems, Legato, Arc Serve, and a few others are working toward the expected data-management increase. And Microsoft? With the release of Windows XP/.NET, Microsoft continues to support high-end storage solutions with increased support for Removable Storage Manager (RSM), Remote Storage Service (RSS), and hardware support.

No one really knows the future, but it will undoubtedly involve Microsoft in some way.

Exploring Windows XP/.NET

Windows XP/.NET includes all of the support for storage we've discussed throughout this book and even includes a few new features, such as volume snapshots, automatic system recovery (ASR), and system restores.

> **NOTE** Windows XP is the first operating system to fully support Microsoft's .NET platform. The combination of XP and .NET will create a more supportive environment for the storage industry because Microsoft is much more aware of the need for 24/7 storage support.

Volume Snapshots

Windows XP includes new functionality in its backup utility: the ability to perform a backup based upon *volume snapshots*. These snapshots (similar to the snapshot utilities discussed in Chapter 7) will create a point-in-time copy of files. The special feature of snapshots is that the backup allows you to back up open files, including open databases and files being worked on by users.

Microsoft claims volume snapshots are *point-in-time* shots that can restore information at a certain moment. When working with this new feature, the term *point in time* struck us as meaning the time we wanted. So, we backed up files that we had open, which worked fine. Then we backed up files that were opened after we made changes to them. Alas, the changes weren't backed up until we saved those changes. Basically, when Microsoft says *point in time,* it is saying that once you initiate your backup, the system will freeze the current position of your volume.

How do you benefit from this? Well, let's say you've worked on a document throughout the day. You changed it quite a bit and saved it, and then went back and worked on it some more. At the time of the backup, let's say you opened the file to work on it again. The backup will continue; however, unlike the previous backup scenarios with Windows Backup where the file would be skipped (thus skipping all changes made for that day), that file would now be backed up as of its latest saved condition, and the user could continue to work. Now that is progress!

A good reason for this type of "freeze" snapshot involves database files. For example, let's say you stop a database, start the backup, and then restart the database. While the backup is going on, a user makes changes to the database. If the changed files are backed up, they may cause inconsistencies in the referential integrity established at the start of the backup when the database was in an offline condition. To maintain consistency,

Microsoft backs up the state of each file in the database as it was at the beginning of the backup (in other words, a point-in-time backup).

This is a nice feature and the default setting for a Windows XP Backup utility; however, you can turn this feature off if you choose.

ERD Replaced with ASR

Automatic System Recovery (ASR) will replace the Emergency Repair Disk (ERD) feature currently in Windows NT/2000. This new tool, although similar in location to 2000's ERD (on the General tab of the Backup utility), handles the recovery of your operating system more quickly.

The ASR takes a snapshot of the operating system partition and saves this to either tape or magnetic (file) storage. At the same time, the ASR creates a floppy with additional configuration information, much like the current ERD.

You can recover your system without going through the current routine of reinstalling the operating system, reinstalling service packs, getting your tape drive to work, and bringing back your latest data. With the ASR you can boot up with your Windows XP CD-ROM, press F5 when requested (which will start off the ASR Wizard), and use the floppy and the tape (if you used tape for your snapshot) to recover your operating system.

The ASR will bring back the original partition information and the operating system itself (including the service packs). From this point, you can restore the data from your last backup. Although this isn't as strong as a true image backup, it is going to make it a whole lot easier than the full server reinstall.

System Restore

This is a feature running in the background with the sole purpose of allowing you to recover your system from a problem that may come from a faulty program or driver. The System Restore will take a snapshot of your System State either every 24 hours by default or when a change is made, such as in the case of a new program being installed. The snapshots are called *restore points*, which roll back the system to the point in time that the snapshot was created to eliminate the faulty program.

Two questions generally arise with this type of solution: First, will this change any of my actual data that I've been working on, such as my documents? No, personal data will not roll back as well. Second, will this impede my system's performance? Of course, what service doesn't? It will be interesting to see the final performance hit benchmarks that come with this "helpful" feature.

> **Rollback Drivers**
>
> Ever install a driver and want to roll it back? The Device Manager with XP includes that functionality now. You can revert to a previously installed driver in the case of an incorrect driver installation. XP has an INF cache that it looks in to replace the older files. Granted, this isn't a storage solution, but it handles a specific type of problem with installing one thing and then wanting the original back.

Looking at Future Technologies

While Microsoft continues to make software changes, advancements will continue in other areas. Third-party software will increase recovery-time solutions. There will be advancements with granular restore issues. There have been, and will continue to be, advancements in the equipment being developed for Storage Area Networks (SANs) and Network Attached Storage (NAS) devices. We look forward to the progress being made in these areas.

In addition to software enhancements, some of the major vendors are pursuing other types of technologies. Let's examine these.

Tunneling and iSCSI (IP Storage)

The Internet Engineering Task Force (IETF) is currently evaluating two approaches to transmitting storage information over IP networks:

- Tunneling Fibre Channel (FC)
- IP Storage (iSCSI)

Tunneling continues using Fibre Channel, the current leader for SAN connectivity. The premise of tunneling is that control codes and data that ordinarily travel over Fibre Channel mediums will be converted from its Fibre Channel format into Internet Protocol (IP) packets. Those packets will be able to go from one FC SAN to another FC SAN, which will allow for a break in the need for Fibre Channel connectivity between distances. That may be difficult to visualize at first, but understand that enterprise storage may encompass the need to have disaster recovery solutions that span huge distances. Fibre Channel is great, but how much better would it be to use existing technologies with tunneling of FC to increase distances without using only FC.

The other method being worked on these days is iSCSI. iSCSI also uses IP as its transport by taking SCSI commands and data to new heights by encapsulating the data into IP packets for use on LAN Ethernet networks or even over WAN/Internet distances. The possibilities are tremendous when Gigabit Ethernet and iSCSI work together. Some are predicting iSCSI means the end of Fibre Channel, but it's still in development, so we wouldn't suggest selling your FC stock just yet.

Jeff Leitner from IBM says this regarding the complexity of such a move:

> "The challenge is to get a specific regiment of ordered commands over the Internet through the "fire-and-forget" approach of TCP-IP. The risk is losing the ability to guarantee the quality of services that we can promise with Fibre Channel, as well as potentially losing the simple interfaces of SCSI."

So, is there really a need for products that encapsulate SCSI? Well, many complain about the high price of Fibre Channel, and a little technological competition will certainly help that. But the fact that SCSI devices are already the staple of storage hardware makes iSCSI an easy match for existing storage systems.

Millipede Technology

Millipede technology is years away from a release date but may be the ultimate resolution to data size limitations for hard disks. Imagine a disk that is about one centimeter long by one centimeter wide with a half centimeter in thickness holding 10Gbs. Difficult to imagine? IBM doesn't think so and is investing in millipede technology.

This is a proposed technology that will one day revolutionize storage capacity (not to mention personal storage such as that of personal MP3 players and mini-computers) because the millipede technology is 100 times denser than modern hard drives.

Millipede uses Atomic Force Microscopy (AFM) to enhance write capabilities with multiple (1024 to be exact) tips on an equal number of cantilevers that will write to a polymer disk. Instead of writing bits by magnetizing regions of a disks surface, millipede technology melts tiny indentations into the recording surface. The tips are heated to 750 degrees Fahrenheit, and they melt holes (which represent bits) in the surface.

The future goal is storage that boasts 500Gbp per square inch. Pretty cool huh? For more information on millipede technology, visit `www.research.ibm.com/journal/rd/443/vettiger.html`.

Optical Improvements

There are many new improvements in the speed and data size of data storage. One area involves the use of a blue (as opposed to red) laser.

The Blue Laser is a type of laser that writes bits with five times greater density than what is currently used for optical media. The blue laser, though, is not easy to manage. Currently, a large, expensive laser is needed, which doesn't quite fit the needs for smaller implementations.

Holographic Storage

A holographic image takes an object and shows different views depending on the angle of the object. From the storage perspective, lasers are able to create pages of electronic patterns within special optical materials that will show a different page of information depending on the angle of storage.

This will not allow more than a surface-level storage of data (like magnetic disks) but rather allows for recording through the entire thickness of the material, increasing storage capacity and transfer rates.

There are actually two laser beams used for holographic storage, one for reference and one for data. The two beams intersect to create changes stored on the medium or read data off the medium. What is the potential for this type of storage? Well, IBM has already proven that a crystal the size of a sugar cube can hold 1GB of data with access rates of one trillion bits per second. Lucent and Imation have joined to work on this type of storage, and they've shown how 125GB of storage could be held on a single removable disk and accessed 25 times faster than current DVD rates. Speeds and storage size are only expected to increase.

The current work on holographic storage is a one-time write, which is great for archival purposes; however, future concepts will include rewritable types of storage.

For more information on this topic, Scientific American has a great article at www.sciam.com/2000/0500issue/0500toigbox5.html.

Virtualization

Virtualization walks side by side with SAN solutions for modern storage problems. The concept is that the physical boundaries of storage should be lifted from off the servers. Rather than having servers hold their magnetic and tape solutions, virtualization allows for pools of devices that control the servers logically. This way, you can emulate the appearance of servers having storage, but the reality is that this storage is located within a storage network pool (a virtual pool) of resources that has been allocated through software.

This may sound like the current definition of what a SAN does, but in reality a SAN is the physical structure that will allow virtualization to work. The true abilities of virtualization have not been written into an architectural platform as of yet. Once structured, servers will not need to care about the storage devices on the SAN; these will be managed centrally and separately from the servers themselves. In other words, you will be able to manipulate your storage (move it, upgrade it, change it) without worrying your servers with the details. Without virtualization, as you already know, the tasks just described would involve shutting down the storage devices and servers and rebooting to reinitialize your devices with the new changes.

Now some have begun to define levels of virtualization by saying that the initial step (the one described previously) is considered *aggregation*, and virtualization is really the next level.

True virtualization seems to be different depending on the vendor. Some say virtualization should include more than a "virtual pool" of storage, but it also has to answer these questions: How do you centrally manage the storage? How do you monitor it for problems? What limitations will be placed on input/output (I/O) bandwidth? How much impact will there be on the processors? Which platforms will be supported in our modern heterogeneous world of storage? These questions are ones to ask before purchasing the devices on the market.

The bottom line is that virtualization provides an easier way to administer the storage devices. The trick is to get the software companies to complete their designs and to get the storage providers to implement some new virtualization tools directly into their devices. But this is easier said than done.

For more information on virtualization, consider some of the new devices being implemented by StorageTek at www.storagetek.com. Other companies are working on this concept and certainly software developers are attempting to put more virtualization features within their data-management software.

> **The Global Storage Center Theory**
>
> Some claim that the ultimate level of virtualization will be the advent of a storage center that allows everyone to access it through any means—everything down to a phone line. This would develop a new type of "e-storage" that companies would invest in to allow for an external storage strategy accessible from any location. This would be great for smaller companies that can house their storage for a fee or for companies that require international storage solutions. Of course, with this type of arrangement there would be a tremendous amount of security in place, but this may be the most cost effective solution of the future of storage.

Additional Technology

Certainly, a great deal more than these few technologies are rocking the storage world. Articles are published every day regarding changes to storage. Large vendors are buying into the hype and creating some of the most amazing technologies, putting their greatest scientists on the job.

Where can you locate the latest and greatest storage news?

First, you can look at www.wwpi.com for breaking storage news. Second, WestWorld Productions publishes great magazines such as *Storage Inc.*, *Storage Management Solutions*, and *Computer Technology Review* (which is always on the cutting edge of storage and a must for those considering a career in enterprise storage solutions). These are all excellent resources for keeping up with storage trends. You should subscribe to them, considering that they are excellent quality and, oh yes…did we mention they are *free*? Well, they are free with an important proviso: You must qualify on the basis of their qualification forms available at wwpi.com.

Finally, another site to look at the overall picture of storage is the Storage Network Industry Association (SNIA), based in Colorado. The site is at www.snia.org, and it provides information on the leanings of the market and the many vendors working through the SNIA. SNIA is currently developing a certification track for engineers to be able to prove their knowledge.

Where Do You Want to Go Today?

This is the infamous Microsoft question. If you've read this book and you see the possibilities, your answer should be "Anywhere I choose."

Plain and simple: Storage is profitable, it's interesting, and the ways to approach it are wide. Even for those who have been in the information system (IS) fields for some time will find it an easy field to get into; however, the content is difficult to master. The primary reason for the difficulty to grasp the storage world is that storage solutions are broken up into three parts: the first is truly developed, the second is in the progress of being developed, the third is the promise of the future that is talked about by marketing persons as if they are ready for shipment.

Storage discussions have been marred by the terms *heterogeneous*, *ubiquitous*, and *exponential* for the last year with additional terms such as *SAN*, *NAS*, and *virtualization* being tossed into the mix. We hope you've seen the need to push past the vocabulary and see the technology.

Enterprise storage solutions make up a large part of the future, affecting the entire computing industry.

Hope you enjoyed the ride!

Glossary

SanSite has provided the primary portion of this glossary, and we thank them.

NUMBERS

8 mm Tape technology based on helical recording techniques. It uses 8 millimeter-wide tape.

A

Access Read, write, or update information on a storage medium, such as disk or tape. The operation of reading, writing, or updating stored information.

Access time The interval between the time a request for data is made by the system and the time the data is available from the drive.

Active Directory Windows 2000 feature that treats every network resource—including users, groups, files, servers, and domains—as an individual object in a hierarchical tree. Based on the Domain Name System (DNS) model.

AIT Advanced Intelligent Tape.

ALDC Adaptive Lossless Data Compression algorithm.

AME Advanced Metal Evaporated media.

AMP Advanced Metal Powder media. Durable metal powder technology. Used for storing high densities of data and for containing embedded information for the Quantum POS system on Super DLT-tape products. Designed by Quantum.

ANSI American National Standards Institute.

API Application Program Interface.

Archive Removing data, usually old or inactive files, from a system and permanently storing it on removable media to reclaim system hard disk space. Because files are physically removed from the system, only one copy of the data exists—unless you back up or replicate the archive media.

To retrieve archived data, find the media on which the data exists, mount the media in the appropriate drive, and retrieve the data to the system.

Archive media can be stored *nearline*—for example, in a tape library or optical jukebox—or *offline* in a secure location, preferably in a fireproof room or vault.

You use an archive software application to move files from an online disk to an offline media to keep track of which media set the files are stored on and to retrieve files to the system.

See also **file migration**.

Archive bit A bit that is turned on or set to 1 to indicate that a file is new or has been modified since the last backup. The archive bit is turned off or set to 0 according to the type of backups you are making.

Enables backup software to keep track of new and changed files. Is more reliable than the date-time stamp because many software applications don't change the date-time stamp when they change the file contents.

See also **incremental backup, differential backup,** and **full backup**.

ARPA Advanced Research Projects Agency of the U.S. government.

Autoloader A system that uses a robotic mechanism to automatically load and unload tape cartridges into a single tape drive. Used to provide unattended data backup and file restoration.

Automation Refers to tape stackers, autoloaders, libraries used in data backup, archiving, hierarchical storage management, and near online storage. A system that generally has storage for multiple tape cartridges, a robotic cartridge-handling system, an electronic control system, software, and one or more tape drives.

B

Backup Copying computer data to an offline location. The more popular backup process copies data from your computer system to tape. Other forms of removable media are suitable.

If the version of the file on your original system becomes inaccessible for any reason, you can restore the data from the backup copy.

Backup uses a software backup utility. This software enables you to copy files, directories, paths, and even drives from a computer system to the backup device and media. After the backup is complete, a file structure of the backup session displays the files on the backup media.

The most common backups are a full, differential, and incremental backups. A typical backup set consists of a full backup followed by either incremental or differential backups.

See also **Grandfather-Father-Son, Tower of Hanoi,** and **disaster recovery**.

Backup interval The period between full backups. A backup set is created during a backup interval.

Backup session One full, incremental, or differential backup event.

See also **backup set**.

Backup set The backup sessions from one full backup to the next full backup, spanning one backup interval. The set may be one full backup, one full backup, and each incremental backup, or it may be one full backup and each differential backup. A backup set is required to perform a complete restore.

A typical backup set interval is Friday to Friday, where the backup set includes the following:

Friday = Full backup

Monday–Thursday = Daily differential or daily incremental backups

Backup window The time available to make backups.

Bandwidth Data transmission speed in bits/s.

Burst transfer rate The number of megabytes transferred per second (MB/s) from the device buffer to the host. Faster than the internal transfer rate (media surface to buffer).

Byte A single character, made up of 8 bits of digital data.

C

Capacity Maximum amount of data that can be stored on media.

Capstan In tape drives, a windlass that rotates to wind tape.

CAV Constant Angular Velocity. A technology used on some DVD drives in combination with Constant Linear Velocity (CLV) to accommodate both CD and DVD disks individually to achieve high-speed data transfer with faster access times. With CAV, the disk rotates at a constant speed regardless of the area of the disk that is being accessed.

CD tower Includes one or more CD-ROM drives (usually four to 28) and an interface to communicate with the computer system.

CD-R Compact Disk–Recordable (write once).

CD-ROM autoloader Includes one CD-ROM drive, a small number of disks (usually fewer than 10), a robotic changer mechanism, and an interface to communicate to the computer system.

CD-ROM jukebox Includes one or more CD-ROM drives, some number of disks held in a structure called a *magazine*, a robotic changer mechanism that moves the CD-ROMs back and forth between the magazine and the drives, and an interface to communicate to the computer system.

CD-RW Compact Disk–Rewritable.

Change Journal The Change Journal allows backup applications to perform incremental backups faster by eliminating the need to scan file systems. Think of the Change Journal as being a virtual notepad. Now imagine if someone wrote the name of each file as it is changed in the notepad. For backup applications, this means that on incremental backups, they can get their list of files right from the journal, without having to scan the file system to get their own list.

Cluster A parallel or distributed collection of interconnected servers used as a single, unified server. Each separate server in the cluster may also be known as a *node*. Redundant nodes are active, often running different applications. They provide static load balancing. If one node fails, the application or resource fails over to another node in the cluster to provide little or no interruption in the service to the users.

Clusters may be in one of the following configurations:

Shared-memory is when memory is accessed and managed by all systems in the cluster.

Shared-disk is when disk storage is accessed and managed by all systems in the cluster. The disk controller is able to take commands from two or more computers. Each computer can read data the other computer has written to the disk.

Shared-nothing is when, from the user's point of view, he does not have to remember drive letters or full pathnames to access his data. His data is always available to him. He has control of his data, no matter what changes the system administrator makes to the system environment. To the user, he is sharing nothing.

See also **fault tolerance.**

CLV Constant Linear Velocity. A technology used on CD-ROMs and most DVD drives to ensure a constant data rate regardless of where on the disk the data is. If the data is closer to the center, the rotation speed of the disk is faster; if the data is closer to the outside the speed is slower.

Compressed capacity The amount of data that can be stored on one data cartridge using data compression. Usually specified in megabytes or gigabytes as a multiple of two or three times the native capacity—for example, 2:1 compression or 3:1 compression.

When comparing the capacity of different types of systems, it is always best to use native capacity.

D

DAT Digital Audio Tape. DAT never caught on in the consumer market, but it became a strong technology in recording and backing up computer data.

Data center A collection of servers and data storage devices, usually in one location, administered by an information systems manager.

Data compression Using an algorithm or formula, data compression removes redundant characters and extra spaces from data as it is stored. Saves data storage space and reduces the time required to store the data. Using the reverse algorithm, compressed data is reconstituted for use by humans or according to the application software requirements.

DDS Developed by Hewlett Packard and Sony, this is the most recognized DAT recording format for the computer industry.

Defragmentation Rearranging pieces of large files on disk so they occupy contiguous or adjacent parts or fragments to improve file-access time.

DFS Distributed File System. A Windows NT 4 feature also included with Windows 2000. Maps physical storage into a logical representation. Consolidates resources, including files, programs, and multiple disk volumes, into one directory tree. Can include file shares on multiple servers around the world. Will interoperate with other file systems. Transparently links volumes and uses alternate volumes. This logical view of storage works with the NT File System (NTFS) and File Allocation Tables (FAT), which organize physical storage space.

Differential backup Partial backup of all changes that have occurred since the last full backup. It is faster to restore from differential backups than from incremental backups because all you need is the last full and differential backups.

During a backup interval, each subsequent daily differential backup is larger than the previous one because it includes all the changes since the full backup. By the last day in your backup interval, your differential backup may be very large.

If large files or a great number of files are changed daily, your daily differential backup may require more than one piece of media.

Copies files where the archive bit is turned on or set to 1. When the file is copied, differential backup leaves the archive bit set to on or 1, so the next differential backup copies the file as well.

See also **full backup** and **incremental backup**.

Disaster recovery A disaster recovery program lets businesses, municipalities, schools, and households get back to normal activities after a catastrophic interruption. Through failover to a parallel system, or by restoration of the failed system, disaster recovery restores the system to its normal operating mode.

Disk mirroring An exact duplication of disk contents on a separate disk to provide fault tolerance or quick access time or both.

DLT Digital Linear Tape.

DNA Direct Network Attached storage.

DVD Digital Video Disk.

E

EIDE Enhanced Integrated Drive Electronics. A standard electronic interface between a computer and its mass storage drives. Is an enhanced version of IDE. Enables addressing a hard disk larger than 528 megabytes. Also enables faster access to the hard drive, support for Direct Memory Access (DMA), and support for additional drives, including CD-ROM and tape devices through ATAPI. Adopted as a standard by American National Standards Institute (ANSI) in 1994. Also called ATA-2 and Fast ATA.

Encrypting File System Encrypting File System is a feature new to NTFS 5 volumes. A need for standardized strong encryption has not only existed for file protection but also for protecting files that have been backed up to remote media. Some backup utilities provide their own native encryption algorithms. With Windows 2000 EFS, you have a solid and secure encryption algorithm that will outlast your backup application.

Encryption Converting data into a cipher to make unauthorized access of the data difficult. Examples of ciphers include substituting for letters and numbers, rotating letters in the alphabet, and using a computer algorithm to rearrange data bits in a digital file.

Enterprise A large computer system that usually includes many personal computers connected by network to servers and remote data storage devices and can even include mainframes.

EPR Enhanced Partial Response channel. Advanced Partial Response Maximum

Likelihood (PRML) channel co-developed by Quantum and Lucent Technology/Bell Labs. Adapted to linear tape products.

F

FAT File Allocation Table filing system that divides the hard disk into clusters of bytes and then files data bit by bit into the clusters. A cluster only stores data from a single application or file. This has the potential to waste disk space. If the hard disk is larger than 2 gigabytes, FAT divides the drive into sections or partitions and treats each partition as a separate drive.

FAT32 File Allocation Table filing system that divides the hard disk into clusters of bytes and then files data bit by bit into the clusters. Because a cluster only stores data from a single application or file, FAT32 creates smaller clusters, reducing the potential for wasted disk space. If the hard disk is larger than 2 gigabytes, FAT32 formats the disk as a single, unpartitioned drive with a single drive letter.

Fault tolerance The ability to offer error-free, nonstop availability, usually by keeping a backup of the primary system. The backup system remains idle until it is needed to serve in place of the primary system.

See also **cluster**.

FC-AL Fibre Channel Arbitrated Loop.

Fibre Channel Based on an American National Standards Institute (ANSI) standard, provides a practical, inexpensive, and expandable method of using fiber-optic cabling for high-speed connections at longer distances to more devices per cable than Small Computer System Interface (SCSI). Is the new network technology of choice for high-end storage. Because Fibre Channel devices and protocols are hot-pluggable, they support dynamic addition and removal of hosts, devices, and paths without interrupting access to other data.

File migration Moving inactive files from a system to nearline storage on a less expensive but slower storage media. File migration keeps system hard disk capacity available for active files without deleting files from the system or archiving files to offline storage.

Files may be migrated from hard disk to optical disk or tape for simple file migration. Or files may be moved through a series of media, for example, from hard disk to optical disk and then to tape for HSM.

Unlike a file that is backed up or archived, a migrated file appears available to the user as though it were still physically on the system. A filename in the form of a file stub, tag, or placeholder remains visible, for example, on Windows Explorer. To recall a migrated file as an active file, the user selects the filename, and the file migration software moves the file back to the system. Except for a longer retrieval time, the file location appears to be unchanged.

Files are migrated when system data reaches a predefined threshold or watermark, which is a percent of total capacity. When the watermark is reached, files are migrated according to predetermined parameters, or migration policy. Migration parameters can include last time accessed, size, type, and others.

See also **HSM**.

File stub Filename on your system for a file that has been moved to secondary or tertiary storage. Appears like a file stored on your system. Enables you to access the file from secondary or tertiary storage as though it were on your system.

Firewall Programs and security policy that prevent unauthorized outside users from accessing a private network or intranet. Also controls which outside resources can be accessed by the intranet users.

Firewall software is usually installed on a gateway server at the network gateway.

A firewall can work with a router program or a proxy server. Working with a router program, a firewall filters all network packets to determine whether or not to forward them to their destination. Working with a proxy server, a firewall screens outgoing requests from network clients and incoming information from outside users.

There are a number of firewall screening methods. One method screens requests to make sure they come from acceptable, previously identified domain names and Internet Protocol (IP) addresses. Another method enables remote users to log onto the private network through secure logon procedures and authentication certificates.

FRS File Replication Service. Windows 2000 replacement for the Windows NT LMRepl service. In Windows 2000, FRS is used by domain controllers to replicate Active Directory and Sysvol data. FRS is also used by the Distributed File System service to replicated data between DFS replica sets.

Form factor The physical size of the tape drive, specified in inches or millimeters. Determines whether the drive fits into a system or operates as an external stand-alone subsystem.

The two most common form factors accommodated by systems are 3.5 inch and 5.25 inch.

Full backup A copy of any data on a system that you designate to be backed up, even data that has not changed since the last full backup. The data can include one file, one directory, or a complete system. Is usually the first backup session in a backup set.

A backup set combines a full backup with differential or incremental backups.

See also **incremental backup** and **differential backup**.

G

Gateway server A network node that acts as an entrance to another network. Gateway node examples include computers that control traffic within a network or at a local Internet Service Provider (ISP).

In the network for an enterprise, a computer server acting as a gateway node is often also acting as a proxy server and a firewall server.

Gigabyte Indicates a billion bytes of data storage capacity. Is 2 to the 30th power, or 1,073,741,824 bytes (decimal notation).

Grandfather-Father-Son A media rotation scheme, where Grandfather is the monthly full backup. Father is the weekly full backup. Son is the daily incremental or differential backup.

A total of 12 media sets are required for this basic rotation scheme, where:

3 grandfather sets, one each for months 1, 2, and 3.

5 father sets, one each for Friday of weeks 1 through 5.

4 son sets, one each for Monday through Thursday of each week.

The media is reused on the day, week, or month matching its label.

H

Hardware For data storage and management, hardware is the drive that mounts media and records and reads data. Includes hard disk, tape, optical disk, and other technology.

Helical recording technology Magnetic tape technology that records and reads digital data in diagonal stripes on a magnetic tape while the tape streams past the spinning head, from one end of the tape to the other without interruption. The tape drive wraps the magnetic tape partially around an angled, rotating drum. The read and write heads are aligned in the drum. The heads spin fast while the tape moves slowly. After any read or write operation, the head stops spinning to avoid excessive wear on the tape.

The diagonal recording pattern enables a very high data density. The read heads are just behind the write heads for "read-while-write verification," which ensures the data integrity of each data stripe.

The combination of spinning head and moving tape provides equal ware across the media.

The time required to stop and start the head spinning and then resynchronize on the data can be many seconds. As a result, helical tape devices are most efficient when they are constantly in use.

VCRs, 8 mm tape drives, and DAT use helical recording.

HiPPI High Performance Parallel Interface.

Host A computer, device, or program defined by its context, as follows:

On the Internet, any computer with full two-way access to other computers on the Internet. Has a unique Internet Protocol (IP) address. With Point to Point Protocol (PPP), you have a unique IP address during any connection to the Internet. During the connection, your computer is a host and a node in a network.

In mainframe computer environments, a mainframe computer, usually called a large server. The mainframe is a host provider of services to workstations attached to it.

In other contexts, a device or program that provides services to a smaller or less capable device or program.

HSM Hierarchical Storage Management software migrates files through a hierarchy of primary, secondary, and tertiary storage. Migration is determined by user-set parameters, such as file age and storage capacity used. Migrated files can be accessed via a file stub, tag, or placeholder on the system.

Data access response time and storage costs determine the appropriate combination of storage devises used in HSM. A typical three-tier strategy may include hard drives as primary storage, rewritable optical as the secondary storage type, and tape as the tertiary storage.

See also **file migration**.

Hub A hub acts like a repeater in that it takes in network requests and then broadcasts them to all the other connections to which it is attached. An analogy would be that a hub is a telephone party line where everyone can talk to each other at the same time. The only catch is that you must wait your turn to talk.

I

IDE Integrated Drive Electronics. Standard electronic interface between a computer motherboard's bus and the computer's disk storage devices. The disk drive controller is built into the logic board in the disk drive. Based on the IBM PC ISA 16-bit bus standard. Adopted as a standard by ANSI in November 1990.

Most computers sold today use an enhanced version of IDE called EIDE.

See also **EIDE** and **SCSI**.

Image backup A backup option that takes a "snapshot" of an entire system by writing a volume image to tape sector by sector, rather than file by file. This method of backup is fast and allows companies to back up critical information in a limited backup window.

Incremental backup A partial backup that supplements a full backup. An incremental backup includes only the files that have changed or been added since the last full or incremental backup.

A common scheme is to make a full backup on Friday and incremental backups Monday through Thursday. When Friday comes around again, you make a new full backup.

On average, an incremental backup takes less time than a differential or full backup because it includes fewer files. However, it takes longer to restore data from an incremental backup because the process requires the last full backup plus each incremental backup to the current. This restores all new files and the latest version of all files changed since the full backup.

A specific incremental backup session may be longer or shorter than its predecessor, depending on the number of file additions and changes that occurred since the preceding incremental backup session. If you change large files or many files, an incremental backup may require more than one piece of backup media.

An incremental backup copies files where the archive bit is turned on or set to 1. When the file is copied, incremental backup resets the archive bit to off or 0.

See also **differential backup** and **full backup**.

Interface A hardware or software protocol, contained in the electronics of the tape controller and tape drive, that manages the exchange of data between the drive and computer.

Internal data rate Speed at which data actually comes off the disk surface onto the buffer on the drive. Increases at 40 percent per year.

Internet A worldwide network of computer servers originally developed by the federal government as a communication system in the event of nuclear war or other wide-scale disaster.

Intranet A private version of the Internet that provides a cost-effective way to publish critical information and provide an interactive communication path for heterogeneous systems.

ISA Industry Standard Architecture. A standard bus architecture associated with the IBM AT motherboard. Enables 16 bits at a time between the motherboard and an expansion slot card and its associated devices.

J

JBOD Just a Bunch Of Disks.

L

Linear recording technology Magnetic tape technology that records and reads digital data in tracks that go the entire length of the one-half inch wide tape. The tape moves past the fixed heads in a straight line. When the end of the tape is reached, the heads are repositioned and the tape moves in the opposite direction to record a new set of tracks on the length of the tape. Has several subsets:

   Parallel tracks (original half-inch reels).

   Serial, serpentine tracks (QIC tape drives).

   Combined parallel and serial tracks (first-generation DLTtape drives).

   Herringbone parallel and serial tracks (next-generation DLTtape drives).

Parallel recording enables error recovery by automatically rewriting bad blocks to parallel channels. Herringbone pattern increases data density.

When the tape stops, neither the tape nor the head is moving. This reduces media wear and also provides a start time well under two seconds.

Is the primary recording technology for digital data for the last 30 years.

DLTtape, LTO, and QIC technologies use linear recording.

LTO Linear Tape Open initiative, proposed by IBM, Hewlett Packard, and Seagate. Multichannel, bidirectional serpentine read-write layout.

M

ME Media Metal Evaporative media, used by Sony in its AIT drives. The developers claim 80 to 100 percent availability of recording material with ME media, which leads to higher density recording.

Media Material used to store data. Most typically it's disk or tape, but it can also be paper. Tape uses magnetic storage technology. Disk may use magnetic or optical storage technology.

Media set All the pieces of media (tape cartridge or optical disk, for example) necessary to contain all the data resulting from a complete backup session. This backup session could be a full backup, an incremental backup, or a differential backup session. In other words, if one piece of media is not large enough (does not have enough capacity) to hold all the data in a particular backup session, then a second, third, and so on piece of media (depending on the size of the backup session) would be required to complete the backup session (hold all the data).

Megabyte Indicates a million bytes of data storage capacity. Is 2 to the 20th power, or 1,048,576 bytes (decimal notation).

Metadata Can mean a set of rules for using a programming language, such as Standard Generalized Markup Language (SGML) and Extensible Markup Language (XML). Can also mean a tag that encloses descriptive language about a collection of data, such as a Hypertext Markup Language (HTML) page.

MIC Memory In Cassette. This is a chip that is also a part of the AIT media that allows the drive to store data that can be used to help access data on tape faster.

Mirroring Having a duplicate set of data in primary storage, usually disk, to provide continuous data access, even if one disk becomes unavailable. There are two methods of redundancy: mirroring and parity striping.

Mirroring maintains full additional copies of the data on separate disks. Duplexing is a special form of mirroring across host controllers. It requires more than one controller and is available only in host-based software arrays.

MO Magneto-Optical Disk. A rewritable optical storage technology that uses a combination of magnetic and optical methods. Data is written on an MO disk by both a laser and a magnet. The laser heats the bit to the Curie point, which is the temperature at which molecules can be realigned when subjected to a magnetic field. A magnet then changes the bit's polarity. Writing takes two passes. An MO disk drive is used for nearline storage.

MRC heads Magneto Resistive Cluster heads. Cluster of small, cost-effective magneto-resistive tape heads that can deliver higher data-transfer rates and capacity than traditional MR heads of equal size. Used by Quantum on Super DLT tape.

N

NAS Network Attached Storage.

Native capacity The amount of data that can be stored on one data cartridge without data compression. Generally specified in megabytes or gigabytes.

For tape libraries, native capacity is the amount of data stored on one tape cartridge multiplied by the number of tape cartridges in the tape library. Because tape cartridges are removable, the capacity of the tape drive is virtually limitless.

NDIS Network Driver Interface Specification. Developed by Microsoft and 3Com to specify communication between communication protocols and network device drivers.

Nearline Referring to data stored on media, often optical disk or tape, so it is available almost immediately to the user. File migration and HSM move files to nearline storage.

See also **online** and **offline**.

Node In a network, a node is a connection point, either a redistribution point or an endpoint for data transmissions. In general, a node has programmed or engineered capability to recognize and process or forward transmissions to other nodes.

NTBackup (or Windows Backup) Software component to Windows 2000 provided by Seagate Software. Focuses on local backup. Supports standard backup and recovery APIs.

NTFS Windows NT system for storing and retrieving files on physical media. Is the equivalent of Windows 95 FAT. Organizes storage space on the hard disk into clusters that range from 512 bytes to 64 kilobytes. NTFS looks for contiguous storage space to hold an entire file, but the file can be divided into scattered clusters. NTFS keeps track of all parts of the file, whether in contiguous or scattered clusters. Works with DFS.

See also **DFS**.

O

Object In object-oriented design, an object is an instance of a class. Different objects of the same class are the concrete representations of the general description set up by the class. Each object may be slightly different in some way from other objects in the class, but all objects in the class share the features defined by the class. For example, in the class tape drives, all the object tape drives use tape, but some use half-inch tape, some use 4-millimeter tape, and some use other types of tape all together. By defining your tape drives, servers, operating systems, and other elements in your system as objects in their separate classes, you're defining a system that is easy to develop and use. Because all objects in a class share some characteristics, it is easy to integrate them into a system. Because an object carries its specific definitions, it's easy to design a system that accommodates diverse objects.

OEM Original Equipment Manufacturer.

Offline Referring to data stored on a medium, such as tape or paper, that is not available immediately to the user.

See also **nearline** and **online**.

Online Referring to data stored on the system so it is available immediately to the user.

See also **nearline** and **offline**.

Operating system Software that controls the basic operation of the computer. Provides the interface between the applications software and the computer hardware.

Optical disk Any storage method that uses a laser to store and retrieve data from media.

Optical jukebox A robotic device with one or more optical disk drives and shelves for optical media storage.

P

PCA Parallel Channel Architecture.

PCMCIA Personal Computer Memory Card International Association.

Peak transfer rate The number of megabytes transferred per second (MB/s) on the bus. Indicates interoperability with other equipment in the system.

PnP Plug and Play. With PnP, you can install a new piece of hardware, and the operating system will detect and identify the hardware. Windows 2000 PnP feature is projected to support hot-swapping.

Policy Criteria that you establish to automate data management. Disk capacity, file age, file type, and file size are examples of data characteristics used to set up data-management policies. Different file migration policies can be specified for different systems in a network. When policies are in place, data-management automation software acts on the data according to the policies.

Primary storage System media that stores data so it is immediately available to the user. Is usually a local hard disk.

Proxy server Separates the outside world, typically the Internet, from a network client. Increases the performance of services, such as Internet requests, and provides a more secure way to receive Internet information.

Push From the master copy on the central server, download an authorized and compatible copy of a piece of software over the network to a networked device.

Q

QIC Quarter-Inch Cartridge. They come in two general classes: full-size, also called *data-cartridge*, and mini-cartridge. These cartridges are designed to use a personal computer's existing floppy disk drive controller instead of a customized controller. Newest set of QIC standards are based on the Travan technology developed by 3M Corporation.

R

RAID Redundant Array of Inexpensive/Independent Disks. Parity striping or parity RAID combines striping with a calculation that enables re-creation of the data on a failed drive.

Recall Gaining access to a file that has been migrated to nearline storage. To recall a migrated file as an active file, the user selects the filename as displayed in the file system, and the file migration software moves the file back to the system. Except for a longer retrieval time, the file location appears to be unchanged.

Recording density The amount of data that can be recorded on the media, expressed as bits per inch (BPI).

RSS Remote Storage Service (RSS) is the Microsoft version of a Hierarchical Storage Manager (HSM). HSMs are great for large file servers running out of room. With an HSM, such as Windows 2000 RSS, you set a maximum capacity, as a percentage, for each hard disk. Once the high watermark (maximum capacity setting) percentage is reached, files that meet an age qualification (days since last accessed) are migrated to a form of remote storage media, such as a tape library.

See also **HSM.**

Reparse points A reparse point is a file attribute. They operate mainly at the I/O subsystem level, which basically means they work with the operating system and are transparent to the end user. When you click a file or folder that contains a reparse point, you are unknowingly redirected somewhere else to retrieve the file's or folder's data. Reparse points are new to Windows 2000 and thus are only supported on NTFS 5 volumes.

Restore Copying a file, directory, path, or drive to a computer system from backup media. A restore uses a backup created by a software backup utility. The backup software displays the file structure of the backup session. You select the file, directory, path, or drive you want to restore and then instruct the backup utility to restore this data to the system.

The data being restored can be as simple as one file or as complex as the entire system.

Retrieve Gaining access to data that has been archived to offline storage. To retrieve archived data, find the media where the data exists, mount the media in the appropriate drive, and retrieve the data to the system.

Rewind speed How fast the tape rewinds from the end to the beginning, expressed as inches per second (inches/s).

ROM A form of memory that cannot be changed in formal operational modes. Many different types are available. Computer control programs are often stored in ROM. ROM is not to be confused with RAM. RAM is not used for permanent information storage

RSM Removable Storage Manager (RSM) is a standard interface in Windows 2000 for accessing removable media, especially media located within changers, jukeboxes, and libraries. It was designed to simplify access to libraries of media in both stand-alone drives and in automated devices.

S

SAN Storage Area Networking.

SCSI Small Computer System Interface standard published by ANSI. It enables you to connect peripheral devices—including disk drives, tape drives, CD-ROM drives, printers, and scanners—to a computer.

Search speed How fast the tape moves when finding a specified file, expressed as inches per second (inches/s).

Secondary storage Media that stores data so it is available to the user, but maybe after a slight delay. Can be optical disk or tape. File migration and Hierarchical Storage Management (HSM) use secondary storage.

Shared-disk clustering Multiple machines simultaneously read and write disks to obtain and update data.

Shared-nothing clustering One machine reads and writes each disk at any time. A non-owner machine that needs to work with data on a disk sends a request to the owner that does the work. Multiple access provides increased system availability. If the owner dies, another machine takes over as the owner.

SIS Single Instance Storage is a feature that reduces the amount of disk space necessary when multiple Remote Installation Service (RIS) images are stored. If you are using RIS to deploy Windows 2000 Professional, SIS will run in the background on your RIS volume.

Sparse Files Files that take advantage of the NTFS 5 Sparse File Attribute can effectively save you a tremendous amount of disk space. Sparse data is considered to be streams of consecutive 0s. If you have data files with large volumes of sparse data, why store every 0? It would save a lot of room if the file system could understand the concept of thousands of consecutive 0s and simply make a note of the sparse strings when the data is saved.

Striping A technique used by RAID and RAIT technology to partition each drive into units. The stripes of the disks in the RAID are interleaved and addressed in order. The function of striping can either improved performance or improve reliability or both.

Sustained transfer rate The number of megabytes transferred per second (MB/s).

T

Tape cartridge The removable module that houses the magnetic tape that a tape drive writes data to and reads data from. Also called a *data cartridge*.

The tape is on reels in the cartridge and can remain entirely inside the cartridge, as with DAT, or can exit the cartridge and travel through the tape drive, as with DLTtape.

The tape drive and the tape cartridge work together as a system to ensure data integrity. A specific type of tape drive requires a specific type of tape cartridge, and the quality and condition of the tape cartridge and its tape are as important to data integrity as the tape drive.

Tape library A system that uses a robotic mechanism to automatically load and unload tape cartridges into one or more tape drives. Distinguishable from stackers and autoloaders in their ability to provide random access to tape cartridges.

See also **autoloader**.

Terabyte One trillion bytes or 1,000 gigabytes.

Threshold The capacity limit established by the user for the system disk. Also called the *watermark*, the threshold causes file migration to occur in systems where disk capacity reaches the threshold.

Tower of Hanoi A backup media rotation scheme named after an ancient Chinese game. In the game, you move a stack of disks from one peg to another peg, disk by disk. A smaller disk can only be placed on a larger disk.

In the backup rotation method, each media set is used a different number of times. A 16-day rotation uses five sets, where the first set is used every other day, and sets 2, 3, and 4 are used every fourth, eighth, and sixteenth days. The fifth media set is used on alternating sixteenth days.

Travan Developed by 3M Corporation. Standardized by the Quarter Inch Cartridge (QIC) consortium. Is backward-compatible with older QIC standards. Doubled the capacities available on QIC tapes by increasing tape length and width.

U

UDF Universal Disk Format. File system that enables files to be added to a CD-R or CD-RW one at a time using packet writing and that enables individual files to be erased from a CD-RW. It also handles large capacity disks, such as DVD.

UPS Uninterruptible Power Supply.

USN Update Sequence Number. Assigned by Microsoft Windows 2000 NT File System (NTFS) to change log process to a file when a change to data or file attributes occurs.

V

VLM Very Large Memory. Windows 2000 supports 64-bit VLM, which lets 64-bit processors access up to 32 gigabytes of RAM. This feature will be part of Intel's 64-bit Merced system.

Volume mount points Volume mount points are similar to junction points, with the exception that they are used to link a folder to a volume (disk drive) instead of linking a folder to another folder.

VSM Virtual Storage Manager.

W

Watermark The capacity limit established by the user for the system disk. Also called the *threshold*, the watermark causes file migration to occur in systems where disk capacity reaches the watermark.

WORM Write-Once, Read-Many optical disk technology for nearline storage.

WSH Windows Scripting Host. A shell that supports multiple scripting languages, including Visual Basic and Java. Provides APIs so developers can create ActiveX-based scripting engines for other languages.

WMI Windows Management Instrumentation. A Web-based Enterprise Management (WBEM-based) mechanism designed by Microsoft for raising and managing events.

Index

Note to the Reader: Throughout this index **boldfaced** page numbers indicate primary discussions of a topic. *Italicized* page numbers indicate illustrations.

A

ablative WORM disks, 34
access operation, 427
access time, 427
active-active clusters, **224**, *225*, **234–235**, *234*
active copper, 153
Active Directory, 427
  backup considerations, **275–277**
  in clustering, **239**
  with Exchange 2000, **360**
  with NAS, **188**
  restoring, **294–296**
Active Directory Installation wizard, 290
Active Directory Sites and Services snap-in
  for domain controllers, 289
  for Recovery Agents groups, **312–313**, *313*
active-passive clusters, **224**, *224*, **232–234**, *232–233*
active portion of SQL transaction logs, 383
active termination, **129–130**
Add a New Replica dialog box, 65, *65*
Add Excluded Files dialog box, 283, *284*
Add Mirror option, 215, *215*, 219
Add New Drive Letter or Path dialog box, 49, *49*
Add New option, 283
/Add option for clusters, 260
Add Recovery Agent Wizard, 317
Add/Remove Snap-in window, 306
Add/Remove Windows Components, 100
Add Standalone Snap-in window, 306
/Adddependency option, 265
/Addowner option, 265
Administrator File Recovery Certificates, **306–309**
Advanced Attributes dialog box, 67, *67*, 303, *304*
Advanced Backup Options dialog box
  for Exchange 5.5, 342, *342*
  for Exchange 2000, 365, *365*

Advanced Intelligent Tape (AIT), **30**
Advanced Metal Power (AMP) media, 427
Advanced Restore Options dialog box, 291–292, *292*
Advanced Restore Options page, 286, *286*
Advanced tab
  for clustering, 258, *258*
  for DHCP, 321, *321*
  for Exchange 5.5, 338, *339*
Affect the Group property, 256
AFM (Atomic Force Microscopy), 423
AIT (Advanced Intelligent Tape), **30**
allocate command, 99
allocated media, 17
allocation policies for media pools, **78**
Allow Failback option, 255
Allow Failback Between option, 253
Allow Failback Immediately option, 253
Allow Users to Assume Primary Role option, 408
Always replace the file on disk option, 286
Always Replace the File on My Computer option, 302
AMP (Advanced Metal Power) media, 427
Append This Backup to the Media option, 364
appliances
  NAS, **186–189**
  SAN, **168–169**
application media pools, 74, **76–77**, *77*
Arbitrated Loop Fibre Channel, **154–156**, *155*
ARC path associations, 272, *272*
archive attribute, **20–21**
archive bit, 428
archiving, **427–428**
ASR (Automatic System Recovery), **421**
Assign the Following Drive Letter option, 244
asymmetric SAN appliances, 168
asynchronous SCSI, **134**

Atomic Force Microscopy (AFM), 423
Authoritative Restore Confirmation dialog box, **294–296**
authoritative restores
  in Exchange 5.5, **351**
  in FRS, **59–61**
  in Windows 2000, **292–294**, *293*
authrest.exe program, 351
autochk.exe file, 270
autoloader system, 428
automatic operations
  cluster restarts, 232
  DHCP database restores, **323–324**, *323–324*
  replication, **65–66**
  WINS backup, **328–329**, *328*
Automatic System Recovery (ASR), **421**
automation, 428
availability
  defined, 17
  SAN, **160–161**, *161*
available media, 17
Axiom's Constant, 36

B

Back Up Database option, 329
backing up. *See* backups
Backup a Database option, 400
Backup Alerts setting, 408
Backup command in T-SQL, **403–405**
Backup Database during Server Shutdown option, 329
Backup dialog box, 278
Backup Domain Controllers (BDCs), 352
Backup Exec program, 351
Backup Express product, 185
backup folder for DHCP, **322–323**
backup intervals, 428
Backup Job Information dialog box
  for Exchange 5.5, 341, *341*, 344, *344*
  for Exchange 2000, **364–365**, *365*
backup markers, 21

Backup media pools, 110, *111*
Backup program, 11
  for Exchange 5.5, 340–344, *341–342*, *344*
  for Exchange 2000, 363–365, *364*
  for nonauthoritative restores, 291
  for RSS data, **110–111**, *110–111*
  for scheduled backups, 281
Backup Progress dialog box, 344, *344*
Backup/Restore tab, 95, *96*
backup sessions, 428
backup sets, **428–429**
Backup tab
  for Exchange 5.5, 340, *341*
  for Exchange 2000, 363–364, *364*
backup windows, 429
Backup Wizard, 278
backups, **274–275**, **428**
  database
    DHCP, 324
    RSM, 96–98, *97*
    RSS, **114**
  encrypted files, 320
  Exchange 5.5, 336–337
    Backup for, 340–344, *341–342*, *344*
    brick-level, 355, *356*
    offline, 337–340, *339*
  Exchange 2000, 363–365, *364–365*
  filters for, 282–283, *283–284*
  full, **275–277**
  NAS, 189
  NDMP, 180
  open files in, 277–278
  restoring. *See* restores
  schedules for, 278–284, *279–284*
  SQL
    differential, **388**
    Enterprise Manager for, **399–403**, *399*, *401–403*
    logical backup devices for, **398–400**, *399–400*
    strategies, **393–398**, *395*
    T-SQL for, **399–400**, *400*, *403–405*
    types, 391–393
  strategies, 20
    NAS, **182–186**, *183–185*
    options, **21–23**, *22*
    rotation, **23–28**
    SQL, **393–398**, *395*
  verifying, **284**
  for WINS, 328–329, *328*

.bak extension, 114
bandwidth, 429
bar code, 18
basic disks, **211–212**, *213*
BDCs (Backup Domain Controllers), 352
BIOS information, documenting, 299
.bkf extension, 340
Blocksize option, 403
Blue Laser, 423
boot.ini file
  fixing, **273**
  with RAID, 218
  replacing, 274
boot sectors, writing, 271
brick-and-mortar companies, 2
brick-level backups
  in Exchange 5.5, **355**, *356*
  in Exchange 2000, 376
bridges in SAN, 157–158
Bring Online option, 250
Brocade Communications Systems
  SAN perspectives, **158–159**
  benefits, **159–164**, *161*, *164*
  switches, **164–166**, *166*
browsing RSS data, **109–111**, *110–111*
BudTool product, 185
Buffer-to-Buffer flow control, 153
bulk logged recovery model, **389–390**
burst rate
  defined, 429
  in SCSI, 139
bus analyzers, 139
bytes, 429

C

CA Identifying Information page, 311, *311*
cables
  cluster, 223, 228
  SCSI, **132–134**, 137
caches in Exchange 5.5, 332
/cancel option, 53
capacity, 429
capital expenditures with SANs, 159
cartridges, cleaning, **91–92**
CAs (Certificate Authorities), **310–311**, *311*
Catalog.wci folder, 55
catalogs, tape, 6
CAV (Constant Angular Velocity) technology, 429
CCS (Common Command Set), 121

CCW (Continuous Composite Write) WORM disks, 34
CD-R (Compact Disc Recordable), 33–34
CD-ROM autoloaders, 429
CD-ROM jukeboxes
  defined, 429
  in RSM, **93**
CD-RW (Compact Disc Rewriteable), 34
CD towers, 429
Central Processing Unit (CPU) for clustering, 229
Centronics50 connectors, 142
.cer extension, 315–317
Certificate Authorities (CAs), **310–311**, *311*
Certificate dialog box, 316, *316*
Certificate Export Wizard, 307–308, *308*, *316*, *317*
Certificate Import Wizard, 308–309, *309*
Certificate Information dialog box, 316
Certificate Request Wizard, 315
Certificate Server, 306, 310–311
Certificate Services option, 310
Certificate Templates folder, 313
certificates, file recovery, **306–309**, *307–309*
  adding, **317–318**, *318*
  exporting, 307–308, *307–308*, **315–316**, *316–317*
  importing, **308–309**, *309*
  requesting, **314–315**
Certificates folder, 308–309
Certificates snap-in, 306
Change Drive Letter and Paths for Data dialog box, 49
Change Drive Letter or Paths dialog box, 244, *245*
Change Journal, 20, **54–55**, **429**
Check Database Integrity option, 407
Check Integrity tab, 94, *95*
Check mode for isinteg, 338
Check and Fix mode for isinteg, 338
checkpoint files, 333, 335
chkdsk command, **270**, *270*
CIFS (Common Internet File System), **176–177**
cipher utility, **68**
circular logging
  in Exchange 5.5, 333, 335, 359
  in Exchange 2000, 363

classes of service in Fibre Channel, 152
CLB (component load balanced) clusters, **226–227**
Cleaner Management Wizard, 92
cleaning cartridges for RSM libraries, **91–92**
cleaning RSM libraries and single drives, **92**, *92*
client file systems in NAS, 173
Cluster Properties dialog box, 249
Cluster Service Configuration Wizard, **245–247**, *246*
Cluster Service option, 247
clusters and clustering, 19, **221–222**, **429–430**
    Cluster Administrator, **247–248**, *248*
        for groups, **248–255**, *251*, *253–254*
        for resources, **255–259**, *257–259*
    cluster command, **259–260**
        cluster group command, **262–263**
        cluster network command, **263**
        cluster node command, **263–264**
        cluster resource command, **265–266**
        options, **260–261**
    configuring, **222–223**
        component load balanced clusters, **226–227**
        network load balanced clusters, **225–226**, *226*
        server clusters, **223–224**, *223–225*
    deployment
        Active Directory issues, **239**
        compatibility and system requirements, **229–230**
        failover planning, **238–239**
        model selection, **230–236**, *231–235*
    installing, **239**
        clustering service, **245–247**, *246*
        domain accounts, **242–244**
        drive letter assignment, **244**, *245*
        failover verification, **247**
        hardware preparation, **240**
        network settings, **241–242**, *242*

resources and groups for, **227–228**, **236–238**
with SANs, 159
single points of failure in, **228–229**
CLV (Constant Linear Velocity) technology, 430
CMOS information, documenting, 299
COM (Component Object Model), 188, 226–227
COM+, 227
Common Command Set (CCS), 121
Common Internet File System (CIFS), **176–177**
communications, cluster, 222
Compact Disc Recordable (CD-R), 33–34
Compact Disc Rewriteable (CD-RW), 34
compatibility, 16
    in clustering deployment, **229–230**
    in SCSI, 125
Completed operator requests, 89
Completing the Certificate Request Wizard window, 315
component load balanced (CLB) clusters, **226–227**
Component Object Model (COM), 188, 226–227
Components tab, 84, *85*
compressed capacity, 430
compression ratios, 36–37
Computer Management
    for Indexing Service, 56, *56*
    for operating system rebuilds, 301
Configure tab, 96
Confirm Attribute Changes dialog box, 304, *304*
conflicts, DHCP, **320–324**, *321*, *323–324*
connectivity, 16
Constant Angular Velocity (CAV) technology, 429
Constant Linear Velocity (CLV) technology, 430
Contains Media of Type option, 78
Continuous Composite Write (CCW) WORM disks, 34
converting basic disks to dynamic disks, **212**, *213*
copper
    in Fibre Channel, **149–150**
    in GBIC, 153

copy backups, 22
    in Exchange 5.5, 343
    in RSS, **108–109**, *108–109*
    in SQL, **388**, **410–411**, *411*
copy command, 270–271
Copy Database Wizard, **388**, **410–411**, *411*
corrupted log files, 350
costs
    in NAS, **172–173**
    in SANs, 159
CPU (Central Processing Unit) for clustering, 229
Create a New Dfs Link dialog box, 64, *65*, **117**, *117*
Create a New Media Pool Properties dialog box, 76–77, *77*
Create a Stand-Alone Dfs Root option, 116
Create an Emergency Repair Disk command, 268
/Create option
    for cluster, 260
    for cluster group, 262
    for cluster resource, 265
Create Media Pool option, 76
Create Volume option, 213, 215–216
Create Volume Wizard, 213, *214*, 215–216
createpool command, 99
cross-platform environments in NAS, 174
crossover cables, 223

D

Dahl, Greg, 173
Dahlmeier, Michael, 35
daily backups, 23, **343**
daisy chains, 123
DAS (Direct Attached Storage), **8–9**, *8*
DAT (Digital Audio Tape), **30–31**, 430
data centers, 430
data compression, 430
Data Consistency Adjuster, **338–340**, *339*, 352
data files in SQL, **383–384**, 393
Data Management Application (DMA), **179–180**
data management software, 16
data protection method, **36–39**
data storage method, **35–39**
data transfer rate, 17

database.edb file, 360
Database Load State setting, 408
Database Maintenance Plan Wizard, 406–410, *406–409*
Database Maintenance Plans object, 406
Database Restore Flag, 323, *323*
database.stm file, 360
databases
    DHCP, 320–324, *321*, *323–324*
    Exchange 5.5
        restore errors, 350
        sets, 334
        structure, 334–336, *336*
    RSM
        backing up and recovering, 96–99, *97*
        integrity checking, 93–94, *94*
        managing, 94–96, *95–96*
    RSS, 114, 279
    SQL, 381–382
        backing up, 394–396, *395*
        copying, 410–411, *411*
        replicated, 397–398
        restoring, 412–414, *414*
    WINS, 329
DBO_Only option, 416
dcpromo program, 61, 290
DDS (Digital Data Storage), 30, 430
deallocate command, 99
deallocated media, 17
deallocation policies for media pools, 78
decryption keys, 305
default filegroups, 384
deferred dismounts, 87
defragmentation, 430
/delete option
    for cluster group, 262
    for cluster resource, 265
Deleted Item Retention
    in Exchange 5.5, 353–355, *354*
    in Exchange 2000, 375–376, *375*
Deleted Items folder, 354, 376
deletepool command, 99
delrp utility, 47–48
Deny Disk Space to Users Exceeding Quota Limit option, 68
dependencies in clustering, 237–238, 256–257
Dependencies tab, 257
Description option, 403
Desired Free Space setting, 100
device drivers for RSM libraries, 82–83, *82*
device-independence in SCSI, 122

Device Info tab, 86, *86*
Device Information tab, 87
Device Manager
    for clustering, 240
    for RSM, 79–80, *80*, 83
    for SCSI, 136, *136*
devices in NAS, 198
Dfs (Distributed File System), 62–63, 430–431
    enabling, 63–64, *64*
    links for, **64**, *65*
    recovery considerations, 326–327, *326*
    replicas in, 65–66, *65*
    and RSS, 114–118, *115–118*
    Structure Tables in, 326–327, *326*
Dfs Root Wizard, 63–64, *64*
dfscmd command, 327
DHCP database recovery, 320–324, *321*, *323–324*
dhcp.mdb file, 322
DHCP Server Properties dialog box, 321, *321*
dhcpserv.dmp file, 322
dial-up connections, 228
differential backups, 21–22, **431**
    in Exchange 5.5, 343
    in SQL, **388**, 392
Differential option for T-SQL backup, 403
differential restores in SQL, 412
differential SCSI, **125–128**, *128*, 130
Digital Audio Tape (DAT), 30–31, 430
Digital Data Storage (DDS), 30, 430
Digital Linear Tape (DLT), 31
Digital Storage Technology (DST), 31
Digital Tape Format (DTF), 32
Digital Versatile Disc Random Access Memory (DVD-RAM), 34
Digital Versatile Disc Read/Write (DVD-RW/DVD+RW), 34
Digital Versatile Disc Recordable (DVD-R), 34
dir.edb (Directory Store) file, **334**
dir.pat file, 333
Direct Attached Storage (DAS), 8–9, *8*
Directory Service/Information Store (DS/IS) Consistency Adjuster, 338–340, *339*, 352
Directory Store (dir.edb) file, **334**
disable command, 271

Disable NetBIOS over TCP/IP option, 241
disabling
    EFS, **318–319**
    services, **271**
disaster recovery, 431. *See also* recovery; restores
disaster tolerance with SANs, 159
/disasterrecovery switch, 370
Disk Management for volume mount points, 49
diskmap utility, **299**, *299*
disks and disk systems
    basic and dynamic, **211–212**, *213*
    cluster, 222
    configuration information for, **299**, *299*
    documentation for, 298
    moving, **216–217**
    quotas, **68–70**, *69–70*
    RAID. *See* RAID (Random/Redundant Array of Independent/Inexpensive Disks)
    RSM, 87, **92**, *92*
    sharing, **167–168**
    spanning, 202
    terminology for, **18**
    usage information, 69
    virtual, **48**
diskuse utility, **69–70**, *70*
dismount command, 99
dismounting, 18
Display a List of Known Drivers option, 82
Distributed File System (Dfs), **62–63**, 430–431
    enabling, 63–64, *64*
    links for, **64**, *65*
    recovery considerations, 326–327, *326*
    replicas in, 65–66, *65*
    and RSS, 114–118, *115–118*
    Structure Tables in, 326–327, *326*
Distribution SQL databases, 397–398
DllCache folder, 51–52
DLT (Digital Linear Tape), 31
DMA (Data Management Application), 179–180
Do Not Permanently Delete Mailboxes and Items option, 376
Do not replace the file on the disk option, 286

Do Not Restart property, 256
documentation
   for clustering, **236–237**
   for disk systems, 298–299, *299*
   for Exchange 2000, **376**
   for SQL backups, 394
domain accounts for clustering, **242–244**
domain-based roots, 63
domain controllers
   in Exchange 5.5, 347, 352
   recovering, **288–294**, *292–293*
doors, 18
down-level client support in RSS, **111–112**
Draw Media from Free Media Pool option, 78
drive letters
   in clustering, **244**, *245*
   displaying, 272
   for mount points, 49
Driver tab, 82
drivers for RSM libraries, **82–83**, *82*
drives. *See* disks and disk systems
DS/IS (Directory Service/Information Store) Consistency Adjuster, **338–340**, *339*, 352
DSADATA folder, 337, 348
DST (Digital Storage Technology), **31**
DTF (Digital Tape Format), **32**
dual fabric arrangements, 161, *161*
duplexing, 205
DVD-R (Digital Versatile Disc Recordable), 34
DVD-RAM (Digital Versatile Disc Random Access Memory), 34
DVD-RW/DVD+RW (Digital Versatile Disc Read/Write), 34
dynamic disks, **211–212**, *213*
dynamic drive sharing, **167–168**
dynamic scalability, 160

E

e-mail inhibited state, 331
E_ports, 152
edb.chk file, 275
.edb database, 333, 335
edb*.log files, 275, 332
edbutil.exe utility, 350
Edit Schedule dialog box, 401, *401*
editing backup schedules, **281**, *282*
EFS (Encrypting File System), **66–68**, *67*, 431
   backing up and restoring files in, 320
   considerations in, **304–305**
   disabling, **318–319**
   encrypting data in, **303–304**, *304*
   Enterprise CAs, **310–311**, *311*
   File Recovery Certificates in, **306–309**, *307–309*
   Recovery Agents in. *See* Recovery Agents
EFS Recovery Agent option, 315
EFS Recovery Certificates dialog box, 313
EIDE (Enhanced Integrated Drive Electronics) interface, 431
8mm tape technology, 427
eject command, 99
Eject Media Wizard, 91
ejectatapi command, 99
electrical compatibility in SCSI, 125
Electromagnetic Interference (EMI), 150
EMC NAS, **199**
Emergency Repair Disks (ERDs), **267–268**
   ASR as replacement for, **421**
   creating, **268–269**, *269*
   for server repair, **273–274**
   Windows 2000 Repair option for, **269–273**, *270*, *272*
enable command, **271**
Enable/Disable option, 196
Enable Library option, 84
Enable Quota Management option, 68
Encrypt Contents to Secure Data option, 67, 303
Encrypted Data Recovery Agents folder, 317–319, *318*
Encrypted Data Recovery Certificates, 306
encryption, 431. *See also* EFS (Encrypting File System); Recovery Agents
End-to-End flow control, 153
Enhanced Integrated Drive Electronics (EIDE) interface, 431
Enhanced Partial Response (EPR) channel, 431–432
Enterprise CAs, **310–311**, *311*
Enterprise Manager for SQL, **385**, *385*
   backups, **399–403**, *399*, *401–403*
   restores, **414–415**, *415–416*
enterprises
   defined, 431
   terminology, **19**

EPR (Enhanced Partial Response) channel, 431–432
Erase All Existing Data option, 346, 348, 352
ERDs (Emergency Repair Disks), **267–268**
   ASR as replacement for, **421**
   creating, **268–269**, *269*
   for server repair, **273–274**
   Windows 2000 Repair option for, **269–273**, *270*, *272*
error messages in diskuse, 69
eseutil utility
   for Exchange 5.5, **350–351**
   for Exchange 2000, 370
Event Viewer
   for Exchange 5.5, 350
   for Exchange 2000, 368, *369*
/evict option, 264
Evict Node option, 250
evicting cluster nodes, **249–250**, 264
Exabyte 8mm tape, **32**
Exchange 5.5, **331–332**
   backups, **336–337**
      Backup for, **340–344**, *341–342*, *344*
      brick-level, **355**, *356*
      offline, **337–340**, *339*
   best practices for, **359**
   database structure and file locations, **334–336**, *336*
   log files, **332–334**
   and NAS, 190
   restores, **345–347**, *345–347*
      full, **347–351**, **356–359**, *358*
      mailbox, **351–355**, *354*, *356*
      offline backups, **337–338**
Exchange 2000
   and Active Directory, 360
   backups, **363–365**, *364–365*
   best practices for, **376**
   and NAS, 190
   resources for, 377
   restores, **365–369**, *366–369*
      full, **369–371**
      mailbox, **371–376**, *375*
   storage groups in, 360, **362**, *362*
   stores in, **361–362**
   System State in, **360–361**, **369–370**
   tips for, **362–363**
Exchange Optimizer, 349
Exclude Files tab, 283, *283*
Exmerge utility, 374
expandability, 16
expanders in SCSI, 126, 132

Expiredate option, 404
expiring passwords, 243–244
Exponential Backup method, 26
Export NTMS Database API, **95**, 97
exporting
 Recovery Certificates, 307–308, **307–308**, **315–316**, **316–317**
 RSM media, **91**
ExportNtmsDatabase API, **95**, 97
Extend Volume option, 216
Extend Volume Wizard, 216
external SCSI cables, **133–134**
external SCSI termination, 130–131, **131**

F

F_ports, 152
Fabric Shorted Path First (FSPF) algorithm, 162
fabrics, **156–157**, *156*, 161, *161*
/Fail option, 265
failback in clustering
 considerations, 239
 settings, 251–255, *254*
Failback tab, *254*, **255**
failover in clustering, 221, 223
 planning, **238–239**
 settings, 251–253, *254*
 verifying, 247
Failover tab, 253, *254*
Fast option, 83
Fast Repair option, **273**
Fast SCSI, **135**
FAT (File Allocation Table) file system, 432
FAT32 file system, 432
fault tolerance, 16, 432
 in Dfs, **65–66**, *65*
 in Exchange 5.5, 335–336
 in RAID 0, 204
 in RAID 1, 205
 in RAID 5, 207
 in RAID 10, 207
 in RAID 50, 209
 in SANs, 159
FCIA (Fibre Channel Industry Association), 148
Fibre Channel, **148**, 432
 benefits, **148–149**
 specifications, **151–153**
 topologies
  Arbitrated Loop, **154–156**, *155*

fabrics, **156–157**, *156*
 Point-to-Point, **154**, *154*
 types, **149–151**, *150*
Fibre Channel Industry Association (FCIA), 148
field replaceable units (FRUs), 165
50-pin SCSI connectors, **133**
File Allocation Table (FAT) file system, 432
file markers, 21
file migration, **432**
File option for T-SQL restore, 417
File Recovery certificates, **306–309**, *307–309*
 exporting, **315–316**, *316–317*
 requesting, **314–315**
File Replication Service (FRS), **59–62**
 defined, 433
 encryption with, 67
file signatures, 51
file stubs, 433
filegroups in SQL, **384–385**, 393
filers in NAS, 172
files
 backing up. *See* backups
 in Exchange 5.5, **334–336**, *336*
 restoring. *See* restores
Files Larger Than setting, 100
FilesNotToBackup key, 282
filters
 for backups, **282–283**, *283–284*
 in operating system rebuilds, **300–301**
 in RSS, **103–104**
Find GUID tab, 96
firewalls, 433
firmware, 34
fixboot command, **271**
fixed hard disks, 35
fixmbr command, **271–272**
FL_ports, 152
floppy disks, 35
flow control in Fibre Channel, 153
folders
 for EFS, 67
 for Indexing Service, **56**, *56*
 restoring, **285–286**, *285–286*
/force option, 264
Foreign state, 217
forklift upgrades, 160
form factor, 433
Format option, 404
Free system media pools, **75**
Friend, Gaylord, 357
FRS (File Replication Service), **59–62**

defined, 433
encryption with, 67
FRUs (field replaceable units), 165
FSPF (Fabric Shorted Path First) algorithm, 162
full backups, 21–22, 433
 Active Directory considerations, **275–277**
 in Exchange 5.5, 342
 options for, **275**
 in SQL, **391–392**, 405
Full option for RSM libraries, 83
full recovery model in SQL, 389
full restores
 in Exchange 5.5, **347–351**, *356–359*, *358*
 in Exchange 2000, **369–371**
 in SQL, 412
fully qualified domain names, 240
future of storage, **419**
 holographic storage, **424**
 millipede technology, **423**
 news about, **425–426**
 optical improvements, **423**
 tunneling and iSCSI, **422–423**
 virtualization, **424–425**
 Windows XP/.NET, **420–422**

G

Gadzoox Networks, 167
Galaxy product, 185, 351, 355, *356*
gateway servers, 433
gateways in SAN, 157
GBICs (Gigabit Interface Converters), **153–154**, 157
General tab
 for clustering, 253, *253*, 257, *257*
 for EFS, 303
 for media pools, 76, *77*
 for recovery certificates, 316, *316*
 for RSM, 83, *84*, 87, *88*
 for RSS, 104–105, *105–106*
 for WINS backups, **328–329**, *328*
Gigabaud Link Module (GLM), **153–154**
Gigabit Ethernet, 149
Gigabit Interface Converters (GBICs), **153–154**, 157
gigabytes, 433
GLM (Gigabaud Link Module), **153–154**
global storage center theory, 425
Globally Unique Identifiers (GUIDs)

defined, 16–17
in RSM, 96
Grandfather-Father-Son rotation
method, **23–26**, **433–434**
Group Policy Objects, 319
groups
for clustering, **227–228**, **236–238**
bringing online and offline,
250–251, *251*
cluster command for,
248–249
creating, **250**
properties of, **251–255**,
253–254
rights for, **248–249**
in Exchange 2000, 360, **362**, *362*
for Recovery Agents, **311–313**,
312–314
growth
in SANs, 160
in storage, **2–7**
GUIDs (Globally Unique Identifiers)
defined, 16–17
in RSM, 96

H

HAL (Hardware Abstraction Layer),
302–303
hardware
defined, 434
in operating system rebuilds,
300–303, *300*, *302*
Hardware Compatibility List (HCL),
229
hardware RAID, **209–210**
hardware zoning, 163
HBAs (Host Bus Adapters), 123, 157
HCL (Hardware Compatibility List),
229
HD50 connectors, 142
HD68 connectors, 142
headless setups, 188
heartbeats in clustering, 222–223
helical recording technology, 29, **434**
heterogeneous NAS appliances, 178
Hierarchical Storage Management
(HSM), 43–44, *44*, **434–435**
HiFD (High Capacity Floppy Disk),
35
high-voltage differential (HVD)
SCSI, **125–128**, *128*
holographic storage, **424**
hop counts in SANs, 162
Host Bus Adapters (HBAs), 123, 157
hosts

defined, **434**
in NDMP, 179
hosts file, 240
hot-pluggable Fibre Channel, 149
hot-spares in Exchange 5.5,
357–359, *358*
HP OmniBack II format, 76
HSM (Hierarchical Storage
Management), 43–44, *44*,
434–435
hubs, 435
in SAN, 157
in SPF, 229
HVD (high-voltage differential)
SCSI, **125–128**, *128*
hybrid cluster model, **235–236**, *235*
HyperTerminal, **193–195**, 197

I

IDE (Integrated Drive Electronics)
interface, 435
IDs
GUIDs, 16–17, 96
SCSI, **124–125**, *124*
SIDs, 347
image backups, 435
Import Foreign Disks option, 217
Import system media pools, **75**
importing
recovery certificates, **308–309**,
309
RSM media, **91**
in-band SAN management, 168
inactive portion of SQL transaction
logs, 383
Include/Exclude Rules tab, 103, *103*
incremental backups, 21–22, **435**
in Exchange 5.5, **343**
scheduling, **280–281**, *281*
Indexing Service, **55–57**, *56–57*
Industry Standard Architecture (ISA),
436
information stores, **334**
INIT option, 404
initiators in SCSI, 122
Inspect Boot Sector option, **274**
Inspect Startup Environment option,
274
installing
clustering, **239**
clustering service, **245–247**,
246
domain accounts, **242–244**
drive letter assignment, **244**,
245

failover verification, **247**
hardware preparation, **240**
network settings, **241–242**,
242
RSS, **100**
Integrated Drive Electronics (IDE)
interface, 435
integrity
of RSM databases, **93–94**, *94*
of SQL backups, 392
intercabinet copper, 149
interfaces, 435
internal data rate, 435
internal SCSI cables, **133**
internal SCSI termination, **130–131**,
131
Internet, 435–436
interoperability in NAS, 174, 180,
188
intracabinet copper, 149
intraday snapshots, 192
intranets, 436
inventories, RSM library, **91**
IP addresses
in clustering, 225–226, 240, 256
DHCP database recovery for,
320–324, *321*, *323–324*
IP Storage (iSCSI), 200, **422–423**
"Is Alive" Poll Interval property, 256
ISA (Industry Standard Architecture),
436
iSCSI (IP Storage), 200, **422–423**
isinteg program, **337–338**, 350
Issue Certificates folder, 315

J

Jaz disks, 35
JBOD (Just a Bunch of Disks),
202–203
jetpack utility, **323**
Join an Existing Site option, 348
junction points, 46–48
Just a Bunch of Disks (JBOD),
202–203

K

Keep_Replication option, 417
Kerberos for NAS, 188
KeysNotToRestore key, 300
KMS (Key Management Service),
377

L

L_ports, 152
label types for OMIDs, 76
LAN backups in NAS, **182–183**, *183*
LAN Connection Properties dialog box, 241–242, *242*
LAN-free backups in NAS, 184
Laser Servo 120 (LS-120) disks, 35
lasers, 423
Last Backup Set option, 367
Last Known Good Configuration option, 274
Last Restore Set option, 370
latency
 in Data Consistency Adjuster, 340
 defined, 17
.ldf files, 383
Leave Database Nonoperational option, 415
Leave Database Operational option, 415
Leave Database Read-Only option, 415
LegacyExchangeDN attribute, 372–373
Leitner, Jeff, 423
length of SCSI cable, 132
libraries
 in media management, 38–39
 for NAS backups, 184, *184*
 for RSM, **82–87**, *82*, *84–86*, *88*
  cleaning, **92**, *92*
  cleaning cartridges for, 91–92
  inventories, 91
 in SANs, **167–168**
 terminology, **18–19**
licensing in clustering, **237**
Limit Reallocations option, 78
linear recording technology, 29, **436**
Linear Tape Open (LTO) initiative, **436**
Linkd utility, **45–46**, *47*
links
 for Dfs, **64**, *65*
 for SPF, 229
/List option, 260
/Listdependencies option, 265
/listinterfaces option
 for cluster network, 263
 for cluster node, 264
/Listowners option, 265
listsvc command, **272**
LMRepl Service, 59

load balancing
 in cluster models, **225–227**, *226*, **234–235**, *234*
 in Dfs, **65–66**
local backups in Exchange 5.5, 336
log shipping, **387–388**, **406–410**, *406–409*
Log Shipping Schedules page, 408, *409*
logic analyzers, 139
logical backup devices, **398–400**, *399–400*
logical block addressing, 120
Logical Disk Manager, 299
logical unit numbers (LUNs), **125**
logs
 Exchange 5.5, **332–334**, 350
 Exchange 2000, 362–363, *362*
 SQL, **382–383**
  backups, **392–393**, 405
  restores, 412
"Looks Alive" Poll Interval property, 256
loop switches, 165
low-voltage differential (LVD) SCSI, **125–128**, *128*
LS-120 (Laser Servo 120) disks, 35
LTO (Linear Tape Open) initiative, **436**
Lunar Flare NAS, 200
LUNs (logical unit numbers), **125**
LVD (low-voltage differential) SCSI, **125–128**, *128*

M

magazines, 18, 426
magnetic discs, **35**
magnetic tape, **29–33**
Magneto-Optical (MO) disks, 34, 437
Magneto Resistive Cluster (MRC) heads, 437
Magstar magnetic tape, **29–30**
Mail applet, 353
Mailbox Reconnect (Mbconn) tool, 373
mailboxes, restoring
 in Exchange 5.5, **351–355**, *354*, *356*
 in Exchange 2000, **371–376**, *375*
maintenance in NAS, 172
makeboot.exe program, 269
Manual Repair option, **273–274**
manual replication, **65–66**
map command, **272**, *272*

mapped drives, **47**, **272**, *272*
mapped shares, 186
Mark as Clean option, 92
Mark the Restored Data as the Primary Data for All Replicas option, 291, 294
master boot records, repairing, 271
Master databases in SQL, **381–382**
 backing up, 396
 restoring, **413–414**, *414*
/maxlogsize option, 261
Mbconn (Mailbox Reconnect) tool, 373
MDBDATA folder, 337, 348
.mdf files, **383–384**
ME (Metal Evaporative) media, 436
media, 436
 management, **35–36**
  examples, **36–38**
  library capacity, **38–39**
  RSS, **105–107**, *106–107*
  terminology, **17**
  types, 17, **28–29**
   magnetic discs, **35**
   magnetic tape, **29–33**
   optical discs, **33–34**
Media Copies tab, 105–107, *106*
Media IDs, 76
media pools, 17
 application, **76–77**, *77*
 containing media pools, **77–78**
 OMIDs for, **75–76**
 security for, **78–79**, *79*
 system, **74–75**
Media Pools folder, 110
Media Properties dialog box, 105, *106*
media sets, **436–437**
Media tab, 84, *85*
Mediadescription option, 404
Medianame option
 for T-SQL backup, 404
 for T-SQL restore, 417
MediaPassword option
 for T-SQL backup, 404
 for T-SQL restore, 417
megabytes, 437
megatransfers per second, 135
Member Of tab, 243
Members tab, 312
Memory In Cassette (MIC) chip, 437
Message Transfer Agents (MTAs), 336
messages, restoring
 in Exchange 5.5, **353**
 in Exchange 2000, **374–375**, *375*

metadata
    defined, 381, 437
    in NAS, 183
metadata cleanup command, 288
Metal Evaporative (ME) media, 436
MIC (Memory In Cassette) chip, 437
microns, 150
Microsoft enterprise networking, 3
Microsoft Tape Format (MTF), 76, 109
millipede technology, 200, 423
mirrored disks, 437
    creating, 214–215, 215
    in RAID 1, 205
    in RAID 10, 207, 208
mixed networks in clustering, 241
mixed termination in SCSI, 130–131, 131
MO (Magneto-Optical) disks, 34, 437
Model databases, backing up, 396
modes in optical cables, 150
mount command, 99
Mount Database After Restore option, 367
mount points, 48–51, 49–50
mounting
    defined, 18
    exports, 186
mountvol utility, 49–51, 50
/move option for cluster group, 262
Move option for T-SQL restore, 417
/Moveto option, 265
moving disks, 216–217
MRC (Magneto Resistive Cluster) heads, 437
Msdb database, 382
MTAs (Message Transfer Agents), 336
MTF (Microsoft Tape Format), 76, 109
multi-mode in GBIC, 153
multimode cable, 150
multiple instances, 387
multiple storage groups, 360

N

N_ports, 152
names
    cluster groups, 251
    Dfs links, 64
Narrow SCSI buses, 123–124
NAS (Network Attached Storage), 9–10, 10, 171–174
    backup strategies, 182–186, 183–185

EMC, 199
    in future, 199–200
    and NDMP, 178–182, 179
    Network Appliance products for, 189–190
        implementing, 193–199, 194–199
        snapshots, 190–192, 191
    and NFS and CIFS, 176–177
    vs. SAN, 174–176, 174–175
    with Windows systems, 186–189
native capacity, 437
.ndf files, 383–384
NDIS (Network Driver Interface Specification), 437
NDMP (Network Data Management Protocol)
    benefits, 180–182
    development of, 178
    operation of, 178–180, 179
    setting up, 195–198, 196–197
ndmpd on command, 195
nearline archiving, 427
nearline storage, 437
NetBackup product, 185
NetBIOS in clustering, 241
NetBIOS over TCP/IP in clustering, 241, 242
netsh dump command, 324
Network Appliance products, 189–190
    implementing, 193–199, 194–199
    snapshots, 190–192, 191
Network Attached Storage. See NAS (Network Attached Storage)
network cards
    in clustering, 241
    in SPF, 228
Network Data Management Protocol (NDMP)
    benefits, 180–182
    development of, 178
    operation of, 178–180, 179
    setting up, 195–198, 196–197
Network Driver Interface Specification (NDIS), 437
Network File System (NFS), 176–177
network load balanced (NLB) clusters, 225–226, 226
networks in clustering, 241, 246, 246
New Dfs Link option, 64, 117
New Dfs Root Wizard, 116, 116, 327

New Maintenance Plans option, 406
New Object-User dialog box, 243
New Replica option, 65
New Technology File System (NTFS), 4–5, 438
NFS (Network File System), 176–177
NICs
    in clustering, 241
    in SPF, 228
NL_ports, 152
NLB (network load balanced) clusters, 225–226, 226
no-rewind devices in NAS, 198
nodes, 438
    cluster, 222
        creating, 246–247
        evicting, 249–250
        pausing and resuming, 249
        preferred, 238–239
        secondary, 232–234, 232–233
    in Fibre Channel, 152
Noformat option, 404
Noinit option, 404
nonauthoritative restores
    in FRS, 61
    steps in, 291–292, 292
Norecovery option, 417
Norewind option
    for T-SQL backup, 404
    for T-SQL restore, 417
normal backups, 21–22
Noskip option, 404
Nounload option
    for T-SQL backup, 404
    for T-SQL restore, 417
NTBackup program, 4–7, 438
ntds.dit file, 275
ntdsutil utility, 288
NTFS (New Technology File System), 4–5, 438
Ntmsdata file, 95
NtmsReg file, 95
NVRAM information, 299

O

Object Structured Query Language (OSQL), 386, 386
objects, 438
OEMs (Original Equipment Manufacturers), 158
offline archiving, 427
offline backups, 337–340, 339
offline media, 19
Offline Message Store (.OST), 334

/offline option
    for cluster group, 262
    for cluster resource, 265
Offline state, 217
offline storage, 438
offsite backup storage, 28
OFM (Open File Manager), 277–278
OMIDs (on-media identifiers), 75–76
online libraries, 18
/online option
    for cluster group, 262
    for cluster resource, 265
Open dialog box, 317, *318*
Open File Manager (OFM), 277–278
open files in backups, 6, 277–278
operating system rebuilds, 297–298
    Dfs recovery, **326–327**
    DHCP database recovery, 320–324, *321*, *323–324*
    diskmap for, **299**, *299*
    EFS. *See* EFS (Encrypting File System); Recovery Agents
    restoring to different hardware, 300–303, *302*
    SIS volume recovery, **324–325**
    WINS, **327–329**, *328*
operating systems, 438
Operator Requests feature, 19, 89–90, *90*
optical cables, 150
optical disks, 33–34, 438
optical improvements, **423**
optical jukeboxes, 438
Options dialog box, 302, *302*
Options tab, 414–415, *416*
organizational units, 296
Original Equipment Manufacturers (OEMs), 158
OSQL (Object Structured Query Language), 386, *386*
.OST (Offline Message Store), **334**
out-of-band SAN management, 168
Out of Sync setting, 408
overhead in NAS, 172
Overwrite option, 400

P

.PAB (Personal Address Book), **334**
pagefile.sys file, 229
pagefiles in clustering, 229
parallel SCSI interface, **125–132**, *128*, *131*, 137

parallel SQL backups, **398**
Parameters tab, 257–258, *259*
parity in RAID, 206
Partial option, 417
partitioning, 202
passive copper, 153
passive termination, 129–130
Password option
    for T-SQL backup, 404
    for T-SQL restore, 417
Password Never Expires option, 243
passwords
    in clustering, **242–245**, 247
    for File Recovery Certificates, 307–308
patch files in Exchange 5.5, **333**, 335
Patch mode for isinteg, 338
/path option for cluster, 261
pause mode in rsm_dbic.exe, 94
/Pause option for cluster node, 264
Pause Node option, 249
Pause RSM option, 94
pausing cluster nodes, **249**
pay-as-you-grow strategy, 160
PBCs (Port Bypass Circuits), 155
PDCs (Primary Domain Controllers), 347
peak transfer rate, 439
Pending Timeout property, 256
performance
    NAS, 172
    SAN, **162**
    SCSI, 139
periods for cluster failovers, 252
peripheral interfaces in SCSI, 122
permissions
    for clustering, 242, **248–249**
    for media pools, 78–79, *79*
    for Recovery Agents groups, 312–313, *313–314*
Personal Address Book (.PAB), **334**
Personal Folder file, 353
Personal Message Store (.PST), **333–334**
personnel costs with SANs, 159
.pfx extension, 307
Physical Locations folder, **79–87**, *82*, *84–86*, *88*
physical media, 17
plans
    for Exchange 2000, 376
    in SANs, 147
Plug and Play (PnP)
    defined, 439
    in NDMP, 181
point-in-time shots, 420

Point-to-Point Fibre Channel, **154**, *154*
policies, 439
Port Bypass Circuits (PBCs), 155
ports
    defined, 17
    in Fibre Channel, 152
Possible Owners option, 255
power in SPF, 229
preferred node in clustering, 238–239
preferred owners in clustering, 234, 250–251, *251*
previous logs in Exchange 5.5, **332–333**
Primary Domain Controllers (PDCs), 347
primary filegroups, 384
primary storage, 439
priority assignments in SCSI, **124–125**
priv.edb (Private Information Store) file, **334**
priv.pat file, 333
private encryption keys, 320
private networks in clustering, 241
Private option in Exchange 5.5 restores, 346
/Privproperties option
    for cluster, 261
    for cluster group, 262
    for cluster network, 263
    for cluster node, 264
/Properties option
    for cluster, 261
    for cluster group, 262
    for cluster network, 263
    for cluster node, 264
    for cluster resource, 265
proxy servers, 439
.PST (Personal Message Store), **333–334**
.pst files, 336, 375
pub.edb (Public Information Store) file, **334**
pub.pat file, 333
Public Key Policies folder, 317
public networks in clustering, 241
Public option in Exchange 5.5 restores, 346
Publication SQL databases, 397–398
/purgecache option, 53
pushing, 439

Q

QIC (quarter-inch cartridges) tape, **32–33**, 76, 439
qtree command, 198
QTrees, **198**, *199*
Query Analyzer, 386
queues for RSM, **88–89**, *89–90*
Quick Restore product, 185
/quiet option, 53
/Quorum option, 261
quorum resources in clustering, 222
Quota tab, 68, *69*
quotas, disk, **68–70**, *69–70*

R

RAID (Random/Redundant Array of Independent/Inexpensive Disks), 19, **201–202**, 439
   hardware, **209–210**
   vs. JBOD, **202–203**
   moving disks, **216–217**
   RAID 0, **203–204**, *204*, *213*, *214*
   RAID 1, **204–206**, *205*, *214–215*, *215*, **218–219**, *219*
   RAID 5, **206–207**, *215*, **220**, *220*
   RAID 10, **207**, *208*
   RAID 50, **208–209**, *208*
   recovery in, **217–220**, *219–220*
   software, **210–216**, *213–215*
   spanned volumes, **216**
Random Access Memory (RAM) for clustering, 229
rdisk utility, 71
Reactivate Disk option, 217
reboots
   with authoritative restores, 293
   in Windows systems, 187
Rebuild Master dialog box, 400, *401*
rebuildm.exe utility, 413
recall, 439
Recall Limit tab, 104
recording density, 439
Recover Deleted Items option, 354, 376
Recover Selected Items option, 376
recovery. *See also* restores
   databases
     RSM, **98–99**
     RSS, **114**
   in RAID, **217–220**, *219–220*
   with SANs, 159
   with SQL transaction logs, 383
Recovery Agents, **305–306**, *305*
   Enterprise CAs, **310–311**, *311*

recovery certificates for, **306–309**, *307–309*, **314–318**, *316–318*
user groups for, **311–313**, *312–314*
recovery certificates in EFS, **306–309**, *307–309*
   adding, **317–318**, *318*
   exporting, 307–308, *307–308*, **315–316**, *316–317*
   importing, **308–309**, *309*
   requesting, **314–315**
Recovery Console, **269–270**
   benefits, **272–273**
   commands, **270–272**, *270*, *272*
recovery models, SQL, **389–390**
Recovery option for T-SQL restore, 417
recovery servers
   in Exchange 5.5, 348
   in Exchange 2000, **371–372**
Recovery tab, 107
redirection with reparse points, 45
redundancy, 17
Redwood tape, 33
refresh command, 99
Refused operator requests, 89
Regback folder, 268, 273
Registry
   backing up, 71, 268
   for backup filters, 282
   in Exchange 5.5 restores, 347
   in operating system rebuilds, 300–301, *300*
   restoring, **273**
   with sfc, **53–54**
reliability
   in NAS, 172
   in Windows systems, 187
Remote Installation Service (RIS), 58, **325**
Remote Storage Diagnostic Utility, **112–113**, *114*
Remote Storage File Analysis Utility, **112**, *112*
Remote Storage Files Not Accessed In setting, 100
Remote Storage media pool, 110
Remote Storage option, 100
Remote Storage Service. *See* RSS (Remote Storage Service)
Remote Storage Setup Wizard, 101, *101*
remotely stored data
   in NTBackup, 6
   in RSS, **109–111**, *110–111*

Removable Storage Manager. *See* RSM (Removable Storage Manager); RSS (Remote Storage Service)
Remove Disk option, 219
Remove Mirror option, 219, *219*
/Removedependency option, 265
/Removeowner option, 265
/Rename option
   for cluster, 261
   for cluster group, 262
   for cluster network, 263
   for cluster resource, 265
Repair folder, 71
Repair Volume option, 220
reparse points, **45**, 440
   delrp for, **47–48**
   Linkd for, **45–46**, *47*
Replace option, 417
Replace the Data on the Media with This Backup option, 364
Replace the file on disk only if it is older than the backup copy option, 286
replicas in Dfs, **65–66**, *65*, 327
replicated SQL databases, **397–398**
replication for domain controller recovery, **288–290**
Replication Policy window, 66
Request New Certificate option, 314
Res1.log file, 275
Rescan Disks option, 217
reserved files in Exchange 5.5, 335
Reset Password command, 243
Reset Password dialog box, 244
Resource Kit, 42
Restart option
   for T-SQL backup, 404
   for T-SQL restore, 417
Restart Period property, 256
Restart Threshold property, 256
Restore command in T-SQL, **416–418**
Restore Database dialog box, 414–415, *415–416*
Restore Database option, 329
Restore Device option, 414
restore.env file, 370
restore points, 421
Restore Progress dialog box, 288, 292–293, 295
   for Exchange 5.5, 346, *347*
   for Exchange 2000, 367, *367*
Restore tab
   for Exchange 5.5, 345, *345*
   for Exchange 2000, 366, *366*

for operating system rebuilds, 302, *302*
for RSS, 110, *111*
Restore Wizard, 285–287, *285–287*, 291, 295
restores, 284, 440
　Active Directory objects, **294–296**
　Dfs, 326–327, *326*
　DHCP databases, **323–324**, *323–324*
　to different hardware, 300–303, *300*, *302*
　domain controllers, **288–294**, *292–293*
　encrypted files, 320
　Exchange 5.5, **345–347**, *345–347*
　　full, **347–351**, **356–359**, *358*
　　mailbox, **351–355**, *354*, *356*
　　offline backups, **337–338**
　Exchange 2000, **365–369**, *366–369*
　　full, **369–371**
　　mailbox, **371–376**, *375*
　files, folders, and volumes, **285–286**, *285–286*
　in FRS, **59–61**
　Registry, 273
　RSM databases, **98–99**
　SIS volumes, **324–325**
　SQL, **411–412**
　　Enterprise Manager for, **414–415**, *415–416*
　　system databases, **412–414**, *414*
　　Transact-SQL for, **416–418**
　system state, **287–288**, *287*
　Windows 2000, **292–294**, *293*
　WINS database, **329**
Restoring Database Store dialog box, **366–367**, *367*
Restoring Microsoft Exchange dialog box, 345–346, *346*
Restricted_User option, 417
/Resume option, 264
Resume Node option, 249
resuming cluster nodes, **249**
Retaindays option, 404
retrieving, 440
Return Media to Free Media Pool option, 78
Return on Investment (ROI), 147
Rewind option
　for T-SQL backup, 404
　for T-SQL restore, 417

rewind speed, 440
rights
　for clustering, 242, **248–249**
　for media pools, **78–79**, *79*
　for Recovery Agents groups, **312–313**, *313–314*
RIPrep images, 58
RIS (Remote Installation Service), 58, 325
Risetup option, 325
RISetup Wizard, 58
Robocopy utility, **61–62**
robotic libraries, 18
ROI (Return on Investment), 147
rollback drivers, **422**
rolling back SQL transactions, 383
rolling forward SQL transactions, 383
ROM, 440
roots in Dfs, **63–64**, *64*
rotation methods, **23–28**
round-robin DNS, **226–227**
routers
　in SAN, **157–158**
　in SPF, 229
rsdiag.exe utility, **112–113**, *114*
rsdir.exe utility, **112**, *112*
RSM (Removable Storage Manager), 19, **42–43**, *43*, 73, 440
　administrative features, 90
　　adding cleaning cartridges to libraries, **91–92**
　　cleaning libraries and single drives, 92, *92*
　　configuring CD-ROM jukeboxes, 93
　　configuring Zip/Jaz drives, 92
　　database backup and recovery, **96–99**, *97*
　　importing and exporting media, 91
　　inventorying libraries, 91
　　rsm.exe, 99
　　rsm_dbic.exe, **93–94**, *94*
　　rsm_dbutil.exe, **94–96**, *95–96*
　configuring, 73, *74*
　　media pools, **74–79**, *77*, *79*
　　operator requests, **89–90**, *90*
　　physical locations, **79–87**, *82*, *84–86*, *88*
　　work queue, **88**, *89*
　RSS with. *See* RSS (Remote Storage Service)
RSM Configuration Wizard, **80–81**
rsm.exe utility, **99**
rsm_dbic.exe utility, **93–94**, *94*

rsm_dbutil.exe utility, **94–96**, *95–96*
RSM Import media pool, 301
rsmconfg.exe utility, **80–81**
RSS (Remote Storage Service), **43–45**, *44*, 439
　administering, 107
　　browsing remotely stored data, **109–111**, *110–111*
　　copying data, **108–109**, *108–109*
　　rsdiag.exe, **112–113**, *114*
　　rsdir.exe, **112**, *112*
　　supporting down-level clients, **111–112**
　configuring
　　first time, **101**, *101–102*
　　installing, 100
　　media, **105–107**, *106–107*
　　properties, **104–105**, *105*
　　volumes, **101–104**, *102–103*
　database backup and recovery, **114**, 279
　and Dfs, **114–118**, *115–118*
Run Cleanup Agent option, 373
Run in a Separate Resource Monitor option, 255

S

SAM (Security Accounts Management) database, 347–348
SANs (Storage Area Networks), **10–11**, *12*, 19, **145–146**, *146*
　appliances, **168–169**
　availability, **160–161**, *161*
　benefits, **146–147**, **159–164**, *161*, *164*
　components, **157–158**
　dynamic drive sharing, **167–168**
　Fibre Channel. *See* Fibre Channel
　vs. NAS, **174–176**, *174–175*
　performance, **162**
　scalability, 147, **160**
　Secure Fabric OS, **164**
　switches, 157, **164–166**, *166*
　vendors, **166–167**
　zoning, **163**, *164*
SASI (Shugart Associates Systems Interface), 120
SCA/SCA-2 connectors, 142
scalability, 16
　SAN, 147, **160**
　SANs zones, 163
Scan for Hardware Changes option, 83

/scanboot option, 53
/scanonce option, 53
Schedule Job dialog box, 280, *281*
Schedule tab, 101, *102*, 104, *105*, 108, *109*
Schedule Jobs tab, 281, *282*
scheduler for snapshots, 192
schedules, backup, **278–284**, *279–284*
   editing, **281**, *282*
   filtered data in, **282–283**, *283–284*
   full, **278–280**, *280*
   incremental, **280–281**, *281*
   for NTBackup, 5
   for RSS, 101, *102*, 104, *105*, **108–109**, *108–109*
   for SQL, 396–397, **400–403**, *401–403*
SCSI (Small Computer System Interface), **119–120**, 440
   bus, **122–125**, *124*
   cables, **132–134**, 137
   documentation for, 298
   hints, **143**
   history, **120–121**
   IDs and LUNs, **124–125**, *124*
   parallel interface, **125–132**, *128*, *131*
   speeds, **134–135**
   termination, **129–132**, *131*, 137–138
   terminology, **122**, *122*, **136–137**, *136*
   troubleshooting, **137–142**
SCSI Architectural Model, 121
SCSI Bus Analyzer, 139
SE (single-ended) SCSI, **125–130**, *128*
search speed, 440
searching indexed files, **57**, *57*
secondary node clusters, **232–234**, *232–233*
secondary storage, 440
Secure Fabric OS, **164**
security
   for clustering, **248–249**
   for media pools, **78–79**, *79*
   for Recovery Agents groups, **312–313**, *313–314*
   for RSM libraries, 86–87
   for SAN, **163–164**, *164*
Security Accounts Management (SAM) database, 347–348
security IDs (SIDs), 347
Security tab

for clustering, 249
for EFS Recovery Certificates, 313
for media pools, **78**, *79*
for RSM libraries, 86–87
Select Databases page, 406, *406*
Select Users dialog box, 313
server-based backups, 336–337
server clusters, **223–224**, *223–225*
Server Message Block (SMB), 177
servers
   in Dfs, **116–118**, *116–118*
   in NDMP, 179
   recovery, 348, **371–372**
   virtual, 222, 227
service packs in Exchange 5.5, 349
services
   disabling, 271
   listing, 272
   in NDMP, 179
set databasebackupinterval command, 324
Set Schedule option, 279–280
/Setowners option, 262
sfc.exe utility, **53–54**
SFC Registry settings, *53–54*
SFCutility, **53–54**
shared-disk clustering, 440
shared-nothing clustering, 440
Ship the Transaction Logs to Other SQL Servers option, 406
Show Services Node option, 312
Shugart Associates Systems Interface (SASI), 120
sides, media, 17
SIDs (security IDs), 347
signatures, file, 51
Silkworm product, 166
simple recovery model in SQL, **390**
single drives, cleaning in RSM, **92**, *92*
single-ended (SE) SCSI, **125–130**, *128*
Single Instance Storage (SIS), **58–59**
   defined, 441
   volume recovery, **324–325**
single-mode fiber, 150, 153
single-node clusters, **231–232**, *231*
single points of failure (SPF), **228–229**
SIS (Single Instance Storage), **58–59**
   defined, 441
   volume recovery, **324–325**
Site Replication Service (SRS), 377
68-pin SCSI connectors, **133**
Skip option, 404
Slingshot switch, 167

slots, 18
Small Computer System Interface. *See* SCSI (Small Computer System Interface)
SMB (Server Message Block), 177
SnapMirror product, 190, 192
SnapRestore product, 190, 192
SnapSchedule product, 192
snapshots
   in NAS, **190–192**, *191*
   in Windows XP/.NET, **420–421**
SNIA (Storage Network Industry Association), 181, 426
SNIA Backup Working group, 181–182
software RAID, **210–216**, *213–215*
software zoning in SANs, 163
spanned volumes, **216**
spares in Exchange 5.5, 357–359, *358*
sparse files, **57–58**, *58*, 441
Specify Backup Disk Directory page, 407, *407*
Specify the Transaction Log Share page, 408, *408*
speeds, SCSI, **134–135**
SPF (single points of failure), **228–229**
SQL, 379–380
   backups
     differential, **388**
     Enterprise Manager for, **399–403**, *399*, *401–403*
     logical backup devices for, **398–400**, *399–400*
     strategies, 393–398, *395*
     T-SQL for, **399–400**, *400*, **403–405**
     types, **391–393**
   basics, **380–381**
   Copy Database Wizard for, **388**
   data files, **383–384**
   databases, **381–382**
     backing up, 394–396, *395*
     copying, **410–411**, *411*
     replicated, **397–398**
     restoring, **412–414**, *414*
   Enterprise Manager for, **385**, *385*
   filegroups, 384–385, 393
   log shipping in, **387–388**, **406–410**, *406–409*
   multiple instances in, 387
   recovery models, 389–390
   restores, **411–412**
     Enterprise Manager for, **414–415**, *415–416*

system databases, **412–414**, *414*
T-SQL for, **416–418**
T-SQL for, **385–386**, *396*
transaction logs, **382–383**
SQL Server Backup dialog box, 400
SRS (Site Replication Service), 377
stand-alone Dfs roots, 63
stand-alone Dfs servers, **116–118**, *116–118*
stand-alone libraries, 18
Standby option, 418
/Start option, 264
Start Restore option, 345
Start Services After Restore option, 346, 352
stateful protocols, 177
stateless connections, 177
static load balancing cluster model, **234–235**, *234*
Stats option
  for T-SQL backup, 405
  for T-SQL restore, 418
/Status option
  for cluster network, 263
  for cluster node, 264
.stm extension, 362
/Stop option, 264
Stop Cluster Service option, 249
Storage Area Networks. *See* SANs (Storage Area Networks)
storage groups, 360, **362**, *362*
Storage Network Industry Association (SNIA), 181, 426
stores in Exchange 2000, **361–362**
Streaming Database File format, 362
stripe sets with parity, 206, 208, *208*
striped volumes, 19, 202, 204
  creating, **213**, *214*
  in RAID 10, 207
striping, 441
Structure Tables in Dfs, **326–327**, *326*
stub files, 44, 433
stubs in SCSI cables, **133**
Submitted operator requests, 89
subordinate CAs, 310
Subscription SQL databases, 397–398
SuperDLT standard, 31
Support Tools, 42
sustained transfer rate, 441
swap files, 229
switches
  in SAN, 157, **164–166**, *166*
  in SPF, 229
symmetric SAN appliances, 168

synchronous SCSI, **135**
sysconfig -t command, 197–198
system attendant, 336
system databases in SQL, **381–382**
  backing up, **394–396**, *395*
  restoring, **412–414**, *414*
System File Checker, **53–54**
system-level SCSI bus, 122
system media pools, **74–75**
System Restore, **421**
System State
  in Exchange 2000, **360–361**, 369–370
  in operating system rebuilds, 300–302
  restoring, **287–288**, *287*
  Windows 2000, **70–71**
System State option, 287, 295
Sysvol data, **290–291**

T

T-SQL (Transact-SQL), **385–386**, *396*
  backups, **399–400**, *400*, **403–405**
  restores, **416–418**
Take Offline option, 250
tape cartridges, 441
tape libraries, 441
targets in SCSI, 122
Tarvan standard, **441–442**
Task Scheduler
  for backups, 281
  for RSS data, **108–109**, *108–109*
TCO (Total Cost of Ownership)
  in NAS, 172
  in SANs, 147
TCP/IP Properties dialog box, 242
Telnet, 197
Tempdb database, **382**
terabytes, 441
Terminal Services option, 310
Terminate Users in Database option, 408
termination, SCSI, **129–132**, *131*, 137–138
terminology, **15–16**
  drive terms, 18
  enterprise terms, 19
  general terms, **16–17**
  library terms, **18–19**
  media terms, 17
TERMPWR line, 131–132, 138
test restores
  in Exchange 5.5, **349–350**
  importance of, 297

thin-client servers, 172
This Database Can Be Overwritten by a Restore option, 373
three-way backups for NAS, **184**, *185*
thresholds
  for cluster failovers, 252
  defined, 441
throughput in SANs, 162
Time Navigator product, 185
timeouts in clustering, 256
timing for failover, 238
TIR (Total Internal Reflection), 150
tolerance. *See* fault tolerance
tombstone lifetime for Active Directory, 276–277
Total Cost of Ownership (TCO)
  in NAS, 172
  in SANs, 147
Total Internal Reflection (TIR), 150
Tower of Hanoi rotation method, **26–27**, 441
traffic in NAS, 183
Transact-SQL (T-SQL), **385–386**, *396*
  backups, **399–400**, *400*, **403–405**
  restores, **416–418**
transaction logs
  Exchange 5.5, **332**
  Exchange 2000, **362–363**, *362*
  SQL, **382–383**
    backups, **392–393**, 405
    restores, 412
transparency in SANs, 147
transports, 18
troubleshooting
  Exchange 5.5 restores, **350**
  SCSI, **137–142**
Truncate Log on Checkpoint option, 394, *395*
trunking in SANs, 162
tunneling, **422–423**

U

U160/m SCSI, **135**
UDF (Universal Disk Format), 442
Ultra SCSI, **135**
Ultra-2 SCSI, **135**
uninterruptible backups, 392
Uninterruptible Power Supplies (UPSs), **228–229**
Universal Disk Format (UDF), 442
Unload option
  for T-SQL backup, 405
  for T-SQL restore, 418

Unrecognized system media pools, 75
Update Driver Wizard, 82
Update Sequence Numbers (USNs), 442
  in Exchange 5.5 restores, 351
  in FRS, 60
Upgrade to Dynamic Disk option, 212, *213*
UPSs (Uninterruptible Power Supplies), 228–229
User Cannot Change Password option, 243
user databases in SQL, **382**, **396–397**
user-defined filegroups, 384
user groups for Recovery Agents, **311–313**, *312–314*
User Properties dialog box, 243
users, disk space usage monitoring, 69
USNs (Update Sequence Numbers), 442
  in Exchange 5.5 restores, 351
  in FRS, 60

V

verbose mode in rsm_dbic.exe, 93
Verbose Output option in rsm_dbutil.exe, 94
Verify Windows 2000 System Files option, **274**
verifying
  backups, **284**
  failover, **247**
/Version option, 261
Very Large Memory (VLM), 442
VHDCI68 connectors, 142
view command, 99
virtual disks, **48**
virtual servers, 222, 227
virtualization
  future of, **424–425**
  in NAS, 200
  in SANs, 147
Vixel Corp, 167
VLM (Very Large Memory), 442
vol command, 198

volume mount points, **48–51**, *49–50*, 442
Volume Properties window, 103, *103*
volumes
  mounting, **48–51**, *49–50*
  restoring, **285–286**, *285–286*
  RSS, **101–104**, *102–103*
  SIS, **324–325**
  snapshots of, **420–421**

W

WAN links in SPF, 229
watermarks, 442
WBEM (Web-Based Enterprise Management), 188
weekly backups, **278–280**, *279–280*
Welcome tab, 278
WFP (Windows File Protection), **51–54**
What to Restore page, 285, *285*
When to Backup setting, 279
Wide SCSI buses, **123–124**
Windows 2000 Repair option, **269–273**, *270*, *272*
Windows 2000 Server Resource Kit, 42
Windows 2000 Server Support Tools, 42
Windows 2000 storage, **11–13**, **41–42**
  Change Journal, **54–55**
  Dfs, **62–66**, *64–65*
  disk quotas, **68–70**, *69–70*
  EFS, **66–68**, *67*
  ERDs for, **273–274**
  FRS, **59–62**
  Indexing Service, **55–57**, *56–57*
  for RAID, **210–216**, *213–215*
  reparse points, **45–48**, *47*
  RSM, **42–43**, *43*
  RSS, **43–45**, *44*
  SIS, **58–59**
  sparse files, **57–58**, *58*
  System State, **70–71**
  volume mount points, **48–51**, *49–50*
  WFP, **51–54**

Windows Backup. *See* Backup program
Windows Backup Restore Wizard, 292
Windows File Protection (WFP), **51–54**
Windows for Workgroups, 4
Windows Management Instrumentation (WMI), 188, 442
Windows NT, 4
Windows-powered NAS appliances, **186–189**
Windows Scripting Host (WSH), 442
Windows systems, NAS with, **186–189**
Windows XP/.NET
  ASR in, **421**
  rollback drivers in, **422**
  System Restore in, **421**
  volume snapshots in, **420–421**
Winlogon key, 53
WINS, **327–328**
  automatic backups for, **328–329**, *328*
  in clustering, 240–241
  restoring, **329**
wins_bak directory, 329
WINS tab, 241, *242*
WINS tool, 329
Wizard Welcome window, 285, 287, 291–292, 295
WMI (Windows Management Instrumentation), 188, 442
work queue for RSM, **88**, *89*
WORM (Write Once Read Many) disks, 34, 442
write-ahead transaction logs, 335
WSH (Windows Scripting Host), 442

Z

Zip disks, 35, **92**
zoning, SAN, **163**, *164*

The Mark Minasi Windows® 2000 Series

The Essential Resource for Windows 2000 Administrators

First Three Titles of an Expanding Series

By Jeremy Moskowitz
0-7821-2881-5 • $49.99

By Christa Anderson
0-7821-2885-8 • $49.99

By J. Peter Bruzzese
and Chris Wolfe
0-7821-2883-1 • $49.99

- **Mark Minasi** serves as the series editor, chooses topics and authors, and reviews each book

- Concise, focused material based upon real-world implementation of Windows 2000 Server

- Designed to provide Windows 2000 Systems Administrators with specific in-depth technical solutions

Mark Minasi, MCSE, is recognized as one of the world's best teachers of NT/2000. He teaches NT/2000 classes in 15 countries. His best-selling *Mastering Windows 2000 Server* books have more than 500,000 copies in print.

TELL US WHAT YOU THINK!

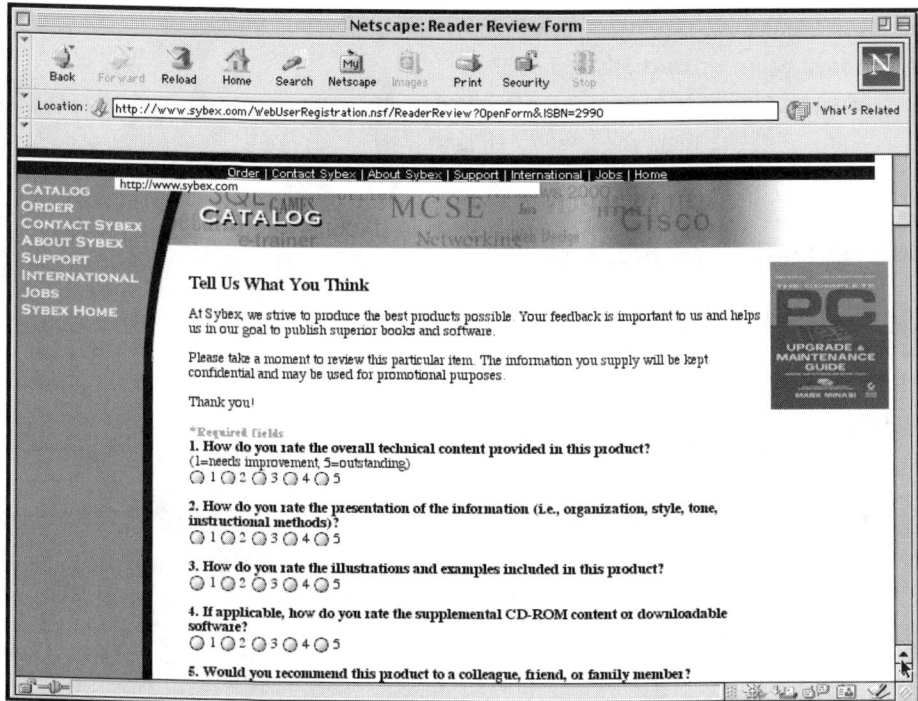

Your feedback is critical to our efforts to provide you with the best books and software on the market. Tell us what you think about the products you've purchased. It's simple:

1. Visit the Sybex website
2. Go to the product page
3. Click on **Submit a Review**
4. Fill out the questionnaire and comments
5. Click **Submit**

With your feedback, we can continue to publish the highest quality computer books and software products that today's busy IT professionals deserve.

www.sybex.com

SYBEX Inc. • 1151 Marina Village Parkway, Alameda, CA 94501 • 510-523-8233

www.sybexetrainer.com
Your #1 Destination for Certification *e*-training!

At Sybex's new online certification training site, **www.sybexetrainer.com**, train online or purchase best-selling Sybex software and books at an incredible value. The site offers an interactive environment and all the tools you need to enhance your skills and reach your certification goals.

Check out these SYBEX *e*-trainer™ products:

VIRTUAL TRAINERS™

Interactive, online courses covering all exam objectives **Starting at $48.99**

VIRTUAL TEST CENTERS™

Online, customizable testing— just like the real exam **Starting at $34.99**

VIRTUAL TESTS™

Quick and convenient online testing for focused preparation **$14.99**

Also Available:

- **VIRTUAL LABS™**
  Simulated network configurations for hands-on practice
- **FLASHCARDS**
  Quick-quizzing software for your Palm or PC
- **SYBEX STUDY GUIDES & EXAM NOTES™**
  Comprehensive coverage of exam topics

Test-drive our **FREE** interactive trials!

SYBEX®
25 YEARS
OF PUBLISHING
EXCELLENCE

www.sybexetrainer.com

Sybex—The Leader in Certification
SYBEX *e*-trainer™ ■ *e*-training ■ *e*-testing ■ *e*-solutions